PHOENIX
SCOTTSDALE & SEDONA

JEFF FICKER

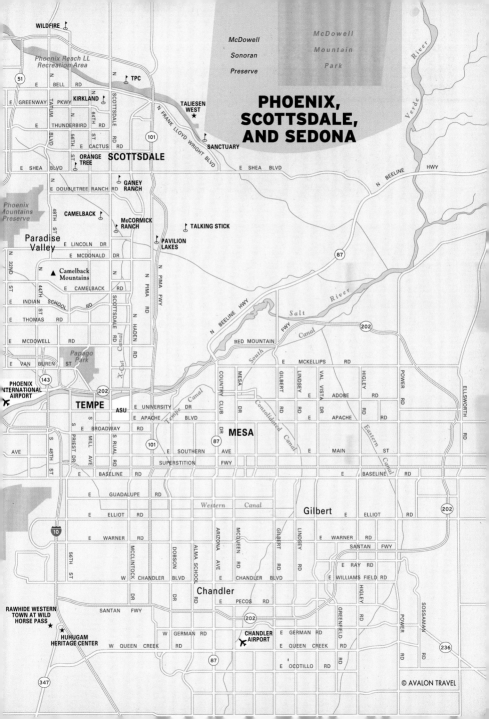

Contents

Discover Phoenix,
Scottsdale & Sedona

Standing at the top of Camelback Mountain, a red sandstone peak that dramatically rises from the center of metropolitan Phoenix, it's easy to appreciate why so many people have migrated to the Valley of the Sun. The city's two great natural resources – light and space – seem infinite, especially at sunset when the sky is streaked with bold swatches of yellow, vermillion, and hot pink.

It's also an extraordinary illustration of how being so popular can utterly transform a landscape. The vast desert floor, once dotted by saguaro cacti and mesquite trees, is now a sweeping expanse of red-tile roofs and slender palm trees, punctuated by lush golf courses, swimming pools, and an efficient grid of streets and freeways. Glass skyscrapers cluster in the city's downtown, marking Phoenix's status as the commercial center of the American Southwest.

That's not to say the Sonoran Desert has been lost to the conquistadors of modern-day development. The rugged, millennia-old landscape is far too tough and enduring to permanently tame. Its rounded boulder formations, mountain ranges, and coyotes and lizards easily coexist in the metropolis of four million people.

Phoenix is where a ranch house and a pool in every backyard are not just an expectation, but a seemingly God-given right, and where sunny

summer days and warm winters have given birth to a resort lifestyle that can often lure a visitor to make a permanent move.

Phoenicians live like they're on vacation, with a hike before work or a late-night swim after a full day. You should join them. Taste the best Sonoran-style cuisine this side of the Mexican border. Enjoy Scottsdale's two favorite pastimes: shopping and nightlife. Discover the rich culture of the Native American tribes who first settled the Valley and still govern independent tribal land. Venture 90 minutes north of Phoenix to the leafy respite of Oak Creek Canyon, and witness the red-rock monoliths of Sedona.

First-time visitors may be surprised to find a desert playground that caters to demanding foodies, diehard shoppers, and outdoor adventurers in search of world-class hiking and biking. Sure, the desert may seem inhospitable, but once you get to know this incredible, beautiful place, you may just consider a move yourself.

Planning Your Trip

▶ WHERE TO GO

Phoenix

The Sonoran Desert's brilliant light and warmth permeate every aspect of Arizona's state capital, now the fifth-largest city in the country. Thanks to more than 325 days of sunshine a year, it's possible to dine alfresco, play golf, or hike year-round. The jagged mountains that surround the Valley of the Sun are prime spots to explore the area's diverse desert landscape. For a little urban fun, downtown Phoenix and the college town of Tempe offer terrific new museums, cultural attractions, and popular restaurants.

Scottsdale

Phoenix's best-known suburb may call itself the "West's Most Western Town," but visitors are immediately struck by its pleasure-loving attitude. Scottsdale prospers thanks in part to its chic resorts, restaurants, and nightspots, along with its desert golf courses and eclectic boutiques selling cowboy boots, trendy brands, and luxury goods. The city's galleries support the country's third-largest art market, and its five-star spas are among the finest in the world. Even architect Frank Lloyd Wright was seduced by the area, building his winter home, Taliesin West, here in the 1930s.

Sedona

It's easy to understand why Sedona is called Red Rock Country. Its massive crimson buttes lure travelers and outdoor lovers with monumental formations and intricate spires. The city's hidden resorts, charming galleries, and rugged Jeep tours cater to visitors' desire to explore its otherworldly prehistoric landscape, which is accentuated by deep-green ponderosa pines and leafy cottonwoods. Historic and cultural sights dot the neighboring Verde Valley, such as the ancient cliffside dwelling Montezuma Castle and the Old West mining town of Jerome.

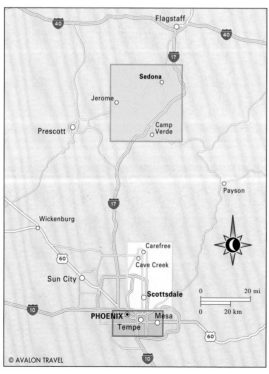

► WHEN TO GO

Locals like to joke that Phoenix and Scottsdale have three seasons: beautiful, hot, and "it can't get any hotter." And though there's some truth to that sentiment, Phoenicians easily adapt in order to take full advantage of the sunny, desert climate year-round.

There's no better time to visit Sedona or the Valley of the Sun than spring. Temperatures peak in the 70s and 80s during the day and cool down to "sweater weather" at night. Residents spend most of their time outdoors, taking advantage of the numerous golf courses, hiking spots, open-air shopping centers, and annual events like Major League Baseball spring training and the FBR Open. Also, the desert bursts to life in an explosion of color thanks to the numerous wildflowers and blooming cacti.

You may actually love Phoenix in the summer when it sizzles—of course, it may be the nosedive in rates at luxury resorts and spas that helps you embrace the heat. The searing temperatures and constant sun leave visitors and residents with little choice but to stake out the closest swimming pool. Cooler mornings

and late nights provide relief, and sudden monsoon storms that build in the desert deliver a refreshing reprieve many evenings.

Fall kicks off the social season. Eager to escape their air-conditioned confines, residents return to their outdoor haunts in October and November, filling up patios and gathering for festivals and concerts.

By winter, the mercury reaches the 50s and 60s, and the sunny, blue skies make Phoenix a mecca for snow-weary travelers. It can get downright chilly in Sedona, and the occasional light dusting of snow of the red rocks is a spectacular sight.

IF YOU HAVE...

- **THREE DAYS:** Visit Phoenix and Scottsdale.
- **FIVE DAYS:** Add Sedona.
- **ONE WEEK:** Add Jerome, Montezuma Castle, and Oak Creek Canyon.

Major League Baseball spring training

patio dining, Phoenician-style

Explore Phoenix, Scottsdale & Sedona

► THE BEST OF THE VALLEY OF THE SUN

Phoenix and Scottsdale make an excellent weekend trip, offering visitors the chance to combine a little culture with their R&R. Don't try to cram in a bunch of "must-see" sights. Instead, savor the Valley like a local, and experience its unique sensibility.

Day 1

Catch an early flight to Phoenix Sky Harbor International Airport and check into your hotel upon arrival. Make your way down to Tempe to have lunch at Four Peaks Brewpub before heading across Tempe Town Lake to get to know the Valley from its geographic heart, Papago Park. The easy climb up its rounded, red-hued butte to the Hole-in-the-Rock formation rewards visitors with a spectacular view of the city.

Within the protected reserve, you'll also find the Desert Botanical Garden, an impressive collection of the diverse cacti and plants that make their home in the Sonoran Desert. Then, visit Pueblo Grande Museum and Archaeological Park, the remains of the ancient Hohokam civilization from which the modern city of Phoenix rose. For dinner consider dining in Central Phoenix at the casual Tee Pee Mexican Restaurant. Afterward, grab a beer and play a little bocce ball at The Vig.

Day 2

Rise with the sun and pick up some fresh orange juice and a Commuter Sandwich at the popular La Grande Orange. Then, head out for a round of golf at one of the city's

the Desert Botanical Garden

WILD WEST ADVENTURE

Sure, it's tempting to kick back by the pool or to spend day after day on the golf course, but Arizona is the land of rugged cowboys and roughneck ranchers. Put down the margarita — the state's wild side is calling, from natural rockslides and mechanical bulls to racetrack driving.

IN THE AIR
Tempt both gravity and death by flying a plane on a "combat mission" over Phoenix's East Valley at **Fighter Combat International.** Even beginners learn to take the stick during in-the-air training in air-combat tactics, "smoke chases," lead-and-follow drills, and weapons training.

IN THE WATER
Take the plunge at Arizona's best swimming hole in **Slide Rock State Park,** situated seven miles north of Sedona. Glide down the 80-foot-long natural rockslide, which was carved into the granite and red sandstone canyon floor by Oak Creek.

ON THE ROAD
Former racer Bob Bondurant and his team coach thousands of students every year at **The Bob Bondurant School of High Performance Driving,** a custom-designed, 60-acre facility near Phoenix's Firebird International Raceway. Single-day courses are designed to implant skills ranging from introductory racing techniques to highway survival.

ON HORSEBACK
Get honest-to-goodness, "no frills" lessons in cowboyin' at **Arizona Cowboy College.** From half-day sessions on horseback riding and roping to the comprehensive six-day course, learn authentic cowboy skills by working at this cattle ranch in Scottsdale.

OFF ROAD
A ride with iconic **Pink Jeep Tours** is the most popular way to romp over Sedona's red rocks. Charismatic guides describe the geology and ecosystem surrounding Sedona as they drive beefed-up Jeep Wranglers over steep boulders and occasionally treacherous passes.

AT NIGHT
Catch a glimpse of the nocturnal desert by donning night-vision goggles with **Desert Storm Hummer Tours** in Scottsdale. Spot bats and coyotes, and hunt for scorpions using UV lights that cause their exoskeletons to glow.

ON A MECHANICAL BULL
Cowboy boots meet high heels at **Saddle Ranch** bar in Scottsdale. Partiers channel their inner urban cowboy by riding the bar's main attraction, a mechanical bull — which is surrounded by an inflatable mat and padded guards.

ON A BIKE
For a moderately challenging half-day trek, try **Submarine Rock Loop** in Sedona. The 10-mile loop starts with a single-track trail that varies between dirt and hard clay, leading to slickrock at Chicken Point and Submarine Rock.

a ride with Pink Jeep Tours in Sedona

SOUTHWESTERN CULTURE AND HERITAGE

Arizona sits at the crossroads of three diverse cultures that are essential to the story of the American West. Discover the region's Native American roots, vibrant Mexican heritage, and cowboy customs, and experience how they have merged to make the region such a vivid place.

Phoenix
SIGHTS

Pueblo Grande Museum and Archaeological Park: The modern city of Phoenix rose from the Hohokam village that stood here from about A.D. 100 to 1400.

Wells Fargo History Museum: For a quick snapshot of the Wild West, duck into this small museum, where visitors will find an authentic 19th-century stagecoach, antique guns, and a softball-size nugget of gold.

Heard Museum: The Heard offers an impressive introduction to Native American art and culture.

Arizona Museum of Natural History: The former Mesa Southwest Museum explores the region's natural and cultural history with hands-on exhibitions, like panning for "gold" and a re-creation of a territorial jail.

ACCOMMODATIONS

Sheraton Wild Horse Pass Resort & Spa: Built on the Gila River Indian Community, the resort reflects the architecture, art, and history of the Pima and Maricopa tribes.

entrance to the Heard Museum

FOOD

Kai: The restaurant taps into the Native American influence on Arizona culture with an innovative menu that consists of indigenous ingredients.

Scottsdale
SIGHTS

Old Town: This collection of restaurants, bars, and Old West-themed boutiques is a little touristy, but you'll still find some historic sites, as well as live music courtesy of singing

championship desert courses or hike the red-sandstone Camelback Mountain, an iconic Valley of the Sun landmark. Spend the rest of your afternoon relaxing, either poolside at your hotel or shopping at the open-air Biltmore Fashion Park shopping center. Have dinner at Pizzeria Bianco, The Tuck Shop, or Barrio Café, independent restaurants that regularly earn praise from foodies. Later, join the locals at Bomberos Café & Wine Bar for a glass of South American wine on the cozy patio.

Day 3

Begin your day in Scottsdale with breakfast at Breakfast Joynt before driving north to Taliesin West, Frank Lloyd Wright's winter home and architecture school, which still trains young apprentices. Learn how Wright's revolutionary work blended modern design and the Sonoran Desert landscape. Have lunch in Old Town Scottsdale at Arcadia Farms, and visit the district's Southwestern boutiques and the Old Adobe Mission, cowboys on horseback and Native American performers.

Old Adobe Mission: Mexican and Yaqui Indian families who settled in the area built Scottsdale's first Catholic church in 1933. Today, the Spanish Colonial Revival church is still used as a spiritual center.

Cave Creek: Miners and ranchers first settled this small, hardscrabble Western town in the 1870s.

ACCOMMODATIONS
Westin Kierland Resort & Spa: The large resort's walls are lined with mementos from Arizona history and culture.

FOOD
Reata Pass: Since its inception in the 1880s as a stagecoach stop, the cowboy steakhouse has been serving meals to hungry travelers in one way or another for more than a century.

Sedona
SIGHTS
Fort Verde State Historic Park: The historic fort is the place to go for a glimpse of the real Old West.

Montezuma Castle National Monument: One of the best-preserved cliff-dwellings in America, the 20-room village served as the home of the Sinagua people from about 1250 to the 1400s.

Jerome: Once dubbed the "Wickedest Town in the West," the hillside community has en-

Montezuma Castle National Monument

dured Prohibition and the boom-and-bust business of mining.

ACCOMMODATIONS
Mii Amo: The destination resort and spa blends holistic wellness treatments, Native American traditions, and luxury pampering.

FOOD
Elote Cafe: Chef Jeff Smedstad has traveled through Mexico for more than 15 years, creating a flavor distillation of the country's diverse cuisine.

Scottsdale's first Catholic church. Head across Scottsdale Road to the art districts of Marshall Way, 5th Avenue, and Main Street, where the city's chic galleries showcase contemporary and Western art. Have dinner at one of downtown's numerous restaurants, such as Cowboy Ciao or The Mission, and barhop among Scottsdale's hip clubs and lounges, including AZ88, Geisha A Go-Go, and Axis/Radius.

Day 4
Have breakfast at Morning Glory Café on your last day. Check out the Desert Modernist Burton Barr Central Library in downtown Phoenix, then get a dose of culture at the Phoenix Art Museum or the Heard Museum, one of the nation's finest collections of Native American art and artifacts. Grab a gourmet Pane Bianco sandwich for lunch before you have to catch your flight home.

► ARIZONA FAMILY ROAD TRIP

Phoenix, Scottsdale, and Sedona offer a diverse range of activities for the whole family. Start in the Valley of the Sun and explore downtown Phoenix's museums and parks. Then, head north to Sedona for a series of outdoor adventures before making your way back to Scottsdale's resorts and Old West fun.

Day 1

Fly into Phoenix Sky Harbor International Airport and check into your resort. You've got plenty of time to explore the city, so spend the afternoon taking advantage of the resort's amenities, which range from water parks and tennis courts to game rooms for kids.

Day 2

There's no better place to begin your trip to Phoenix than at its ancient foundations, the Pueblo Grande Museum and Archaeological Park. Go inside reconstructed pit homes and learn how archaeologists dig for artifacts by getting your own hands dirty. Head to neighboring Tempe Town Lake, where you can rent paddleboats or let the little ones run wild in the water-soaked Splash Playground. Have lunch at one of Mill Avenue's many restaurants, such as Bison Witches Bar and Deli. Cross back over the lake to Papago Park to tour the Phoenix Zoo, where you can touch stingrays or duck into the walk-through Monkey Village. In the evening, sample the tacos, chimichangas, and fajitas at Macayo's Depot Cantina.

Day 3

Begin your third day in the Valley at Matt's Big Breakfast, a downtown Phoenix breakfast joint known for its fresh orange juice, hash browns, thick-cut bacon, and scrambled eggs with salami. Afterward, visit the Arizona State Capitol, restored to its original look in 1912, the year of Arizona's statehood. Nearby, the Arizona Mining and Mineral Museum showcases the state's geological wealth with

Pueblo Grande Museum and Archaeological Park, Phoenix

Arizona Science Center, Phoenix

sparkling gemstones, prehistoric fossils, and enormous excavation equipment. Consider a picnic lunch at Civic Space Park, where kids play in the grass or splash around in the water features, or Encanto Park, home of Enchanted Island Amusement Park. If it's a little too cool (or hot), grab a bite at CityBakery at the Arizona Science Center, a delightfully interactive museum in Heritage and Science Park. Younger kids may prefer the Children's Museum of Phoenix, across 7th Street. Older teens may enjoy a tour of Phoenix's progressive art and design at the Phoenix Art Museum and the Burton Barr Central Library, which offers brilliant views of the Phoenix skyline. Tonight, try dinner at one of downtown's pizzerias, like Cibo or the renowned Pizzeria Bianco.

Day 4

It's time to immerse yourself in the Sonoran Desert, with a morning hike in South Mountain Park, the world's largest municipal park. Hunt for ancient Native American petroglyphs or explore the pristine trails on horseback. Reward your adventurous spirit with a hearty, gourmet meal at the open-air The Farm at South Mountain. Explore more of South Phoenix at the mountainside Mystery Castle, a private home built from objects found in the desert, or you may want to take the kids to Rawhide Western Town. The 1880s-themed Old West town features dusty streets, stagecoach rides, and old-fashioned carnival games. After lunch, pan for "gold," visit a territorial jail, and scope out the three-story Dinosaur Mountain at the Arizona Museum of Natural History in Mesa. Then, consider dinner at Caffe Boa and a stroll along Mill Avenue.

Day 5

Today, discover Arizona's rich Native American history. Start out at the Heard Museum, an impressive introduction to Arizona's original inhabitants and culture. Then, head north on I-17 to Montezuma Castle National Monument. The stunning five-story pueblo, perched cliffside near Camp Verde, was once inhabited by the ancient Sinagua people. Just up the interstate, you can witness more of their ingenuity at Montezuma Well, one of Arizona's unique geological wonders, which is fed by 1.5 million gallons of water every day by underground springs.

From there, take I-17 to Highway 179 and explore the red rocks of Sedona. As you drive into town, admire the monolithic Bell Rock, Courthouse Butte, and Cathedral Rock. Pull over in the Village of Oak Creek to have lunch at the Village Griddle. Fortified, stop in at Chapel of the

UNEXPECTED ARIZONA

The West's pioneering spirit and eccentric personality are alive and well in Arizona. Check out the manmade lakes, the quirky public art pieces, and the old ghost town where hippies and bikers now roam the streets.

PHOENIX

Mystery Castle: Mary Lou Gulley still welcomes visitors into her home, an eccentric "castle" her father built in the 1930s and '40s from found objects like rocks, adobe, glass, auto parts, and even petroglyphs.

Civic Space Park: *Her Secret Is Patience,* a massive fabric-net sculpture that hangs over the park from steel rings, resembles a saguaro cactus blossom – or a giant jellyfish, depending on your perspective.

Tempe Town Lake: The city of Tempe converted two miles of the usually dry Salt River into a reservoir lake for boating, rowing, and fishing, thanks to a series of inflatable rubber dams.

SCOTTSDALE

Cosanti: Visit this small artists' village and bell foundry by Paolo Soleri, Frank Lloyd Wright's former student, which includes a subterranean "Earth House," outdoor studios, and student dorms.

McCormick-Stillman Railroad Park: Antique engines and train cars dot this popular city park, where children and train buffs can ride a scale reproduction of a narrow-gauge railroad.

Cave Creek: You're more likely today to find yuppie bikers and artists than cattlemen in this former Old West town. Still, the community manages to retain much of its 1880s character at Frontier Town.

the bells of Cosanti

SEDONA

Snoopy Rock: Kids get a kick out of the red-rock formation from the perspective of Uptown Sedona, where they recognize the famous beagle asleep on his back. Lucy Rock is nearby.

Sedona Air Tours: Take to the skies in a vintage Red Waco biplane, which can accommodate two passengers at a time, with a pilot providing commentary about the changing landscape.

Jerome: Hippies, artists, and bikers have transformed the old mining town into an eclectic mix of galleries, hotels, restaurants, and saloons.

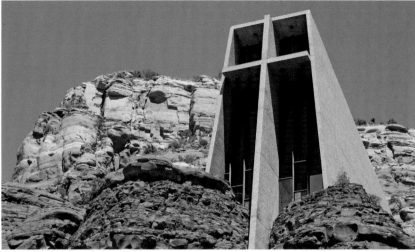

Chapel of the Holy Cross, just south of Sedona

Holy Cross, an elegant, Modernist church that appears to rise out of the red rocks, offering panoramic views of Sedona. Check into your hotel, and after dinner at Elote Cafe, consider a stargazing adventure with an astronomer who will guide you around Arizona's nighttime sky.

Day 6

Have breakfast at Coffee Pot Restaurant and explore one of Sedona's protected parks, like Red Rock State Park or Crescent Moon Recreation Area, which features postcard views of Oak Creek and Cathedral Rock. Also, you can't come to Sedona without venturing into the backcountry on one of the ubiquitous Jeep tours. The guided journeys are a fun way to explore out-of-the-way formations and learn about Sedona's unique geology and wildlife. After lunch at Oak Creek Brewery and Grill at Tlaquepaque, head north on Highway 89A to the leafy refuge of Oak Creek Canyon. Hike the picturesque forest trails or plunge down the 80-foot-long natural chute at Slide Rock State Park.

Day 7

Take a side trip to the Old West mining town of Jerome. The hillside community was once called the "Wickedest Town in the West," and today it's a National Historic Landmark, welcoming visitors with a host of small cafés, shops, galleries, and saloons. Have lunch at Mile High Grill & Spirits and visit the Mine Museum before driving back to the Valley of the Sun. Consider a stop at Dead Horse Ranch State Park, a lush stretch of Verde River that offers hiking, mountain biking, fishing, and equestrian areas. Make the 90-minute drive back to Scottsdale, where you check into one of the city's sprawling resorts.

Day 8

Reacquaint yourself with the Valley of the Sun at Camelback Mountain. The moderately difficult trails are among the best in the area, although you may want to take the little ones to McCormick-Stillman Railroad Park, where they can ride the popular train or beautifully restored carousel. After lunch at Chloe's Corner, head to Frank Lloyd

Oak Creek Canyon

Jerome's Mine Museum

Scottsdale's Old Town

Wright's desert masterpiece, Taliesin West, for a tour of the architect's winter home. Then, keep heading north on Scottsdale Road to Frontier Town in Cave Creek. Embrace the Wild West spirit and have dinner at Reata Pass, a cowboy steakhouse that oozes real Western atmosphere.

Day 9

Today, you want to camp out at your resort to enjoy the pools, tennis courts, and golf courses. However, if you're looking for a little adventure, float down the Salt or Verde River on a guided rafting tour. Tonight, have dinner at Old Town Tortilla Factory, then explore the hidden nocturnal desert with the aid of night-vision goggles on an outing with Desert Storm Hummer Tours. You'll never be so excited to see coyotes and scorpions.

Day 10

On your last day in Scottsdale, dine at The Breakfast Club and Barrista Bar and explore the Western-themed streets of Old Town to pick up last-minute souvenirs and gifts. Hop on and off the free Scottsdale Trolley, which stops in the three arts districts and at Scottsdale Fashion Square. Grab lunch at The Orange Table before you have to catch your flight home.

▶ DESERT CHIC

Brilliant light, rugged mountains, sculptural plant life—few landscapes create such an evocative setting, but the Sonoran Desert also has a luxurious, cosmopolitan side, which lures pleasure-seekers and stressed-out vacationers to its resorts, golf courses, and award-winning restaurants and five-star spas. Sip prickly pear margaritas amid the boulders and adobe villas of Scottsdale before retreating north to Sedona's red rocks.

Day 1

Arrive at Phoenix Sky Harbor International Airport and head to Papago Park to get your bearings of this sprawling city. The park's rounded, red-rock formation is an easy ascent, and its views of the desert metropolis are well worth the little bit of effort. Visit the park's Desert Botanical Garden to learn about spiny cacti, green-bark palo verde trees, and colorful wildflowers. Afterward, head north on Scottsdale Road to see these indigenous plants in their native environment at the Four Seasons Scottsdale at Troon North, a desert sanctuary inspired by old adobe villas and nestled into the foothills of Pinnacle Peak. Relax on the veranda overlooking the Valley of the Sun and enjoy—literally—the fruits of the desert in a delicious prickly pear margarita. Have dinner at one of the resort's restaurants, or order room service for a romantic meal on your private balcony.

Day 2

Wake up early to experience the desert at sunrise. Consider a leisurely hike up Pinnacle Peak or a round of golf at Troon North Golf Club, one of the Valley's best championship desert courses. Have lunch at Chloe's Corner, and reward your efforts and soothe any aching muscles at one of Scottsdale's deluxe spas, like the canyon-inspired Willow Stream Spa or the renowned Golden Door Spa, which is set against the Boulders Resort's namesake rock formation and features treatments rooted in Native American traditions. The spa also offers rock-climbing clinics for the more adventurous. Once you're feeling relaxed, head over to Kierland Commons, an outdoor shopping center in North Scottsdale, to browse for gifts or to find a cozy restaurant for dinner.

Day 3

Spend the morning shopping at Scottsdale Fashion Square and SouthBridge in downtown Scottsdale. Grab brunch at Arcadia Farms, a charming cottage that serves fresh sandwiches, soups, and salads. Afterward, drive across Scottsdale Road to Old Town for more shopping. You can also get a dose of historical and modern culture at the Old Adobe Mission and the Scottsdale Museum of Contemporary Art, which is highlighted by Skyspace, an exhibition by installation artist James Turrell that ingeniously frames Arizona's changing sky. If you're hungry for more art, downtown's galleries are among the finest in the country, showcasing edgy modern pieces along with traditional Southwestern art. You're in the heart of Scottsdale's dining and nightlife scene, so spend your evening sampling the city's numerous options, such as Roaring Fork and Olive & Ivy.

Day 4

Horseback ride this morning through the desert and mountain passes of Tonto National Forest with Spur Cross Stables. Customize your horseback adventure or select one of several themed options. Afterward, enjoy lunch at Zinc Bistro and perhaps a quick siesta. Re-energized, drive south on Scottsdale Road to Paradise Valley, where Paolo Soleri's quirky Cosanti bell foundry and artist community reveals the architect's theories on environmentally responsible design. As evening approaches, enjoy a handcrafted cocktail at Sanctuary on Camelback Mountain Resort & Spa's stylish Jade Bar, where you can catch Mummy Mountain bathed in a desert sunset. Enjoy a Western-inspired dinner at the historic Lon's at the Hermosa Inn or go modern at the sleek Bourbon Steak.

horseback riding with Spur Cross Stables

entrance to Tlaquepaque Arts and Crafts Village

Day 5

Even the quintessentially American architect Frank Lloyd Wright was seduced by the desert. Tour his winter home, Taliesin West, a stone, sand, and glass masterpiece that incorporates indigenous materials and blends indoor and outdoor spaces. Afterward, get a brief introduction to Native American art, culture, and design at the Heard Museum North, an intimate branch of the respected Indian museum in downtown Phoenix. Have lunch at the charming El Encanto, then drive north to the high desert of Sedona, where massive red-rock buttes reveal Arizona's rich geological diversity. Once you get into town, head west on Highway 89A to Boynton Canyon, where the hacienda-inspired Enchantment Resort and Mii Amo spa are enveloped by the canyon's soaring cliff walls. You may never want to leave, though you should for dinner at El Portal Sedona.

Day 6

This morning, survey the red-rock buttes from the sky while floating in a hot-air balloon over Sedona, giving a bit of perspective of the vast scale of the region's rocky formations. Once you descend and enjoy the complimentary champagne breakfast, be sure to visit the Chapel of the Holy Cross, where a local artist and Frank Lloyd Wright's son created a stunning church that seems to emerge from its red-rock foundations. You then have plenty of time to shop the small boutiques and galleries at Tlaquepaque Arts and Crafts Village. Tonight, dine creekside at L'Auberge Restaurant on Oak Creek.

Day 7

Have breakfast at Secret Garden Café at Tlaquepaque, and spend the morning perusing the shops in Uptown or the artists' studios on Gallery Row, where you may find a piece of colorful pottery or a handmade Navajo rug to take home. Enjoy a picnic lunch at Sedona Memories, and drive back to Phoenix to catch a late flight home.

PHOENIX

Abandon your expectations of Phoenix. The desert metropolis, once dismissed as an ever-sprawling suburb, is transforming into a cultural hub, building a host of new, architecturally significant museums, developing arts districts, and weaving together communities with a new light-rail network.

To visitors, the Valley of the Sun is a recreational nirvana, where warm days by the pool or on the links melt into a blazing sea of color at sunset. This heady mix of sun and fun has tempted many to make a permanent move. But Phoenicians, like most city dwellers, aren't content to simply waste away in a dreamy haze of margaritas. The pioneering spirit is alive and well in the country's fifth-largest city, and Phoenicians are determined to create a vibrant, culturally relevant city on par with its Sun Belt sisters in Miami, Austin, and Los Angeles. They want their ice cream cake, and they'll eat it, too.

The dramatic landscape and Western spirit have conspired to create a unique destination. Sure, you'll find prickly cacti, lots of sunshine, and all the things you think you already know about Phoenix, but you'll also discover a unique sensibility. Get to know the city and its residents by having brunch at the Farm at South Mountain or simply lounge by the pool to savor that favorite Phoenician punch line—"the dry heat."

Phoenix shouldn't be explored as a succession of tourist sites à la New York or Washington, D.C. Instead, think of the city as a collection of experiences: the scent of orange blossoms in the spring or the sound of gravel beneath

© MICA THOMAS MULLOY

PHOENIX

HIGHLIGHTS

Heritage and Science Park: Get a glimpse of Phoenix's original Victorian-era townsite. Heritage Square's eight historic homes now house small museums and popular restaurants and bars, and its futuristic Arizona Science Center is the perfect spot to escape the summer heat (page 32).

Heard Museum: Perhaps the finest collection of Native American art in the world, the Heard Museum is one of Arizona's great treasures. Learn about the incredibly rich culture of the state's original inhabitants (page 34).

Phoenix Art Museum: A $50 million expansion has helped transform the museum into a sleek, stylish cultural institution. The museum's galleries feature a diverse selection of American, European, and Latin American artists, as well as Asian art and fashion design (page 36).

Burton Barr Central Library: This iconic building's rectangular, rusted-steel facade has come to define the region's Desert Modernism architecture movement. Be sure to peek inside and check out the views (page 37).

Hole-in-the-Rock: Join Phoenicians who gather in Papago Park to hike this rounded, red-rock formation that was once used by the ancient Hohokam civilization for astronomy (page 38).

Desert Botanical Garden: Get a taste of the Sonoran Desert without leaving the city. The garden easily claims the world's largest collection of desert plants, with some 21,000 cacti, shrubs, trees, and colorful wildflowers (page 39).

Pueblo Grande Museum and Archaeological Park: Discover Phoenix's ancient roots. The site of a Hohokam village that stood here from about A.D. 100 to 1400, Pueblo Grande offers a fascinating into the city's past (page 40).

Arizona Museum of Natural History: Pan for gold, visit a territorial jail, and scope out the mammoth dinosaur fossils. This fun, interactive museum explores Arizona's natural and cultural history (page 45).

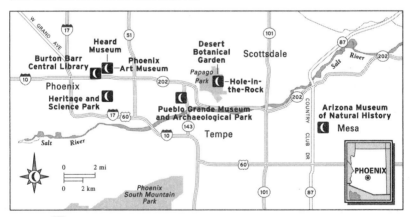

LOOK FOR ▐ TO FIND RECOMMENDED SIGHTS, ACTIVITIES, DINING, AND LODGING.

© MICA THOMAS MULLOY

Piestewa Peak at the Phoenix Mountains Preserve

your feet as you climb Piestewa Peak. Sample authentic corn tortillas and carne asada at the small taquerias that dot the city, or discover the ancient culture of the region's Native American people at the Heard Museum. These subtle—often hidden—pleasures will linger long after a suntan begins to fade.

PLANNING YOUR TIME

You'll need at least three days to see Phoenix, balancing a few cultural sights with the bounty of outdoor activities. Consider a hike or round of golf in the morning and afternoon visits to the Phoenix Art Museum, Heritage Square, or the world-renowned Heard Museum, a rich repository of Native American art and artifacts. However, you should really take a week to make the most of a trip to the Valley of the Sun. Phoenix, Scottsdale, and the surrounding suburbs each offer pockets of pedestrian-friendly neighborhoods to explore, and you'll

want to make sure you have plenty of time to relax and enjoy the sunshine.

Families, couples, and groups of friends won't struggle to find activities that appeal to their tastes. Most of the year, kids spend morning, noon, and, yes, night, in the Valley's pools and water parks, a recreational specialty found at many resorts. When the weather is a bit cooler, though, the Phoenix Zoo and the Old West–themed Rawhide Western Town can be fun diversions. Adults, too, won't mind spending time poolside, with a tasty beverage and good book in hand. Be sure to make some time to immerse yourself in the Sonoran Desert landscape, though. Hikers, mountain bikers, and horseback riders of all levels will appreciate the cactus-dotted peaks that rise throughout the city. You can even get a taste of this rugged landscape without leaving the city's paved sidewalks at the Desert Botanical Garden and Papago Park.

The Valley of the Sun is huge, covering 2,000 square miles. The area's four million residents crisscross the city daily thanks to a large web of freeways. Fortunately for visitors, many of the best sights, parks, restaurants, and shops are clustered in a central strip running from South Mountain through downtown Phoenix and Tempe to North Scottsdale. To explore the city, you'll definitely need a car—and you'll become quite familiar with the main commuter arteries: I-10, Highway 101 and Highway 202, and Central Avenue and Camelback Road.

The weather, in all likelihood, will shape what you do and when you do it. Phoenix is heavenly October through April, when warm days and cool evenings attract most visitors. It can even get a little cold in the winter, with the occasional nighttime temperature drop below freezing. Summer is a much different story. Count on triple-digit temps June through September, making a swimming pool or air-conditioned escape mandatory. Don't be frightened, though. The desert's arid climate means you'll actually be shivering when you emerge from a pool, and an early morning hike

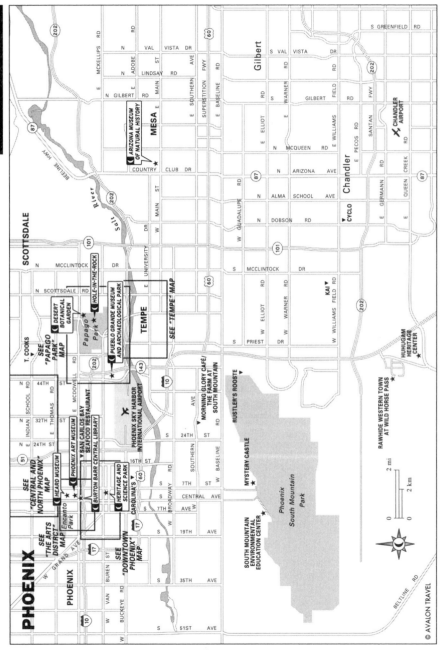

or round of golf means you won't be trapped inside. It's also the opportunity to indulge at luxury resorts for bargain prices.

HISTORY

Phoenix is called a "young" city so often that it's easy to forget that there's an entire ancient civilization buried underneath it. Native Americans have called the Sonoran Desert home for thousands of years, but the Hohokam people dug the first irrigation canals fed by the Salt River about 2,000 years ago. They improved and expanded the system over centuries using nothing but wood and stone tools, simple leveling devices, and their own labor. Some canals were as long as 20 miles and carried thousands of gallons of water through a complex series of main lines, laterals, and small ditches. At its height around 1300, the system watered more than 10,000 acres scattered across most of what is now metro Phoenix. The Hohokam's corn, beans, squash, and cotton crops supported as many as 50,000 people, making the Salt River valley one of the largest settlements in prehistoric North America. But after 1,500 years of growth, Hohokam society began a slow collapse, likely triggered by a combination of drought, environmental stresses, and war. By the end of 1400s, the people had abandoned their pueblos and canals for small farming villages scattered across the region.

Modern Phoenix wasn't born until 1867, when a man named Jack Swilling passed through and saw that the Salt River Valley looked like a good place for farming. The broad, fertile valley was filled with desert grasses, mesquite, willow, and cottonwood trees, and best of all, the wide, winding river that flowed down out of the mountains to the northeast. So after the one-time army scout, gold miner, cattle rancher, and saloon owner returned home to Wickenburg, a mining town about 50 miles northwest of present-day Phoenix, he got financial backing from a group of local residents and organized a company to dig irrigation canals and establish farms in the remote valley.

THE VALLEY OF THE SUN

Phoenix, now the fifth-largest city in the country, is just a part of an immense metropolitan area known as the Valley of the Sun – and it's not just a tourism slogan. "The Valley," as locals call it, is surrounded by a series of mountain ranges, and after decades of suburban sprawl, it is creeping beyond the valley floor. Just since 2000, more than 1 million people have moved here. Developers have consumed huge swaths of agricultural land and pristine desert. Formerly independent cities and towns now blend from one into another, connected by a giant grid of freeways. In fact, the United States Census Bureau now designates all of Maricopa and Pinal Counties as part of the Phoenix metropolitan area, a mammoth conglomeration of 60-plus municipalities, Native American lands, and 4.2 million people.

The East Valley was the first to experience a huge surge of arrivals in the 1980s and '90s, when small cities like Chandler and former agricultural centers like Gilbert, Queen Creek, and Apache Junction became stucco-home boomtowns. Bedroom communities like Fountain Hills and Ahwatukee practically sprang up overnight. Scottsdale in the Northeast Valley also experienced significant growing pains, annexing huge portions of land.

A decade later, master-planned communities – like Anthem in the north, Gold Canyon in the east, and Maricopa in the south – pushed further into the desert. Developers in the West Valley turned huge tracts of land into subdivisions that now house hundreds of thousands of people. Glendale and the retirement community of Sun City were soon engulfed by Surprise, Avondale, Goodyear, Peoria, and Buckeye. Leaders have had to scramble to find the best ways to turn their small towns in big ones. However, the housing bust in 2008 complicated matters, with the West Valley becoming one of the hardest-hit areas in the country.

It wasn't long before he and the dozens of settlers who followed discovered that digging up the Hohokam canal system was an easier way to bring water to their fields than starting from scratch. So it was that an erudite settler named Darrell Duppa suggested they name their new town Phoenix, after the mythical bird that rises from its own ashes after being consumed by flame.

By 1900, the young town's population had grown to 5,554 thanks to a long growing season and new railroads centered on historic Union Station downtown that took farmers' crops all across the United States. Modern technology didn't solve all their problems, though. Snowmelt and rain regularly sent the Salt River over its banks, including the worst flood on record in February 1901, which swelled the river to three miles wide in some places, wiping out crops, houses, and the all-important railroad bridge. The brand-new territorial capitol west of downtown was inundated, too, destroying many early records. Luckily, President Theodore Roosevelt was ready to ride to the rescue with a bold plan and several million dollars.

Roosevelt tasked the newly formed federal Bureau of Reclamation with building a hydroelectric dam on the Salt River in 1911 to control flooding and generate electricity. It was the first project the new agency tackled, and though it tamed the free-flowing river by diverting the whole flow from its banks into an expanded canal system, it led to one of the city's first big boom periods. With an economy fueled by the "Five C's"—citrus, cotton, cattle, copper, and climate—Phoenix's population mushroomed to nearly 30,000 people by 1920, then added almost 20,000 more by 1930, matching the Hohokam's previous record of 50,000 inhabitants in just 50 years. The boom had barely begun, though.

Following World War II, returning soldiers—many of whom had trained at the airbases that sprang up around Phoenix thanks to its sunny, flying-friendly weather—flocked to the area and its burgeoning aerospace industry. As air-conditioning became widely available and early technology-manufacturing companies also moved here in search of cheap land, the population grew past 100,000 by 1950 and neared an almost-unimaginable 440,000 by 1960.

Today, some 1.5 million live in Phoenix, making it the fifth-largest city in the nation behind New York City, Los Angeles, Chicago, and Houston. Growth has come with a price, however. Many residents see pollution and the destruction of pristine desert sapping their quality of life as suburban sprawl forces them to spend hours commuting or going about everyday tasks. But the same spirit that drove Phoenicians to build a metropolis in less than 150 years is pushing them to dream up new solutions, and it's anyone's guess what seemingly impossible feats the residents of this dynamic city will tackle next.

Sights

Phoenix, now the fifth-largest city in the U.S., is a sprawling expanse of neighborhoods and suburbs, and its attractions are scattered throughout the city. You'll need a car to navigate the Valley of the Sun, though the new light-rail system conveniently connects some of the most popular sights, including the Heard Museum, the Phoenix Art Museum, the Arizona Science Center, and Tempe's Mill Avenue neighborhood.

DOWNTOWN AND THE ARTS DISTRICT

Like any Old West town worth its salt, Phoenix has had to endure the boom and bust of life in the desert since its founding in 1870. However, unlike some of its ghost town brethren, Phoenix has a knack for reemerging from hard times. Tombstone may be "the town too tough to die," but downtown Phoenix is the metropolis that always seems to rise again.

PHOENIX

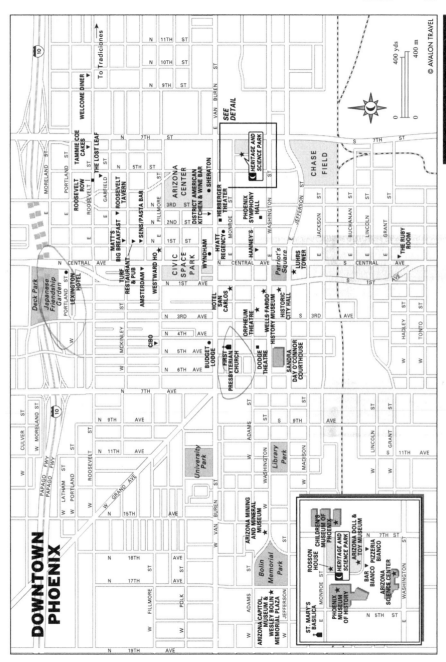

DOWNTOWN PHOENIX

To Tradiciones

WELCOME DINER

TAMMIE COE CAKES

THE LOST LEAF

ROOSEVELT ROW

ROOSEVELT TAVERN

MATT'S BIG BREAKFAST

SENS/PASTA BAR

ARIZONA CENTER

DISTRICT AMERICAN KITCHEN & WINE BAR

SHERATON

HERBERGER THEATER

PHOENIX SYMPHONY HALL

HYATT REGENCY

HANNEY'S

LEXINGTON HOTEL

TURF RESTAURANT & PUB

AMSTERDAM

WESTWARD HO

CIVIC SPACE PARK

WYNDHAM

Patriot's Square

LUHRS TOWER

THE RUBY ROOM

Japanese Friendship Garden

Deck Park

HOTEL SAN CARLOS

ORPHEUM THEATRE

WELLS FARGO HISTORY MUSEUM

HISTORIC CITY HALL

CIBO

BUDGET LODGE

FIRST PRESBYTERIAN CHURCH

DODGE THEATRE

SANDRA DAY O'CONNOR COURTHOUSE

University Park

ARIZONA MINING AND MINERAL MUSEUM

Library Park

Bolin Memorial Park

ARIZONA CAPITOL MUSEUM & WESLEY BOLIN MEMORIAL PLAZA

ST. MARY'S BASILICA

SEE DETAIL

HERITAGE AND SCIENCE PARK

CHASE FIELD

400 yds

400 m

© AVALON TRAVEL

Inset (SEE DETAIL):

ROSSON HOUSE

CHILDREN'S MUSEUM OF PHOENIX

HERITAGE AND SCIENCE PARK

ARIZONA DOLL & TOY MUSEUM

BAR BIANCO

PIZZERIA BIANCO

ARIZONA SCIENCE CENTER

PHOENIX MUSEUM OF HISTORY

EXPLORING PHOENIX'S ARCHITECTURE

Changing architectural styles in Phoenix's neighborhoods and commercial districts are like tree rings tracking the city's growth. Because it grew so big so fast, many neighborhoods in Phoenix were built all of a piece by developers. The resulting "master-planned communities" can make it seem like all the city has to offer are cookie-cutter ranch houses or red-tile roofs, but nothing could be further from the truth. The warm, sunny climate has encouraged architectural innovation since the first people moved to the Sonoran Desert, and today is no exception.

Phoenix Prehistory (A.D. 1-1450): More than 2,000 years ago, the Hohokam people started building a system of irrigation canals fed by the Salt River. For the next millennium and a half, they built villages, pit houses, and walled pueblos that housed as many as 50,000 people in what is now metro Phoenix, making it one of the largest ancient population centers in North America. The society collapsed in mid-1400s, and of most of their buildings are gone or buried, but visitors can walk through the ruins of a large, 800-year-old platform mound at **Pueblo Grande Museum and Archaeological Park** (4619 E. Washington St., 602/495-0901, www.phoenix.gov, 9 A.M.-5 P.M. Mon.-Sat., 1-5 P.M. Sun., closed Sun. and Mon. May-Sept., $6 adults, $3 children 6-17). The earthen-walled structure evokes how these resourceful people adapted to life in the desert.

Turn of the 20th Century (1880-1915): The 19th-century houses huddled on **Heritage Square** (115 N. 6th St., 602/262-5071, www.phoenix.gov/parks) show the roots of the modern city. Home to the merchants and traders who served what was then a valley of farmers and ranchers, they are the only extant residential structures from the city's original townsite. The sturdy, red-brick homes with ample verandahs are now inhabited by a mix of restaurants, bars, and museums. The **Rosson House** (115 N. 6th St., 602/262-5029, 10 A.M.-4 P.M. Wed., 1-4 P.M. Thurs., 10 A.M.-4 P.M. Fri.-Sat., noon-4 P.M. Sun., $5 adults, $2 children 6-12), a Victorian mansion built in 1895, is open for public tours.

The Roaring Twenties (1920-1935): A half-mile stretch of Central Avenue between Jefferson and Fillmore Streets downtown displays the architectural ambitions from this perennial boomtown's first growth spurt in the 1920s. The renaissance-revival **Hotel San Carlos** (220 N. Central Ave., 602/253-4121, www.hotelsancarlos.com) and the Art Deco **Westward Ho** (618 N. Central Ave.) both debuted in 1928 as luxury hotels that have attracted Hollywood stars, gangsters, and politicians over the ensuing decades (take a look at the famous-guest list on the sidewalk outside the San Carlos). The 14-story, Art Deco **Luhrs Tower** (45 W. Jefferson St.) rose a year later in 1929. Across the street, Phoenix's 1928 **Historic City Hall** (125 W. Washington St.) makes the idea of occupying one of the jail cells on the upper levels almost appealing. The **First Presbyterian Church** (402 W. Monroe St., 602/254-6356, www.historicfirst.org) and the **Orpheum Theatre** (203 W. Adams St., 602/262-7272, www.phoenix.gov) both inject Spanish Revival with a little Moorish style, and it's possible to get tours of both. Simply ask around at the church, and you might get lucky. Free theater tours run the second Tuesday of the month, but call the Friends of the Orpheum Theatre (602/262-6025, www.friendsoftheorpheumtheatre.org) to confirm dates and times.

Midcentury Identity (1948-1970): Phoenix came of age following World War II as its population exploded, and the city's wealth of midcentury architecture shows it. Frank Lloyd Wright lived in Arizona for decades, designing a number of buildings around town, including his winter home and workshop, **Taliesin West** (12621 N. Frank Lloyd Wright Blvd., 480/860-2700, www.franklloydwright.org, 8:30 A.M.-5:30 P.M. daily). It's open for tours daily, as is **Cosanti,** designed by Wright acolyte Paolo Soleri (6433 E. Doubletree Ranch Rd., 480/948-6145, www.arcosanti.org, 9 A.M.-5 P.M. Mon.-Sat., 11 A.M.-5 P.M. Sun., free). Good examples of midcentury commercial buildings include the 1964 **Phoenix Financial Center** (3443 N. Central Ave.), which has a facade designed to look like a computer punch

© MICA THOMAS MULLOY

Burton Barr Central Library, a prime example of Desert Modernism architecture

card, and **Hanny's,** which was downtown's first "modern" department store in 1948 and now houses a restaurant of the same name (40 N. 1st St., 602/252-2285, http://hannys.net). But the best places to see how new owners have updated that icon of the Atomic Age, the ranch house, are two neighborhoods near the Phoenix Mountains Preserve. A drive around **Paradise Gardens** – generally bounded by 36th and 33rd Streets to the east and west and Gold Dust and Mountain View Roads to the north and south – shows off the work of locally revered architect Al Beadle. **Marlen Gardens** – which sits between Bethany Home and Montebello Roads along 10th and 11th Streets – was designed and built by the equally beloved Arizona architect Ralph Haver. The group Modern Phoenix (www.modern phoenix.net) arranges tours of residences several times a year.

Desert Modern (1990-present): Dozens of Phoenix offices and houses have earned the attention of the design world over the past few years thanks to their blending of indoor/outdoor spaces, innovative use of materials, and embrace of light and space. But a lot of it is, unfortunately, private. The best publicly accessible examples of this Desert Modernism are a trio of public libraries (www.phoenixpublic library.org): the Will Bruder-designed **Burton Barr Central Library** (1221 N. Central Ave.), the Richard+Bauer-designed **Desert Broom Library** (29710 N. Cave Creek Rd.), and the Gould Evans and Wendell Burnette-designed **Palo Verde Branch Library** (4402 N. 51st Ave.). Other ways to catch a glimpse of spectacular houses include driving around nicer neighborhoods, particularly near the mountains, or scanning real estate websites such as www.azarchitecture.com for open houses.

(Contributed by David Proffitt, architectural journalist)

Following decades of suburban flight and urban decay, businesses and, more importantly, people, are returning. An estimated $3 billion was spent redeveloping the 90-block area dubbed **Copper Square** (602/495-1500, www.coppersquare.com), and it seems to be paying off, albeit slowly. Much as in the city's early days, when farmers and ranchers would come to town for a show or to pick up supplies, suburbanites are flocking to downtown's stadiums, museums, and concert venues, and even supporting new restaurants and bars. The construction of a new convention center and Arizona State University's downtown campus has brought some nighttime pedestrian traffic to the once-empty streets. Plus, the light rail has given downtown another shot in the arm. If you have any questions or need directions—downtown is built in an easy-to-navigate grid—look for one of the Copper Square "ambassadors," easily identifiable in an orange shirt.

© MICA THOMAS MULLOY

Arizona State Capitol

Arizona State Capitol

Arizona's territorial capital bounced between Prescott and Tucson before finally settling in Phoenix in 1889. In an effort to prove to the federal government that Arizona was ready for statehood, the territorial legislature constructed the capitol building between 1898 and 1901. The design, based on a rejected concept for the Mississippi State Capitol, was modified by legislators, who scaled back its size and added features appropriate for Arizona's desert climate, like thick masonry walls for insulation and ventilating windows. They also painted the dome copper as a tribute to the mineral that served as an essential economic resource.

As the state grew, so did the demands on the building. Part-time Arizona resident Frank Lloyd Wright submitted plans in 1957 for a massive Arizona Capitol Complex, which would have transferred the legislature, governor, and Supreme Court from downtown to Papago Park—at a whopping cost of $5 million. It was immediately rejected. (You can see one of the proposed 125-foot-tall spires for the project at Scottsdale and Frank Lloyd Wright

Boulevards in North Scottsdale.) Instead, the state House and Senate were relocated into bunker-like buildings on either side of the capitol in 1960, and the governor moved to the Executive Tower behind the capitol.

A renovation in 1981 restored the building to its original look from 1912, the year of Arizona's statehood, and the dome was finally given a proper copper plating: 4.8 million pennies-worth, a fitting number for the 48th state. That same year, the **Arizona Capitol Museum** (1700 W. Washington St., 602/926-3620, www.lib.az.us/museum, 9 a.m.–4 p.m. Mon.–Fri., closed Sat.–Sun., free) was opened, allowing visitors to see the old House and Senate chambers, offices of the governor, and exhibitions about Arizona's history. There is also a small display chronicling the USS *Arizona*. The rapidly growing state is contemplating another overhaul in honor of its centennial in 2012. Many are calling for a radical transformation of the buildings and the adjacent **Wesley Bolin Memorial Plaza,** though tight budgets likely will delay those plans.

Arizona Mining and Mineral Museum

Texas may have its black gold, but Arizona made its underground fortune in the mines. Get a load of the state's haul at the Arizona Mining and Mineral Museum (1502 W. Washington St., 602/771-1611, http://mines. az.gov, 8 A.M.–5 P.M. Mon.–Fri., 11 A.M.–4 P.M. Sat., $2 adults, children 17 and under free), which showcases more than 3,000 minerals, rocks, fossils, and mining artifacts, including an eight-foot specimen of copper and rocks from the first moon landing. The sparkling gemstones and iridescent semiprecious stones are real show-stoppers, and kids will love the enormous excavation and mining equipment.

Civic Space Park

Part of an effort by city leaders to transform downtown into a vibrant urban space, the new Civic Space Park (424 N. Central Ave., 602/262-4734, www.phoenix.gov/parks, 5:30 A.M.–11 P.M. daily, free) brings some green design to the neighborhood, with rolling lawns, dancing water fountains, and leafy trees that are expected to shade as much as 70 percent of the park once they mature.

Her Secret Is Patience, a massive fabric-net

PHOENIX POINTS OF PRIDE

A city still trying to define its identity, Phoenix has created a list of 32 sights that "contribute to the quality of life in the Valley." Among the parks, historic residences, cultural buildings, and natural attractions that residents voted for:

- Arizona Biltmore Resort & Spa
- Burton Barr Central Library
- Camelback Mountain
- Desert Botanical Garden
- Encanto Park
- Heard Museum
- Herberger Theater
- Heritage Square
- Japanese Friendship Garden
- Mystery Castle
- Orpheum Theatre
- Papago Park/Hole-in-the-Rock
- Phoenix Zoo
- Pueblo Grande Museum and Archaeological Park
- South Mountain Park

- St. Mary's Basilica
- Tovrea Castle and Carraro Cactus Garden
- Wrigley Mansion

© MICA THOMAS MULLOY

St. Mary's Basilica

sculpture that hangs over the park from steel rings, has garnered some controversy, both because of its abstract shape and its $2.4 million price tag. Artist Janet Echelman—who named the piece after a line in a Ralph Waldo Emerson poem: "Adopt the pace of nature; her secret is patience"—says Arizona's monsoon clouds and saguaro cactus blossoms inspired her, though some liken the funnel-shaped sculpture more to a giant jellyfish or purple tornado. Either way, the kinetic sculpture billows in the wind and literally shines at night, when powerful lights cause the painted nets to glow brilliant shades of violet and orange. In fact, it's the three-acre park's transformation when the sun sets that makes it so unique. A dozen LED-lit poles put on a show at the south end of the park while whimsical water features for kids glow purple. There is even space for movies and small concerts, which attract students from Arizona State University's adjacent downtown campus. The requisite energy demands are offset by solar panels on the park's shade structures during the day.

Wells Fargo History Museum

For a quick snapshot of the Wild West, duck into the Wells Fargo History Museum (145 W. Adams St., 602/378-1852, www.wellsfargohistory.com/museums, 9 A.M.–5 P.M. Mon.–Fri., free), where you'll be greeted by an icon of Arizona's history—an authentic 19th-century stagecoach that still bears the scars of a hard life roaming the West's bumpy trails. The small collection of memorabilia includes antique guns, Western artwork by N.C. Wyeth and Frederic Remington, and a softball-size nugget of gold. Plus, kids can try their hands at the telegraph or climb aboard a replica stagecoach.

St. Mary's Basilica

When Phoenix's citizens built their first Catholic church in 1881, I suspect only the most devout could have imagined a papal visit some 100 years later. That original structure, constructed from hand-formed adobe, was replaced in 1902 by St. Mary's Basilica (231 N. 3rd St., 602/354-2100, www.stmarysbasilica.org, 9 A.M.–4 P.M. Mon.–Fri., 10 A.M.–6 A.M. Sat., 8 A.M.–2 P.M. Sun., free), a Spanish Colonial Revival church that still holds mass every day. Pope John Paul II named St. Mary's a minor basilica in 1985, and two years later he visited the church on a trip to Phoenix. The basilica's collection of stained glass windows is the largest in the state, and its bright interior is worth a quick stop.

Heritage and Science Park

Heritage Square (115 N. 6th St., 602/262-5071, www.phoenix.gov/parks) is a bit of an anomaly in car-loving, tear-it-down-and-build-something-new Phoenix. The historic park protects the only remaining residential buildings from Phoenix's original 1870 townsite. Today, the eight historic structures house small museums, offices, shops, and restaurants. **Rosson House** (115 N. 6th St., 602/262-5029, www.phoenix.gov/parks, 10 A.M.–4 P.M. Wed., 1–4 P.M. Thurs., 10 A.M.–4 P.M. Fri.–Sat.,

© MICA THOMAS MULLOY

The 1895 Rosson House was one of Victorian Phoenix's most ornate homes.

noon–4 P.M. Sun., $5 adults, $2 children 6–12) is the most ornate, and even when it was built in 1895 by Roland and Flora Rosson for $7,525, the Victorian home's octagonal turret and shaded veranda were considered extravagant. Flora, who came from a wealthy family, had bought the entire city block, allowing plenty of space for the 2,800-square-foot home's 10 rooms, which have been restored with period furnishings and pressed-tin ceilings. Docent-guided tours are available.

Nearby, the 1901 Stevens House is now home of the **Arizona Doll & Toy Museum** (602 E. Adams, 602/253-9337, 10 A.M.–4 P.M. Tues.–Sat., noon–4 P.M. Sun., $3 adults, $1 children under 12), which showcases antique dolls, vintage toys, and a reproduction of a turn-of-the-20th-century one-room schoolhouse.

PHOENIX MUSEUM OF HISTORY
It can be easy to forget that Phoenix began as a small, dusty frontier town no bigger than Tombstone or Jerome. The Phoenix Museum of History (105 N. 5th St., 602/253-2734, www.pmoh.org, 10 A.M.–5 P.M. Tues.–Sat., $6 adults, $3 children 7–12) traces the city's evolution from Victorian settlement to the fifth-largest city in the country, with interactive exhibitions on everyday life for early pioneers, as well as the Latinos and Native American people who helped shape the city. The 40,000-item collection of costumes, paintings, household items, transportation materials, tools and equipment, and personal artifacts is an important trove for the city.

ARIZONA SCIENCE CENTER
One of the best museums in the Valley and a hit with kids, the Arizona Science Center (600 E. Washington St., 602/716-2000, www.azscience.org, 10 A.M.–5 P.M. daily, $12 adults, $10 children 3–17) packs 350 interactive exhibits into 40,000 square feet of gallery space, making science seem cool and a little dangerous: Climb a rock wall, race up a pulley system, make clouds, or lie on a bed of 1,000 nails. Noted architect Antoine Predock designed the sprawling concrete-and-metal

Arizona Science Center

© MICA THOMAS MULLOY

building, creating soaring spaces for the large displays. The museum's high-tech IMAX theater and planetarium feature a series of shows throughout the day, and nationally traveling exhibitions regularly make a pit stop here. The on-site **CityBakery** (602/257-8860, 9 A.M.–4 P.M. daily, $6–11) is a great place to grab an after-museum lunch or snack, with lots of gourmet sandwiches and salads that grownups will love.

Children's Museum of Phoenix
It seems fitting that Jackson Pollock's old elementary school should find new life as the splashy Children's Museum of Phoenix (215 N. 7th St., 602/253-0501, www.childrensmuseumofphoenix.org, 9 A.M.–4 P.M. daily, $9), a hands-on, 70,000-square-foot gallery dedicated to little ones 10 and under. Would-be Picassos and Pollocks will find more than finger-paints here, though. In 2008, the historic Monroe School Building was transformed into a playground designed to "engage the minds, muscles, and imaginations of children." Kids can navigate through the Noodle Forest, climb

up a makeshift tree house, pedal through a tricycle car wash, or simply enjoy a little reading in the comfy Book Loft. It's a great place for exploring on a hot day.

Heard Museum

For thousands of years, native people have made their home in the Southwest, creating an incredibly rich and much-underappreciated culture. The Heard Museum (2301 N. Central Ave., 602/252-8848, www.heard.org, 9:30 A.M.–5 P.M. daily, $10 adults, $3 children 6–12) documents their millennia-old traditions, offering an impressive introduction to Native American art and Arizona's original inhabitants. Experience what it is like to live in a Navajo hogan, or learn how the intricate weavings and beadwork found in many clothes, baskets, and rugs reflect a tribe's unique history. There are also intricate sand paintings, Barry Goldwater's collection of 437 Hopi kachina dolls, and boldly imaginative works by contemporary artists, as well as exhibitions

documenting the indignities of those forced to live on reservations and boarding schools in the 19th and 20th centuries.

The museum started as the personal collection of Dwight and Maie Heard, who built the first incarnation of the Spanish Colonial building on their private grounds in 1929 to house the art and artifacts that had begun to overtake their home. Dwight died of a heart attack as the display cabinets were being installed, but Maie forged ahead, overseeing the museum until her death in 1951. The Heard has been significantly expanded over the years, and its grounds, beautifully landscaped with native plants and trees, also provide space for music and dance performances, special events, and festivals, like the annual Indian Fair and Market. The gift shop sells art and jewelry by Native American artisans, and its Southwestern-inspired restaurant, **Arcadia Farms** (602/251-0204, 9:30 A.M.–3 P.M. daily, $9–13), is a satellite of the popular Scottsdale café.

© CRAIG SMITH, COURTESY OF THE HEARD MUSEUM/GREATER PHOENIX CVB

Heard Museum

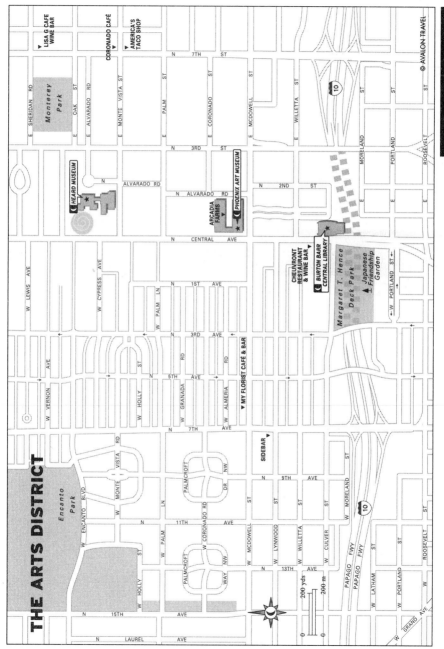

PHOENIX

© AVALON TRAVEL

THE ARTS DISTRICT

LISA G CAFE
WINE BAR
CORONADO CAFÉ
AMERICA'S
TACO SHOP

HEARD MUSEUM

PHOENIX ART MUSEUM
ARCADIA FARMS

CHELMONT
RESTAURANT
& WINE BAR
BURTON BARR
CENTRAL LIBRARY

Japanese
Friendship
Garden

Margaret T. Hence
Deck Park

MY FLORIST CAFÉ & BAR

SIDEBAR

Monterey
Park

Encanto
Park

E SHERIDAN RD
OAK ST
E ALVARADO RD
E MONTE VISTA ST
E PALM ST
E CORONADO ST
E McDOWELL ST
E WILLETTA ST
MORELAND
PORTLAND
ROOSEVELT

N 7TH ST
ST
ST
ST
ST
ST
10

N 3RD ST
ALVARADO RD
N ALVARADO RD
N 2ND ST
N CENTRAL AVE

W LEWIS AVE
W CYPRESS AVE
N 1ST AVE
W PORTLAND ST

N PALM LN
W PALM
AVE
N 3RD AVE
ST
N 5TH AVE
W HOLLY
W GRANADA RD
W ALMERIA RD
N 7TH AVE

W VERNON AVE

W ENCANTO BLVD
N MONTE VISTA RD
PALMCROFT DR NW
W CORONADO RD
MCDOWELL ST
LYNWOOD ST
WILLETTA ST
MORELAND ST
10

N 9TH AVE

N 11TH AVE
W PALM LN
PALMCROFT NW
W CULVER ST

PAPAGO FWY
PAPAGO FWY
LATHAM ST
PORTLAND ST
ROOSEVELT

W HOLLY ST
PALMCROFT WAY
N 13TH AVE
W GRAND AVE

N 15TH AVE
LAUREL AVE

200 yds
200 m
0
0

© MICA THOMAS MULLOY

◖ Phoenix Art Museum

Like many regional art museums, the Phoenix Art Museum (1625 N. Central Ave., 602/257-1222, www.phxart.org, 10 A.M.–9 P.M. Wed., 10 A.M.–5 P.M. Thurs.–Sat., noon–5 P.M. Sun., $10 adults, $4 children ages 6–17) limped by for years with a small but respectable collection of art, featuring secondary works by well-known masters and a few excellent pieces by lesser-known artists. That all changed in 1996 when the museum launched an ambitious makeover that has transformed the institution, nearly tripling its size and bringing new focus to its acquisitions and exhibitions. A later $50 million expansion added a grassy sculpture garden and a dramatic, glass-enclosed lobby and entry plaza.

Throughout the museum, you'll find a broad cross-section of art, with American, European, and Latin American artists like Claude Monet, Pablo Picasso, Georgia O'Keeffe, Mark Rothko, and Frida Kahlo, as well as a nicely curated Asian art gallery. A new four-level wing has added space for large-scale contemporary pieces, photography, and the museum's 4,500-piece fashion design collection, with garments by Balenciaga, Chanel, Dior, and Yves Saint Laurent. Be sure to make some time to see the exhibition The Art of Philip Curtis, which highlights the work of the former WPA artist who moved to Arizona in 1937 to spearhead the Phoenix Art Center, the precursor to today's museum. His whimsical and provocative paintings are reminiscent of Norman Rockwell, and they reveal his love of Arizona's mining towns.

The museum regularly hosts film screenings and live concerts, as well as blockbuster traveling exhibitions, which have featured Impressionism, Rembrandt, Richard Avedon, and the glassworks of Dale Chihuly. The café, **Arcadia Farms** (602/257-2191, 11 A.M.–2:30 P.M. Tues., 10 A.M.–5 P.M. Wed.–Sun., $9–13) is a great place to grab lunch.

Encanto Park

Encanto Park (2605 N. 15th Ave., 602/261-8991, http://phoenix.gov/parks, 5:30 A.M.–11 P.M., free) has been a Phoenix favorite for generations. On most weekends, you'll see kids running toward the playground, young couples lying under shady trees, and large families hauling coolers and bags of food to the old picnic tables. The 222-acre "enchanted" park was designed to be a leafy oasis for escaping the heat, and its quaint neighborhood of Spanish Colonial homes and historic bungalows still feels connected to the Phoenix of 50 years ago. There are plenty of amenities—basketball and tennis courts, softball fields, and a municipal swimming pool and golf course—but it's the small lagoon that gives the park its unique character.

PHOENIX INDIAN SCHOOL

In 1891, the Phoenix Indian School opened, part of the federal government's plan to assimilate Native Americans. It was one of several boarding schools established around the country to force Indian children to speak English, cut their hair, wear Anglo clothes, and attend church. Students were also required to abandon their tribal traditions and leave their families behind, a particularly difficult sacrifice for the close-knit Native American communities.

By 1900, the co-ed school had grown to 698 students from 23 tribes across the West. Its 160-acre campus had a large schoolhouse, dining hall, several dormitories, and workspace to teach vocation skills. It finally closed in 1990, and a decade later, a third of the land was redeveloped as the **Steele Indian School Park** (300 E. Indian School Rd., 602/495-0739, www.phoenix.gov/parks, 6 A.M.-10 P.M. daily). Only three of the school's original buildings remain, including the restored Memorial Hall, an auditorium that was opened in 1922 to honor Native American students who had fought in World War I. Fittingly, Native Americans now gather at the park for tribal celebrations and festivals, and it's also the site of Phoenix's annual Fourth of July fireworks event.

Head down to the boathouse and rent a paddleboat or canoe ($8 for 30 minutes). Encanto also is home to the **Enchanted Island Amusement Park** (1202 W. Encanto Blvd., 602/254-1200, www.enchantedisland.com, open Wed.–Sun., $1 per ride), which offers a charming collection of rides, bumper boats, games, and a carousel. Check the website for detailed information on hours and prices.

Burton Barr Central Library

Phoenix embarked on a cultural renaissance in 1988, when voters approved an ambitious, architecturally daring series of public works projects that included the Phoenix Art Museum and Burton Barr Central Library (1221 N. Central Ave., 602/262-4636, www.phoenixpubliclibrary.org, 10 A.M.–9 P.M. Mon.–Thurs., 10 A.M.–6 P.M. Fri.–Sat., noon–6 P.M. Sun.). The iconic building's rectangular, rusted-steel facade resembles a red-hued mesa. Phoenix architect Will Bruder, a pioneer in the region's Desert Modernism movement, gracefully incorporated natural daylight throughout the design, including a glass-and-steel central stairwell and elevator atrium, called the "Crystal Canyon." On the equinox, the sun shines directly through overhead skylights in the fifth-floor reading room, lighting its graceful, white columns and creating a stunning show.

Japanese Friendship Garden

Dorothy, we're not in Phoenix anymore. The tranquil Japanese Friendship Garden (1125 N. 3rd Ave., 602/256-3204, www.japanesefriendshipgarden.org, 10 A.M.–3 P.M. Tues.–Sun., closed Jun.–Aug., $5 adults, $3 children) is a pleasant contrast to the desert cityscape that surrounds it, with some 50 varieties of plants, flowing streams, a koi pond, and a 12-foot waterfall. This joint effort between Phoenix and its sister city, Himeji, Japan, is tucked into the southwestern end of **Margaret T. Hance Deck Park** (on top of the I-10 freeway tunnel, between Central and 3rd Avenues). Enter through the bamboo gate and follow the pathway through the perfectly manicured grounds, which feature yellow and purple irises, lush water lilies, and artfully placed boulders. Some allowances for the desert climate have been made, like the neatly trimmed bonsai trees that are shaped from hardy olive trees. You can join a tea ceremony the second Saturday of the month during regular public hours, though reservations are required for the $20 teahouse experience.

PAPAGO PARK

Think of it as Phoenix's answer to New York's Central Park, a natural refuge in the middle of the city, where residents can hike, fish, or play a round of golf. Papago Park (625 N. Galvin Pkwy., 602-256-3220, www.phoenix. gov/parks, 5 A.M.–11 P.M. daily, free) is one of the city's great resources, and the large desert sanctuary's paved trails, small lake, baseball stadium, and softball fields have made it a popular destination, not to mention its museums and cultural attractions like the Phoenix Zoo and Desert Botanical Garden.

Hole-in-the-Rock

You can see Papago's rounded, red-hued buttes from the surrounding communities of Phoenix, Tempe, and Scottsdale, but the sandstone formations should be explored up close, especially the unique "holes," which were formed by water erosion over millions of years. Be sure to make the short, easy trek to the landmark Hole-in-the-Rock, a natural formation through which you can survey the city. Phoenix's first residents, the Hohokam, used the formation for astronomy and to track the seasonal movements of the sun. You can also make the short walk to **Hunt's Tomb,** a white pyramid that serves as the final resting place of Arizona's first governor.

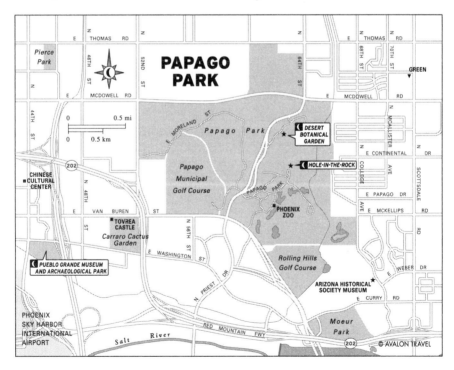

Phoenix, seen through the feature known as Hole-in-the-Rock at Papago Park

Arizona Historical Society Museum

Some wild things have happened in Arizona—Old West gunfights, copper rushes, gubernatorial impeachments—and the state's version of the National Archives has been there to document it from the beginning. The first territorial legislature created the Arizona Historical Society in 1864, and, since then, the institution has been chronicling the state's history as it happened. Today, four museums across Arizona preserve some three million artifacts, with the facility at Papago Park (1300 N. College Ave., 480/929-0292, www.arizonahistoricalsociety.org, 10 A.M.–4 P.M. Tues.–Sat., noon–4 P.M. Sun., $5 adults, $4 children 12–18) specializing in the Phoenix area and the 20th century. A particularly interesting exhibition documents how the state came of age during World War II with the bombing of the USS *Arizona* at Pearl Harbor. In fact, you can learn how Camp Papago Park, not too far from the museum, experienced the largest mass escape of POWs in the United States. Admission to the museum is free on the first Saturday of each month.

Desert Botanical Garden

First-time visitors to the Sonoran Desert often expect to find a lifeless expanse of sandy dunes. A trip to the Desert Botanical Garden (1201 N. Galvin Pkwy., 480/941-1225, www.dbg.org, 8 A.M.–8 P.M. daily Oct.–May, 7 A.M.–8 P.M. daily Jun.–Sept., $15 adults, $5 children 3–12) quickly dispels any myths about a Sahara in the Southwest. With some 21,000 cacti, agaves, succulents, shrubs, trees, and colorful wildflowers, the garden easily claims the world's largest, if not finest, collection of desert plants, including 139 rare, threatened, or endangered species. About a third of the living collection is native to the region, with the remaining plants originating from Australia, South America, and Mexico. The park began in 1939 with a mission "to exhibit, to conserve, to study, and to disseminate knowledge of the

© ADAM RODRIGUEZ/COURTESY OF THE DESERT BOTANICAL GARDE

The Desert Botanical Garden features the world's largest collection of desert plants.

arid-land plants of the world." Since then, it has evolved beyond a plant refuge, offering classes and hosting a series of social events throughout the year that range from spring concerts to arts festivals.

Try to come early in the day or late in the evening, when the sunlight is incredible. Or, for a different perspective, flashlight tours are held during the summer, a fun opportunity for children to see the nocturnal desert's nighthawks, snakes, insects, and night-blooming flowers. Of course, the springtime wildflowers are always a highlight, and the annual Las Noches de las Luminarias has become a Phoenix holiday tradition.

Phoenix Zoo

Lions, tigers, and giant desert tortoises—oh, my! The Phoenix Zoo (455 N. Galvin Pkwy., 602/273-1341, www.phoenixzoo.org, 9 A.M.–5 P.M. daily, $16 adults, $6 children 2–17) is one of the nation's largest privately owned zoological parks, with some 1,300

birds, slithering reptiles, and furry mammals from around the world. You'll find classic animal habitats with elephants, zebras, and playful orangutans, but it's the newer exhibits that are blurring the boundaries of the animal kingdom, like Monkey Village, where visitors can walk through a cageless enclosure where a dozen squirrel monkeys hop from tree to tree. For an extra $3, you can plunge your hand into Stingray Bay and feed a school of small sharks and stingrays. Or set your little ones free in Yakulla Caverns to explore the geologically themed water park's dripping stalactites and refreshing waterfalls. June through September, the zoo is open weekdays 7 A.M.–2 P.M., and until 4 P.M. on weekends.

◖ Pueblo Grande Museum and Archaeological Park

Like Rome's Forum or Beijing's Forbidden City, this is where the modern metropolis of Phoenix honors the ancient foundations from which it rose. Pueblo Grande Museum and Archaeological Park (4619 E. Washington St., 602/495-0901, www.pueblogrande.com, 9 A.M.–5 P.M. Mon.–Sat., 1–5 P.M. Sun., closed Sun. and Mon. May–Sept., $6 adults, $3 children 6–17) is the site of a Hohokam village that stood here from about A.D. 100 to 1400, supporting as many as 1,000 people. It now sits in the middle of a desert metropolis, but the valley looked quite different then, when water flowing through the Salt River fed lush plants along its banks, as well as a complex system of canals that irrigated crops. Those well-engineered waterways would serve as a framework for the rebirth of Phoenix in the 1860s—and today's canals still parallel their original paths.

The Hohokam lived in wood-framed homes, built over shallow pits and covered with adobe. Because these natural materials were so vulnerable to erosion, none of Phoenix's early dwellings still exist, though you're now able to go inside full-size replicas of these adobe pit houses. You can also see an excavated ballcourt and an example of an adobe compound,

Pueblo Grande Museum and Archaeological Park

homes that families would surround with large walls to create private courtyards—a practice adopted into Mexican architecture and modern suburban housing developments. The recently renovated museum highlights the Hohokam's tools, shell and stone jewelry, and unique red-on-buff pottery. There are also interactive exhibits that examine how archaeologists dig at sites and sort through relics to piece together the history of an ancient civilization. A warning: There isn't much shade at the site, so be sure to visit on a cool day or early in the morning.

Tovrea Castle and Carraro Cactus Garden

Many Phoenicians regularly drive by Tovrea Castle (5041 E. Van Buren St., 602/256-3220, www.phoenix.gov/parks) on Highway 202 (Loop 202) and have no idea what it is, but the three-tier wedding cake-style house is hard to miss. In 1928, Italian immigrant Alessio Carraro purchased 277 acres of undeveloped land east of downtown Phoenix, armed with grand plans for the desert hilltop. He envisioned a luxury housing development that would be crowned by a massive cactus garden and a posh resort, which he designed as a rococo castle inspired by his native Italy. Those dreams were soon dashed, though, when Edward and Della Tovrea began ranching land adjacent to his would-be oasis—the addition of a slaughterhouse didn't help matters. With few options, Carraro sold the castle to an anonymous buyer in 1931: Della Tovrea. Edward died the following year, and Della would live in the castle most of her life until 1969, when burglars broke into the home and beat the 80-year-old woman. She eventually died from her injuries. Today, the city of Phoenix has renovated the abandoned home and garden, which has been replanted with 5,000 cacti, including 352 saguaros. The garden just opened to the public for the first time, and the restored castle is expected to commence tours in spring 2010. Call for details.

PHOENIX

TEMPE AND THE EAST VALLEY

The vibrant college town of Tempe came of age during the past decade, staking its claim as a progressive, culturally minded community. Surrounded by the cities of Phoenix, Scottsdale, Mesa, and Chandler, the 40-square-mile city can no longer spread into the desert like other Valley suburbs. Instead, it's meeting the demands of a growing population by slowly casting away the shackles of suburbia to become a city where residential, retail, and commercial buildings coexist rather than retreat to their respective neighborhoods. The city's developers, recognizing the success of pedestrian-oriented **Mill Avenue**—a popular spot for dining and shopping—are now moving beyond the street's nostalgic red-brick buildings and creating a modern cityscape along Tempe Town Lake. That said, the city isn't new to experimental design. In 1971, the city unveiled the **Tempe Municipal Building** (31 E. 5th St., 480/967-2001, www.tempe.gov), an inverted glass-walled pyramid that shades itself from the summer sun. More recently, the **Tempe Center for the Arts** (700 W. Rio Salado Pkwy., 480/350-2829, www.tempe.gov/TCA, 10 a.m.–6 p.m. Tues.–Fri., 11 a.m.–6 p.m. Sat., free) made a splash on the banks of Tempe Town Lake, with an elaborate silver roof reminiscent of local mountain ranges.

Still, Tempe hasn't bulldozed its past. At the northern end of Mill Avenue, you can see the tall silos and remains of the **Hayden Flour Mill.** Charles Hayden originally built the river-powered mill in 1874. His Hayden Ferry connected Phoenix from the north banks of the Salt River to a road to Tucson. A small community grew up along this "Mill Avenue," and you can still see the old brick buildings and quaint bungalows and ranch houses that popped up here.

Tempe Town Lake

If you build it, they will come—or so city leaders hoped in 1989 when they adopted the ambitious Rio Salado Master Plan, which converted two miles of the usually dry Salt River into a reservoir lake for boating, rowing, and fishing. The resulting Tempe Town Lake (620 N. Mill Ave., 480/350-8625, www.tempe.gov/lake, free) opened a decade later, created by

© MICA THOMAS MULLOY

Tempe Town Lake and Mill Avenue Bridge

PHOENIX

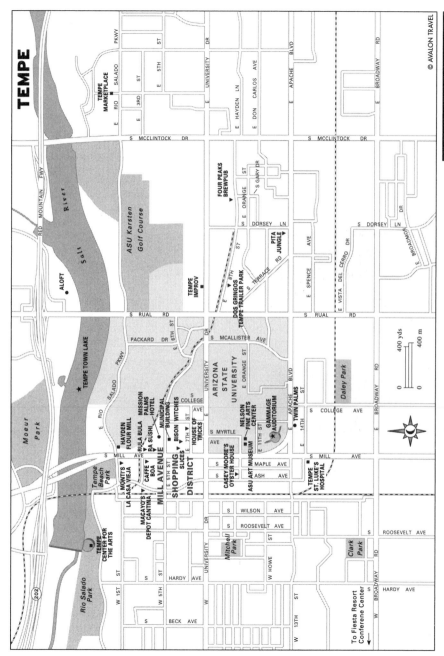

TEMPE

© AVALON TRAVEL

ALOFT

Salt River

Red Mountain Fwy

ASU Karsten Golf Course

TEMPE MARKETPLACE

E RIO SALADO PKWY
E 3RD ST
E 5TH ST
E SALADO ST
UNIVERSITY DR

S MCCLINTOCK DR

E HAYDEN LN
S DON CARLOS AVE
E APACHE BLVD

E BROADWAY RD

FOUR PEAKS BREWPUB
E ORANGE ST
S GARY DR

S DORSEY LN

PITA JUNGLE

E SPENCE AVE

E VISTA DEL CERRO DR

S DORSEY LN

E BROADMOR DR

TEMPE IMPROV

DOS GRINGOS
TEMPE TRAILER PARK
E 8TH ST
S TERRACE RD

S RUAL RD

S MCCLINTOCK DR

S RUAL RD

TEMPE TOWN LAKE

PACKARD DR
E 6TH ST

S McALLISTER AVE

S McALLISTER AVE

Moeur Park

HAYDEN FLOUR MILL
MISSION PALMS HOTEL
RULA BULA
RA SUSHI
MUNICIPAL BUILDING
BISON WITCHES
HOUSE OF TRICKS

ARIZONA STATE UNIVERSITY

E ORANGE ST

UNIVERSITY DR
S COLLEGE AVE

NELSON FINE ARTS CENTER
GAMMAGE AUDITORIUM

TWIN PALMS

E APACHE BLVD

S MYRTLE AVE

E 11TH ST

E 14TH ST

S COLLEGE AVE

E BROADWAY RD

Daley Park

MILL AVENUE SHOPPING DISTRICT

MONTI'S
LA CASA VIEJA
CAFFE BOA
SLICES

MACAYO'S DEPOT CANTINA

CASEY MOORE'S OYSTER HOUSE
ASU ART MUSEUM

S MAPLE AVE
S ASH AVE

TEMPE ST. LUKE'S HOSPITAL

S MILL AVE

E 5TH ST
E 7TH ST

Tempe Beach Park

TEMPE CENTER FOR THE ARTS

Rio Salado Park

202

S MILL AVE

UNIVERSITY DR

S WILSON AVE
S ROOSEVELT AVE

W HOWE ST

Mitchell Park

S ROOSEVELT AVE

Clark Park

HARDY AVE

W 1ST ST
W 5TH ST

S HARDY AVE
S HARDY RD

W 13TH ST

BECK AVE

To Fiesta Resort Conferene Center →

0   400 yds
0   400 m

PHOENIX

inflatable rubber dams and encircled by five miles of paths for biking and jogging. The adjacent **Tempe Beach Park** has become one of the Valley's prime spots for festivals, concerts, and events, and little ones will love the $1.3 million **Splash Playground** (10 A.M.–7 P.M. daily Apr.–Sept., free) when the temperatures start to climb. The monsoon-inspired water park features rain showers, misters, waterfalls, and large squirt guns.

Arizona State University

Much of Tempe's progressive attitude—and the abundance of cheap restaurants, bars, and shops—can be credited to the presence of Arizona State University's main campus (University Dr. and Mill Ave., 480/965-9011, www.asu.edu). ASU was founded as the Tempe Normal School in 1885 while Arizona was still a territory. Since then, it has mushroomed into the largest public research university in the country, with 67,000 students on four campuses in the Valley.

Those interested in design and architecture should head south on Mill Avenue to see two significant buildings. The **Nelson Fine Arts Center** is a Modernist concrete complex that is perfectly suited to its desert home, drawing inspiration from Native American architecture and creating brilliant subterranean spaces that highlight the desert's stark contrasts of light and shadow. Inside, the **ASU Art Museum** (51 E. 10th St., 480/965-2787, http://asuartmuseum.asu.edu, 11 A.M.–5 P.M. Tues.–Sat., free), has a modest collection that features contemporary, Latin American, and ceramic pieces.

Just south, you'll find **Gammage Auditorium** (1200 S. Forest Ave., 480/965-5062, www.asugammage.com, open for performances), the last public commission of Frank Lloyd Wright. Based on an old design for an opera house in Baghdad, Iraq, Wright modified the concept for its new home on the edge of ASU's campus. "I believe this is the site," he said. "The structure should be circular in design, and yes, with outstretched arms, saying 'Welcome to ASU.'" Those arms became flying buttresses that serve as pedestrian ramps and echo the building's interlocking-circle motif. Both Wright and ASU president Grady Gammage, who is credited

© MESA ARIZONA CVB

The Arizona Museum of Natural History appeals to both kids and adults.

with landing the commission, died before its completion in 1964.

◖ Arizona Museum of Natural History

One of the Valley's best-kept secrets, the Arizona Museum of Natural History (53 N. MacDonald, 480/644-2230, www.azmnh.org, 10 A.M.–5 P.M. Tues.–Fri., 11 A.M.–5 P.M. Sat., 1–5 P.M. Sun., $10 adults, $6 children 3–12) appeals to kids—dinosaurs!—and even adults who aren't "museum people." Formerly known as the Mesa Southwest Museum, it explores the region's natural and cultural history with plenty of hands-on, interactive, sound-and-light, try-this-on excitement. Pan for "gold," visit a territorial jail, and scope out the three-story Dinosaur Mountain, complete with a simulated flash flood and mechanical creatures. Those of us who revel in the nerdy joy of museums will love the in-depth exhibits on prehistoric Native American life and the assembled mammoth and mastodon fossils. The museum also cares for the **Mesa Grande** mound, where as many as 2,000 Hohokam people once lived.

AHWATUKEE AND SOUTH PHOENIX

Southern Phoenix and its affluent bedroom community of Ahwatukee (pronounced ah-wuh-TOO-kee) are home—primarily—to a sea of stucco housing developments. There are a few sites, though, that are worth checking out.

South Mountain Park

The largest urban park in the country—and perhaps the world—South Mountain Park (10919 S. Central Ave., 602/495-0222, 5 A.M.–10 P.M. daily, free) is where many Valley residents escape from the city to hike, bike, horseback ride, and picnic. Don't expect large grassy meadows or shady forested hideaways, though. This is 16,500 acres of bona fide Sonoran Desert, preserving hardy creosote bushes, palo verde trees, and dozens of varieties of cactus. You may even come across a few

critters, like jackrabbits and the snakes, scorpions, and co in the park tend to come ou much cooler, but you shoul out for them). The park also of petroglyphs and pictogra..., ated by the Hohokam and other indigenous tribes. These small drawings, carved or painted onto stones, depict people, animals, and geometric patterns, and anthropologists theorize they may have been a means of recording history, part of religious ceremonies, or even ancient street signs or border markings.

If you're not interested in exploring the more than 50 miles of trails on foot or by bike, there are a few scenic drives, including a 5-mile winding road that snakes its way up the mountain to the popular Dobbins Lookout at the summit, where the panoramic views reveal Phoenix's sprawling suburban growth. For more information about the park's wildlife or where to find rock art, visit the **South Mountain Environmental Education Center** (10409 S. Central Ave., 602/495-5078, 7 A.M.–1 P.M. Fri.–Sat.).

Mystery Castle

"Life Visits a Mystery Castle," proclaimed the cover of *Life* magazine in 1948, featuring a teenage Mary Lou Gulley on a spiral staircase that overlooked the eccentric house her father, Boyce Luther Gulley, had built. The name Mystery Castle stuck (800 E. Mineral Rd., 602/268-1581, 11 A.M.–4 P.M. Thurs.–Sun. Oct.–May, $5), and Gulley is still welcoming visitors into her home. In 1930 Boyce had abandoned his wife and daughter in Seattle, moving to the dry climate of Phoenix after being diagnosed with tuberculosis. He built Mystery Castle from a hodgepodge of found objects: rocks, adobe, glass, auto parts, even petroglyphs. He had been inspired by his daughter, who would cry when her sandcastles were washed away by the tide and ask her father to build her one in the desert large enough to live in. When he died in 1945, a lawyer contacted Mary Lou and her mother, and they moved into the eccentric castle. Today, you can tour the 18 rooms, furnished with quirky pieces

WHAT ARE THOSE RED LIGHTS IN SOUTH PHOENIX?

Scan the Valley's horizon at night, and you can't help but notice a cluster of red twinkling lights in South Phoenix. These blinking spires mark the **South Mountain Antenna Farm,** a city beacon of 30-plus towers that beam radio and television transmissions from the mountaintop. The antennas provide more than music, news, and sports, though, as the red lights serve as an important navigational marker for pilots flying into nearby Sky Harbor Airport. They also seem to be a magnet for residents who drive at night to the top of South Mountain, the highest point in the Valley, for a panoramic view of the Valley bathed in shimmering lights.

designed by Boyce as well as an original sofa designed by Frank Lloyd Wright. When Mary Lou is feeling up to it, she'll help out on tours. To reach the castle, head south on 7th Street, past Baseline Road, and make a left where the road dead-ends at South Mountain. The home is closed June through September.

Rawhide Western Town at Wild Horse Pass

Rawhide Western Town (5700 W. North Loop Rd., 480/502-5600, www.rawhide.com, 5:30–9 P.M. Thurs.–Sun., free) moved from North Scottsdale to the Gila River Indian Community a few years ago, but it's still delivering 1880s-themed family fun. Check out the stunt shows in the dusty streets, or try your luck on the mechanical bull. Of course, there are easier rides in town, such as the desert train or stagecoach tours guided by a trained mule team. It's all a little hokey, but having an "old-time" photo made or browsing the candies at Sweet Sally's Confections is a lot of fun. Admission to the park is free, but there are small fees for any of the activities or games. Or, you can buy an all-day Town Pass for $15.

Also, March though May, visitors can experience an old-fashioned chuck-wagon cookout under the stars ($45 adults, $19 children 4–11), which includes a hayride, live music, line-dancing instruction, and a marshmallow roast around the campfire.

Nearby, the **Huhugam Heritage Center** (4759 N. Maricopa Rd., 520/796-3500, www.huhugam.com, 10 A.M.–4 P.M. Tues.–Sat., $5 adults, $2 children 6–12) honors the other figures of the Old West: Native Americans. Operated by the Gila River Indian Community's Akimel O'odham (Pima) and Pee Posh (Maricopa) tribes, the museum's small exhibits trace the cultural heritage of their ancestors. However, it's the museum's strikingly modern architecture and ethnobotanical garden of desert plants that make it special.

WEST VALLEY
Deer Valley Rock Art Center

Long before the Valley's urban sprawl began creeping into Northwest Phoenix, ancient Native Americans made the Valley their home. These indigenous people literally left their mark on the landscape, carving more than 1,500 petroglyphs onto the basalt boulder formations in the Hedgpeth Hills. This impressive concentration of rock art is a fascinating and revealing look at the civilization that once thrived here, and the petroglyphs—geometric and anthropomorphic drawings carved onto rock—give a peek into their stories, religious rites, and hunting practices. The Deer Valley Rock Art Center (3711 W. Deer Valley Rd., 623/582-8007, http://dvrac.asu.edu, 9 A.M.–5 P.M. Tues.–Sat., noon–5 P.M. Sun. Oct.–Apr., 8 A.M.–2 P.M. Tues.–Sun. May–Sept., $7 adults, $3 children) is more than archaeological site, though. The 47-acre park also serves as a nature preserve for native wildlife and an ethnobotanical garden for the hardy crops that have been cultivated in Arizona for thousands of years, including corn, beans, chile peppers, onions, squash, and cotton. Visitors may want to bring a pair of binoculars or rent some at the center to view the more distant petroglyphs.

Entertainment and Events

Frequently overshadowed by Scottsdale's trendy clubs, Phoenix's nightlife takes a bit more work to find. As a resident, though, I prefer to meet up with friends at one of Phoenix's hip but low-key bars and lounges. If you're in town at the beginning of each month, you may want to consider joining art-lovers and hipsters at the First Fridays artwalk in downtown's Roosevelt Historic District.

NIGHTLIFE
Downtown
BARS AND PUBS

Downtown Phoenix recently got its wish: a convenient, modern pub in which to grab a beer after work. **Turf Restaurant & Pub** (705 N. 1st St., 602/296-5043, 10 A.M.–2 A.M. daily) has big booths, high-top tables, and a large patio ideal for relaxing after a long day or catching up with friends on the weekend. The dark interior and concrete floors give the bar a bit of style,

and its decent selection of beers and live music Thursday, Friday, and Saturday nights are a rarity for downtown. There's a full menu with classic pub fare, which makes it an especially appealing option for late-night snacks.

Going to the **Roosevelt Tavern** (816 N. 3rd St., 602/254-2561, 5 P.M.–midnight Tues.–Thurs., 5 P.M.–2 A.M. Fri.–Sat., 5 P.M.–midnight Sun.) is a lot like going to your buddy's place—if your friend converted a historic home into a tavern complete with a look-in cooler, full range of local and regional beers on draft, varied wine selection, and large array of bottled beer. For those looking to mingle with strangers, the bar or the conversation friendly table in the back is perfect. A more intimate setting is found in the front rooms, complete with candlelight and sofa. Snack choices include hearty sandwiches, a salad, and a full cheese plate. For drinks, try the hoppy Roosevelt House beer, the smooth Scrimshaw Pilsner, or any of

© MICA THOMAS MULLOY

Roosevelt Tavern

the featured wines. Hungry? Give the classic grilled cheese and tomato soup combo a try.

Killing time before a game at Chase Field? Grab a pint or a classic gin and tonic at **The Rose & Crown** (628 E. Adams St., 602/256-0223, 4 P.M.–2 A.M. Mon., 11 A.M.–2 A.M. Tues.–Sun.) in Heritage Square. The converted historic home has a full bar, imports galore from the British Isles, and an excellent patio and lawn for enjoying the weather when it's nice outside. The pool table, darts, and pop art paintings of Queen Elizabeth and Winston Churchill add some fun British style to the turn-of-the-20th-century bungalow.

LOUNGES AND WINE BARS
Like a good speakeasy, **Sidebar** (1514 N. 7th Ave., 602/254-1646, 4 P.M.–2 A.M. Mon.–Fri., 5:30 P.M.–2 A.M. Sat.–Sun.) can be tough to find. Enter through the side door on 7th

Avenue and climb the stairs to the swank, loft-like space, where you'll find a stylish mix of exposed-brick walls, funky lights, and flatscreen TVs playing black-and-white films. The laid-back vibe appeals to many residents, and it's not uncommon to see a meeting of up-and-coming politicos next to a couple on a date or a group of friends celebrating a birthday. The large lineup of specialty cocktails, dozens of beers, and 40-plus wines should appeal to most.

The sleek and contemporary **Hanney's** (40 N. 1st St., 602/252-2285, 11 A.M.–1:30 A.M. Mon.–Fri., 5 P.M.–1:30 A.M. Sat.–Sun.) recently emerged from the shell of an old Phoenix department store. When it opened in 1947 as an upscale men's store, the building was praised for bringing the clean lines of Modernism to downtown Phoenix. A three-year renovation has preserved much of the building's original character and given it a glossy update with

THE WRIGLEY MANSION

A Valley landmark, the Wrigley Mansion sits atop a small hill in Central Phoenix's Biltmore neighborhood, like a Spanish Colonial citadel safeguarding million-dollar homes and golf courses. Chewing-gum magnate William Wrigley Jr. built the 24-room, 16,000-square-foot mansion in 1931 as a "winter cottage" and gave it to his wife, Ada, for a 50th anniversary present. The couple only stayed a month or two a year, as the mansion was the smallest of the family's five homes.

Today, the "cottage" houses the private Wrigley Mansion Club, which re-opened in 2003 after undergoing a $2 million renovation that added dining space and a bar. Long gone are the days when the Wrigley family wintered at the house while they managed their fortunes, a business and real estate empire that included California's Catalina Island and the Arizona Biltmore Resort. And though the home's pristine desert view has evolved into a sprawling cityscape since then, the mansion retains much of its original 1930s appeal, from hand-carved doors to an elegant rotunda ceiling. Even the mansion's 17 bathrooms, which

reflect the Art Deco tastes of the era, were carefully restored, reviving the chartreuse, turquoise, black, and royal blue tiles that were made in the Wrigley family kiln.

The recent addition also preserves the home's historical architectural details, including a two-story patio and balcony that formed the mansion's northern facade. The space has been converted into an intimate lounge and restaurant, **Geordie's at the Wrigley Mansion** (2501 E. Telawa Trail, 602/955-4079, lunch 11 A.M.–3 P.M. Tues.-Sat., dinner 5-9 P.M. Fri.-Sat., lounge 4 P.M.–midnight Fri.-Sat., brunch Sun. 10 A.M.–3 P.M.), named after the mansion's last owner, the late heir to the Spam fortune, George "Geordie" Hormel, and it serves as a sort of observation deck with big picture windows offering unobstructed views of the city lights at night. Due to neighborhood zoning restrictions, the Wrigley Mansion must operate as a private club, and the Hormels have instituted an egalitarian $10 yearly fee that is donated to Valley charities. However, non-members can enjoy a guided tour, drinks, or the Sunday brunch.

© JEFF FICKER

Hanney's is a stylish downtown option for dinner or a late-night cocktail.

chocolate-brown leather banquettes, taupe walls, and small votive candles that flicker on the white marble tables. The classic cocktails are an excellent complement, and its "abandoned" elevator shaft and maze-like bathrooms are fun additions.

Hotel bars can be hit or miss. Fortunately, **District American Kitchen and Wine Bar** (320 N. 3rd St., 602/817-5400, 11 A.M. to midnight daily) at the Sheraton Phoenix Downtown brings a bit of style—and a topnotch bar menu—to the table. The District specializes in American wines, beers, and cocktails, which are meant to complement the hearty, Western-inspired menu. Enjoy one of the microbrews on tap, like the local Four Peaks amber, and order the AZ Sweet Shrimp Po' Boy Sliders with andouille sausage and celery root. The prices here aren't cheap, but the live music on the weekends makes this chic lounge with low-slung furniture and floor-to-ceiling windows a fun place to settle in.

Wine and cheese. What more do you need?

Cheuvront Restaurant & Wine Bar (1326 N. Central Ave., 602/307-0022, 11 A.M.–10 P.M. Mon.–Thurs., 11 A.M.–midnight Fri., 4 P.M.–midnight Sat., 4 P.M.–9 P.M. Sun.) serves a changing lineup of some 40 artisan cheeses from around the world—creamy camembert, nutty *manchego,* robust gorgonzola—which are thoughtfully paired with an extensive wine list that recently earned a Wine Spectator Award of Excellence. Throw caution to the wind and order one of the international wine flights, like "fruit-forward whites" or "zinfandels." Cheuvront's is a popular spot for a post-work drink and or late-evening nightcap, thanks in part to its urban, loft-like decor and convenient access to the light rail.

LIVE MUSIC
Phoenix's hip downtowners have made **The Lost Leaf** (915 N. 5th St., 602/258-0014, www.thelostleaf.org, 5 P.M.–2 A.M. daily) a regular hangout, thanks in part to its low-key vibe and regularly rotating series of local

artwork. The small, converted bungalow maintains much of the house's original character, including its hardwood floors, exposed brick walls, and former kitchen, which now serves as a bar with more than 100 types of beer and 20 wines. Most nights, The Lost Leaf features live music by regional or underground acts, like the Haymarket Squares, as well as the occasional improv act or poetry reading. And its intimate setting always makes for a good spot for conversation.

Experience the Valley's local music scene at **The Ruby Room** (717 S. Central Ave., 602/258-6900, www.myspace.com/therubyroomlounge, 3 P.M.–2 A.M. daily). Its easy-to-miss exterior in South Phoenix's rundown warehouse district may not seem like much, but step inside and the scarlet walls and vintage nudes give the club the delightfully unwholesome atmosphere of a rockabilly bordello, luring Betty Page wannabes and tattoo-sleeved scenesters. The music can be loud, and the quarters cramped—and if you have a problem with it, tough.

GAY AND LESBIAN

Amsterdam (718 N. Central Ave., 602/258-6122, www.amsterdambar.com, 4 P.M.–2 A.M. daily) is the heart of the Valley's gay nightlife scene, but with so few dance clubs in Phoenix, everyone is welcome here. Clubbers will find a large dance floor fueled by thumping pop and house music, as well as expensive martinis. The over-the-top interior can be a bit much, but the large patio is a comfortable place to hang out, especially on a warm night.

Central Phoenix
BARS AND PUBS

A little Scottsdale style has managed to slip into Central Phoenix. **The Vig** (4041 N. 40th St., 602/553-7227, 11 A.M.–midnight. Sun.–Wed., 11 A.M.–2 A.M. Thurs.–Sat.) has become the place to go for folks who want Desert Modernist design with their cocktails and European beer. The restaurant and bar are always busy, though it's The Vig's "backyard" that has made it such a hotspot. On weekends, a DJ spins tunes on the large, shady patio, and

friends battle it out on the bocce ball court. Despite all of the polish, the "modern tavern" is pretty relaxed and a nice place to start your evening or to finish it up with a nightcap.

Who hasn't thought a 1960s rec room would make a perfect dive bar? Thankfully, someone had a little follow-through. **Shady's Lounge** (2701 E. Indian School Rd., 602/956-8998, 11 A.M.–2 A.M. daily) has become a wood-paneled hipster haven, complete with pool table, well-stocked jukebox, and requisite beer selection, including Stella, New Castle, and Guinness on tap. The bar is small to be sure, but the laidback crowd is colorful and eager to chat. As one of the regulars, Heidi, will tell you: Never a dull moment, never a dull conversation.

Phoenix loves its pubs, and the **George & Dragon** (4240 N. Central Ave., 602/241-0018, 11 A.M.–2 A.M. daily) is the most British of the bunch, with stone walls and fireplaces, Union Jack flags, and an impressive selection of English, Welsh, and Scottish beers. In fact, the "GnD" promises the "largest selection of imported draught beer and scotch in the Phoenix area." So why not grab yourself a Tetley's and an order of bangers and mash? You could do worse—and an irascible but lovable staff is happy to tell you so.

Phoenix is a sports town, and there's no better place to catch a big game with a couple hundred of your closest friends than **Half Moon Sports Grill** (2121 E. Highland Ave., 602/977-2700, www.halfmoonsportsgrill.com, 11 A.M.–2 A.M. daily). Thanks to big screens galore throughout the restaurant, bar, and patio, you'll find plenty of opportunities to follow a host of games and tourneys. The ambience and food are decidedly more upscale than your traditional sports bar, though the selection of beer is up to the test of most connoisseurs. And why the name Half Moon? You'll figure out the cheeky reference when you get there.

Rosie McCaffrey's Irish Pub (906 E. Camelback Rd., 602/241-1916, 11 A.M.–2 A.M. Mon.–Sat., 11 A.M.–midnight Sun.) is big, loud, and always a lot of fun—perfect for a Friday night. Yes, it can be too crowded and the band too loud, but with Smithwick's on tap and Jameson at the ready, it's an easy cross to bear. Try to grab a booth in the back or a table out front if you'd like a quieter place to chat. **The Swizzle Inn** (5835 N. 16th St., 602/277-7775, 10 A.M.–2 A.M. daily) offers everything you want in a dive bar. Cheap, strong drinks? Check. A dartboard and pool table? Check. Johnny Cash on the jukebox, a sassy bartender named Darlene, and an eccentric group of regulars who welcome newbies? Check, check, *and* check. This hole-in-the-wall bar feels like a neighborhood hangout because it is. I've even heard of people living at "the Swiz" for an entire weekend, sustaining themselves on the potluck dishes and ever-flowing cocktails. As the sign says, "swizzle in and swagger out."

After a hike up neighboring Piestewa Peak, a little time on **Aunt Childa's** patio (7330 N. Dreamy Draw Dr., 602/944-1286, 11 A.M.–1 A.M. daily) with a margarita or three could be just the cure for sore muscles. The old hacienda-style restaurant has three outdoor bars, and there's live music Wednesday and Friday nights.

LOUNGES AND WINE BARS

Dark, sleek, and sexy, the **Merc Bar** (2525 E. Camelback Rd., 602/508-9449, www.mercbar.com, 4 P.M.–2 A.M. Mon.–Fri., 6 P.M.–2 A.M. Sat.–Sun.) is Phoenix's finest watering hole, a chic, modern lounge that exudes quiet elegance. Softly lit lanterns and flickering votives reflect off the bar's polished copper tables, creating a warm glow and the ambiance of a hidden Manhattan speakeasy—though this bar is tucked into the Esplanade Center at 24th Street and Camelback. You'll find well-heeled locals, Scottsdale party girls, and guests from the neighboring Ritz-Carlton sipping glasses of Veuve Clicquot and aged Scotch. In all, the mix of expensive cocktails and seen-and-be-seen preening can be quite pretentious and a whole lotta fun.

In-the-know Phoenicians have made the **Clarendon Rooftop Bar** (401 W. Clarendon Ave., 602/252-736) one of their favorite hangouts, particularly at sunset when the city seems to glow and the sky is streaked with oranges and reds. The mod lounge, which is perched on the eastern roof of The Clarendon Hotel, features a view of the Phoenix skyline that few watering holes are able to top. The bar is closed in the summer, and hours vary throughout the year, so be sure to call ahead. **Bomberos Café & Wine Bar** (8801 N. Central Ave., 602/687-8466, 7 A.M.–midnight Mon.–Thurs., 7 A.M.–1 A.M. Fri.–Sat., 7 A.M.–3 P.M. Sun.) is one of those neighborhood hangouts that regulars love to take their friends to. Owners Oscar and Kristi have converted an old North Phoenix firehouse into a hip, laidback wine bar, featuring polished concrete floors, large garage doors that open onto the sidewalk, and a cozy back patio with comfy couches and a fire pit for cool evenings. *Bomberos* means "firemen" in Spanish, and Uruguay native Oscar brings a bit of South American flair to the diverse selection of wine and beer. Order a refreshing glass of the white La Playa and sample the bruschetta. I'll probably be next to you enjoying the same thing.

LIVE MUSIC

This is a place with some character—and quite a few characters. **Char's Has the Blues** (4631 N. 7th Ave., 602/230-0205, www.charshastheblues.com, 7:30 P.M.–2 A.M. daily)—as well as live funk, soul, and jazz seven nights a week. Head inside the small converted cottage, grab yourself a stiff drink at the bar, and find your way to the softly lit dance floor to do that thing you do. There's also a pool table and darts if you left your dancing shoes at home. Oh, and be sure to call ahead and ask when you can catch the stylish funk-sploitations of Soul Power, the best R&B/soul cover band this side of Detroit.

For top blues acts and killer live music, there's only one spot in the Valley to go. **The Rhythm Room** (1019 E. Indian School Rd., 602/265-4842, www.rhythmroom.com, 8 P.M.–1 A.M. Sun.–Thurs., 8 P.M.–2 A.M. Fri.–Sat.) is a dark, intimate club that highlights some of the best jazz, bluegrass, and roots musicians, as well as touring acts that range from Bob Schneider and Cary Brothers to MGMT. If you work up an appetite on the dance floor, you can head out back most nights to pick up a sweet-and-smoky sandwich or plate of ribs at **Rack Shack BBQ** (602/279-0772, 6–11 P.M. Wed.–Thurs., 6 P.M.–2 A.M. Fri.–Sat.).

GAY AND LESBIAN

Kobalt (3110 N. Central Ave. Ste. 125, 602/264-5307, www.kobaltbarphoenix.com, 10 P.M.–2 A.M. Mon.–Fri., 11 A.M.–2 A.M. Sat.–Sun.) at Park Central Mall is another trendy destination for Valley gays and lesbians. A bit more laidback than Amsterdam, the lounge has a nice outdoor patio and features themed nights that range from trivia and movies to the popular karaoke on Sunday and Tuesday nights. It may also be the only bar in town with a daily happy hour from noon to 8 P.M.

Yee-haw! You don't have to be a real cowgirl to enjoy a little two-steppin' at **Cash Inn Country** (2140 E. McDowell Rd., 602/244-9943, www.cashinncountry.net, 2 P.M.–1 A.M. Tues.–Thurs., 2 P.M.–2 A.M. Fri., noon–2 A.M. Sat., noon–1 A.M. Sun.). Phoenix's "down-home lesbian country nightclub" offers free line-dancing lessons every Thursday at 7 P.M., and the Wednesday night poker tournaments make this ladies' saloon a fun place to grab a cheap beer. The rest of the week you'll find live music, latin dancing, or a DJ spinning tunes next to the pool tables and dart boards.

Men who'd like to give their cowboy boots a workout should head to **Charlie's** (727 W. Camelback Rd., 602/265-0224, www.charliesphoenix.com, 2 P.M.–2 A.M. Mon.–Fri., noon–2 A.M. Sat.–Sun.), home of the Arizona Gay Rodeo Association. The recently expanded bar now features a larger dance floor to boot, scoot, and boogie.

Tempe and the East Valley
BARS AND PUBS
Casey Moore's Oyster House (850 S. Ash Ave., 480/968-9935, 11 A.M.–2 A.M. Mon.–Sat., 11 A.M.–midnight Sun.) is a Tempe mainstay, where college students and professors share an enormous patio with hipsters and hippies. The old creaky house-turned-restaurant is rumored

to be haunted, and you may just see a ghost in one of the upstairs bedrooms, which have been converted into small dining rooms for private parties. Still, the real action is outside or in the bar, where you can get one of two dozen beers on tap and a cheap cocktail. The fresh oysters and appetizers aren't half bad, either.

Graduates of neighboring Arizona State University make a point of visiting **Four Peaks Brewpub** (1340 E. 8th St., 480/303-9967, 11 A.M.–2 A.M. Mon.–Sat., 10 A.M.–2 A.M. Sun.) when they return to their old stomping grounds in Tempe. The popular brewpub is a bit of a legend, and with so many delicious ales, stouts, and pilsners, who can blame their enthusiasm? The amber Kilt Lifter Scottish-style ale is served at restaurants and bars throughout the Valley, and the refreshing Hefeweizen, Hop Knot IPA, and seasonal brews are just as tasty. Be forewarned: There is no air-conditioning, so make sure you sample the brews when the weather is pleasant. Pints are $3 at happy hour, which runs 3–7 P.M.

Dos Gringos Tempe Trailer Park (1001 E. 8th St., 480/968-7879, 11 A.M.–2 A.M. daily) can seem like spring break in a Mexican beach town: cheap drinks, loud music, and the occasional college kid gone wild. Nevertheless, it's a fun place to enjoy a beer or margarita with friends, as the cheap prices and occasional live music bring out a bit of Cinco de Mayo's festive spirit. Head upstairs to the large balcony, which overlooks most of the outdoor bar. You won't want to miss the people-watching below.

Follow the sound of the energetic live band into **Rula Bula** (401 S. Mill Ave., 480/929-9500, 11 A.M.–2 A.M. daily). The lively Irish pub oozes Gaelic charm and honors the building's roots as an old saddlery and harness shop with plenty of tools, dark woods, and old engravings of horses. You'll feel right at home among the friendly regulars at the large oak bar from Ireland, or you may want to grab a table outside on the inviting patio. If you can tear yourself away from the comprehensive beer list, treat yourself to the Bailey's cheesecake or whiskey-spiked bread pudding that will have you thanking St. Patrick himself.

CASINOS

While newcomers to Arizona once tried to strike it rich in the mines, today, visitors can go for big payouts at the Gila River Indian Community's three casinos south of Phoenix. **Wild Horse Pass Casino** (5550 W. Wild Horse Pass, 800/946-4452, www.wingilariver.com) is the closest casino to the city and the largest. In addition to live poker, blackjack, and 875 slot machines, it offers live entertainment like comedians Joan Rivers and Sinbad. **Lone Butte Casino** (1200 S. 56th St., 800/946-4452, www.wingilariver.com) near Chandler features 850 slot machines and 24 Las Vegas-style table games, including blackjack and Pai Gow. Southwest of downtown Phoenix and near Laveen, you can try your luck at **Vee Quiva Casino** (6443 N. Komatke, 800/946-4452, www.wingilariver.com), which has slots, bingo, table games, and a 14-table poker room with daily tournaments.

COMEDY

When it's 114 degrees outside, you need a dry sense of humor. Join the locals at the always air-conditioned **Tempe Improv** (930 E. University Dr. Ste. 201, 480/921-9877, www.tempeimprov.com, 8 P.M.–midnight Thurs.–Sat., 8–10 P.M. Sun.), the Valley's outpost of the national comedy-club chain. Most weekends you can catch touring comedians, as well as standup masters like Bob Saget, Kathy Griffin, and Jerry Seinfeld.

PERFORMING ARTS

The Valley has a slew of venues for catching a play, concert, or dance performance. **Phoenix Symphony Hall** (75 N. 2nd St., 602/495-1117) is home to two of the city's most respected cultural institutions. For a dose of Verdi and Puccini, the **Arizona Opera** (602/266-7464, www.azopera.com) produces lavish spectacles that range from traditional to the occasionally experimental. The **Phoenix Symphony** (602/495-1999, www.phoenixsymphony.org) performs classics, chamber orchestra, and symphony pops throughout the year. Also, in downtown Phoenix, the **Herberger Theater**

Orpheum Theatre

(222 E. Monroe St., 602/254-7399, www.herbergertheater.org) stages a host of performances by Valley drama and dance groups.

The ornate **Orpheum Theatre** (203 W. Adams St., 602/534-5600) is once again wowing audiences. A massive $14 million renovation restored the historic theater's Baroque architectural details, and its auditorium creates the illusion of sitting in an outdoor Spanish courtyard, complete with a ceiling that changes from a blue sky with floating clouds to a golden sunset and a starry firmament. Nearby, Broadway shows, comedy acts, and concerts by Jay-Z, Coldplay, and Diana Krall take the stage at **Dodge Theatre** (400 W. Washington St., 602/379-2800, www.dodgetheatre.com). **Celebrity Theatre** (440 N. 32nd St., 602/267-1600, www.celebritytheatre.com) is one of the best venues to catch a show in Phoenix. Its in-the-round stage and small theater guarantee that "no seat is farther than 75 feet from the stage." Recent performers

© CITY OF TEMPE/GREATER PHOENIX CVB

the Tempe Festival of the Arts on Mill Avenue

include Smokey Robinson, Lucinda Williams, Tony Bennett, and Dwight Yoakam.

In the East Valley, the modern **Tempe Center for the Arts** (700 W. Rio Salado Pkwy., 480/350-2829, www.tempe.gov/TCA) overlooks Tempe Town Lake, and its two theaters stage performances by local arts and children's organizations. The Frank Lloyd Wright–designed **Gammage Auditorium** (1200 S. Forest Ave., 480/965-5062, www.asugammage.com) regularly hosts touring Broadway musicals and plays, as well as concerts and lectures. Further east, the boldly designed **Mesa Arts Center** (1 E. Main St., 480/644-6500, www.mesaartscenter.com) has four theaters for visiting acts and regional arts groups like the **Southwest Shakespeare Company** (480/641-7039, www.swshakespeare.org).

FESTIVALS AND EVENTS
January
The year kicks off with the **Fiesta Bowl** (1 Cardinals Way, 480/350-0900, www. fiestabowl.org) at the University of Phoenix Stadium in Glendale. The big game, which is part of the Bowl Championship Series, is preceded by the **Fiesta Bowl Parade** in Central Phoenix, with dozens of floats, bands, cheerleaders, balloons, and equestrian groups.

A few weeks later in mid-January, the **P.F. Chang's Rock 'N' Roll Arizona Marathon** (800/311-1255, www.rnraz.com) runs through Phoenix, Scottsdale, and Tempe. Now one of the most popular races in the country, the event also features more than 60 bands performing along the route.

February
In mid-February, book lovers converge on the **VNSA Book Sale** (1826 W. McDowell Rd., 602/265-6805, www.vnsabooksale. org) at the Arizona State Fairgrounds, featuring more than half a million used, rare, and out-of-print books. Also in February, the **Arizona Renaissance Festival** (12601 E. Hwy. 60, 520/463-2600) descends upon

Apache Junction in the far East Valley, for two months of ye olde fun. Enjoy raucous jousting tournaments, rides, live shows, and giant turkey legs fit for Henry VIII.

March

The **Heard Museum Guild & Indian Market** (2301 N. Central Ave., 602/252-8848, www. heard.org) in March is the state's largest festival of Native American arts and crafts. An estimated 20,000 serious collectors and curious browsers attend the annual event, where they are able to purchase original artwork and enjoy authentic food and entertainment.

Later in the month, downtown Tempe celebrates a series of outdoor events, including the **Great Arizona Beer Festival** (80 W. Rio Salado Pkwy., 480/774-8300, www.azbeer.com). The **Tempe Festival of the Arts** (Mill Ave. and University Dr., 480/921-2300, www.downtowntempe.com) transforms Mill Avenue into a pedestrian-only zone, lined with artists' booths, food stalls, and concert stages.

And for some quirky fun, head out to Chandler in the middle of the month for the **Ostrich Festival & Parade** (2250 S. McQueen Rd., 480/963-4571, www.ostrichfestival.com), which features live races, a carnival, and lots of food and entertainment.

April

Hollywood comes to town in April for the **Phoenix Film Festival** (7000 E. Mayo Blvd., 602/955-6444, www.phoenixfilmfestival. org). You can check out soon-to-be released features as well as documentaries, shorts, and independent and foreign films. Past attendees include Ed Burns, Peter Fonda, director John Waters, and, of course, the ever-connected Kevin Bacon.

If music is more your thing, the two-day **Tempe Music Festival** (80 W. Rio Salado Pkwy., 480/970-3378, www.tempemusicfestival. com) brings big acts like John Mayer, Kid Rock, Jeff Beck, and Fergie to Tempe Beach Park.

October

Events tend to grind to a screeching halt when the temperatures climb into the triple digits during summer, but they start up again with a bang in October at the **Arizona State Fair** (1826 W. McDowell Rd., 602/252-6771, www. azstatefair.com). The two-week carnival combines rides, deep-fried food, big-name concerts, and farm animal exhibitions for a bit of classic Americana.

At the end of the month, the Valley's Latino community celebrates **Dia de los Muertos,** or Day of the Dead. There are regular exhibitions and events at the Mesa Arts Center (1 E. Main St., 480/644-6500, www.mesaartscenter.com) and the Burton Barr Central Library (1221 N. Central Ave., 602/262-4636, www.phoenix-publiclibrary.org).

November-December

By mid-November, most of the Valley is gearing up for elaborate holiday events, like **Las Noches de las Luminarias** (1201 N. Galvin Pkwy., 480/941-1225, www.dbg.org) at the Desert Botanical Garden. Luminarias are a Southwestern tradition, and thousands of the small votives in paper bags are lit throughout the grounds of the desert garden, creating a spectacular sight. Also, **ZooLights** (455 N. Galvin Pkwy., 602/273-1341, www.phoenixzoo.org) delights kids with elaborate light displays, carousel rides, and hot cocoa at the Phoenix Zoo.

In the West Valley, **Glendale Glitter and Glow** (58th Ave. and Glendale Ave., 623/930-2299, www.glendaleaz.com) dazzles visitors in the city's historic district with twinkling lights and illuminated hot-air balloons. At the end of the month, Tempe lures college football fans with the **Insight Bowl** (500 E. Veterans Way, 480/350-0900, www.fiestabowl.org) at ASU's Sun Devil Stadium and the wild **Tempe Insight Fiesta Bowl Block Party** (Mill Ave. and University Dr., 480/350-0900, www.fiestabowl.org), one of the nation's largest New Year's Eve celebrations.

Shopping

Phoenix helped pioneer the outdoor mall when the upscale Biltmore Fashion Park opened in the 1960s, and the retail landmark is still one of the city's few pedestrian-friendly enclaves. Shoppers who are looking for funky mom-and-pop stores and vintage boutiques should head downtown or to Central Phoenix, which offers some surprisingly affordable retail options. Also, Mill Avenue's shops in Tempe attract students at neighboring Arizona State University.

DOWNTOWN
Shopping Districts and Centers
ARIZONA CENTER

The outdoor Arizona Center (400 E. Van Buren St., 602/271-4000, 10 A.M.–9 P.M. Mon.–Sat., 11 A.M.–5 P.M. Sun.) is a pleasant mix of restaurants, bars, and shops surrounded by downtown Phoenix's office towers. There's even a 24-screen multiplex movie theater—perfect for escaping the heat. The complex's tourist-oriented stores are handy if you're searching for Arizona souvenirs and gifts, like tiny cacti, t-shirts, and trinkets with Kokopelli. Sadly, residents often overlook its best feature: a small, shady garden with benches, waterfalls, and a tranquil pond. It's a nice place to enjoy a picnic lunch or catch a few rays.

ROOSEVELT ROW

The small collection of independent shops, galleries, and restaurants that make up Roosevelt Row (602/614-8727, www.rooseveltrow.org) has tried to do the impossible: transform downtown Phoenix into a vibrant, pedestrian-friendly neighborhood. And after nearly two decades, their Herculean efforts appear to be working. Twice a week, the **Downtown Phoenix Public Market** (721 N. Central Ave., www.foodconnect.org/phoenixmarket, 4–8 P.M. Wed., 8 A.M.–noon Sat.) pops up near Central Avenue and McKinley Street, made up of local farmers and artisans selling organic produce and homemade goods.

The monthly **First Friday artwalk** (602/256-7539, www.artlink.com, 6–10 P.M.) fills Roosevelt Street from Grand Avenue to 16th Street, with people darting in and out of the neighborhood's small galleries, artist studios, and live/work spaces that have sprung up. Some of the smaller shops come and go, but **Modified Arts** (407 E. Roosevelt St., 602/462-5516, http://modified.org, hours vary) remains a leading force in Phoenix's alternative arts scene, featuring musical performances in addition to rotating gallery selections.

The collective, artist-run space **Eye Lounge** (419 E. Roosevelt St., 602/430-1490, 9 A.M.–5 P.M. Tues.–Thurs., 9 A.M.–9 P.M. Fri., 1–5 P.M. Sat.) promotes the works of local emerging artists, making it an excellent opportunity to invest in a piece on the ground floor. There are a few independent stores of note

© MICA THOMAS MULLOY

Modified Arts

on Roosevelt, including **Made Art Boutique** (922 N. 5th St., 602/256-6233, 10 A.M.–6 P.M. Mon.–Thurs., 10 A.M.–9 P.M. Fri.), which sells fun books, t-shirts, jewelry, and artwork. Just south, **Bunky Boutique** (812 N. 3rd St., 602/252-1323, 11 A.M.–7 P.M. Tues.–Fri., 11–6 P.M. Sat.) has become a Phoenix retail darling with an eclectic selection of men's, women's, and children's clothing and accessories. Well-known labels and independent designers are represented, and hours change throughout the year.

CENTRAL PHOENIX
Shopping Districts and Centers
BILTMORE FASHION PARK
Biltmore Fashion Park (24th St. and Camelback Rd., 602/955-8400, www.shopbiltmore.com, 10 A.M.–7 P.M. Mon.–Wed., 10 A.M.–8 P.M. Thurs.–Fri., 10 A.M.–6 P.M. Sat., noon–6 P.M. Sun.) is more than a mall. Since opening in 1963, the open-air shopping center has become a sort of public square in Phoenix's posh Biltmore neighborhood, attracting many of the city's residents to its upscale shops, landscaped courtyards, and popular restaurants. **Macy's** and **Borders** anchor the western end of the complex. Next door, **Saks Fifth Avenue** overlooks a grassy lawn, attracting well-heeled clients who visit the store's mini-boutiques dedicated to Chanel, Gucci, Louis Vuitton, and Prada. Under the Biltmore's shaded canopies you'll find other big-name brands like Escada, Ralph Lauren, Apple, and Elizabeth Arden Red Door Spa. A controversial remodel has transformed the much-beloved midcentury landmark's design, though it did add a new underground pedestrian walkway that connects the center to additional restaurants, a movie theater, and The Ritz-Carlton on the other side of Camelback Road.

7TH AVENUE MELROSE DISTRICT
The Melrose District has become the city's thrift-store haven. Among the half-dozen antiques stores, **Retro Redux** (4303 N. 7th Ave., 602/234-0120, 11 A.M.–6 P.M. Wed.–Sun.) sells old-school clothing, dishware, and

furniture. Nearby, the **Phoenix Metro Retro** (708 W. Hazelwood St., 602/279-0702, www. phoenixmetroretro.com, 10 A.M.–4 P.M. Sat.) opens Saturdays for a warehouse sale of affordable midcentury modern furniture. **Hollywood Regency** (708 W. Montecito Ave., 602/277-5765, 11 A.M.–6 P.M. Wed.–Sat.) is regularly named the best vintage shop in Phoenix, with women's clothing from the 1940s to the '80s.

CHINESE CULTURAL CENTER
Think of it as Phoenix's answer to Chinatown. The COFCO Chinese Cultural Center (668 N. 44th St., 602/273-7268, www.phxchinatown.com) brings a bit of the Far East to the Sonoran Desert, with graceful pagodas, traditional arches, small gardens, and restaurants serving Mandarin, Sichuan, and Shanghai-style cuisine. Stroll the grounds and visit the small shops, like **Golden Gifts** (602/275-1311, 10 A.M.–7 P.M. Mon.–Sat., noon–7 P.M. Sun.) and the **Chinese Herbal Shop** (602/244-9885, 10 A.M.–7 P.M. daily). Be sure to make some time to pop into the mammoth **Super L Ranch Market** (602/225-2288, 9 A.M.–9 P.M. daily), which features rows of imported goods, crisp produce, and tanks with live fish to guarantee a fresh "catch."

Clothing
A few mod, independent shops are clustered around Camelback Road and Central Avenue, like **Frances** (10 W. Camelback Rd., 602/279-5467, www.francesvintage.com, 10 A.M.–6 P.M. Mon.–Sat., noon–5 P.M. Sun.), where shoppers will find an eclectic mix of goods reflecting the boutique's vintage-inspired aesthetic, like embroidered blouses, men's wallets, retro paper goods, soy candles, and fun gifts for kids and adults.

Gifts and Toys
Domo arigato, Mr. Roboto, for this one-of-a-kind boutique in Central Phoenix. **Red Hot Robot** (14 W. Camelback Rd., 602/264-8560, www.redhotrobot.net, noon–7 P.M. Tues.–Sat., noon–5 P.M. Sun.) stocks Japanese pop-inspired books, clothing, art, and "designer toys."

Owner Jason Kiningham has created a whimsical "toy gallery + cultureshop" that kids and adults will appreciate. Check out the imported vinyl figures and prints, as well as the quirky pieces designed by Arizona artists.

Home Furnishings

For hip furniture and housewares, **Haus Modern Living** (4700 N. Central Ave. Ste. 102, 602/277-0111, www.hausmodernliving. com, 10 A.M.–6 P.M. Tues.–Sat., noon–5 P.M. Sun.) supplies Barcelona chairs, Jonathan Adler ceramics, Alessi home accessories, and trendy pieces by Philippe Starck.

Red Modern Furniture (201 E. Camelback Rd., 602/256-9620, redmodernfurniture.com, 10 A.M.–6 P.M. Mon.–Sat., noon–5 P.M. Sun.) is the place to go for original vintage pieces by Eero Saarinen, Arne Jacobsen, Knoll, Henredon, Gio Ponti, and Charles and Ray Eames. This hidden gem is a resource for some the nation's top interior designers and collectors. Inside the boutique, you'll find Mint, a beautifully curated collection of vintage clothing and accessories by brands like Gucci, Dior, and Louis Vuitton.

Music

Video killed the radio star, and the Internet is slowly killing the music shop. Fortunately, **Stinkweeds** (12 W. Camelback Rd., 602/248-9461, www.stinkweeds.com, 11 A.M.–8 P.M. Mon.–Sat., noon–6 P.M. Sun.) keeps hope alive for Valley music lovers as one of the city's last independent record shops, specializing in up-and-coming bands, imports, and music from independent labels.

NORTH PHOENIX
Shopping Districts and Centers
DESERT RIDGE

Behold yet another of Phoenix's outdoor "lifestyle centers" (a.k.a. megamalls); at 1.2 million square feet, Desert Ridge (21001 N. Tatum Blvd., 480/419-8088, www.shopdesertridge. com, 11 A.M.–9 P.M. Mon.–Sat., 11 A.M.–6 P.M. Sun.) seems to have a super-chain for every need and taste. You'll find clothing stores

like Old Navy, American Eagle Outfitters, and Hollister, as well as specialty shops like Learning Express and Sunglass Hut, a handy resource in the desert. There's also an 18-screen movie theater, bungee jumping, and a super-arcade and bowling alley at Dave & Busters.

OUTLETS AT ANTHEM

On the northern edge of town, a bargain hunter's paradise unfolds in the desert. The Outlets at Anthem (4250 W. Anthem Way, 623/465-9500, 10 A.M.–8 P.M. Mon.–Sat., 10 A.M.–7 P.M. Sun., www.outletsanthem.com) is home to 75 brand-name stores loaded with merchandise at significantly reduced prices. Traveling cheap? You'll find Banana Republic, Gap, J. Crew and Calvin Klein duds marked down by up to 70 percent. The shops are clean. The styles are new. A food court with just about anything you're looking for will keep you full enough to search out every last deal for affordable but fashionable sunglasses and kitchenware. A 50,000-square-foot expansion means you'll need all the energy you can get.

TEMPE AND THE EAST VALLEY
Shopping Districts and Centers
MILL AVENUE

A Main Street for Arizona State University, Mill Avenue became a little too popular for its own good in the 1990s, when high rents chased out mom-and-pop shops and bars. National chains moved into the red-brick buildings, but only a few, like **Urban Outfitters** and **American Apparel,** were able to survive the shopping habits of this eclectic crowd of students and suburbanites. Stores may come and go, but "Mill Ave." continues to serve as one of the city's few spots for streetside shopping.

TEMPE MARKETPLACE

A couple of miles north, you'll find the sprawling Tempe Marketplace (Highway 202 and McClintock, 480/966-9338). The mega-complex of chain retailers boasts a lot of names you'll recognize from the mall, like Gap, Levi's, and Barnes & Noble, as well as a movie theater and dozens of restaurants and bars. Its light shows, outdoor fireplaces, and unique water features make it a great place to hang out at night, especially for its free Third Thursday concerts.

Bookstores
One of the stores that fled Mill Avenue, **Changing Hands Bookstore** (6428 S. McClintock Dr., 480/730-0205, 10 A.M.–9 P.M. Mon.–Fri., 9 A.M.–9 P.M. Sat., 10 A.M.–7 P.M. Sun.) features 12,000 square feet of new and used books, specializing in contemporary fiction. Known for its regular events, the store's impressive roster of signings include David Sedaris, Jimmy Carter, Hillary Clinton, Elizabeth Gilbert, and *Fight Club* author Chuck Palahniuk. Collectors can find rare and modern first editions like Harper Lee's *To Kill a Mockingbird,* as well as signed copies of Jonathan Fanzen's *The Corrections* and Nick Hornby's *About a Boy.*

Clothing
The younger crowd will appreciate the compact **Here on the Corner** (714 S. College Ave., 480/377-0100, 11 A.M.–7 P.M. daily), near the campus of Arizona State University. The boutique's trendy finds include denim from Frankie B and William Rast, eco-friendly handbags, and funky t-shirts, and accessories. Nearby, **Buffalo Exchange** (227 W. University Dr., 480/968-2557, www.buffaloexchange.com, 10 A.M.–9 P.M. Mon.–Sat., 11 A.M.–7 P.M. Sun.) sells an eclectic mix of new and used clothing. Hunt for vintage concert shirts, leather jackets, funky accessories, and high-end brand names.

Denim junkies, welcome to heaven. Chandler's **Moody Blues** (3355 W. Chandler Boulevard Ste. 4, 480/558-7494, 10 A.M.–7 P.M. Mon.–Sat., noon–5 P.M. Sun.) offers a staggering selection of jeans, many of which cannot be found anyplace else in the Valley. The

friendly staff is happy to help you find your perfect fit and color, with styles ranging from skinny rock-star to boot cut, faded indigo to whiskered dark rinses. There are also plenty of other fashionable finds, including chic dresses and tops for women and cool shirts for men.

Farmers Markets
If only every grocery shopping experience could be this charming. The family-owned **Guadalupe Farmer's Market** (9210 S. Avenida del Yaqui, 480/730-1945, 9 A.M.–6 P.M. Mon.–Sat., 9 A.M.–5 P.M. Sun.) sells locally grown fruits and vegetables, as well as Latin American specialties like fresh tortillas, roasted chiles, and homemade salsas and jams. There's also a large selection of dried spices and Arizona honey that make terrific gifts. This small market is tucked into the community of Guadalupe, a one-square-mile town predominantly inhabited by Yaqui Indian and Latino residents. Shoppers may also want to make time to stop into the **Mercado Mexico** (8212 S. Avenida del Yaqui, 480/831-5925), which sells imported products from south of the border, like ceramics and paper goods.

WEST VALLEY
Shopping Districts and Centers
HISTORIC DOWNTOWN GLENDALE
The quaint Historic Downtown Glendale has become a mecca for Arizona antiquers, thanks to its two shopping districts of Old Towne (Glendale Ave. and 58th Ave.) and Caitlin Court (Myrtle Ave. and 58th Ave.). This pedestrian-friendly neighborhood features old bungalows with white picket fences and shady trees that have been converted into small specialty shops, like **Country Maiden** (7146 N. 58th Ave., 623/930-7303, 10 A.M.–5 P.M. Mon.–Sat.) and **The Cottage Garden** (7142 N. 58th Ave., 623/847-3232, 10 A.M.–4 P.M. Tues.–Sat.).

Sports and Recreation

Few cities in the world offer such a rich selection of activities for outdoor lovers. Phoenix and the city's surrounding suburbs will seem like Nirvana for diehard golfers, hikers, and bikers. And don't let the summer heat stop you from taking advantage of the city's incredible landscapes. Many Phoenicians set their alarm clocks early in the summer, when cool morning temperatures make a round of golf or jog along the city's canals downright pleasant.

AIR ADVENTURES AND BALLOONING

With more than 300 sunny days a year, Phoenix is a pilot's paradise. See what all the fuss is about while getting a bird's-eye view of the spectacular desert scenery by taking a glider ride at **Arizona Soaring** (22548 N. Sailport Way, Maricopa, 520/568-2602, www.azsoaring.com). Twenty-minute flights start at $105 and come with or without aerobatics like loops and spins.

Act out all your *Top Gun* fantasies at **Fighter Combat International** (5865 S. Sossaman Rd., Mesa, 866/359-4273, www.fightercombat.com), where you can tempt both gravity and death by flying a plane on a "combat mission." Even beginners learn to take the stick during in-the-air training in air-combat tactics, "smoke chases," lead-and-follow drills, and weapons training. As they say, "only the bullets aren't real." Prices range from $755 for a three- to four-hour adventure to more than $4,000 for a multiday experience.

A Balloon Experience by Hot Air Expeditions (480/502-6999, www.hotairexpeditions.com) flies its balloons about 400 feet above the desert floor, low enough to see critters like jackrabbits, roadrunners, and coyotes. But the best part might come after landing: A red-carpet welcome that includes either a champagne breakfast or full dinner catered by award-winning Arizona chef Vincent Gerithault's restaurant, Vincent's, awaits. The company is FAA-certified and offers free hotel transfers. The three-hour trips cost about $175.

Aerogelic Ballooning (866/353-8329, www.aerogelicballooning.com) focuses on small balloons that hold two, four, or six people for flights over the Sonoran Desert outside of Phoenix, or other, more unusual flight paths. "Dawn patrol" flights start half an hour before sunrise to show the city's lights as they wink out for the day, while the White Mountains flight soars over the high mountains northeast of Phoenix and one of the largest ponderosa pine forests in the nation. Packages range $169–315.

DESERT AND JEEP TOURS

Hit pay dirt by learning how to pan gold and gemstones with **Arrowhead Desert Tours** (602/942-3361, www.azdeserttours.com). A genuine prospector drives tenderfeet to backcountry streams that may give up garnets or even "the color." The company provides all the equipment, and guides explain how to use it. **Phoenix Tours** (800/303-5185, www.phoenixtours.us) leads Jeep tours of everything from the Apache Trail in the Superstition Mountains to a daylong Sedona trip or a nocturnal, night-vision scope adventure. Drivers will pick you up at your hotel or residence and drive you out to the desert, where guides will cover the history and ecology of the tour area. Prices range $45–500 depending on the trip.

BIKING AND JOGGING

Phoenix's 181 miles of canals give it one of the most extensive biking and running-trail systems anywhere. One of the best paths in town is along the gravel banks of the **Arizona Canal** between Scottsdale Road and Central Avenue. The full distance is just over 11 miles, but luckily, the best parts are at either end: Crunch past Scottsdale hotels and neighborhoods carved out of old citrus groves near 68th Street or canal-side public art and the Biltmore Hotel on the stretch between Central Avenue and 24th Street.

One of the best introductions to mountain biking in the Sonoran Desert is the **Desert Classic** trail at South Mountain Park. The 9-mile out-and-back trail (find the trailhead at 9904 S. 48th St., near Guadalupe Road, phoenix.gov/parks/hiksogud.html) runs the gamut of terrain from steep-sided washes to single-track speedways and even a few rocky, technical climbs without becoming impossible for bikers with at least intermediate skills. Anyone looking for more of a challenge can take a right on the **National Trail**—where the rocky, steep descents make for one of the toughest rides in the state—to make a loop back to the parking area.

Roadies will find it nearly impossible to get a traffic-free pedaling fix in Phoenix, but one of the city's rare paved hill climbs is on **Valle Vista Road** on the south side of Camelback Mountain. The best approach is from the south, either on 48th Street or 56th Street, because the streets link up to form a loop back to wherever you parked your car (or even to the light-rail stop at 44th Street and Washington).

HIKING AND ROCK CLIMBING

No visit to Phoenix would be complete without climbing **Piestewa Peak**. The short but challenging Summit Trail rises just over 1,200 feet in 1.2 miles, but it's worth it. The peak offers panoramic views of the city stretched out for miles in every direction, and when the wind carries the scent of creosote and citrus blossoms up from the valley below, it can be hard to begin the clamber back down. On weekend mornings, the trail becomes a mountainside promenade as throngs of tanned, supple hikers and runners (and those who wish to be so) make even panting by the side of the trail interesting. But it is the quieter weekdays when jackrabbits, Gila monsters, geckos, and the occasional rattlesnake or coyote come out to sun themselves among the

© MICA THOMAS MULLOY

Phoenix Mountains Preserve and Piestewa Peak

cacti and desert trees that pepper the hillsides. To reach the trailhead, turn east onto Squaw Peak Drive from Lincoln Drive between 22nd and 24th streets.

The other must-hike destination is **South Mountain Regional Park.** Its 61,000 acres of mountains, arroyos, and flats crisscrossed by 51 miles of hiking trails make this the largest municipal park in the United States. San Juan Road leads to the highest peak in the range, where you'll find New Deal-era picnic areas and a series of short hikes through the hills. For the more ambitious, the Alta Trail starts near the park entrance and runs along a ridge, offering 4.5 miles of some of the most stunning city views anywhere. Coyotes, javelina, and rattlesnakes make regular appearances in the park, so be alert and give them a wide berth. The park entrance and main ranger station are on Central Avenue south of Dobbins Road.

Farther north, the 10.7-mile Charles Christiansen Memorial Trail (Trail 100) linking North Mountain, Shaw Butte, and Dreamy Draw is too long for most people to hike in a single go, but it serves as the spine of the entire **Phoenix Mountains Preserve** trail network and is a good jumping-off point to explore canyons and washes that feel like they're far from the surrounding city. Find information on the flora and fauna and get maps at the **North Mountain Visitors Center** (12950 N. 7th St., 602/495-5540, www.phoenix.gov/parks, 7 A.M.–1 P.M. Sat.–Sun.).

Hiking "quickies" seldom lead to anything interesting, let alone iconic, but the Hole-in-the-Rock trail at **Papago Park** is the exception. The easy, 835-foot trail shoots up to a tunnel-like hole in the sandstone that houses an ancient Hohokam Indian solar calendar. The entrancing views of downtown Phoenix make this one of the best places anywhere to watch a colorful Southwestern sunset. Get there by turning off the Galvin Parkway onto the Papago Park/Phoenix Zoo road. The trail begins from a picnic area on the northern end of the Ranger Office Loop road.

The **Phoenix Parks and Recreation** department also organizes hikes (free with a

© ADAM RODRIGUEZ/GREATER PHOENIX CVB

red buttes in Papago Park

city Recreation Card, available for a one-time fee of $20, $10 for residents) through all of its mountain parks, guided by experts on the plants, birds, petroglyphs, and history of central Arizona. Get a full schedule or sign up for a hike at www.online.activecommunities.com/phoenix. **Take a Hike Arizona** (866/615-2748, www.takeahikearizona.com) also leads guided hikes to all destinations around metro Phoenix. Half-day excursions start at $65. Full-day hikes of five hours or more run about $99. Prices include snacks, lunch, and guides.

The steep canyons and rock spires that shape the mountains around Phoenix are a playground for rock climbers, but the sandstone terrain is often treacherous. Guide outfits **Ascend Guide Services** (800/227-2363, www.amdest.com) and **360 Adventures** (602/795-1877, www.360-adventures.com) offer instruction and equipment for beginners and the lay of the land for experts. Prices for full-day rock-climbing or canyoneering trips range $120–400 per person depending on the activity and size of the group.

GOLF

Welcome to the Southwest's golf capital. Phoenix and neighboring Scottsdale lure professionals and amateurs alike, with one of the finest collections of courses in the world. Its championship greens dot the city, and residents practically live on the links—some literally, thanks to dozens of golf course communities. Arizona State University graduates Phil Mickelson, Billy Mayfair, and Grace Park refined their skills here, and Tom Lehman and Annika Sörenstam were compelled by the constant sunshine and topnotch fairways to move here.

Scottsdale's luxury desert courses may be more well-known, but Phoenix offers quality for a good price. Here you'll find a broad mix of traditional and desert courses, as well as some unique landmarks. Many courses close their lawns for a few weeks in the fall and spring for re-seeding between seasons, so be sure to call ahead and ask when you make a tee time. Like hotel and resort rates, greens fees tumble as the heat rises, with even the best courses charging a fraction of their winter prices in the summer. Call ahead for current fees.

One of the best golf experiences in the state features courses designed by two legends. **Wildfire Golf Club** (5350 E. Marriott Dr., 480/473-0205, www.wildfiregolf.com) at the JW Marriott Desert Ridge Resort showcases two 18-hole desert courses designed by giants Arnold Palmer and Nick Faldo. The scenic Palmer Signature Course has expansive fairways and rolling greens, while the Faldo Championship Course treats golfers to large bent-grass greens, tee boxes, and a bewildering 106 sand bunkers. If you'd prefer to hit a few balls and take in the views of the McDowell Mountains, though, grab a bucket at the 13,000-square-foot practice green, complete with bunkers and pitching areas.

A little bit closer to town, **Lookout Mountain Golf Club** (11111 N. 7th St., 602/866-6356, www.pointehilton.com) at the Pointe Hilton Tapatio Cliffs Resort is a par-71, 18-hole championship course that wraps around North Mountain Park and the Lookout Mountain Preserve, giving golfers a chance to appreciate the occasional Sonoran Desert rabbit or coyote along with their birdies and eagles. The medium-length course should appeal to most skill levels, though the back nine features a few challenging target holes. The well-regarded golf academy may be a good place to grab a few lessons if you're new to the game, and its practice area has its own pitching green and separate chipping and putting areas.

Looking for a green with a view? **Papago Golf Course** (5595 E. Moreland St., 602/275-8428, www.papagogolfcourse.net) has become one of the most loved slices of turf in the Valley since opening in 1963. Golf course architect William Francis "Billy" Bell, whose roster of 100-plus courses includes Torrey Pines, designed it to highlight the so-close-you-can-touch-it views of the red-hued Papago Buttes, Camelback Mountain, and downtown Phoenix. And the course is now better than ever, having

AQUA VITAE

Summer in the Sonoran Desert means hot, sunny days and warm nights. To combat the triple-digit temperatures, Phoenicians find relief in the region's most valuable resource: water.

- **Pools:** Arizona without swimming pools is like New York City without hot-dog carts. And with more than 50 public pools and thousands of backyard swimming holes scattered throughout the Phoenix metropolitan area, finding one of these shimmering oases isn't too hard. Most hotels and resorts have at least one pool, though the most elegant has to be the main pool at **The Phoenician** (6000 E. Camelback Rd., 480/941-8200, www.thephoenician.com), which is lined with mother-of-pearl tiles. Sorry, it's only open to guests, though you can take a peek if you have dinner or a cocktail at the hotel.

- **Misters:** Where would Phoenix patios be without the mister? You'll see them producing a fine mist of water at homes, restaurants, and bars throughout the city. This simple machine produces water droplets as fine as the diameter of a human hair, and when they make contact with the dry desert air, the droplets "flash evaporate," resulting in a dip in temperature by as much as 25 degrees – and all with just a slight increase in noticeable humidity.

- **Lakes:** Thanks to a series of dams around the Valley, there are seven large lakes within an easy drive of Phoenix. The most convenient body of water, though, has to be **Tempe Town Lake** (620 N. Mill Ave., 480/350-8625, www.tempe.gov/lake, free). Created by inflatable rubber dams along the Salt River, the manmade lake is a popular gathering spot for festivals, joggers, and rowing clubs. You can rent a paddleboat at the park or let the little ones enjoy the

re-opened after a $5.8 million renovation that reshaped and added bunkers, reseeded the lawns, restored its lakes, and trimmed mature trees along the fairways. This city-owned course is one of Phoenix's best golf values.

Arizona State University boasts one of the finest collegiate golf programs in the country, so it's little surprise that their home course in Tempe should earn 4.5 stars from *Golf Digest*. The challenging **ASU Karsten Golf Club** (1125 E. Rio Salado Pkwy., 480/921-8070, www.asukarsten.com) may force you to use every club in your bag, but with four sets of tees, you don't have to be PGA-bound to make par—or at least have fun. Designer Pete Dye incorporated his trademark mounding and inspired pot bunkers, as well as lakes, rolling hills, and well-protected greens. The Scottish links-style course books well in advance, so be sure to call early for a tee time.

If you're tired of seeing cacti lining the fairways, try **Raven Golf Club at South Mountain** (3636 E. Baseline Rd., 602/243-3636, www.theravensouthmountain.com). The traditional course features thousands of mature trees, including large African sumacs and 6,000 pine trees. You'll find water hazards, strategically placed bunkers, and a few challenging target holes. Raven regularly earns nods for its incomparable service and Kent Chase Golf Academy, which offers private instruction and group classes.

The **Legacy Golf Resort** (6808 S. 32nd St., 888/828-3673, www.shellhospitality.com) in South Phoenix was named one of the "Top 10 Golf Courses to Play in Phoenix" by *Golf Digest*. Old structures from the 7,500-acre ranch of Dwight B. Heard—founder of the Heard Museum—now line the 18-hole desert golf course, where you'll find manicured greens and views of South Mountain and the downtown Phoenix skyline. Group instruction

Splash Playground water park (10 A.M.-7 P.M. daily, Apr.-Sept., free).

- **Water Parks:** In summer, nothing beats the heat like gliding down a slide into a clear pool of water. There are a half-dozen water parks throughout the Valley, including a few at the larger resorts, but only **Wet 'n' Wild** (4243 W. Pinnacle Peak Rd., 623/201-2000, http://phoenix.mywetnwild.com, $35 adults 12-64, $27 seniors and children 3-11) can claim the title of "Arizona's largest." The Glendale retreat opened in summer 2009 with $30 million worth of slides, rides, and splish-splashin' good times.

- **Rivers:** Many Phoenicians regularly make the 20-minute commute northeast of the Valley to the mountain-fed Salt River. Tubers can float by majestic sandstone cliffs, spiraling hawks, wading blue herons, and towering saguaro cactus – as well as beer-soaked partiers on the river and jacked-up

trucks blasting classic rock on the shore. It's an inimitable experience, and tour company **Salt River Recreation** (480/984-3305, www.saltrivertubing.com) will rent you a tube and give you a ride in an old school bus to and from the river for $15 a person.

- **Fountains:** Head out to the aptly named suburb of Fountain Hills to see the Valley's answer to Old Faithful, **The Fountain,** a 560-foot-tall jet of water. One of the world's tallest fountains, the slender column rises *only* 330 feet most days in the center of **Fountain Park** (12925 N. Saguaro Blvd., 480/816-5151) for 15 minutes at the top of every hour (9 A.M. to 9 P.M.). On special occasions, the town turns on all three pumps to send it soaring to its maximum height of 56 stories. To see it, visit the park, which has a great playground for children. Take Shea Boulevard 15 minutes east from central Scottsdale and turn north on Saguaro Boulevard.

is available, as are private lessons by LPGA professionals Lynn Marriott and Pia Nilsson, who are regularly named among the best instructors in the country.

A recent makeover transformed South Phoenix's Phantom Horse Golf Club into the **Arizona Grand Golf Course** (8000 S. Arizona Grand Pkwy., 602/431-6480, www.arizonagrandresort.com). The unconventional fairways wrap around South Mountain Park, creating dramatic elevation changes, unusual slopes, and stunning views. The ingenious design features a traditional front nine before switching over to a desert back nine, which can be an exhilarating change during a mid-game slump.

Many say this is where Arizona's reputation as a mecca for golfers began. **San Marcos Golf Resort** (1 N. San Marcos Pl., 480/963-3358, www.sanmarcosresort.com) opened in 1913, and its big draw was the state's first course with grass greens. Over the years, presidents

and celebrities have played its wide, forgiving fairways, and more than a few have found their balls in its numerous bunkers. The Chandler landmark is a good value and should be considered if you're staying in the East Valley.

By the time you lose your second ball, you'll ask yourself where so much damn water came from in the middle of the desert. Chandler's **Ocotillo Golf Resort** (3751 S. Clubhouse Dr., 480/917-6660, www.ocotillogolf.com) is one of the state's most individual courses, as 24 of its 27 holes feature water hazards—from small lakes and cascading waterfalls to a few "island holes." Still, the challenging course is beautiful, and many say it's one of the best-manicured in the city. Games can be pricy, especially in the winter.

Trust me, it's worth the drive. Take Highway 60 well beyond Mesa and Gilbert to **Gold Canyon Golf Resort** (6100 S. Kings Ranch Rd., 480/982-9449, www.gcgr.com), a spectacular course tucked into the Superstition Mountains. *Sports Illustrated* named it one of the country's most underrated courses, thanks to nosebleed elevation changes, mountain views, and lush, green fairways lined by pristine desert. Its 18-hole Dinosaur Mountain Course snakes through mountain passes, while the Sidewinder wraps around the foothills. You'll pay a bit for all of this scenery, but why not splurge?

HORSEBACK RIDING

The easiest place to set up an equine adventure is at **Ponderosa Stables & South Mountain Stables** in South Mountain Park (10215 S. Central Ave., 602/286-1261, http://arizona-horses.com). The experienced trail guides lead rides almost everywhere through the 16,000-acre park, as well as special sunrise and sunset rides that include breakfast or dinner seven days a week, all year long. Trail rides start at $30 a person for one hour and can change depending on the size of the group. Morning reservations are recommended, especially for summer days when the temperature can top 100 degrees.

Driving out to the far eastern edge of town makes **Saguaro Lake Trail Rides** (13020 Bush Hwy., 480/984-0335, www.saguarolaketrail-rides.com) more of an all-day destination than a place to drop in, but the lush canyons, towering rock spires, and, yes, an actual lake make the area one of the more scenic spots to ride horses. Rides run anywhere from $38 to $110 per person.

On the west side, step into the saddle at **White Tanks Riding Stables** (20300 W. Olive Ave., 623/935-7455, www.whitetanksriding.com). The staff can round up horses for trail rides, "Dutch oven" dinner rides, and even pony rides for kids. Rates start at $37 per person for an hour.

TUBING AND WATER PARKS

Tubing in the Salt River northeast of Phoenix is a fascinating combination of relaxing and trashy. On the two- to four-hour trips, tubers

float along the banks of the lower Salt River, where you'll experience an interesting mix of wildlife and some raucous partiers. The tour company **Salt River Recreation** (480/984-3305, www.saltrivertubing.com, $15) will rent you a tube and give you a ride to and from the parking lot. Take Highway 202 (Loop 202) to Power Road in east Mesa and drive seven miles north.

As might be expected in a town where summertime temperatures regularly top 100 degrees, metro Phoenix has a wealth of water parks. The three biggest all feature the requisite water slides, wave pools, and tubing areas, but each has a slightly different focus. The claim to fame of **Big Surf** (1500 N. McClintock Dr., 480/947-2477, $26 adult, $19.50 child) is a wave pool big enough to allow actual surfing, as featured in the 1987 movie *North Shore.* **Golfland Sunsplash** (155 W. Hampton Ave., 480/834-8319, www.golfland.com/mesa, $26 adult, $19.50 child) in Mesa has a dozen different water slides but a less powerful wave pool. And the newest destination, **Wet 'n' Wild** (4243 W. Pinnacle Peak Rd., 623/201-2000, http://phoenix.mywetnwild.com, $35 adult, $27 child), opened in summer 2009 with $30 million worth of slides and white-water rafting rides in Glendale.

SPECTATOR SPORTS
Auto Racing

Half a dozen times a year, the roar of NASCAR comes to the **Phoenix International Raceway** (7602 S. Avondale Blvd., Avondale, 866/408-RACE, www.phoenixraceway.com). The facility was renovated in 2008 and sports several bars and restaurants, including the new Speed Cantina, but its upscale makeover didn't break with stock-car tradition. Fans still can camp on the grounds all weekend in an RV while watching dozens of high-speed racecars turn left really, really quickly. Unreserved RV parking spots are $60 for the weekend.

Baseball

The **Arizona Diamondbacks** won a World

AUTO RACING CLASSES AND FUN

Drivers in Phoenix sometimes seem like they're trying out for a spot on a Grand Prix racing team, but Bob Bondurant is the real thing. The former racer for Carol Shelby and Team Ferrari coaches thousands of students every year at **The Bob Bondurant School of High Performance Driving** (20000 S. Maricopa Rd., 800/842-7223, www.bondurant.com), his custom-designed, 60-acre facility near Phoenix's Firebird International Raceway. Single-day courses are designed to impart skills ranging from introductory racing techniques to highway survival. Multiday courses cover all kinds of training, including military and security hazard-avoidance strategies and general high-performance driving "experiences." Fees start at $400 and rise to well over $5,000.

A similar though less expensive (and less intense) experience that also involves beer and video games can be had at the **F1 Race Factory** (317 S. 48th St., 602/302-7223, www.f1racefactory.com). Their "European racing carts" can hit speeds upwards of 45 mph, and video cameras and timed clocks keep careful track of who wins and loses for later bragging rights. Fees for single races start at $30, and an all-day pass is $75.

Series in 2001—just four years after the team was formed during Major League Baseball's 1997 expansion—and Phoenicians have loved them ever since. In typical Arizona style, **Chase Field** (401 E. Jefferson St., Phoenix, 602/514-8400, http://arizona.diamondbacks. mlb.com) in downtown Phoenix has a retractable roof that can be opened on balmy spring and fall days and closed during the heat of summer. There's also a pool in right field. Really. Single-game tickets can be had for as little as $5, but prices rise quickly to as much as $250 for box seats. Scalping is legal in Arizona, so check websites and the streets around the

field (prices often drop once the game starts) to find deals.

The crack of the bat also comes earlier to Arizona than most other places thanks to the Cactus League. A dozen teams arrive in late February and stay through March (or the first week of April) at their **spring training** (www. cactusleague.com) homes in metro Phoenix, including the Chicago Cubs, Chicago White Sox, Cleveland Indians, Kansas City Royals, Los Angeles Angels of Anaheim, Los Angeles Dodgers, Milwaukee Brewers, Oakland Athletics, San Diego Padres, San Francisco Giants, Seattle Mariners, and Texas Rangers. Two more—the Arizona Diamondbacks and Colorado Rockies—winter 90 minutes south in Tucson. Games are often more casual than in "The Show," and the small fields give fans a chance to get a close look at superstars and up-and-comers both.

Basketball

Next door to Chase Field sits **US Airways Center** (201 E. Jefferson St., 602/379-2000, www.usairwayscenter.com), the home of both Phoenix's professional basketball teams: The **Phoenix Suns** (602/379-SUNS, www.nba. com/suns) and the **Phoenix Mercury** (602/252-WNBA, www.wnba.com/mercury). Tickets for the Suns start around $40 for nosebleed seats and go up to $500 or more for courtside.

Football

The **Arizona Cardinals** (602/379-0102, www. azcardinals.com) spent years in the National Football League's rankings cellar before making their first Super Bowl appearance ever in 2009. They put up a good fight, but many long-suffering fans would say it's typical of the team to lose their lead—and the game—at the last minute. However, the team's home at **University of Phoenix Stadium** (1 Cardinals Dr.) in Glendale is spectacular. The round shape of the building is designed to mimic the Sonoran Desert's native barrel cactus, and it not only features a retractable roof but also has a retractable field that can slide out to catch the sunshine.

SPRING SWINGS

If you're a baseball fan, then you've probably planned out your ideal vacation. No, not Hawaii, South America, or Mount Everest. Baseball fans just want to jump in the car and make the drive from coast to coast, taking in a game at every Major League Baseball ballpark. The alternative is to spend a week in the Valley of the Sun during **spring training** (www.cactusleague.com).

For baseball fans, it's an annual rite as quintessential as peanuts and Cracker Jacks. Beginning in February, 15 Major League Baseball teams descend upon Arizona, allowing fans to catch a game – or two – every day until early April. There really isn't a bad ballpark in the Cactus League. Each place has its own unique qualities. The key is to pick out a couple of teams you want to see and then plan accordingly. Remember to get there early, because most of the big-name players leave the game after a couple of innings, but that's also when you'll see the stars of tomorrow.

The **Los Angeles Dodgers** and **Chicago White Sox** share the brand-new **Camelback Ranch** (10710 W. Camelback Rd., 623/877-8585) stadium in Glendale. The park is about 10 miles west of Phoenix, right across Highway 101 (Loop 101) from the Westgate City Center and University of Phoenix Stadium. Outside, you'll find a nice lake to walk around, and be sure to check out the replicas of Ebbets Field and Comiskey Park.

Take the 101 to the I-10 east, and you're likely to spot more than a few Ohio license plates. The **Cincinnati Reds** and **Cleveland Indians** just moved to the new **Goodyear Ballpark** (1933 S. Ballpark Way, 623/882-3120), in Goodyear, a town 20 miles southwest of Phoenix that's named for the Ohio-based tire company. You can enjoy a view of the Sierra Estrella and White Tank Mountains from some seats in the ballpark.

Follow the smell of brats a few minutes east

© MICA THOMAS MULLOY

Every spring, 15 Major League Baseball teams descend upon the Valley of the Sun for spring training.

on the I-10. The **Milwaukee Brewers** are the only tenant at **Maryvale Stadium** (3600 N. 51st Ave., 623/245-5555), built in 1998. It's in one of Phoenix's older neighborhoods, but the park itself is one of the most serene in the Cactus League. Tickets are usually available, and even if the game is out-of-hand, be sure to stick around for the popular sausage race.

Continue on I-10 toward Tucson and you will be able to see right field in **Tempe Diablo Stadium** (2200 W. Alameda Dr., 480/350-5205) from the freeway. The stadium has hosted spring training games since the 1960s, and it underwent a $20 million renovation in 2006. The **Los Angeles Angels of Anaheim** consistently lead the Cactus League in attendance. This is a popular pastime for Arizona State University students.

The **Oakland A's** also play a stone's throw from campus at **Phoenix Municipal "Muni" Stadium** (5999 E. Van Buren, 602/392-0074), which recently underwent a major renovation – and another one is on the way. Seats offers great views of Papago Park's six-million-year-old rock formations.

Keep heading east on Highway 202 (Loop 202), and you'll come across the toughest ticket in the Cactus League. **Hohokam Park** (1235 N. Center St., 480/964-4467) is the spring training home of the **Chicago Cubs,** the team that earns a fanatical following despite a less-than-stellar World Series record. The stadium was built in 1987 but has a very retro '50s feel. It's the best place in the Cactus League to get autographs and pictures with the players.

Heading back west on Highway 202 (Loop 202), stop off smack dab in the middle of Scottsdale, home of the **San Francisco Giants.** There is a really cool picture on the press box wall from when the Red Sox used to train at the old stadium in the 1950s, when the stadium was in the middle of a farm. There's really never a bad time to take in a game at **Scottsdale Stadium** (7408 E. Osborn Rd., 480/312-2580), with all the dinner and entertainment options now right outside the park.

Back on the west side, exit Highway 101 at Bell Road. The **Seattle Mariners** and **San**

Superstars like Ken Griffey Jr. get back into the swing every spring.

Diego Padres play a couple blocks to the south at **Peoria Sports Complex** (16101 N. 83rd Ave., 623/773-8700). Many consider the park the best in the Cactus League. Every seat feels like it's right on top of the action, and you don't feel crammed if it's a sellout crowd. It also features the best lawn seating in the city.

Head north on Bell Road and you'll end up in Surprise, home of the **Texas Rangers** and **Kansas City Royals. Surprise Recreation Campus** (15850 N. Bullard Ave., 623/222-2222) is a hike from Phoenix but it's the best place to bring a family. There's plenty of room to play catch and tailgate in the parking lot. It's also a great park to walk around while the game is going on because you can always see the action.

The **Arizona Diamondbacks** and **Colorado Rockies** train in Tucson, about 90 minutes south of Phoenix. Both teams will be moving to the Valley, though, in 2011.

(Contributed by Mark McClune,
host/reporter, FOX Sports Arizona)

Horseracing

Thoroughbred horses win, place, and show on the mile and a quarter track at **Turf Paradise** (1501 W. Bell Rd., 602/942-1101, www.turfparadise.com) five days a week October through May. Races generally start shortly after noon or at 1 P.M. in the spring, but the track is open 9 A.M.–7 P.M. daily for horse workouts and simulcast races from tracks around the country. The 1,000-seat grandstand is air-conditioned, natch, and the Turf Club (only a $5 admission) serves food and cocktails. The management calls the dress code "country club casual," but this isn't the South, so big hats are optional.

Ice Hockey

To experience a temporary cold snap during Phoenix's not-exactly-frosty winters, either head for the mountains north and east of town or to Jobing.com Arena (9400 W. Maryland Ave., Glendale, www.jobingarena.com) to cheer on the town's National Hockey League team, the **Phoenix Coyotes** (480/563-PUCK, http://coyotes.nhl.com), at least for now. The team may be moving to—where else?—Canada.

SPAS

While Scottsdale might be better known for its world-class spas, Phoenix has much to offer in the art of luxuriating. Buffing and pampering abound in the capital city, and while old-school resorts have been making their guests look and feel great for decades, some new hotspots are attracting spa-goers to their spacious surroundings and ever-expanding lists of amenities.

A tried-and-true classic, the **Arizona Biltmore Spa** (2400 E. Missouri Ave., 602/950-0086, www.arizonabiltmore.com/spa, 5:30 A.M.–8:30 P.M. daily) specializes in massage and body and skin care treatments, but also offers guests the use of a full-service salon, fitness center, bicycles, and not one but seven tennis courts. Located on the grounds of the famed Arizona Biltmore Resort & Spa, for which Frank Lloyd Wright served as the consulting architect, the spa now offers signature "green experience" treatments, utilizing chemical-free, organic products that minister to physical, mental, and spiritual health. Guests may enjoy outdoor retreat areas in the gardens and choose from a wealth of classes, including yoga, aqua aerobics, sculpting, and power step.

Just down the street is **Alvadora Spa** at the Royal Palms Resort (5200 E. Camelback Rd., 602/840-3610, www.royalpalmshotel.com, 9 A.M.–6 P.M. Sun.–Thurs., 8 A.M.–8 P.M. Fri.–Sat.), which exudes a Mediterranean charm. A recipient of the Mobil Four Star Spa Award every year since 2004, Alvadora also has the distinction of being a SpaFinder "Best for Romance" winner. It serves up classic menu items such as deep tissue, shiatsu, and aromatherapy massages; water therapies; and skin treatments, along with a variety of signature citrus treatments, including the Citrus Grove Facial, Orange Blossom Body Buff, and Simply Citrus mani-pedis. The fitness center is open 24 hours a day, with personal training sessions and yoga, stretch, tai chi, and meditation classes.

The water-inspired **Revive Spa** at the JW Marriott Desert Ridge Resort (5350 E. Marriott Dr., 480/293-5000, www.spa.jwdesertridgeresort.com, 8 A.M.–7:30 P.M. daily) is where ancient rituals coalesce with new, cutting-edge techniques. A water feature flows beneath a skylight that serves as a floor above the lobby's impressive two-story rotunda, reminding spa-goers of water's soothing powers. Custom packages are available for a unique and well-rounded experience, such as the Gentleman's Escape, billed as the perfect way for a guy to rejuvenate. The treatment includes a special bath, 80-minute therapeutic massage, and a Guy's Total Wellness Facial. For women, such treatments are de rigueur, but there are also unique options such as the Detoxifier, the Arizona Experience featuring hot stones, and the Turquoise and Revive packages, utilizing turquoise gemstones and oils and lotions from the Revive Herb Garden, respectively.

In Chandler, just south of Phoenix, **Aji Spa** at the Sheraton Wild Horse Pass Resort & Spa (5594 West Wild Horse Pass Blvd., Chandler, 602/225-0100, www.wildhorsepassresort.

com, 5:30 A.M.–7:30 P.M. daily) offers authentic Native American treatments that are inspired and implemented by tribal elders from the local Gila River Indian Community's Pima and Maricopa tribes. Try the Sacred Salt Energy Balance, Burden Basket Pima Meditation, or Pima Medicine Massage, in which a therapeutic treatment incorporates energy anatomy and ancient techniques to create a relaxed atmosphere conducive to spiritual healing. In addition to more traditional massages and treatments, Aji Spa also hosts indigenous cultural activities such as sage offerings, Native American art tours, and a Harmony Keeper Meditation Class.

Accommodations

Thanks to a growing downtown and a brand-new convention center, Phoenix offers several hotel options. You'll likely want to choose one of downtown's high-rise towers (which offer convenient light-rail access) or one of the popular and quintessentially Arizona resorts in the Camelback Corridor. The resorts tend to be a bit pricier than their hotel brethren, but they offer a mini-oasis of manicured grounds, multiple swimming pools, and adjacent golf courses. Their lavish amenities are well worth a few extra dollars a night. In summer, rates at all Phoenix hotels are dramatically discounted, as much as half off or more.

DOWNTOWN
$50-100
Finding affordable digs downtown without veering into less-desirable areas can be a challenge. The **Lexington Hotel Central Phoenix** (1100 N. Central Ave., 602/252-2100, www.central-phoenixinn.com, $90–125 d) is a decent budget option, though. You won't get much in the way of style, but its location next to a small park and light-rail station couldn't be any nicer or more convenient. There's a continental breakfast in the morning, and even a small heated outdoor pool and Jacuzzi. You'd likely pay $50 more for one of the comparable chains.

If you simply need cheap and clean, the **Budget Lodge Downtown Phoenix** (402 W. Van Buren St., 602/254-7247, www.budget-lodgedowntownphx.com, $50–60 d) fits the bill. Don't expect much in the way of style, but the decent rooms, large balconies, and spotless bathrooms may outweigh the less-than-stellar neighborhood for some travelers.

$100-250
Bombshells Mae West and Marilyn Monroe slept here. So did Ingrid Bergman, Humphrey Bogart, and Cary Grant. The **Hotel San Carlos** (202 N. Central Ave., 602/253-4121, www.hotelsancarlos.com, $145–180 d) is a Valley landmark that now gives guests a taste

The Hotel San Carlos is a Phoenix landmark.

of old Phoenix. When the Italian Renaissance-style hotel opened in 1928, it featured luxury amenities like elevators and air-conditioning, a first in Phoenix. Today, guests will find lots of charm and the idiosyncrasies of a historic hotel: tiny bathrooms, "quaint" rooms, and even a few ghosts. The bar and rooftop pool are popular spots for parties on the weekend, and despite its having lost its golden age luster, you won't find this much character in any other downtown hotel.

If you prefer fresh and modern over historic and quirky, try the new **C Sheraton Phoenix Downtown** (340 N. 3rd St., 602/262-2500, www.sheratonphoenixdowntown.com, $225–300 d). The $350 million, city-owned hotel is part of a massive revitalization of Copper Square, which includes a brand-new convention center. It's also an ambitious attempt to revamp the Sheraton brand, thanks to its hip lounge and contemporary rooms that are styled with neutral furnishings, warm dark woods, and modern touches like flat-panel televisions. You'll find a small outdoor pool and on-site fitness center at this 1,000-room, 31-story hotel, the largest in Arizona. It's the best bet for most who want to stay in the heart of downtown.

A $6 million remodel has given the **Wyndham Phoenix** (50 E. Adams St., 800/359-7253, www.phxhotel.com, $225–300 d) a contemporary makeover. Its large rooms are terrific for business travelers looking for free Wi-Fi, ergonomic Herman Miller Aeron desk chairs, and an on-site Starbucks. The rooms are clean, the bathrooms are large, and the service is top-drawer. Next door, the **Hyatt Regency Phoenix** (122 N. 2nd St., 602/252-1234, www.phoenix.hyatt.com, $225–300 d) is highlighted by a soaring atrium and panoramic views of Phoenix from its 712 rooms. The small outdoor pool and spa are pretty ordinary, though be sure to make some time to have a meal or even just a drink at its revolving restaurant, The Compass. You won't find a better way to take in the city.

Situated just north of downtown and about 10 minutes from the airport, the **Hilton Suites Phoenix** (10 E. Thomas Rd., 602/222-1111, www.hilton.com, $150–200 d) is a terrific selection for business travelers looking for value and convenience. The handy light-rail stop just outside the front door makes commuting to the convention center and downtown's restaurants rather easy, though guests can also take advantage of the complimentary shuttle service. The hotel's 11-story atrium provides a light-filled retreat, complete with a pleasant garden and small pond, and its tasteful all-suite rooms, which were remodeled in 2008, feature large bathrooms, flat-panel televisions, and wet bar areas with a microwave and refrigerator. Many also offer views of the downtown skyline.

The **Holiday Inn Phoenix Downtown North** (212 W. Osborn Rd., 602/595-4444, www.ichotelsgroup.com, $110–160 d) breaks out of the beige-on-beige corporate mold with comfortable, modern rooms decorated in crisp whites, chocolate browns, and bold reds. Parking can be challenging, but once you get to your room, you're able to select a pillow that suits your preference, from firm to fluffy down. The recently renovated property also features a small pool, gym, and business center.

CENTRAL PHOENIX
$50-100

Near Piestewa Peak and Highway 51, **Best Western InnSuites** (1615 E. Northern Ave., 602/997-6285, http://phoenix.innsuites.com, $80–125 d) offers an excellent value. Budget travelers and families will appreciate the in-room refrigerator, microwave, and complimentary breakfast buffet each morning, not to mention the large swimming pool and hot tub in the central courtyard. Still not convinced? There is a free nightly happy hour 5–7 P.M.

ZenYard Guest House (830 E. Maryland Ave., 602/680-7631, www.zenyard.com, $60–90 d) is an eccentric alternative to the city's plethora of chain hotels and resorts. The offbeat bed-and-breakfast is tucked into a north-central Phoenix neighborhood, and it offers daily yoga classes, on-call massage therapy, and organic continental breakfasts. The mid-20th-century ranch house has been decorated with small Asian touches, such as a koi pond near the pool and hot tub. There are three suites from which to choose.

$100-250

Looking for a little L.A. style in Central Phoenix? **The Clarendon Hotel** (401 W. Clarendon Ave., 602/252-7363, www.theclarendon.net, $115–275 d) is a funky, boutique alternative to the midprice chains that permeate the area, attracting the likes of the Black Eyed Peas, AC/DC, and The Rolling Stones. The recently renovated property, which is still a little rough around the edges, features mod rooms with flat-panel TVs and free Wi-Fi. Most rooms open onto the property's star attraction, the Oasis, a hip courtyard pool and 50-person Jacuzzi with striped tile, two-story glass water walls, and lounge-y cabana furniture. At night, the pool's floor twinkles with 1,000 illuminated starry lights, and the rooftop bar transforms into an open-air lounge popular with locals in search of strong cocktails and impressive views of the downtown skyline.

Bed-and-breakfasts are a rare breed in Phoenix, though **Maricopa Manor** (15 W. Pasadena Ave., 602/274-6302, www.maricopamanor.com, $190–240 d) happily picks up the slack. Its seven unique suites are enhanced by gas fireplaces and French doors that open onto charming, palm tree-lined courtyards. The 1928 Arts and Crafts-style bungalow creates an inviting space in which to relax between hikes and shopping expeditions, thanks to small touches like potted plants and colorful flowers around its pool and sundeck. For a little Southwestern flavor, try to reserve the sunflower-yellow Siesta Suite, which features carved Mexican Colonial furniture, hand-painted Talavera tile, and a small sunroom with a twin daybed for a third guest. In the morning, breakfast is delivered to guest rooms in picnic baskets, allowing a leisurely meal on your private patio.

The **Embassy Suites Phoenix-Biltmore** (2630 E. Camelback Rd., 602/955-3992, www.embassysuites.com, $175–225 d) is conveniently situated next door to Biltmore Fashion Park's shops and restaurants. Unlike its posh neighbors, The Ritz-Carlton and Arizona Biltmore Resort, this Camelback Corridor hotel is a relatively inexpensive option, complete with complimentary made-to-order breakfasts and evening cocktail hour. The recently renovated rooms, pleasant atrium, and outdoor pool are popular with families and business travelers.

Conveniently situated near the Biltmore neighborhood, **Courtyard Phoenix Camelback** (2101 E. Camelback Rd., 602/955-5200, www.camelbackcourtyard.com, $160–200 d) is within easy reach of numerous restaurants and shops, like those at Town and Country Shopping Center and Biltmore Fashion Park. The four-story, midlevel hotel has been renovated, and many of its comfortable, modern rooms overlook a nicely landscaped pool and courtyard. Also, it offers a few amenities that offset the less-than-economical price: complimentary Wi-Fi, upgraded bedding, and a pullout sofa for an extra sleeping space.

Hotel Highland at Biltmore (2310 E. Highland Ave., 800/956-5221, www.hotelhighlandatbiltmore.com, $150–200 d) underwent a major remodel in 2009, updating the former Phoenix Inn Suites with modern furnishings and plasma televisions. Its moniker as an "urban-desert boutique hotel" is a bit of a stretch, but the 120-room property does offer a little more style than a run-of-the-mill motel. Guests can enjoy a swim in the courtyard swimming pool or make the short walk to the Biltmore Fashion Park's restaurants and shops.

Over $250

The Ritz-Carlton (2401 E. Camelback Rd., 602/468-0700, www.ritzcarlton.com, $400–550 d) delivers impeccable service and all the grand European style for which the hotel group is famous, including formal marble foyers, gilt frames, silk brocade fabrics, and Egyptian cotton linens. The pink-stucco tower is the hotel de rigueur for pop stars and athletes passing through town, though less-famous guests will also appreciate the sky-high views of

Camelback Mountain and the Phoenix skyline. And should it be too hot to enjoy the open-air shopping at Biltmore Fashion Park across the street, take a dip in the second-floor pool, which is surrounded by the neighborhood's glass towers, a distinctly urban experience in this desert metropolis.

Resorts

Tucked into an upscale residential neighborhood, the 1929 ((**Arizona Biltmore Resort & Spa** (2400 E. Missouri Ave., 602/955-6600, www.arizonabiltmore.com, $205–675 d) is a Phoenix landmark. The Art Deco gem elegantly blends geometric forms and Southwest touches, a credit to its architect, Albert Chase McArthur, a student of Frank Lloyd Wright. The Biltmore has attracted presidents, old Hollywood movie stars, and former guests of the Wrigley family, whose winter home still sits atop a hill neighboring the property. Even composer Irving Berlin was an occasional guest, penning "White Christmas" while sitting poolside. For those who are not content to lounge by one of the resort's eight pools or hit the links at the two adjacent PGA golf courses, the Biltmore offers a full docket of activities that range from wine-tasting and cigar rolling to family-friendly marshmallow roasts and pottery-painting classes.

Unlike Scottsdale's large, sprawling resorts, the romantic ((**Royal Palms Resort and Spa** (5200 E. Camelback Rd., 800/672-6011, www.royalpalmshotel.com, $400–600 d) is understated, elegant, and intimate. The Mediterranean–style hideaway features stone courtyards with potted flowers and tiled fountains, and its casitas and villas are decorated with Spanish Colonial furniture, rich colors, and Old World accents. It's the ultimate couple's getaway spot. You won't find better ambiance in the city, nor is it easy to top its Alvadora Spa and T. Cook's restaurant. Best of all, the former private estate sits at the base of Camelback Mountain, an easy 10-minute drive on Camelback Road to the Biltmore neighborhood or Old Town Scottsdale.

Not all of the Valley's amenity-laden resorts

Charming courtyards and blossoming gardens give Royal Palms Resort and Spa the atmosphere of a lavish private residence in Old World Europe.

are expensive. The mountainside **Pointe Hilton at Squaw Peak** (7677 N. 16th St., 602/997-2626, www.pointehilton.com, $160–200 d) is a perfect vacation destination for families, especially in the summer when the property becomes an aquatic oasis. Kids will revel in the Hole-in-the-Wall River Ranch's multiple pools, waterfall-fed lagoon, half-mile lazy river for tubing, 130-foot slide, and "dive-in" movies. There's also an 18-hole miniature putting course and hands-on Coyote Camp. The spa and tennis courts aren't bad, either. And thanks to a $24 million dollar renovation, the all-suite hotel has a host of layouts that can accommodate big parties or large broods.

The **Pointe Hilton Tapatio Cliffs Resort** (11111 N. 7th St., 602/866-7500, www.pointe-hilton.com, $160–190 d) is also a great budget option. A $25 million renovation has given a bit of polish to the north-central Phoenix property. The large, mountainside resort feels cocooned from the city, offering a host of outdoor activities, like hiking at the adjacent North Mountain Park and golfing at Lookout Mountain course. Its Falls Water Village features multiple pools, streams, waterfalls, private cabanas, and a 138-foot slide. Not to be outdone, the restaurants are just as pleasurable, especially the sleek Different Pointe of View, which wows diners with a "mile-high view" of Phoenix.

SOUTH PHOENIX
Resorts

It can be hard to get a sense of Arizona's native culture when you spend your days poolside or on the golf course. Fortunately, the **Sheraton Wild Horse Pass Resort & Spa** (5594 W. Wild Horse Pass Blvd., 602/225-0100, www.wildhorsepassresort.com, $275–350 d) incorporates much of the Sonoran Desert's indigenous culture and wildlife into its design, while still providing a AAA Four Diamond spa and Five Diamond restaurant. Built on the Gila River Indian Community, the resort reflects the architecture, art, and history of the Pima and Maricopa tribes. It's named after the wild horses that still roam the community's land south of Phoenix. Though it's a 10-minute

drive from Chandler and 25 minutes from downtown Phoenix, you'll find plenty to do, like play golf, ride horses, or visit the neighboring casino. The boat rides and indoor boulder formation can feel a little Disney-like at times, but the setting is gorgeous.

Arizona Grand Resort (8000 S. Arizona Grand Pkwy., 602/438-9000, www.arizonagrandresort.com, $375–500 d) just completed a $52 million remodel, and the 740-suite property has never looked better. The family-friendly Arizona Grand has all the amenities found at most resorts—a championship golf course, spa, fitness classes—but it's the Oasis Water Park that has kids and adults buzzing. Many spend days at a time, braving the ocean-like wave pool, tubing the lazy river, or plunging down the three eight-story water slides. At the end of the day, the large suites provide plenty of room for the whole gang—although Mom and Dad may want to grab a drink in the new lobby, which overlooks the golf course's rolling hills.

NORTH PHOENIX
Resorts

Everything about the 🄲 **JW Marriott Desert Ridge Resort & Spa** (5350 E. Marriott Dr., 480/293-3939, www.jwdesertridgeresort.com, $525–700 d) is enormous, from the soaring lobby and 950 rooms to its 10 restaurants and Revive Spa. Even the poolside margaritas are big (25 ounces). It boasts the title of Arizona's largest resort, but it carries its size well, with clean, modern lines that give a nod to the Southwest's indigenous architecture. There are also subtle Western details, like leather couches, light-colored stone, and delicate ironwork. The massive meeting space frequently hosts multiple conferences and trade shows at once, but you're just as likely to see leisure travelers and families at the four pools or on the golf courses designed by Jack Nicklaus and Nick Faldo.

TEMPE AND THE EAST VALLEY
$50-100

The cheap and uninspiring **Twin Palms**

(225 E. Apache Blvd., 480/967-9431, www. twinpalmshotel.com, $80–150 d) is conveniently situated across the street from Arizona State University's campus and Gammage Auditorium. It's a perfectly respectable option, and the 1980s Southwestern decor has its charms. Guests also have access to the mammoth ASU fitness center across the street.

$100-250

There's nothing worse than being stuck in a bland, vanilla box when you travel. Thankfully, the **Fiesta Resort Conference Center** (2100 S. Priest Dr., 480/967-1441, www.fiestainnresort.com, $140–200 d) is an unexpected bit of character in the midlevel price range. The Frank Lloyd Wright–inspired resort is nicely maintained, and its 270 rooms just received a much-needed updating. Thankfully, though, the public spaces retain much of their vintage character, with stacked concrete blocks, warm woods, and stained-glass accents. Guests can soak up the sun at the pool, which is surrounded by green lawns and tall palm trees.

Tempe Mission Palms Hotel (60 E. 5th St., 480/894-1400, www.missionpalms.com, $225–300 d) is a solid choice if you're in town to catch a game at Sun Devil Stadium. You can't beat the hotel's Mill Avenue location, which houses dozens of bars and restaurants just outside the front door. The hotel itself is rather dated, though its rooftop terrace pool and tennis court are great places to hang out and survey Tempe and the adjacent ASU campus.

Over $250

The W Hotel's younger, funkier sibling, **Aloft** (951 E. Playa Del Norte Dr., 480/621-3300, www.alofthotels.com, $325–375 d) packs a bit of style into its Tempe Town Lake location. The loft-inspired space plays up its urban appeal with light woods, exposed ducts, and a hip patio with neon-green lounges and trendy lighting. Guests check in at a self-serve kiosk before heading up to the bright, airy rooms. Even the walk-in showers, loaded with Bliss Spa products, benefit from natural light. The

outdoor pool, sleek gym, WXYZ bar, and small lounge with a hot-pink pool table add to the sleek L.A. vibe.

Resorts

Perched on a desert hilltop, **The Buttes** (2000 Westcourt Way, 602/225-9000, www.marriott.com/phxtm, $225–275 d) burrows into its rugged locale, incorporating rock formations right into lobby walls and its two pools. It's hard to forget that you're in the middle of the desert and a big city here, as the small resort offers spectacular views of the Valley, especially from its beautifully designed Top of the Rock restaurant. The I-10 freeway runs along the base of the mountain, which can detract from the skyline at rush hour, but thanks to its elevated height, you won't hear a thing.

An East Valley landmark, the **Crowne Plaza San Marcos Golf Resort** (1 N. San Marcos Pl., 480/812-0900, www.sanmarcosresort.com, $140–170 d) has been welcoming guests since Dr. A.J. Chandler opened the hotel in his namesake town in 1913. Chandler's friend, Frank Lloyd Wright, helped oversee the construction of the California Mission-style resort, and he was just one of a succession of celebrities to spend time at the San Carlos, including President Herbert Hoover, Fred Astaire, Joan Crawford, and Bing Crosby. Today, the resort has lost a bit of its luster, but its beautiful lobby and large rooms are a good value. Plus, you can still enjoy the historic golf course, which was the first in the state with grass greens.

Gold Canyon Golf Resort (6100 S. Kings Ranch Rd., 480/982-9090, www.gcgr.com, $125–150 d) isn't for everyone, but diehard golfers and travelers hoping to retreat into the desert will love this secluded property in the East Valley community of Gold Canyon, which is about 50 minutes from the airport. Surrounded by the rugged Superstition Mountains, the resort's white adobe-style buildings gleam in the Sonoran Desert setting, and the expansive views of the cacti and palo verde trees that dot the landscape would cost three times as much in North Scottsdale. The real highlight is Gold Canyon's two championship desert courses, which *Sports Illustrated* named among the 10 most underrated in the country.

WEST VALLEY
Resorts
For a taste of old Arizona, try the **Wigwam Golf Resort & Spa** (300 Wigwam Blvd., 623/935-3811, www.wigwamresort.com, $280–350 d) in the West Valley community of Litchfield Park. The Wigwam began as a winter guest ranch in 1929 for Goodyear tire executives and their families. Today, it's a AAA Four Diamond resort with three 18-hole championship golf courses, nine tennis courts, three swimming pools, and an Elizabeth Arden Red Door Spa. The elegant Southwestern property—lushly landscape with green lawns and slender palm trees—features casita-style rooms decorated with wood furnishings, Mexican ceramic tile, slate floors, and copper and leather fixtures.

Food

For years, Phoenix suffered from a dearth of quality, innovative restaurants, as most of the city's groundbreaking restaurateurs and chefs preferred to set up shop in Scottsdale. Happily, the times have changed, and a host of culinary mavericks have transformed the city's dining scene.

DOWNTOWN
American
🄲 **The Tuck Shop** (2245 N. 12th St., 602/354-2980, 5–10 p.m. Tues.–Sat., $9–18) is still one of Phoenix's best-kept secrets. It seems like only in-the-know foodies frequent this Desert Modernist remodel of a 1950s-era building in the Coronado neighborhood. Architect/owner D.J. Fernandes serves up "neighborhood comfort food" in a casually chic setting, and the menu's tapas-inspired small plates are quite simply phenomenal. Bring some friends and order up a medley of dishes, like the Spanish *patatas bravas* with aioli, mac and cheese with crispy prosciutto and lobster, or the soon-to-be-legendary fried chicken with cheddar waffles and braised greens. The handcrafted cocktails are just as thoughtful. Try the gin and house-made tonic, garnished with a ribbon of shaved cucumber.

Durant's (2611 N. Central Ave., 602/264-5967, 11 a.m.–10 p.m. Mon.–Thurs., 11 a.m.–11 p.m. Fri., 5–11 p.m. Sat., 5–10 p.m. Sun., $20–40) is a classic in every sense of the word. From its ever-so-dry martinis to its deep-red decor, the pink-stuccoed steakhouse is a bona fide local landmark that has changed little since then-newlyweds Marilyn Monroe and Joe DiMaggio dined there in 1954. Enter like locals through the kitchen in the back, and take a peek at the thick steaks and oysters Rockefeller

© MICA THOMAS MULLOY

Marilyn Monroe and Joe DiMaggio celebrated their nuptials at Durant's.

before heading into the dining room. Don't be surprised if you bump into the governor—it is a favorite haunt of Arizona politicos.

Next door, Phoenix urbanites flock to **Switch** (2603 N. Central Ave., 602/264-2295, 11 A.M.–midnight Mon.–Fri., 10 A.M.–midnight Sat.–Sun., $8–15), a breakfast joint turned trendy lounge. The blue-on-blue mod decor and hip music provide a background for burgers, salads, pitas, and innovative sandwiches. Switch caters to a younger crowd, though it's packed at lunch with downtown workers of all ages. The restaurant prides itself on its house-made sangria, crepes, and flaky baked galettes. You can sit at the community bar, on the patio, or in the lounge-like dining room.

A former flower shop, **My Florist Café & Bar** (534 W. McDowell Rd., 602/254-0333, 7 A.M.–midnight daily, $9–14) offers quiet mornings over coffee, late-night drinks, and a tasty selection of salads and sandwiches in between. Its stylish, modern dining room and the memorable piano serenades of Nicole Pesce have made My Florist a popular spot to unwind

with a cheese plate and glass of wine. Try the turkey and brie sandwich or the asparagus salad with caramelized onions, artichoke hearts, feta cheese, and a lemon-thyme dressing.

A refurbished bungalow now serves as the home of the **Lisa G Cafe Wine Bar** (2337 N. 7th St., 602/253-9201, 11 A.M.–2 P.M. Mon.–Fri., 5–10 P.M. Tues.–Thurs., 5–midnight Fri.–Sat., $9–12). It's a fitting choice for chef/owner Lisa Giungo, who has spent a lifetime cooking for family and friends—not mention some of the best restaurants in town—and her adorable family photos only add to homey atmosphere. Rustic sandwiches and fresh salads make the small, stylish café a terrific lunchtime spot, though it's always a popular destination for a casual evening meal. Regulars swear by Lisa's Bowl of Balls, a family recipe of beef, pork, and veal, while vegetarians swoon for the eggplant, zucchini, blue cheese, and pine nut empanadas.

Asian

Lively and modern, **Sens** (705 N. 1st St., 602/340-9777, 11 A.M.–2 P.M. Mon.–Fri.,

My Florist Café & Bar

© JEFF FICKER

5 P.M.–midnight Mon.–Thurs., 5 P.M.–2 A.M. Fri.–Sat., $8–14) breathes life into a once stagnant downtown neighborhood. Sens was carved out of an abandoned office plaza that has quickly become a vibrant spot for new pubs and restaurants. Chef Johnny Chu has brought creativity and talent to this Asian tapas bar, where the signature dish, sizzling volcano beef, is seared on a hot stone. Try the quail seasoned with rock salt, or the red-curry tofu that comes to the table simmering in a clay pot. The bar features exotic foreign beers and an extensive sake selection, so it's a perfect stop on your way to the theater, or for a quick, but upscale, late-night snack.

Breakfast and Lunch

Wallet-friendly **Matt's Big Breakfast** (801 N. 1st St., 602/254-1074, 6:30 A.M.–2:30 P.M. Tues.–Sun., $5–8) is Phoenix's best breakfast joint, hands down. The small, brick diner is bright and sunny, and its pleasant orange counter, vintage barstools, and mod 1950s decor are the perfect backdrop for griddlecakes and homemade hash browns. Owners Matt and Erenia insist on quality, fresh ingredients, which means the orange juice is squeezed each morning and the eggs come from cage-free chickens. There's usually a short wait at the popular restaurant, but you won't mind once you sit down for the salami scramble or to sample the lunchtime offerings.

You'll feel like you've stepped back in time at the **Welcome Diner** (924 E. Roosevelt St., 602/495-1111, 11 A.M.–3 P.M. Tues.–Sat., $4–8). The tiny nine-stool building was built in Wichita, Kansas, in 1945, and was trucked across the country to serve up burgers and grilled cheese on Route 66 in Williams, Arizona, before it made its way to downtown Phoenix in 1980. Today, the Depression-era diner has received a stylish update, and it serves up classics, as well as playful treats like the cup of Sweet Toast—battered Texas toast cooked in peanut oil and served with organic maple syrup. The Garfield egg sandwich, hot dogs, burgers, hand-cut fries, and organic sodas are just as tasty.

Congratulations, you found it: the best carne

© JEFF FICKER

Matt's Big Breakfast

asada in town. The short menu at **America's Taco Shop** (2041 N. 7th St., 602/682-5627, 8 A.M.–9 P.M. Mon.–Thurs., 8 A.M.–10 P.M. Fri.–Sat., 10 A.M.–9 P.M. Sun., $4–7) revolves around this marinated, flame-broiled beef, which you can get wrapped in tacos and burritos or topped on tostadas, quesadillas, and fluffy tortas. Non-meat eaters can enjoy the veggie quesadilla or bean and cheese burrito, though whatever you get, you'll want an order of the rich and creamy flan. The bright converted bungalow is a terrific breakfast or lunch spot, especially on Fridays and Saturdays when chef/owner America Corrales prepares her zesty ceviche, a combination of diced fresh white shrimp, tomatoes, cucumbers, red onions, serrano chiles, cilantro, and lime. If you've grown tired of the greasy tacos and refried beans many American restaurants pass off as "authentic" Mexican food, give this charming shop a try.

Desserts

Brides and sugar addicts clamor for the artfully sculpted confections at **Tammie Coe Cakes** (610 E. Roosevelt Ste. 145, 602/253-0829, 6:30 A.M.–6 P.M. Mon.–Fri., 10 A.M.–6 P.M. Sat., 7 A.M.–1 P.M. Sun., $2–8). Satisfy that sweet-tooth with an Ooey Gooey Cupcake, frosted brownie, and triple-dipped chocolate-covered strawberry. If you're looking for something a bit more substantive, grab a filling Box Lunch ($10), which includes a sandwich, chips, and a cookie. And heck, why wait until the end of your meal? Start with the cookie.

Italian

It was no surprise when chef Chris Bianco won the James Beard Award in 2003 for his wood-fired pizzas. Since then, [**Pizzeria Bianco** (623 E. Adams St., 602/258-8300, 5–10 P.M. Tues.–Sat., $10–14) has become a culinary legend in Phoenix. Jerry Seinfeld, Oprah, and Martha Stewart are fans, and *Esquire* magazine named his thin-crust pies the best pizza in the country. A Slow Food Movement champion, Bianco uses only the freshest ingredients, including herbs cultivated next to the 1929 machine shop the restaurant now inhabits. As for the menu, the sausage-topped Wiseguy and classic Margherita with homemade mozzarella

Pizzeria Bianco

are impeccable. Aficionados covet the Rosa, a so-good-I-want-it-on-my-deathbed combination of red onion, parmigiano reggiano, rosemary, and Arizona pistachios. And though the pizza may be the most popular choice on the menu, the roasted antipasto and fresh salads are well worth the infamous wait—and that can be a two-, three-, or even four-hour experience. Best advice: Line up before the doors open at 5 P.M. and enjoy a glass of wine or a beer next door at **Bar Bianco** (609 E. Adams St., 602/528 3699, 4–11 P.M. Tues.–Sat.). If you have to ask if it's really worth the wait, don't bother coming. I don't want you getting a table before me.

Don't let the nondescript building fool you. **Pasta Bar** (705 N. 1st St., 602/687-8704, 11 A.M.–midnight Sun.–Thurs., 11 A.M.–2 A.M. Fri.–Sat., $9–15) has some of the freshest, most elegantly prepared pasta in the Valley. Wade Moises, who cooked at Mario Batali's Lupa and Babbo restaurants, has traded in his old duties at North Scottsdale's Sassi to pursue this downtown creation. The buffalo mozzarella with basil pesto, heirloom tomatoes, and anchovies is an excellent starter. Moises' handmade pasta dishes are served Italian style, in four-ounce portions lightly tossed with authentic sauces like carbonara, puttanesca, and *al cedro,* a deceptively simple mix of lemon, Italian butter, and parmigiano cheese.

It takes an Italian to craft artisanal pizzas this delicious—and unlike at Bianco, there usually isn't much of a wait at the family-owned **Cibo** (603 N. 5th Ave., 602/441-2697, 11 A.M.–2 P.M. Mon.–Fri., 5–10 P.M. Tues.–Thurs., 5–11 P.M. Fri.–Sat., $9–13). The salads, antipasto, and wood-fired pizzas feature locally grown produce and premium prosciutto and parmigiano reggiano cheese imported from Italy. It's all simply prepared and often topped with a light drizzle of olive oil. There are more than a dozen pizzas from which to choose—the Diavola with tomato sauce, mozzarella, and spicy salami offers a bit of a kick. Dine outside on the large patio or inside the charming 1913 bungalow. Either way, be sure to save room for a Nutella crepe.

Mexican and Southwest

Barrio Café (2814 N. 16th St., 602/636-0240, 11 A.M.–10 P.M. Tues.–Thurs., 11 A.M.–10:30 Fri., 5–10:30 P.M. Sat., and 3–9 P.M. Sun., $10–20) will have you saying *hola.* Chef Silvana Salcido Esparza proves there's more to Mexican food than Sonoran tacos and refried beans, with a culinary tour of the country's best dishes. Start with the pomegranate-seed guacamole, prepared tableside, and survey the small restaurant's award-winning menu. Consider the *cochinita pibil,* a 12-hour roasted pork with *achiote rojo* and sour oranges from the Yucatán Peninsula. The amazing *pollo poblano,*—a tender chicken breast with roasted peppers, caramelized onions, and *queso fresco* in a tomatillo buerre blanc—will make you a convert to Mexico's other cuisines. The Sunday brunch 11 A.M.–3 P.M. is also a treat.

Coronado Café (2201 N. 7th St., 602/258-5149, 11 A.M.–2:30 P.M. Mon.–Sat., 5–9 P.M. Tues.–Thurs., 5–10 P.M. Fri.–Sat., $14–18) delivers an artfully crafted assortment of rustic pizzas, fresh fish, slow-roasted meats, and the occasional "comfort" dish like the bourbon and cherry BBQ chicken, served with fork-mashed potatoes and grilled squash. The converted Craftsman-style bungalow's hardwood floors and charming bar provide a romantic atmosphere for a special dinner. Delicious sandwiches, soups, and salads are perfect at lunch.

It doesn't look like much from the outside, but once you step into **San Carlos Bay Seafood Restaurant** (1901 E. McDowell Rd., 602/340-0892, 9 A.M.–9 P.M. daily, $10–18), you'll think you've landed in a small café on the Sonoran coast of Mexico. Start with a cold Pacifico beer and the Seven Seas cocktail, a buffet of tasty ocean creatures. The spicy seafood stews are extraordinary, but you won't want to miss filling up on fresh tortillas topped with garlic shrimp. This is a place the locals frequent, and the mariachis on the weekends are not for the benefit of tourists.

Big, festive, and family-friendly, the hacienda-style **Tradiciones** (1602 E. Roosevelt St., 602/254-1719, 11 A.M.–8:30 P.M. Tues.–Thurs., 11 A.M.–10 P.M. Fri.–Sun., $9–17) provides lots of south-of-the-border ambience in downtown Phoenix. Dive into a bowl of warm tortilla chips, and take in the courtyard's ceramic tiles, tin lamps, fountain, and multi-colored pennants. The sizzling fajitas, seafood enchiladas, and burros with shredded beef are tasty, but it's the grilled rib-eye, topped with a spicy chipotle cream sauce, that will have you saying *delicioso*. Most nights, a mariachi trio serenades diners.

CENTRAL AND NORTH PHOENIX
American

Postino (3939 E. Campbell Ave., 602/852-3939, 11 A.M.–11 P.M. Mon.–Thurs., 11 A.M.–midnight Fri.–Sat., 11 A.M.–10 P.M. Sun., $5–12) has been a mainstay on the Phoenix dining scene since its first location opened on Campbell Avenue in the Arcadia neighborhood back in 2001. Serving delicious and affordable sandwiches, salads, and mix-and-match bruschettas, Postino—housed in a historic building that once served as a post office, hence the name—provides a lovely ambience with floor-to-ceiling windows and alfresco dining on the patio. A wide selection of wine and beer complements a casual-yet-notable menu. A second location, known as **Postino Central** (5144 N. Central Ave., 602/274-5144), opened in Phoenix's historic Medlock district in 2009.

Friends and families alike flock to **La Grande Orange Pizzeria** (4410 N. 40th St., 602/840-7777, 6:30 A.M.–10 P.M. daily, $7–14) for pizzas that locals argue are among the best in the city. This neighborhood delight is one of a trio of restaurant concepts that make the corner of Campbell Avenue and 40th Street a madhouse on Saturdays and Sundays and a must-visit for any traveling foodie. If you want to try a little of everything, come with a group and order multiple pizzas. Just make sure to get the Padre, with savory prosciutto, fresh ricotta, fig, and arugula. After dinner, stop by the grocery for gifts ranging from wine to pet products and potted plants.

Part of the local restaurant empire that includes La Grande Orange and Postino,

Chelsea's Kitchen (5040 N. 40th St., 602/957-2555, 11 A.M.–10 P.M. Mon.–Sat., 10 A.M.–9 P.M. Sun., $12–27) starts with a great patio and builds from there. The sleek interior manages to be both lively and private, especially in the tall leather booths, but the canal-side outdoor space is the showstopper. Gorgeous views of the sunset and the city below make it easy to linger over a pitcher of Chelsea's signature white sangria (made with pinot grigio) or a plateful of swordfish tacos. Or go for the wood-fired rotisserie chicken with house-made spatzle or the ahi tuna burger. Whatever you choose, Chelsea's delivers in a very stylish package.

If you knew the wonders of sweet-potato fries before all of your friends, **Delux** (3146 E. Camelback Rd., 602/522-2288, 11 A.M.–2 A.M. daily, $7–13) is the burger joint for you. This hip spot dishes up fancified versions of burgers, hot dogs, and sandwiches that are actually worth the price. Try the Delux burger topped with blue and gruyère cheese, organic arugula, carmelized onion, and applewood bacon on a locally made demi-baguette for a red-meat treat. Don't forget the side of fries, either. They're served in a miniature shopping cart and come in regular and sweet potato varieties. The restaurant looks like it could double as a nightclub, and thankfully it keeps nightclub hours, too. It's open until 2 A.M. in a town where late-night dining options are all too rare.

A recent addition to Biltmore Fashion Park, **True Food Kitchen** (2502 E. Camelback Rd. Ste. 135, 602/774-3488, 11 A.M.–9 P.M. Sun.–Thurs., 11 A.M.–10 P.M. Fri.–Sat., $10–21) is an innovative collaboration between holistic-health guru Dr. Andrew Weil and Arizona's uber-restaurateur Sam Fox. The fresh, flavorful menu—which promises "globally inspired cuisine that nourishes body, mind, and spirit"—incorporates many health-conscious, eco-friendly movements that have transformed the way many people eat. Chefs use healthy fats like olive oil, prepare wheat-free pasta with brown and white rice, and serve Alaskan black cod, which has more Omega-3s than salmon.

Much of the organic, seasonal produce is locally grown, and the chicken and turkey are certified hormone- and antibiotic-free. And not to worry—with dishes like goat cheese ravioli and steak tacos topped with avocado and tomatillo salsa, meals are as tasty as they are nutritious.

In the heart of north-central Phoenix, the **Rokerij** (6335 N. 16th St., 602/287-8900, 11 A.M.–midnight Mon.–Fri., 4 P.M.–midnight Sat.–Sun., $12–32) has quickly become a staple for fine food. Before dinner, go downstairs to the basement bar; it's a perfect sanctuary on a hot summer day. In the winter, a fireplace transforms the room into a cozy cocktail den. Bottles of wine are half price Sunday through Tuesday. Making a decision at dinner will be the hardest part of the night. The rotisserie pork green chile enchiladas—amazing. Grilled beef tenderloin smothered with Dungeness crab and jalapeño hollandaise—even better.

Asian

Sushi, meet happy hour. These two are a perfect match at **Zen 32** (3160 E. Camelback Rd.,

602/954-8700, 11 A.M.–2 A.M. daily, $7–25), a Biltmore neighborhood hangout that provides a fresh assortment of sushi and sashimi, along with spring rolls, pot stickers, spicy calamari, and soft-shell crab. The post-work bash from 4:30 to 6:30 P.M. includes killer drink specials and free California and spicy tuna rolls in the bar. It kicks back up again at 10 P.M. for the late-night crowd, which usually spills over onto the patio. Vegetarians and meat eaters will find a medley of Asian fusion dishes that range from vegetable tempura and miso soup to yaki soba noodles and the teriyaki-topped Zen burger.

Cherry Blossom Noodle Café (914 E. Camelback Rd. Ste. 1, 602/248-9090, 11 A.M.–9:30 P.M. Sun.–Thurs.; 11 A.M.–10:30 P.M. Fri.–Sat., $6–15) is the closest you'll find to traditional Japanese food in the Valley. But with udon noodles and *yakisoba* this good, who needs the competition? Cherry Blossom specializes in Asian noodle dishes—and a few Italian items—as well as salads, sushi, tofu, and homemade soups. The *tonkotsu* ramen with barbecue pork is a Tokyo-worthy dish that newbies to Japanese cuisine will find quite approachable. And in another quirky twist, the free homemade banana bread is a delicious nosh while you peruse the menu.

Breakfast, Lunch, and Snacks

Stopping in to **Scramble** (9832 N. 7th St., 602/374-2294, 6 A.M.–2 P.M. daily, $5–12) for breakfast or lunch feels like visiting an impossibly good school cafeteria, only better. Diners walk up to the counter to order morning mainstays such as buttermilk pancakes, eggs Benedict, and omelets, as well as a few surprises such as "brizzas"—a Scramble creation that puts eggs, bacon, chorizo, and other breakfast toppings on a pizza—and pigs in a blanket—sausage links wrapped in multigrain pancakes. The modern self-serve space is bright, airy, and everything you wish your school had been.

◖ La Grande Orange (4410 N. 40th St., 602/840-7777, 6:30 A.M.–10 P.M. daily, $6–12) is one of those magical neighborhood joints where young and old, couples and families, big

© JEFF FICKER

Postino is housed in a former post office.

PHOENIX

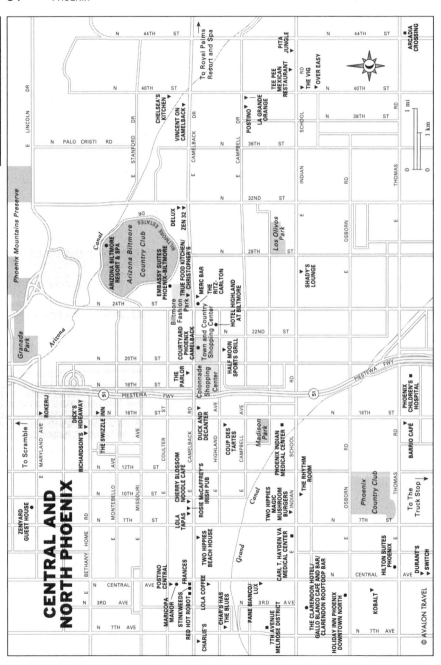

CENTRAL AND NORTH PHOENIX

ARCADIA CROSSING

To Royal Palms Resort and Spa

PITA JUNGLE

TEE PEE MEXICAN RESTAURANT

THE VIG

OVER EASY

CHELSEA'S KITCHEN

VINCENT ON CAMELBACK

POSTINO

LA GRANDE ORANGE

1 mi

1 km

DELUX

ZEN 32

Phoenix Mountains Preserve

Canal

ARIZONA BILTMORE RESORT & SPA

Arizona Biltmore Country Club

EMBASSY SUITES PHOENIX–BILTMORE

TRUE FOOD KITCHEN

CHRISTOPHER'S

MERC BAR

THE RITZ-CARLTON

SHADY'S LOUNGE

Los Olivos Park

Biltmore Fashion Park

HOTEL HIGHLAND AT BILTMORE

Granada Park

Arizona Canal

COURTYARD PHOENIX CAMELBACK

Biltmore Town and Country Shopping Center

HALF MOON SPORTS GRILL

Colonnade Shopping Center

THE PARLOR

PIESTEWA FWY

DUCK AND DECANTER

Madison Park

PHOENIX CHILDREN'S HOSPITAL

ROKERIJ

DICK'S HIDEAWAY

RICHARDSON'S

THE SWIZZLE INN

To Scramble

COUP DES TARTES

PHOENIX INDIAN MEDICAL CENTER

BARRIO CAFÉ

CHERRY BLOSSOM NOODLE CAFÉ

THE RHYTHM ROOM

ZENYARD GUEST HOUSE

LOLA TAPAS

ROSIE McCAFFREY'S IRISH PUB

TWO HIPPIES MAGIC MUSHROOM BURGERS

Phoenix Country Club

To The Truck Stop

POSTINO CENTRAL

FRANCES

TWO HIPPIES BEACH HOUSE

CARL T. HAYDEN VA MEDICAL CENTER

HILTON SUITES PHOENIX

DURANT'S

SWITCH

MARICOPA MANOR

STINKWEEDS

RED HOT ROBOT

LOLA COFFEE

CHAR'S HAS THE BLUES

PANE BIANCO/ LUX

THE CLARENDON HOTEL/ GALLO BLANCO CAFE AND BAR/ CLARENDON ROOFTOP BAR

KOBALT

CHARLIE'S

7TH AVENUE MELROSE DISTRICT

HOLIDAY INN PHOENIX DOWNTOWN NORTH

AVALON TRAVEL

© AVALON TRAVEL

groups of friends and quiet newspaper readers can all sit down and enjoy themselves. Drop in early in the morning for the trademark fresh-squeezed O.J., and try out the Commuter Sandwich, served on LGO's signature English muffins. Later in the day, pop back in to grab a quick salad or warm Cubano sandwich. The hip market also offers a fun selection of gifts and wine, and its coffee bar is among the best in the city—give the Spanish latte a try if you don't believe me. Parking can be a (big) hassle, but once you sit down on the shady patio for first-rate people-watching, you won't mind the inconvenience.

Even non-morning people like starting their day at **Over Easy** (4037 N. 40th St., 602/468-3447, 6:30–11:30 A.M. daily, $4–9). The sunny yellow interior and bright patio provide a pleasant setting for cheesy omelets, waffles, and big, fluffy pancakes. Got a sweet tooth? The brioche French toast topped with caramelized banana and pecans is divine, as is the iced coffee with cinnamon, cardamom, sweetened condensed milk, and mint. Get here early or expect to wait for a table at the small café.

If trendy urban coffee joints get your juices flowing on a Sunday morning, **Lola Coffee** (4700 N. Central Ave., 602/265-5652, 7 A.M.–7 P.M. Mon.–Thurs., 7 A.M.–10 P.M. Fri.–Sat., 7 A.M.–2 P.M. Sun., $2–7) is your kind of place. The café is usually full of boisterous, good-looking caffeine addicts. Its plush couches and big family-style table are more suited to conversation than to serious work. You won't find a lot of food options at Lola, but the coffee is serious—seriously good—and the homemade pastries are, quite literally, a treat. If the weather is nice, enjoy a seat outside and watch the light rail cars quietly roll downtown.

Duck and Decanter (1651 E. Camelback Rd., 602/274-5429, 7 A.M.–7 P.M. Sat.–Wed., 7 A.M.–9 P.M. Thurs.–Fri., $5–8) is a Camelback classic. The popular brown-bag lunch put this gourmet sandwich shop on Phoenix's culinary map in the 1970s. Since then, the wine bar, assortment of European beers, and well-stocked deli and cheese shop

have earned it a loyal following—not to mention the reasonable prices, which mean weekly trips for many. The mile-high sandwiches come with a choice of nine breads, and the fresh salads are splashed with seasoned rice vinegar. You can get your meal to go, but you should join the neighborhood regulars on the large, shaded patio. You'll also find European imports and Arizona-made products like cactus candies in the culinary shop.

Finding a cheap, delicious place to have lunch can be hard. But with $2 tacos, **Two Hippies Beach House** (501 E. Camelback Rd., 602/277-0399, 10:30 A.M.–8 P.M. Mon.–Sat., $2–7) makes it easy. The "shack" prepares simple but extraordinarily tasty chicken, fish, pork, and carne asada, wrapped in tortillas and stacked with pinto beans, cheese, cabbage, tomatoes, and onions. Pair them with one of the flavored lemonades and you've got yourself a solid meal. A mile south, go all-American with burgers, hot dogs, and chicken sandwiches at **Two Hippies Magic Mushroom Burgers** (802 E. Indian School Rd., 602/265-3525, 10 A.M.–4 P.M. Mon.–Sat., $3–7). The fresh-cut fries and hot wings are pretty good.

Although its older sibling, Pizzeria Bianco, gets most of the attention, **Pane Bianco** (4404 N. Central Ave., 602/234-2100, 11 A.M.–3 P.M. Tues.–Sat., $7–9), Chris Bianco's lunchtime sandwich and salad shop, is just as worthy of high praise and a slew of accolades. Bianco's genius is his simplicity, and at his lunch stop, the choice is limited to a perfect four sandwiches and two salads. The *soppressata* with aged provolone and roasted peppers is the standout, but everything here is exemplary, perhaps most notably the wood-fired focaccia bread that offers a glimpse into Bianco's renowned pizzas. Make sure to check out the market sandwich, which is the only changing item on the menu; it could be thick-sliced bacon or roast lamb. Bianco is a strong supporter of local growers, and his food reflects this sensibility with its incredible freshness and delicious taste.

A mix of house-roasted coffee, tempting baked goods, and midcentury Modernist furniture attracts the local hipsterati and those looking for a good cuppa joe alike to **Lux** (4404 N. Central Ave., 602/696-9976, 7 A.M.–10 P.M. daily, $2–5). Baristas pride themselves on remembering names and drink orders after just a couple of visits, and regulars do keep coming back. Repeated visits often reveal the same groups of people gabbing at the tables as they get a caffeine fix or munching on sandwiches from Pane Bianco next door.

French

Dining spots don't get much more romantic than **Coup des Tartes** (4626 N. 16th St., 602/212-1082, 11 A.M.–2 P.M. Mon.–Fri., 5:30–10:30 P.M. Tues.–Sat., $16–34). The bungalow that houses this delightful French bistro looks unassuming from the outside, but its cozy interior is pitch-perfect for first dates, anniversaries, and all manner of intimate meals. The menu changes regularly but almost always includes classic treatments of lamb, duck, and fish. If summer chicken is on the menu, don't hesitate. Its mix of herbs and citrus is the perfect pick-me-up for hot summer days. Two other "don'ts": Don't forget the restaurant's BYOB policy, and don't skimp on the appetizers or desserts. The cheese plate and house-made tarts are good enough to make you and your date swoon.

Christopher's (2502 E. Camelback Rd., 602/522-2344, 11 A.M.–10 P.M. daily, $12–28) recently re-emerged with a hip look and a new locale at the Biltmore Fashion Park—and it seems the change has reinvigorated its creator, James Beard Award–winning chef Christopher Gross. The French bistro-inspired menu still includes his cult favorites—red bell pepper soup, goat cheese salad, foie gras, specialty pizzas—but he's debuted a more casual side at the restaurant's **Crush Lounge,** where you get half off the menu during happy hour (3–6 P.M.). Give the vanilla-dusted scallops, shallot rings, mac 'n' cheese au gratin, and bowls of sweet, truffled, and curried fries a try.

Italian

The Parlor (1916 E. Camelback Rd., 602/248-2480, 11 A.M.–10 P.M. Mon.–Thurs., 11 A.M.–midnight Fri.–Sat., $8–16), a stylish new pizzeria in the Camelback Corridor, quickly won over Phoenicians when it opened in 2009. A glamorous makeover has preserved a few

The Parlor

© JEFF FICKER

retro details from the building's previous life as the Salon de Venus, though its sleek new look—with polished-concrete floors and recycled-wood tables—has made the restaurant a hit, especially the popular bar (don't miss the refreshing basil gimlet). The kitchen serves Italian favorites, including a pappardelle bolognese with meat sauce, shaved pecorino, and rosemary oil, as well as a delicious selection of salads that you'll want to share. Order one of the wood-fired pizzas, like the Pesto or the Smokey, which is topped with ricotta, olive tapenade, arugula, and smoked prosciutto.

Mediterranean and Middle Eastern

Welcome to the **Pita Jungle** (4340 E. Indian School Rd., 602/955-7482, 10:30 A.M.–10 P.M. daily, $7–15). The Central Phoenix branch of this ever-growing Valley culinary empire attracts a busy lunch and dinner crowd thanks to its inexpensive, healthy, Middle Eastern-inspired menu. The eclectic assortment includes gyros, falafels, and warm lavash, as well as salads and veggie burgers. The Mediterranean-roasted chicken *shawarma* is a garlicky, pita-wrapped masterpiece. Oh, please note: Best. Hummus. Ever.

It's all about ambience at **T. Cooks** (5200 E. Camelback Rd., 602/808-0766, 11 A.M.–2 P.M. and 5:30–10 P.M. daily, $26–38), a romantic hideaway at the Royal Palms Resort. The cozy, Spanish Colonial dining room is complemented by a Southwest-meets-Mediterranean menu, featuring seasonal dishes, fresh fish, and fire-roasted meats. The lobster bisque garnished with fennel foam is just one of the subtle, uniquely crafted dishes. Phoenicians regularly gather at the Sunday morning brunches for lemon brioche French toast, eggs Benedict, vanilla-scented pancakes, and mimosas.

Mexican and Southwest

Once you discover **C Richardson's** (1582 E. Bethany Home Rd., 602/265-5886, 11 A.M.–midnight Mon.–Fri., 9 A.M.–midnight Sat.–Sun., $10–28), you'll be a convert to New Mexico's own Southwestern cuisine: roasted chiles, gooey melted cheese, and smoky, grilled meats. You could easily make an entire meal of a small salad and the jumbo shrimp quesadilla with red pepper sauce and cheese, or the must-try posole, a spicy stew of hominy and pork in a zesty red-chile broth. Of course, then you'd miss out on the enchiladas and Pasta Heidi's green chile linguine in a smoky chipotle cream sauce. In the same plaza, the compact **Dick's Hideaway** (6008 N. 16th St., 602/265-5886, 8 A.M.–1 A.M. Mon.–Fri., 7 A.M.–1 A.M. Sat.–Sun.) offers the same menu, but in a dark, rustic setting that feels a bit like a modern saloon. Pull up a stool at the polished copper bar and order a drink from the extensive beer and wine list. Both restaurants serve fantastic brunches.

You know your enchiladas are good when the president of the United States shows up at the door. George W. Bush ate at the **Tee Pee Mexican Restaurant** (4144 E. Indian School Rd., 602/956-0178, 11 A.M.–10 P.M. Mon.–Sat., 11 A.M.–9 P.M. Sun., $6–13) in 2004, but Phoenicians have been coming to this hole-in-the-wall for authentic Mexican food for almost 50 years. The Tee Pee is known for its chile rellenos, which come to the table as an intimidating, but tasty, mountain of cheese and chile peppers. The menu is affordable and diverse, but be prepared for tight quarters. The original orange booths are separated by a single divider, which means you'll get to know your neighbor. Oh, and President Bush dined on two enchiladas, rice, and beans.

Chef Vincent Guerithault and his eponymous **Vincent on Camelback** (3930 E. Camelback Rd. Ste. 204, 602/224-0225, 11:30 A.M.–2 P.M. and 5–10 P.M. Mon.–Fri., 5–10 P.M. Sat., $30–36) are local classics. The James Beard Award winner combines Southwestern ingredients with French technique. The elegant restaurant is perennially popular for its signature appetizers—like duck tamale with Anaheim chile and raisins—creative entrées, and delicious selection of Grand Marnier, tequila, lemon, and raspberry soufflés.

The casual, hip vibe and deliciously simple menu inspired by Mexican street food have made **Gallo Blanco Café and Bar** (401 W.

Clarendon Ave., 602/274-4774, 7 A.M.–10 P.M. Sun.–Thurs., 7 A.M.–11 P.M. Fri.–Sat., $4–11) a popular choice for locals. Start with the made-to-order guacamole and the *elote callejero*, grilled corn on the cob with fresh *cotija* cheese and smoked paprika. You'll also want to sample the small homemade tacos, which range from seasonal veggies to *cochinita*, local pork marinated in achiote, oranges, garlic, and guajillo chiles. The small bar and restaurant in The Clarendon Hotel is also a great spot for an inexpensive breakfast, like the egg sandwich, topped with spicy chorizo and fresh avocado.

One of the best things about being a border state is the quality of the Mexican food. **Via de Los Santos Mexican Café** (9120 N. Central Ave., 602/997-6239, 11 A.M.–9:30 P.M. Mon.–Thurs., 11 A.M.–10:30 P.M. Fri., 11 A.M.–9:30 P.M. Sat., 11 A.M.–8:30 P.M. Sun., $6–17) is no exception. The café, known for its quality margaritas (which start at $2), boasts a selection of more than 200 different tequilas. But it is the food that keeps the patrons coming back. Beloved for its low prices and tasty Sonoran-style Mexican dishes, this Sunnyslope eatery is frequented for its well-marinated chicken enchiladas and the deep-fried perfection of its *machaca* chimichangas.

Spanish

Phoenix is home to countless Mexican restaurants, but it was only recently blessed with an authentic, fine Spanish eatery in **Lola Tapas** (800 E. Camelback Rd., 602/265-4519, 5–10 P.M. Tues.–Sat., $4–14). Specializing in cuisine from the Andalucia region in the south of Spain, Lola's serves terrific sangria, along with small plates of mouthwatering dishes such as serrano ham with *manchego* cheese and marcona almonds, spicy chickpeas and spinach, and daily specials. The wine list boasts *vino blanco* like Albariño and Spanish reds, as well as a choice of sherries—*olé!*

AHWATUKEE AND SOUTH PHOENIX
Breakfast and Lunch
The Farm at South Mountain (6106 S. 32nd

St.) is a slice of classic Arizona—and sadly, the rural, agricultural setting is nearing extinction in Phoenix. Fortunately for residents and visitors, though, the farm's restaurants still showcase the city's former rural beauty. Students, families, the Scottsdale brunching set—well, it seems like everyone raves about the **Morning Glory Café** (602/276-8804, 8 A.M.–noon Tues.–Fri., 8 A.M.–1 P.M. Sat.–Sun., closed summers, $8–15). The open-air restaurant isn't fancy, but the farm-fresh food is spectacular: cowboy chili and eggs, white truffle scrambled eggs, and rustic French toast, topped with candied walnuts and warm syrup. Even enjoying a simple cup of coffee while sitting under the old pecan trees is the perfect way to unwind after a hike up South Mountain. Also on the property, **The Farm Kitchen** (602/276-7288, 10 A.M.–3 P.M. Tues.–Sun., closed summers, $6–12) features soups, salads, and sandwiches for a lunchtime picnic. Head south of Southern on 32nd Street, and pull into the charming farmstead's gravel driveway.

Mexican and Southwest
Kai (5594 W. Wild Horse Pass Blvd., 602/385-5726, 6–9 P.M. Tues.–Fri., 5:30–10 P.M. Sat., $20–47), which means "seed" in the Pima language, taps into the Native American influence on Arizona culture and cuisine. The brainchild of Tucson restaurateur Janos Wilder, the restaurant at the Wild Horse Pass Resort hits high marks with an innovative menu that consists of indigenous ingredients produced on the Gila River Indian Community's land. The butter-braised lobster served with avocado mousse on frybread and veal ribeye rubbed with sandalwood, dry mole, and green-chile sand create an epic, uniquely Arizona experience. Give the eight-course tasting menu a try if you're feeling adventurous, not to mention hungry. The AAA Five Diamond restaurant is rather formal—which in Arizona means no jeans or shorts. Also, Kai closes for four weeks in August.

There are scores of great places to grab good tacos and enchiladas in the Valley, but **Carolina's** (1202 E. Mohave St., 602/252-1503, 7 A.M.–8:30 P.M. Mon.–Sat., $3–7) is among the very best, with fresh, made-from-scratch Mexican food. The less-than-stellar neighborhood and slightly dumpy building belie the care that is given to the homemade tortillas, guacamole, and salsa. To really experience Carolina Valenzuela's original recipes, order one of the hearty combination platters, which include tamales, *machaca,* flautas, and tostadas.

Steakhouse

Cowpokes crave **Rustler's Rooste** (8383 S. 48th St., 602/431-6474, 4–10 P.M. daily, $15–28). This giant barnlike restaurant is perched on South Mountain and offers splendid views of Phoenix. The two-story waterfall, giant live steer, and hefty servings of steak, ribs, and corn on the cob force even the most urban epicurean to pick up a country twang and salivate for good ole chuckhouse grub. Oh, and the best part? You can avoid the stairs and instead opt for a two-story slide that whizzes eaters between floors. The restaurant is full of gimmicks, but the great atmosphere and live music are pure fun.

TEMPE AND THE EAST VALLEY
American

House of Tricks (114 E. 7th St., 480/968-1114, 11 A.M.–10 P.M. Mon.–Fri., 5–10 P.M. Sat., $21–29) is one of Tempe's best restaurants. Tucked behind big, shady trees, the 1920s cottage offers casual charms and sophisticated New American dishes with French, Asian, and Southwestern flavors. Enjoy a glass of wine in the outdoor Garden Bar, or opt for a cozy dinner inside. The eclectic, seasonal menu features starters like crab and mango salad with yellow bell peppers, cilantro, and honey-lime vinaigrette. The herb-crusted lamb porterhouse and spiced ahi tuna on toasted couscous are just as flavorful.

Monti's La Casa Vieja (100 S. Mill Ave., 480/967-7594, 11 A.M.–10 P.M. Sun.–Thurs., 11 A.M.–11 P.M. Fri.–Sat., $8–32) is an Arizona institution. The adobe building is among the oldest in the city. It was the boyhood home of longtime Arizona congressman Carl T. Hayden, whose father ran a ferry across the Salt River before it was dammed in 1911, and it's been a restaurant in one form or another for well over 100 years. The focus on stick-to-your-ribs dishes like prime rib, pork chops, and ribs would satisfy even the restaurant's most ravenous pioneer patrons, and the kitchen isn't bad with seafood, either. If you try just one thing, though, make it the ground sirloin sandwich served on cheese toast with a side of the restaurant's justifiably famous Roman bread.

Four Peaks Brewpub (1340 E. 8th St., 480/303-9967, 11 A.M.–2 A.M. Mon.–Sat., 10 A.M.–2 A.M. Sun., $5–17) is a regular on "best of" lists for tasty bar food and locally brewed ales. Set in an 1892 red-brick, mission-style building just off the beaten path in Tempe, the brewery shows off its floor-to-ceiling steel casks in the back and a chalkboard with the day's brews in the front, including alcohol-content percentage. Savor the Kiltlifter, a three-time medalist at the Great American Beer Festival, for its flavor and provocative moniker. If hunger strikes, try the pub's Southwest burger topped with chiles and jalapeño dressing. Or indulge your deep-fried fantasies with the 8th Street Ale Chicken Strips, the only chicken tenders you can order without feeling like you have an immature palate.

College students don't mess around when it comes their sandwiches. They want their meat and veggies stacked high and their portions huge. Luckily, **Bison Witches Bar and Deli** (21 E. 6th St. Ste. 146, 480/894-9104, 11 A.M.–2 A.M. daily, $5–9) is well up to the challenge. A Tucson legend, Bison Witches' Tempe location is a cheap, casual spot for lunch or dinner. You'll find traditional bar appetizers and a few salads, but regulars know it's all about the Half and Half—a filling half sandwich paired with one of five soups in a giant bread bowl. Grab a beer while you decide which mix-and-match option to enjoy. The chunky chicken salad on wheat with the potato bacon soup? Or perhaps the reuben on rye with the Boston clam chowder?

Asian

For tasty, accessible Vietnamese and pan-Asian cuisine, **Cyclo** (1919 W. Chandler Blvd., 480/963-4490, 11 A.M.–2:30 P.M. and 5–9 P.M. Tues.–Thurs., 11 A.M.–2:30 P.M. and 5–10 P.M. Fri.–Sat., $5–12) can't be beat. The decor is surprisingly stylish for the strip-mall setting—imagine the riotous colors of Saigon let loose in an Ikea—and the owner, Justina, is a hoot. The food is also first-class. The *goi du du* (green papaya salad), *canh ga* (spicy chicken wings), and *pho xe lua* (beef noodle soup) never disappoint, especially if they're paired with a Vietnamese coffee brewed into a glass of condensed milk at the table. And just for the record, the name (pronounced SEE-klo) is the Vietnamese word for a three-wheeled pedicab.

Sushi in the desert? Sure, and at **RA Sushi** (411 S. Mill Ave., 480/303-9800, 11 A.M.–11 P.M. daily, $3–22), the fish is FedEx'd fresh—overnight. Add a backbeat that wafts through the dining room and a distinct energy, supplied by a Mill Avenue address and proximity to ASU, and dinner at RA is akin to an entire night on the town. The bar is always packed with revelers, and the sushi bar and dining tables serve up some of the Valley's best sushi, sashimi, noodles, and tempura. The drinks are nothing to sneeze at, either, featuring a bunch of beers and an array of sakes, including a "saketini" and "sake sangria," as well as an extensive cocktail list. The sushi house was bought by Benihana a few years ago, and there are now RAs across the city and country.

Italian

Just off the main drag on Mill Avenue, **Caffe Boa** (398 S. Mill Ave. Ste. 110, 480/968-9112, 11 A.M.–10 P.M. Mon.–Wed., 11 A.M.–11 P.M. Thurs.–Sat., noon–10 P.M. Sun., $14–32) is a longtime favorite. The stylish restaurant's exposed brick walls, dark hardwood floors, and elegant, modern light fixtures are chic, but the overall mood is quite casual. Boa's seasonal menu can swing from a light organic Persian cucumber salad tossed with a mint-and-yogurt dressing in the summer to braised meats and rich sauces in the winter. The handmade agnolotti ravioli filled with grilled portabello and cremini mushrooms in a creamy tomato sauce is always a winner.

Plop me down with the pepperoni and cheese from **Slices** (11 E. 6th St., 480/966-4681, 11 A.M.–10 P.M. Sun.–Wed., 11 A.M.–3 A.M. Thurs.–Sat., $3–5) and I'm in heaven. There's nothing swank about this small, New York-style, grab-a-big-slice-and-fold-it pizza joint, which prepares a changing lineup of a dozen pies, including chicken parmesan, potato and bacon, chipotle veggie, and the Greek, salty combination of olive, feta cheese, and onion. Order a slice (or two) at the counter and fine-tune with a quick shake of crushed red pepper, garlic powder, or oregano. Hungry college students swarm to this crowded shop off of Mill Avenue, especially late at night, though a newer location at **Tempe Marketplace** (2000 E. Rio Salado Pkwy., 480/966-2021, 11 A.M.–10 P.M. Sun.–Wed., 11 A.M.–11:30 P.M. Thurs.–Sat., $3–5) is winning over fans as well.

Mexican

Housed in Tempe's old train station, **Macayo's Depot Cantina** (300 S. Ash Ave., 480/966-6677, 10 A.M.–midnight daily, $6–14) is a festive Mexican restaurant just west of Mill Avenue's main drag. It's a convenient lunch or dinner option for visitors to the popular shopping district or neighboring Tempe Town Lake and Papago Park. Lunch specials feature shredded beef tacos, tamales, and chicken chimichangas, though Macayo's fajitas and spicy Baja specialties are certainly worth a taste. The large, colorful restaurant is best known for its crowded happy hours from 4 to 6 P.M., particularly on Fridays, when college students and office workers are anxious to jumpstart their weekends at the open-air bar and patio.

Middle Eastern

The first **Pita Jungle** (1250 E. Apache Blvd., 480/804-0234, 10:30 A.M.–10 P.M. Mon.–Fri., 9 A.M.–10 P.M. Sat.–Sun., $6–15) opened in a funky strip mall near the Arizona State campus with a goal of attracting the burgeoning market of healthful eaters. And it did. In 15 years, the eatery expanded to nine restaurants across the state. The quirky, Mediterranean-inspired decor blends seamlessly with the eatery's menu of hummus, baba ghanoush, and feta- and olive-topped lavash pizzas. Regulars swear by the chicken *shawarma*. The restaurant is well suited for mixed company—that is, vegetarians and carnivores—because it offers multiple meatless options, including three types of veggie burgers, as well as a selection of beef, chicken, and lamb dishes.

Vegetarian

Vegans can rejoice and carnivores can relax at **Green** (2240 N. Scottsdale Rd., 480/941-9003, 11 A.M.–9 P.M. Mon.–Sat., $6–8). The casual restaurant features 100 percent vegan "comfort food" like burgers, pizzas, po-boys, and noodle bowls made with mock meat and vegan cheeses. There are also gluten-free options for nearly everything on the menu. If this sounds more like a diet than a meal, close your eyes and take a bite. The spicy Buffalo wings, "steak" po-boys, and kung pao bowls are tasty enough to please even the most hard-core meat eater.

Information and Services

TOURIST INFORMATION

The **Greater Phoenix Convention & Visitors Bureau** (602/254-6500, www.visitphoenix.com) is a great place to start for additional information about the Valley of the Sun. Its **Downtown Phoenix Visitor Information Center** (125 N. 2nd St. Ste. 120, 8 A.M.–5 P.M. Mon.–Fri.) is conveniently located across from the main entrance of the Hyatt Regency Phoenix.

LIBRARIES

The Phoenix Public Library has 16 branches across the city, including the **Burton Barr Central Library** (1221 N. Central Ave., 602/262-4636, www.phoenixpubliclibrary.org, 10 A.M.–9 P.M. Mon.–Thurs., 10 A.M.–6 P.M. Fri.–Sat., noon–6 P.M. Sun.). You'll find computer terminals for easy access to the Internet, as well as an array of resources. The newer branches are almost as architecturally interesting as Burton Barr and worth a mini-tour, particularly **Agave** (23550 N. 36th Ave), **Desert Broom** (29710 N. Cave Creek Rd.), **Palo** **Verde** (4402 N. 51st Ave.), and **Juniper** (1825 W. Union Hills Dr.). Call the main number with questions or for hours.

HOSPITALS AND EMERGENCY SERVICES

In an emergency, dial 911 for immediate assistance. **St. Joseph's Hospital and Medical Center** (350 W. Thomas Rd., 602/406-3000, www.stjosephs-phx.org) is Phoenix's premier hospital and home of the Barrow Neurological Institute as well as a Level 1 trauma center. Nearby, **Phoenix Children's Hospital** (1919 E. Thomas Rd., 602/546-1000, www.phoenixchildrens.com) is one of the 10 largest children's hospitals in the country, offering a host of pediatric specialties, including neonatology, neurosciences, and Level 1 trauma. **Banner Health** (602/230-2273, www.bannerhealth.com) operates more than two dozen clinics and medical centers around the Valley, ranging from specialized services to general health care.

Getting There and Around

AIR

Phoenix Sky Harbor International Airport (3400 E. Sky Harbor Blvd., 602/273-3300, www.phxskyharbor.com) is a major regional hub for national and international flights. Tempe-based US Airways (800/428-4322, www.usairways.com) is the hometown airline, but more than 20 carriers fly to Sky Harbor's terminals 2, 3, and 4, including British Airways and Hawaiian Airlines. Shuttles connect the three terminals, as well as parking lots, the Rental Car Center, and the light rail's 44th Street stop.

CAR
Rental Cars

You'll need a vehicle to get around Phoenix, especially if you plan to explore the Valley of the Sun's diverse attractions scattered around the city. Take the free shuttle from any of the terminals to the **Rental Car Center** (1805 E. Sky Harbor Circle, 602/683-3741). You'll find major companies, like **Budget** (602/267-4000, www.budget.com), **Hertz** (602/267-8822, www.hertz.com), and **Enterprise** (602/489-6898), which have convenient drop-off centers around Phoenix and Scottsdale and offers free pickup service. It can be hard to find a gas station near the rental car center, so be sure to fill up before returning your vehicle.

Limos, Shuttles, and Taxis

Join a shared-van ride to your resort or hotel with the reliable **SuperShuttle** (602/232-4610, www.supershuttle.com). Its bright blue vans are easy to spot at each of Sky Harbor's terminals.

AAA Sedans (602/454-7433) has a fleet of town cars that can ferry you to downtown Phoenix for about $50, plus tip. **Desert Knights Sedans & Limousines** (480/348-0600, www.desertknights.com) provides taxis, sedans, limos, and luxury minibuses, which can be a practical option for families or groups.

Also, you can grab a taxi at Sky Harbor with one of three contracted companies: **AAA Cab** (602/437-4000), **AllState** (602/275-8888), and **Discount** (602/266-1110). And if you want to hit the town at night, try **Courier Cab** (602/232-2222).

PUBLIC TRANSPORTATION
Light Rail

The Valley's 20-mile light-rail system opened in December 2008, and it has proven to be popular with commuters, bar-hoppers, and visitors alike. Trains wend from 19th Avenue and Bethany Home Road in Phoenix, through downtown and Tempe's Mill Avenue, before ending one mile into Mesa. It stops at many of the city's most popular attractions, including the Heard Museum and Phoenix Art Museum, the Phoenix Convention Center, and Sun Devil Stadium in Tempe. Trains run daily, every 10 to 20 minutes. The last full trip begins at 11 P.M., and on Friday and Saturday nights, the hours are extended to 2 A.M. Fares start at $1.75 for a one-ride trip, and multi-ride passes are available.

Bus

The **Valley Metro** (602/262-7433, www.valleymetro.org) public transportation network connects the entire Phoenix metropolitan area. In addition to the light-rail line, its buses run throughout the city. Visit the website for a comprehensive schedule, map, and fares.

SCOTTSDALE

Unlike Phoenix's other suburban communities, Scottsdale easily stands on its own. The city has been tanned, toned, bleached, and buffed to enjoy the good life, and its residents happily comply. Scottsdale sits in the northeast of the Valley of the Sun, the glamorous, overindulged sibling to Phoenix's family of suburbs. And like any spoiled child, Scottsdale demands the spotlight, luring residents and visitors to its resorts, restaurants, nightspots, five-star spas, and eclectic boutiques.

Scottsdale is divided into three areas. The compact, southern part of the city, downtown, is where you'll find Old Town and the arts districts of 5th Avenue and Marshall Way, as well as the city's best shops and nightlife venues. The area is bordered by the college town of Tempe to the south and by Phoenix to the west.

The central part of Scottsdale extends east, featuring an indistinguishable sprawl of housing developments and strip malls called the Shea Corridor. You'll also find the community of Paradise Valley, the Valley's answer to Beverly Hills and home to big-name celebrities and five-star resorts.

Within the last decade, the northern half of the city has become one of the most sought-after areas in the region and has begun to creep into formerly pristine desert and the relatively isolated arts communities of Cave Creek and Carefree. Fortunately, developers have taken a more enlightened approach to the city's growth, sparing much of the area's indigenous wildlife.

Despite its flashy exterior (and occasionally hedonistic impulses), Scottsdale is still firmly

SCOTTSDALE

HIGHLIGHTS

◖ Scottsdale Museum of Contemporary Art (SMoCA): This intimate museum of modern art, architecture, and design stands out in the capital of cowboy art. The permanent *Knight Rise* installation, which distorts your perception of Arizona's wide blue sky, is the highlight (page 99).

◖ Camelback Mountain: You can't miss the iconic "kneeling camel" profile. The red-sandstone-and-granite peak rises at the center of the Valley of the Sun and is a top draw for hikers and rock climbers (page 100).

◖ Taliesin West: Frank Lloyd Wright's winter home blends the architect's trademark techniques and design motifs with the desert landscape. Tour the National Landmark, which is still a working architecture school and home to members of the Wright Foundation (page 102).

◖ Nightlife: Scottsdale's downtown transforms from a shoppers' paradise to a social hub when the sun goes down. The city's world-class restaurants and sizzling bars, lounges, and clubs are famous – and occasionally infamous – for their posh crowds and steep prices (page 104).

◖ Art Galleries: Scottsdale commands the country's third-largest art market, and its three arts districts showcase Southwestern pieces and avant-garde works (page 114).

◖ Golf: The city courses tee up some of the best golf in the world. Be sure to play one of the sprawling desert courses, which contrast lush fairways with the natural, rocky landscape (page 118).

◖ Spas: Scottsdale's opulent spas impress even the most jaded spa-goers. Revel in the outdoor showers, Native American-inspired treatments, healing mineral pools, and chic decor (page 121).

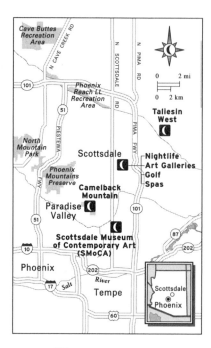

LOOK FOR ◖ TO FIND RECOMMENDED SIGHTS, ACTIVITIES, DINING, AND LODGING.

rooted in its decades-old slogan as "The West's Most Western Town." The city is bordered to the east by mountains and the agricultural land of the Salt River Pima–Maricopa Indian Community, which has kept the city's sprawling tendencies in check. It's still one of the few spaces in metropolitan Phoenix where you can truly feel like you are living in the desert—perhaps the city's greatest luxury.

PLANNING YOUR TIME

Don't rush your time in Scottsdale. Relax and imagine that your life really consists of endless days of soaking up sunshine, sipping tequila, and dining alfresco at topnotch restaurants that forgo the formality of suits and ties. After all, this is the city that invented resort casual—both in terms of attire and attitude.

Half the fun of Scottsdale is knowing you

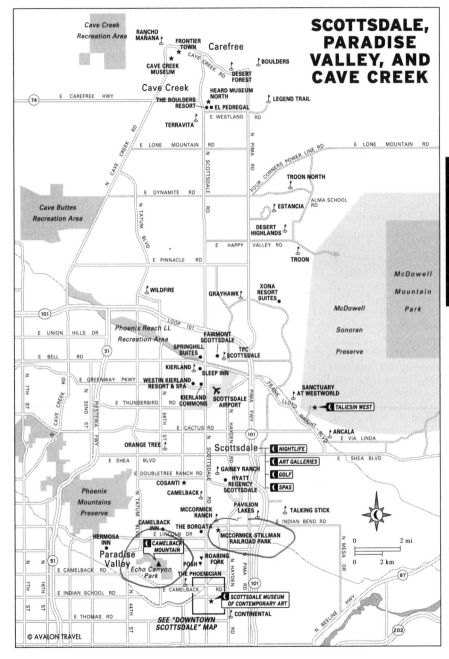

SCOTTSDALE, PARADISE VALLEY, AND CAVE CREEK

SCOTTSDALE

Cave Creek
Recreation Area

RANCHO MAÑANA

FRONTIER TOWN

Carefree

Cave Creek

CAVE CREEK MUSEUM

BOULDERS

DESERT FOREST

E CAVE CREEK RD

Cave Creek

HEARD MUSEUM NORTH

LEGEND TRAIL

74   E CAREFREE HWY

THE BOULDERS RESORT

EL PEDREGAL

E WESTLAND   RD

TERRAVITA

E LONE   MOUNTAIN   RD

E LONE   MOUNTAIN   RD

N SCOTTSDALE

N PIMA   RD

FOUR CORNERS POWER LINE RD

Cave Buttes
Recreation Area

E DYNAMITE   RD

TROON NORTH

N TATUM   BLVD

ESTANCIA

ALMA SCHOOL RD

E HAPPY   VALLEY RD

DESERT HIGHLANDS

McDowell

Mountain

E PINNACLE   RD

TROON

Park

101

WILDFIRE

GRAYHAWK

XONA RESORT SUITES

McDowell

Sonoran

E UNION   HILLS   DR

Phoenix Reach LL
Recreation Area

LOOP 101

FAIRMONT SCOTTSDALE

Preserve

51

E BELL   RD

SPRINGHILL SUITES

TPC SCOTTSDALE

N 7TH   ST

E GREENWAY   PKWY

KIERLAND

SLEEP INN

WESTIN KIERLAND RESORT & SPA

N CAVE CREEK RD

N 32ND   ST

PIESTEWA   FWY

E THUNDERBIRD   RD

KIERLAND COMMONS

SCOTTSDALE AIRPORT

N PIMA

N FRANK LLOYD WRIGHT BLVD

SANCTUARY AT WESTWORLD

TALIESIN WEST

56TH   ST

E CACTUS RD

N HAYDEN   RD

ORANGE TREE

ANCALA

E VIA   LINDA

101

Scottsdale

NIGHTLIFE

N SCOTTSDALE   RD

E SHEA   BLVD

E SHEA   BLVD

ART GALLERIES

Phoenix
Mountains
Preserve

E DOUBLETREE RANCH DR

GAINEY RANCH

GOLF

N TATUM   BLVD

COSANTI

HYATT REGENCY SCOTTSDALE

SPAS

CAMELBACK

MCCORMICK RANCH

PAVILION LAKES

TALKING STICK

HERMOSA INN

CAMELBACK INN

THE BORGATA

E LINCOLN DR

MCCORMICK-STILLMAN RAILROAD PARK

E INDIAN BEND RD

N MESA   DR

0   2 mi

51

CAMELBACK MOUNTAIN

Paradise Valley

Echo Canyon Park

E CAMELBACK   RD

ROARING FORK

POSH

0   2 km

N 7TH   ST

16TH   ST

THE PHOENICIAN

N PIMA

87

E INDIAN SCHOOL   RD

44TH   ST

E CAMELBACK   RD.

101

E THOMAS   RD

SCOTTSDALE MUSEUM OF CONTEMPORARY ART

CONTINENTAL

N BEELINE   HWY

202

© AVALON TRAVEL

SEE "DOWNTOWN SCOTTSDALE" MAP

don't have to be anywhere or doing anything. You could easily spend a week enjoying days by the pool, playing rounds of golf, browsing in galleries, and getting pampered at one of the city's five-star spas.

If you only have a weekend, though, be sure to see Frank Lloyd Wright's winter home, Taliesin West, before witnessing the clash of civilizations in Old Town. The eclectic mix of expensive galleries, trendy clubs, yuppie biker bars, and boutiques selling Western and Native American kitsch creates some the best people-watching this side of the Rocky Mountains. Bars and restaurants literally slide away their glass walls from November through April, giving you a front row seat to the streetside spectacle.

Visiting during the summer's triple-digit heat will force you to change your plans—both in terms of what you do and when you do it. But that's not a bad thing. Take a cue from the natives—both wildlife and residents—who switch to a more nocturnal schedule from May well into October. Wake at dawn to take advantage of an early tee time or a sunrise hike at one of Scottsdale's craggy peaks. Then, spend your afternoons in one of the city's air-conditioned oases, like Scottsdale Fashion Square mall. When late afternoon hits, make like a lizard and find some shade for a nap (the thermometer hits its hottest point around 4 P.M.).

Come out to play in the evening when the sun dips below the horizon and the desert's beige tones and blue sky give way to a rich burst of color. The Technicolor sunsets are just a preview of the evening's lime-green margaritas, vibrant Southwestern cuisine, and flashy lounges and clubs. And as the temperature drops 20 degrees throughout the night, let the warm, weightless air convince you living in the desert can be heaven.

HISTORY

The city of Scottsdale may look new, but its roots date back to the ancient Hohokam civilization, which first inhabited the Salt River Valley circa 300 B.C. When the Hohokam mysteriously abandoned their villages in the 1500s,

their canals served as a foundation for the Pima Indian village known as Vasai Svasoni, or "rotting hay." Although it wasn't the most appealing name, the area proved to be an enduring home for the Pima, who still live in the Salt River Pima–Indian Community, which borders Scottsdale's city limits.

In 1888, U.S. Army chaplain Winfield Scott bought 640 acres of rocky, desert land northeast of Phoenix. At $2.50 an acre, the purchase may be the Valley's best land deal on record. Scott saw the cheap desert land and its still-functioning canals as rife with opportunity, as well an ideal climate to recover from wounds he had sustained in the Civil War.

Scott and his wife, Helen, became the first of a succession of New Yorkers who would abandon the East Coast's cold, gray winters—and tell their friends about it. Scott used his oratory gifts to convince other families to move to his fledgling community of Orangedale. You can still see the olive trees Scott planted to mark the border of his original 40-acre orange grove down the center of 2nd Street and Civic Center Boulevard (across from the Scottsdale Center for the Performing Arts and Scottsdale Stadium). The citrus trees didn't prove to be as hardy, dying in a drought in the late 1890s.

During the next few decades, the small community attracted cowboys, ranchers and miners, as well as Native Americans looking to trade goods and tuberculosis patients seeking the dry desert air to recover from their respiratory ailments.

The mild winter climate and stark landscape even lured famed architect Frank Lloyd Wright, who was in Phoenix to consult on the design of the Arizona Biltmore Resort. Wright was so taken by the Sonoran Desert that he established his "winter camp," Taliesin West, at the base of the McDowell Mountains in 1937. The rocky desert site would serve as a constant source of inspiration until his death in 1959.

Following World War II, airmen who had trained at Scottsdale Airfield returned to the city, bringing their families and green lawns from the Midwest. The growing community, which was officially incorporated in 1951, attracted burgeoning high-tech corporations, like Motorola in 1956. Bill Keane, Scottsdale's answer to *Peanuts* creator Charles Schultz, reflected the postwar suburban boom in his comic strip, *Family Circus.*

Scottsdale became the first city in the nation to enact a sign ordinance in 1969, which restricted the size and height of billboards—a controversial measure that was even challenged at the U.S. Supreme Court.

New resorts and the availability of air-conditioning only increased Scottsdale's popularity. City leaders annexed huge swaths of land in the north, areas once roamed only by ranchers and wildlife. Developers happily created large master-planned communities with amenities like parks and golf courses, attracting retirees and young families. The skyrocketing home prices, new business parks, and chichi art galleries and shopping centers earned the increasingly affluent city the nickname "Snottsdale" by residents of neighboring communities.

Since the 1950s, Scottsdale has grown from 2,000 residents to nearly a quarter of a million. It seems the country's "Most Livable City," as it was deemed by the United States Conference of Mayors in 1993, has become one of its most desired.

Sights

Scottsdale's biggest attraction is the city's unapologetic resort lifestyle. You'll want to spend your time like the locals: shopping, eating and drinking, browsing art galleries, hitting the links, and hiking some of the region's most interesting desert mountains. Indulge at one of the world-class spas, and make time to visit Frank Lloyd Wright's winter home, Taliesin West.

DOWNTOWN
Old Town

There's no better place to begin a tour of "The West's Most Western Town." This touristy hodgepodge of restaurants, bars, and Old West–themed boutiques is a little cheesy, but you'll find some historic sites along with the kitschy shopping and art. And even if you're not a big shopper, the live music courtesy of singing cowboys on horseback and Native American performers makes for a fun "only in Arizona" experience.

Start at the beautifully landscaped **Scottsdale Civic Center Mall,** a 21-acre park ringed by chic hotels and restaurants, hole-in-the-wall bars, arts venues, and the city hall and library. The walkways, shaded by mesquite trees, and cool fountains attract visitors and residents year-round. You're likely to see friends playing chess in the sunken garden or a young girl posing for pictures in an elaborate white dress for her *quinceañera* (a Mexican coming-of-age ceremony held on a girl's 15th birthday).

Scottsdale bills itself as "The West's Most Western Town."

SCOTTSDALE

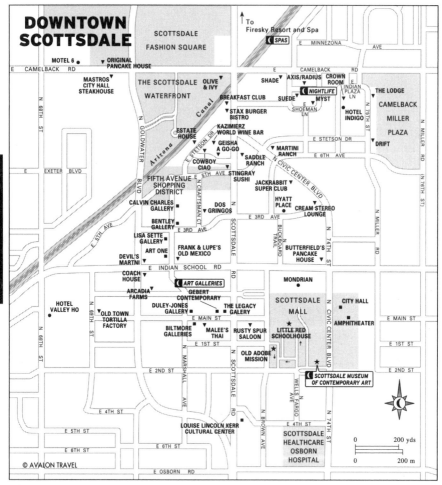

DOWNTOWN SCOTTSDALE

To
Firesky Resort and Spa

SPAS

E   MINNEZONA   AVE

SCOTTSDALE
FASHION SQUARE

MOTEL 6   ORIGINAL
                 PANCAKE HOUSE
E   CAMELBACK   RD   E   CAMELBACK   RD
          MASTROS   AXIS/RADIUS   CROWN
          CITY HALL   THE SCOTTSDALE   OLIVE   SHADE   ROOM
          STEAKHOUSE   WATERFRONT   & IVY   NIGHTLIFE   INDIAN   THE LODGE
                                           BREAKFAST CLUB   SUEDE   MYST   PLAZA
                                                                 SHOEMAN   HOTEL   CAMELBACK
                              STAX BURGER   LN   INDIGO   MILLER
                              BISTRO   PLAZA
                         KAZIMIERZ
                         WORLD WINE BAR   DRIFT
          ESTATE
          HOUSE   GEISHA   MARTINI
                         A GO-GO   RANCH
                                    SADDLE   E   6TH   AVE
                    COWBOY   RANCH
                    CIAO
          FIFTH AVENUE   STINGRAY
          SHOPPING   SUSHI   JACKRABBIT
          DISTRICT   SUPER CLUB
          CALVIN CHARLES   DOS   HYATT
          GALLERY   GRINGOS   PLACE   CREAM STEREO
                                                         LOUNGE
          BENTLEY
          GALLERY   E 3RD   AVE   E 3RD   AVE
          LISA SETTE
          GALLERY   BUTTERFIELD'S
          ART ONE   FRANK & LUPE'S   PANCAKE
          DEVIL'S   OLD MEXICO   HOUSE
          MARTNI
          COACH   E   INDIAN   SCHOOL   RD
          HOUSE
          ARCADIA   ART GALLERIES   MONDRIAN
          FARMS   GEBERT
                     CONTEMPORARY
          OLD TOWN   DULEY-JONES   THE LEGACY   SCOTTSDALE   CITY HALL
          TORTILLA   GALLERY   GALERY   MALL
          FACTORY   E MAIN ST   AMPHITHEATER   E MAIN ST
          BILTMORE   MALEE'S   RUSTY SPUR   LITTLE RED
          GALLERIES   THAI   SALOON   SCHOOLHOUSE   E 1ST ST
HOTEL   E 1ST   ST
VALLEY HO   OLD ADOBE
          E 2ND   ST   MISSION   E 2ND ST
                                              SCOTTSDALE MUSEUM
                                              OF CONTEMPORARY ART

          E 4TH   ST
          E 5TH ST   E 4TH ST
                    LOUISE LINCOLN KERR
                    CULTURAL CENTER   SCOTTSDALE
          E 6TH ST   HEALTHCARE   0   200 yds
                                             OSBORN
© AVALON TRAVEL   E OSBORN   RD   HOSPITAL   0   200 m

Across from the statue of Winfield and Helen Scott on the western end of the mall, you'll find the **Little Red Schoolhouse** (7333 E. Scottsdale Mall, 480/945-4499, www. scottsdalemuseum.org, 10 A.M.–5 P.M. Wed.–Sat., noon–8 P.M. Sun., closed July–Aug. and holidays), the original 1909 Scottsdale Grammar School that now houses the Scottsdale Historical Society. Inside, artifacts from the Scotts' home and a collection of historic photographs illustrate the city's modest beginnings as a territorial farm community.

Head east to the outdoor **amphitheater,** a popular site for festivals and outdoor concerts. You can see Robert Indiana's iconic *Love* sculpture on the lawn, along with a host of other public artworks.

On the far eastern end of the plaza, you'll see the Scottsdale **City Hall,** designed by native Arizonan Benny Gonzales, whose mid-20th-century modern interpretation of traditional Southwest design transformed the region's architecture.

◖ SCOTTSDALE MUSEUM OF CONTEMPORARY ART (SMOCA)

On the southern end of the mall, next to the Scottsdale Center for the Performing Arts, you'll see the city's best piece of contemporary architecture. SMoCA (7374 E. 2nd St., 480/994-2787, www.smoca.org, 10 A.M.–5 P.M. Tues.–Wed., 10 A.M.–8 P.M. Thurs., 10 A.M.–5 P.M. Fri.–Sat., noon–5 P.M. Sun., $7 adults, $5 students, kids under 15 free, admission free Thurs.) specializes in modern art, architecture, and design, providing a refuge for avant-garde art lovers in the land of cowboy paintings. Take a walk around the building before heading in. The "eggplant gray" stucco is meant to evoke the McDowell Mountain Range to the east while the shimmering steel facade reflects the frequently blue Arizona sky.

Inside, Will Bruder, the Desert Modernist architect behind Phoenix's Burton Barr Central Library, deftly converted five theaters of an old cinema into a series of flexible galleries. The ever-changing lineup of exhibitions can be a bit hit or miss, though the museum's perma outdoor installation, *Knight Rise,* never disap points. Gaze through an oculus in the ceiling, similar to Rome's Pantheon. The smooth, gray dome distorts your perception of sky, focusing your attention on the changing colors, from the morning's bright blues and evening's deep purples to gathering gray clouds on a stormy day.

OLD ADOBE MISSION

Established originally as Our Lady of Perpetual Help, Scottsdale's first Catholic church was built in 1933 by Mexican and Yaqui Indian families who settled in the area. Today, the Old Adobe Mission (1st St. and Brown Ave., 480/947-4331, www.olphaz.com, 10 A.M.–4 P.M. daily, Oct.–May, free admission, closed summers) is being restored to its former glory and is still used as a spiritual center. The brilliant white facade and domed bell tower of the Spanish Colonial Revival church were designed to resemble the Mission of San Xavier del Bac, south of Tucson. Peek inside to see the building's original adobe bricks

Scottsdale Museum of Contemporary Art (SMoCA)

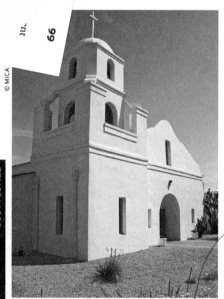

© MICA

the Old Adobe Mission, Scottsdale's first Catholic church

through a small cutaway in the plaster on the north wall. The bricks—which were made by blending local soil, straw, and water, then molded and baked in the sun—allow the walls to "breathe," moderating the church's temperature in both the summer and winter.

CENTRAL SCOTTSDALE AND PARADISE VALLEY
◀ Camelback Mountain

It doesn't require a great deal of imagination to make out the "kneeling camel" profile. Camelback Mountain, the Valley's most iconic landmark, straddles the communities of Phoenix, Scottsdale, and Paradise Valley, luring some 300,000 hikers to its red sandstone and granite cliffs every year.

The park preserves a 76-acre piece of the Sonoran Desert in the heart of the city, where bighorn sheep once scaled the dramatic rock formations and the ancient Hohokam civilization practiced religious rituals.

The federal government set aside Camelback as an Indian reservation until the late 1800s,

and it slipped into private hands in the 1940s. Finally, in 1968 private citizens, led by Sen. Barry Goldwater, arranged a land exchange that protected the mountain from future development. The event was marked by President Lyndon B. Johnson and Lady Bird Johnson, who walked the mountain in high heels.

Today, a good portion of Camelback has been protected for recreation, though multimillion dollar homes and posh resorts climb its base. For visitors not heading out to the desert, it's an excellent opportunity to see Sonoran critters like spiny lizards, roadrunners, rabbits, and, yes, the possible rattlesnake, in their native environment.

To get an up-close view of Camelback, explore the **Echo Canyon Recreation Area** (5700 N. Echo Canyon Pkwy., 602/256-3220, phoenix.gov/parks/hikecmlb.html) at the "camel's head," where you'll find **Praying Monk** rock. The freestanding, 80-foot-high rock tower, which looks like the camel's eyelashes from a distance, is a popular spot for rock climbers.

Taking one of the two trails to the 2,704-foot summit is not recommended for beginning hikers, but more confident climbers will be rewarded with 360-degree views of the Valley and the surrounding mountain ranges. The always-busy trailheads are open daily from sunrise to sunset, but parking is limited.

Cosanti

Paolo Soleri moved from Italy in 1947 to Scottsdale for a fellowship with Frank Lloyd Wright at Taliesin West. More than a half century later, Soleri has emerged as one of the region's most innovative architects, with an organic style that merges Wright's aesthetics with Native American influences. Cosanti (6433 E. Doubletree Ranch Rd., 480/948-6145, www.cosanti.com, 9 A.M.–5 P.M. Mon.–Sat., 11 A.M.–5 P.M. Sun., free) serves as Soleri's gallery, studio, and home, and reflects many of his theories on environmentally responsible design. The small village includes his original subterranean "Earth House," outdoor studios, student dorms, and a performance space, set amidst terraced courtyards and shaded paths.

ROCK YOUR WORLD

There's no better way to get in touch with the rocky Sonoran Desert than with these quintessential Scottsdale experiences.

- Hike Camelback Mountain's Echo Canyon Summit Trail for an up-close look at the 80-foot-tall **Praying Monk rock outcropping.**

- Enjoy a margarita, on the rocks, of course, at the Fairmont Scottsdale's **Stone Rose Lounge** (7575 E. Princess Dr., 480/585-4848). The swank bar by nightlife guru Rande Gerber (a.k.a. "Mr. Cindy Crawford") features two bars, including an open-air lounge that seems to float over a pool of water and white stones.

- Tee off at **Boulders Golf Club** (34631 N. Tom Darlington Rd., 480/488-9009, www.theboulders.com). The South Course's signature fifth-hole green sits at the base of a dramatic 12 million-year-old rock formation, which beckons rock climbers of all skill levels.

- Catch a **rock concert at Martini Ranch** (7295 E. Stetson Dr., 480/970-0500, 9 P.M.-1 A.M. Thurs., 8 P.M.-2 A.M. Fri.-Sun.). Coldplay, Kid Rock, Mandy Moore, and the French pop band Phoenix have all played the nightclub's intimate Main Stage. If there isn't a touring act in town, house band Rock Lobster covers retro Top 40 hits on the weekends.

- Relax with a Signature Massage at **The Spa at Camelback Inn** (5402 E. Lincoln Dr., 480/596-7040, www.camelbackspa.com, 6:15 A.M.-7:30 P.M. daily), which combines aromatherapy, reflexology, and a hot-and-cold **stone massage.** The Native American-inspired treatment places semiprecious stones on the chakras while cold aquamarine stones are used to massage facial contours.

- Snack on the Baja flatbread at **Kazimierz World Wine Bar** (7137 E. Stetson Dr., 480/946-3004, 6 P.M.-2 A.M. daily), a pizza-like appetizer topped by chipotle-orange **rock shrimp,** buffalo mozzarella, and *pepitas.* The walls of the wine bar-speakeasy are covered with stone, and the lounge's 3,000 vintages wow connoisseurs.

Much of Soleri's Arcosanti, an experimental artists' community 70 miles north of Phoenix, is funded by the sale of his "windbells." These metal and ceramic wind chimes, which start at $25, are designed and forged at Cosanti's on-site foundry and ceramics studio. The bronze casting process can be viewed weekday mornings.

McCormick-Stillman Railroad Park

Children and train buffs love McCormick-Stillman Railroad Park (7301 E. Indian Bend Rd., 480/312-2312, www.therailroadpark.com, open daily, closed Thanksgiving and Christmas), a popular city park near Paradise Valley that began as the personal ranch of Anne and Fowler McCormick, a grandson of John D. Rockefeller. Today, visitors can ride a scale reproduction of a Colorado narrow-gauge railroad that Anne's son, Guy Stillman, donated to the park (rumor has it Walt Disney tried to buy the railroad for one of his parks). The train carries passengers on a one-mile loop through a desert Xeriscape arboretum.

The park has an air of Old Americana meets Old West to it, with a general store selling hand-dipped ice cream and an adobe-style playground. The beautifully restored carousel and shaded ramadas make it a popular spot for parties, concerts, and events throughout the year.

Antique engines and train cars dot the property, including a Pullman car that was used by every president from Herbert Hoover to Dwight Eisenhower. Be sure to check out the "Merci Train," one of 49 boxcars donated by France to thank Americans for their aid after World War II. The cars were originally loaded with personal belongings that ranged from wooden shoes and toys to wedding dresses and war medals from dead soldiers. Admission to the park is free, with $1 tickets required to ride the train and carousel and to visit the museum exhibition. The train and carousel schedules vary per month. Check the website for detailed information on hours.

NORTH SCOTTSDALE
◖ Taliesin West

A literal hothouse for design, Frank Lloyd Wright's winter home, Taliesin West (12621 N. Frank Lloyd Wright Blvd., 480/860-2700, www.franklloydwright.org, 8:30 A.M.–5:30 P.M. daily), is the perfect synthesis of architecture and the desert.

Wright's use of local sand, gravel, and stone (what he called "desert masonry") creates the impression that the complex emerged out of the ground. He masterfully incorporated the environment by integrating indoor and outdoor spaces, diffusing harsh sunlight through canvas ceilings, and creating asymmetrical lines evocative of the surrounding mountains. The effect is simply stunning.

In 1927, Wright first came to Phoenix from his Wisconsin home, Taliesin, to serve as a consultant on the Arizona Biltmore. The architect was

© SCOTTSDALE CONVENTION & VISITORS BUREAU

Frank Lloyd Wright's Taliesin West

so captivated by the desert landscape and light that in 1937 he used the money from his Falling Water commission to purchase 600 acres of land in the foothills of the McDowell Mountains.

Wright's original "winter camp" evolved into a small cooperative community, where his architecture school apprentices helped with the building of Taliesin West and lived on-site in communal sleeping spaces. They were expected to study, help with chores, and even perform in Cabaret Theater and Music Pavilion, as Wright thought his students should be well-rounded individuals.

Some students chose to live in tents around the property, where they could experiment with their own designs and building techniques. This practice grew into a more formalized program of "apprentice shelters" that continues today, with older structures eventually being razed to make room for the designs of new students.

The insular community resembled a soap opera with its entangled affairs and desire to create a utopian society. In fact, the drama continues today, as members of the Frank Lloyd Wright Foundation, some in their 70s and 80s, still live on the property, protecting the vision of "Mr. Wright."

Today, the National Historic Landmark serves as the headquarters of the Wright foundation and its school of architecture. Guided tours, which vary throughout the year, are required to explore the property and range from a two-hour apprentice shelter tour to the Night Lights on the Desert. The popular 90-minute Insights tour ($32) showcases Wright's private living quarters and canvas-roofed office, where he designed many of his masterpieces, including the Guggenheim Museum and Tempe's Gammage Auditorium. Discounts are available for students, seniors, and large groups, as well as during the summer. Call ahead or visit the website for details.

Heard Museum North

Long before East Coast and Midwestern settlers began flooding into the Sonoran Desert, Native American tribes made their home in and around North Scottsdale's McDowell Mountains for two millennia. A visit to the Heard Museum North (32633 N. Scottsdale Rd., 480/488-9817, www.heard.org/north, 10 A.M.–5 P.M. Mon.–Sat., 11 A.M.–5 P.M. Sun., $5 adults, $4 seniors, $2 students, children under 6 free) provides a reminder that these indigenous people created a rich and unique culture.

The small museum's two galleries showcase items from the renowned collections of the Heard Museum in downtown Phoenix, including pots and bowls, kachina dolls, paintings, sculpture, and jewelry. It's easy to write off these ubiquitous treasures as Southwestern clichés, but their omnipresence documents the diverse tribes throughout Arizona.

The museum's shop gives folks the opportunity to purchase traditional and contemporary pottery, textiles, baskets, and artwork directly from Native American artisans.

Make sure to appreciate this stunning bit of desert just south of Carefree on Scottsdale Road. You'll see the rounded rock formations that gave the neighboring Boulders Resort its name. Don't be surprised to see javelina, desert rabbits, or quail walking through still rather undeveloped areas. Walk next door to the adobe-inspired **El Pedregal** shopping center, where you'll find shops, restaurants, and the occasional festival in its open-air courtyard.

Cave Creek

You're more likely today to find yuppie bikers and artist studios than cattlemen in Cave Creek, but the town manages to retain more of its Old West character than any other Valley community.

This hardscrabble outpost, first settled by miners and ranchers in the 1870s, has changed significantly. In the 1920s, tuberculosis camps first popped up in Cave Creek, as those suffering from lung ailments thought the dry desert air would cure them. By the 1940s and '50s, dude ranches took over old homesteads, and the visitors have been coming ever since.

You can get a sense of Cave Creek's Old West past and have a little tourist fun at **Frontier Town** (6245 E. Cave Creek Rd., 480/488-3317, www.frontiertownaz.com), an "1880s-style theme town." Sure, it's a little hokey, but you can't help but smile while walking the wooden boardwalks and dodging hitching posts and antique wagons on your way to grab a beer.

© MICA THOMAS MULLOY

Cave Creek

In the 1930s and '40s, the WPA set up camp, providing living quarters for workers building Bartlett Lake and Horseshoe Dams. Today, Frontier Town is home to restaurants with live music on the patio, gift shops, and even an old-time barber shop. The Leather Mill gift shop is housed in one of the original WPA cabins.

For an authentic slice of the Old West, the **Cave Creek Museum** (6140 E. Skyline Dr., 480/488-2764, cavecreekmuseum.com, 1–4:30 P.M. Wed.–Sun.) is just down the street from Frontier Town. You can see the last tuberculosis cabin in the state of Arizona, one of 16 cabins originally found in a 1920s camp.

Entertainment and Events

Scottsdale may not be the "city that never sleeps," but it sure goes to bed tired. Its pleasure-loving residents and visitors happily fill their days with weeklong culinary events and international film festivals while their evenings simmer with energy at performing arts venues, before coming to a full boil at the dozens of nightclubs and lounges that lure the Valley's self-indulgent party set, as well athletes and pop stars who regularly serve as tabloid fodder.

That's not to say you won't find less style-conscious venues where you can have fun. The Old West's saloons and gambling halls manage to live on. Cowboy bars still attract boot-wearing regulars to their live shows and honky-tonk dance floors, and casinos at the neighboring Indian communities now offer glittery slot machines along with a bit of old-fashioned poker.

🅒 NIGHTLIFE

With the exception of Las Vegas, no other city in the Southwest offers a nightlife with as much glitz as Scottsdale. The see-and-be-seen bars, thumping clubs, and trendy lounges are primarily located downtown. Put on your clubbing finest, as you'll be given the once-over by your fellow patrons (and probably a few bouncers). This is where the Gucci-loving set comes to preen and play.

Bars and Pubs

AZ88 (7353 Scottsdale Mall, 480/994-5576, 11:30 A.M.–1:30 A.M. Mon.–Fri., 5 P.M.–1:30 A.M. Sat.–Sun.) is a great place to eat, drink, and be seen. With its killer comfort food and first-class martinis, the perennial

Scottsdale favorite attracts older couples on their way to a show, as well as trendy scenesters who descend on the bar and mod all-white patio after 8 P.M. Try the classic French 75 martini or Pimm's Cup and scope out the chic glass-and-white-wall decor, which provides a minimalist backdrop for the over-the-top and always changing art installations.

The neighboring **Brackin's Bar** (7320 E. Scottsdale Mall, 480/945-2882, noon–midnight daily) is a more laid-back option. This comfortable hideaway, tucked into the grassy lawn of the Scottsdale Mall, is a great place to treat yourself to a late-afternoon drink. There's live music on the weekends, and the cozy fireplaces on its two patios are perfect for cooler evenings. And with $3 beers and cheap cocktails, you'd barely know you're in Old Town.

It's always fascinating when two worlds collide, and there's no better place to see the Old West meet high heels and hair product than at **Saddle Ranch** (4321 N. Scottsdale Rd., 480/429-2263, 11 A.M.–2:30 A.M. Mon.–Fri., 8 A.M.–2:30 A.M. Sat. and Sun.). But, hey, when in Rome…Take a shot of whisky and let out your inner urban cowboy by riding the bar's main attraction, a mechanical bull—which is thankfully surrounded by an inflatable mat and padded guards to protect from serious injuries.

The Polynesian-themed **Drift** (4341 N. 75th St., 480/949-8454, 11:30 A.M.–2 A.M.) invites patrons into its throwback lair by the glow of tiki lamps and a mammoth tropical aquarium behind the bar. The 1960s-flavored lounge serves up boldly colored drinks with the requisite umbrellas and fruit, and the two-for-one happy hour (4–7 P.M.) provides the perfect excuse to order a retro punch cocktail and flaming pupu platter.

Like a lone cabin in the woods, **The Lodge** (4422 N. 75th St., 480/945-0828, 11 A.M.–2 A.M. Mon.–Sat., 10:30 A.M.–2 A.M. Sun.) provides a warm retreat in the cold, glitzy forest of downtown's nightclub district. Look for the family of hand-carved Sasquatches at the entrance, and head into the cozy watering hole to order a drink at the honey-colored "log" bar. Don't be fooled by the pool table, small arcade, and wood-paneled walls—this is still Scottsdale, so expect an upscale crowd and a respectable menu. Nonetheless, the rustic decor is a charming alternative to the neighborhood's minimalist lounges, and it's hard to beat Bingo Tuesdays and Fish Fry Fridays.

Crown Room (7419 E. Indian Plaza, 480/423-0117, 5 P.M.–2 A.M. Mon.–Sat., 5 P.M.–midnight Sun.) offers low-key ambience, great drinks, and an inspired lounge decor in the city's nightclub epicenter. The martini bar shakes up an extensive menu of cocktails, from cosmos and manhattans to its signature cookie-dough martini, and the 30-something crowd is a little less clubby than you'll find at neighboring bars.

Wannabe Axl Roses and Whitney Houstons who may be a little shy will love the private karaoke rooms at **Geisha A Go-Go** (7150 E. 6th Ave., 480/699-0055, 5 P.M.–2 A.M. Tues.–Sun.), a rock 'n' roll Japanese bistro. Order Japanese beer or fruity Hello Kitty cocktails in the dark, wood-paneled bar, which serves as a Zen "rock" garden complete with bonsai tree and portraits of Jimi Hendrix and Jim Morrison. Couples and groups up to 20 people can rent the rooms by the hour (rates starting at $20 per hour for a four-person room), and reservations are recommended.

Yes, Virginia, there is a cool dive bar in the heart of trendy Scottsdale. Duck into **Coach House** (7011 E. Indian School Rd., 480/990-3433, 6 A.M.–2 A.M. Mon.–Sat., 10 A.M.–2 A.M. Sun.) Halloween through New Year's Eve to witness a holiday drinking miracle: thousands of Christmas lights covering the walls and ceiling of this tiny old wooden house. The bar is a popular destination year-round, though, attracting an impressively diverse mix of bar hoppers, club goers, and old regulars. Make a new friend over darts or pinball, or grab a seat on the patio.

Inspired by Mexico's casual beach bars, **Dos Gringos** (4209 N. Craftsman Ct., 480/423-3800, 11 A.M.–2 A.M. daily) packs in 20-something singles looking for cheap drinks and potential love. The raucous, open-air bar has three patios, and the kitchen serves Mexican standbys until close.

The chic **Olive & Ivy** (7135 E. Camelback Rd., 480/751-2200, 11 A.M.–midnight Sun.–Thurs., 11 A.M.–1 A.M. Fri.–Sat.) is a great place to see Scottsdale's professional set at play. The upscale Mediterranean restaurant offers decent food, but its posh decor and large outdoor lounge overlooking the Scottsdale Waterfront's Arizona Canal have made it a place to mingle. The people-watching hits its prime at 10 P.M., when a steady stream of styled 30- and 40-somethings sidle up to the bar for Grey Goose martinis.

Lounges and Wine Bars

Enjoy a drink at **Jade Bar** (5700 E. McDonald Dr., 480/948-2100, 10 A.M.–2 A.M. daily) early in evening, when you can catch Mummy Mountain bathed in a desert sunset. This chic, modern bar at Paradise Valley's Sanctuary on Camelback Mountain Resort & Spa is a stylish alternative to the gaudy lounges of Old Town. Try one of the signature cocktails, like the Celery Serano Margarita or the Grapefruit & Basil, a blend of lemongrass simple syrup, vodka, basil leaves, and fresh grapefruit juice.

If you're looking for great wine and a more adult crowd, **Kazimierz World Wine Bar** (7137 E. Stetson Dr., 480/946-3004, 6 P.M.–2 A.M. daily) provides an unpretentious retreat for friends or a romantic date. Serious wine lovers will appreciate the listing of 3,000 wines from around the world, which has earned regular recognition from *Wine Spectator* magazine for its depth and value. Curl up on one of the plush sofas and pair an Arizona varietal with one of the delicious Egyptian flatbreads. Be forewarned, though; "Kazbar" isn't easy to find: "Like all good speakeasys, the entrance is hidden in the rear."

Get ready—**Shade** (7277 E. Camelback Rd., 480/970-2100, 10 A.M.–2 A.M. daily) is Scottsdale at its $15 martini-loving, Louis Vuitton handbag-carrying, trendy jean-wearing finest. The uber-glam lounge at the W Scottsdale Hotel has become a nightlife staple, and on any given evening, you could be crashing some Hollywood celebrity's birthday party or the debut of a Valley resident on a reality TV show. If you can get past the velvet rope and unnecessarily rude bouncers, you'll be treated to some prime Scottsdale people-watching. Step outside to experience its poolside sibling Sunset Beach, a rooftop "beach bar" with white daybeds, "lounging pods," and spectacular views of the city.

Suede (7333 E. Indian Plaza, 480/970-6969, 7 P.M.–2 A.M. Wed.–Sat., 9 P.M.–2 A.M. Sun.) has been a nightlife fixture for years, thanks in part to the upscale atmosphere and namesake fabric that covers the furniture and walls. Don't let the Art Deco-inspired decor, cherrywood floor, and chandeliers fool you—this isn't a stuffy lounge for the older set. The dance floor is usually jammed with partiers, with music that ranges from house to lounge to top 40 and hip-hop, and its open patio is a heavenly retreat if you find someone to strike up a conversation with.

Dance Clubs and Live Music

A Scottsdale mainstay, **Martini Ranch** (7295 E. Stetson Dr., 480/970-0500, 9 P.M.–1 A.M. Thurs., 8 P.M.–2 A.M. Fri.–Sun.) covers a lot of bases if you're not sure where to begin your evening in downtown. Downstairs, you'll find one of the popular house bands covering '90s hits or heavy-metal favorites. Head outside to the patio for a drink before going upstairs to the Shaker Room, where you can dance to top 40 hits. Less pompous than some of Scottsdale's other nightclubs, it has become a solid venue for national acts looking for an intimate place to perform.

Welcome to the beating, cologne-scented heart of the city's nightlife scene. **Axis/**

Radius (7340 E. Indian Plaza, 480/970-1112, 9 P.M.–2 A.M. Thurs.–Sat.) is the quintessential Scottsdale club: beautiful people, large patios, velvet ropes, and expensive drinks. As nightclubs and bars come and go, this tireless legend manages to pack in hundreds of revelers weekend after weekend. A glass catwalk connects the two-clubs-in-one complex—top 40 and dance music on the left and hip-hop on the right.

Myst (7340 E. Shoeman Ln., 480/970-5000, 9 P.M.–2 A.M. Thurs.–Sat.) pumps out house music until close, and often imports well-known DJs like Paul van Dyk and Richard Vission. Wend your way through the sprawling, multilevel club and enjoy a cocktail in the sunken lounge or in the all-white Milk Room. Celebs and athletes, like Shaquille O'Neal, often host parties in this extravagant land of go-go dancers and limos.

Listen for the strumming guitars and clacking castanets on the Scottsdale Mall. **Pepin** (7363 E. Scottsdale Mall, 480/990-9026, 4 P.M.–2 A.M. Tues.–Sun.) presents live flamenco shows Friday and Saturday evenings during dinner, then clears out half the restaurant to make room for salsa dancing, which begins at 10 P.M. on Fridays and Saturdays, and at 9 P.M. on Sundays. You'll find dancers of all levels, but you can also take salsa and tango lessons throughout the week (call ahead for days and times).

The burlesque craze hit Scottsdale a few years ago with the opening of **Jackrabbit Supper Club** (4280 N. Drinkwater Blvd., 480/429-4494, 9 P.M.–2 A.M. Thurs.–Sat.). Today, the spray-on-tan crowd still enjoys the nightly—and quite tame—striptease shows that are choreographed to live jazz music. It's all a lot of campy fun, with acts ranging from belly dancers to va-va-voom bombshells clad in vintage-inspired lingerie. In between shows, the dance floor fills up with club-goers. And should things get a little too warm inside, head out to the patio, which has hosted the likes of Britney Spears and Arizona Cardinal Matt Leinart.

Bikini-clad women dancing in a tableside bathtub—you can decide if this crosses the line of tastefulness at **Cream Stereo Lounge**

(4252 N. Drinkwater Blvd., 602/222-9922, 8 P.M.–2 A.M. Wed.–Sun.). Billowy white curtains and a sleek white-on-white interior give this club a posh, minimalist feel, and its thumping house music and impressive sound system lure an energetic dance crowd. Still, the small club's pricy drinks and unfriendly doorman may not be everyone's cup of tea—well, more like Red Bull and vodka here—but the scene is something to behold.

You don't have to wear tight jeans or sport a tattoo sleeve to appreciate **The Rogue** (423 N. Scottsdale Rd., 480/947-3580, 8 A.M.–2 A.M. Mon.–Thurs., 6 A.M.–2 A.M. Fri.–Sat., 10 A.M.–2 A.M. Sun.). This trendy dive bar in South Scottsdale attracts skinny hipsters in funky glasses and punked-out kids to its small dance floor, where the DJ spins the likes of The Cure, Pat Benatar, and The Smiths. Grab a Pabst Blue Ribbon or a Stella Artois at the bar, and scope out one of the booths for some fun people-watching.

If you're looking for a quintessential slice of lounge-lovin' Scottsdale, head to **Devil's Martini** (4175 N. Goldwater Blvd., 480/947-7171, 5 P.M.–2 A.M. Thurs.–Fri., 8 P.M.–2 A.M. Sat.). You'll find an army of highlighted blondes in strappy tops and heels, and well-gelled guys in the requisite jeans and button-down shirts. Sure, it can all be a little pretentious, but it can be perversely fun. And should the just-out-of-college regulars seem a little young, a slightly older crowd gathers at the North Scottsdale location (10825 N. Scottsdale Rd., 480/348-1666, 5 P.M.–2 A.M. Thurs.–Fri., 8 P.M.–2 A.M. Sat.).

Anthropologists should gather at North Scottsdale's **Barcelona** (15440 N. Greenway Hayden Loop, 480/603-0370, 4 P.M.–2 A.M. Tues.–Sun.) to study the courtship rituals between the 40-somethings in Arizona. The oversized indoor/outdoor restaurant and nightclub offers live jazz and R&B in the evenings, and the dining room transforms into a dance club with a top 40 cover band after 10 P.M. The dress: "resort elegance."

Cowboy Bars and Saloons

An original stagecoach stop between Fort McDowell and Phoenix, **Greasewood Flat** (27375 N. Alma School Pkwy., 480/585-9430, 11 A.M.–1 A.M. daily) is a North Scottsdale landmark, serving up cold beers and barbecue grub for years. The popular open-air bar is the perfect place to grab a drink and chat at the picnic tables with bikers, real-life cowboys, and well-to-do locals. Dance to live music under the stars on the weekend, or bundle up next to one of the campfires on cool evenings.

Hang your hat, along with the hundred others that dangle from the rafters, at **Handlebar-J Restaurant and Saloon** (7116 Becker Lane, 480/948-0110, 11 A.M.–2 A.M. Mon.–Sat., 5 P.M.–2 A.M. Sun.). The country-western bar offers live music every night, and its outdoor bar can't be beat. Even if you're not a fan of country music, you can't help but have a great time with the locals who pack the dance floor seven nights a week. Even Loretta Lynn and Lyle Lovett have been known to pop in. Handlebar-J offers country dance lessons Monday, Wednesday, Thursday, and Sunday nights at 7 P.M.

"Scottsdale's Oldest Saloon," **Rusty Spur Saloon** (7245 E. Main St., 480/425-7787, 11 A.M.–2 A.M. daily) is a no-fuss option tucked into a former bank in Old Town—the original vault now stores alcohol. There's live entertainment every day, though it can quickly get crowded.

CASINOS

Thanks to two neighboring Native American communities, Scottsdale is within easy access of three big casinos, offering gaming 24 hours a day. And because the gaming houses are on sovereign tribal land, smoking is allowed indoors.

Operated by the Salt River Pima–Maricopa Indian Community, **Casino Arizona** (480/850-7777, www.casinoaz.com) has two locations just off the Highway 101 (Loop 101). The largest, **Casino Arizona at Salt River** (Highway 101 and McKellips Rd.) has more than a thousand slot machines, in addition to two blackjack rooms and a keno parlor. For a break from the din of the casino, the 250-seat theater regularly books national acts, and its Showstoppers Live event/show features impersonations of classic music acts like Elvis, Madonna, and The Four Tops.

Less than 10 minutes up the road, Lady Luck pays off better at **Casino Arizona at Indian Bend** (Highway 101 and Indian Bend Rd.), with its 637 slots, 42 blackjack tables, keno, off-track betting, and decent poker room.

The **Fort McDowell Casino** (10424 N. Fort McDowell Rd., 480/837-1424, www.fortmcdowellcasino.com), operated by the Fort McDowell Yavapai Nation, is a little bit further out of town. Take Shea Boulevard 20 minutes east to State Route 87 (Beeline Highway) toward the town of Fountain Hills, and turn left on Fort McDowell Road. More than 800 gaming machines, 55 table and poker games, live keno, and regular bingo and poker tournaments throughout the week should keep any gambler busy.

PERFORMING ARTS

The **Scottsdale Center for the Performing Arts** (7380 E. 2nd St., 480/994-2787, www.scottsdaleperformingarts.org) showcases a host of live events, from theater and comedy to music and dancing. The SCA's white Modernist pavilion, which just underwent an extensive renovation, and its stages have featured a diverse roster of touring acts, like Etta James, Dave Brubeck, Kronos Quartet, and David Sedaris. Larger shows are held at its **Virginia G. Piper Theater** (7380 E. 2nd St., 480/994-2787), but you'll also find touring acts and local performers at **Stage 2** (7380 E. 2nd St., 480/994-ARTS, www.scottsdaleperformingarts.org) and **Theater 4301** (corner of Drinkwater Blvd. and 5th Ave., 480/994-2787, www.scottsdaleperformingarts.org), which are both located in the Galleria Corporate Centre.

The open-air **amphitheater** (75th St. and Main St., 480/994-ARTS, www.scottsdaleperformingarts.org), just outside SCA on Scottsdale Mall's grassy lawn, provides a lovely setting for concerts. Be sure to catch **Native Trails,** a free show by elaborately costumed Native American performers, which gives attendees the opportunity see a traditional powwow and hoop dancing Thursday and Saturday afternoons, January through early April.

For 50 years, the **Louise Lincoln Kerr Cultural Center** (6110 N. Scottsdale Rd.,

Eldred Matt, a dancer in Scottsdale's *Native Trails*

480/596-2660, www.asukerr.com) has served as an artist colony for emerging musicians, artists, and writers. Today, Kerr's beautifully maintained adobe home and guesthouses provide an intimate setting for jazz, choral, and chamber music performances.

FESTIVALS AND EVENTS

Thanks to the near-perfect weather in the winter and spring, it's not hard to catch a fun outdoor festival well into April.

January

The **Barrett Jackson Auto Auction** (16601 N. Pima Rd., 480/663-6255, www.barrett-jackson. com) kicks off the social calendar with an impressive showcase of luxury and historic vehicles. The weeklong event at the WestWorld complex in North Scottsdale is one of the largest and best-attended auto auctions in the world.

The annual **Celebration of Fine Art** (southeast corner of Scottsdale Rd. and Mayo Blvd., 480/443-7695, www.celebrateart.com) runs January through March, when big white tents dot the desert near Scottsdale Road and Highway 101 (Loop 101). Some 100 artists set up their studios, allowing browsers and buyers to peruse an extensive collection of Western and contemporary paintings, sculptures, glass, ceramics, and jewelry.

SCOTTSDALE

THE GREATEST SHOW ON GRASS

The **FBR Open** (www.phoenixopen.com) is the biggest party in town – and the largest event on the PGA Tour, luring nearly a half million people to TPC Scottsdale over the course of a week.

The infamous annual event, usually held in late January or early February, is not your traditional, polite-applause tournament. In fact, it's more like a nightclub on the fairway. You're as likely to see seniors with scorecards as 20-somethings in tube tops and heels, barhopping from beer gardens to VIP skyboxes. The plentiful bars and young crowds fuel a raucous party atmosphere, so much so that Tiger Woods, who sunk a legendary hole-in-one on the 16th hole, has vowed not to return.

TPC Scottsdale's Stadium Course was specifically designed to accommodate an "unlimited number of people." And by the final day, that can mean as many as 50,000 fans gathered around the 18th hole to watch pros like Phil Mickelson and Vijay Singh sink a tournament-winning putt.

Golf is only part of the draw, though, with half the crowd arriving when the sun sets and the putting is over. These latecomers flock to the Birds Nest, a party tent where big-name bands entertain thousands of carousers with drinks.

The Thunderbirds, a group of the Valley's leading businessmen, have hosted the event since 1939, making it one of the five oldest events on the PGA tour. It's the philanthropic group's biggest fundraiser, netting more than $50 million for Arizona charities. Admission begins at $25 per day, though there are additional fees for skyboxes and entrance to the after-hours Birds Nest.

© SCOTTSDALE CONVENTION & VISITORS BUREAU

© SCOTTSDALE CONVENTION & VISITORS BUREAU

Pony Express riders at Parada del Sol Rodeo

February

A bit of old Arizona that manages to hang on, **Parada del Sol Rodeo** (various venues, 480/990-3179, www.paradadelsol.org) reminds Scottsdale residents in late February that despite the BMWs and designer sunglasses, this is still the Wild West. The month-long event includes a Pony Express ride, dances, and live country music, culminating in a professional rodeo and the "World's Largest Horsedrawn Parade" in Old Town.

Also in February, the 50-year-old **Scottsdale Arabian Horse Show** (16601 N. Pima Rd., 480/515-1500, www.scottsdaleshow.com) gathers some 2,000 Arabian horses at WestWorld for 10 days of shows, competitions, demonstrations, and seminars.

March

The three-day **Scottsdale Arts Festival** (3939 N. Drinkwater Blvd., 480/874-4699, www.scottsdaleartsfestival.org) in March gathers 200 jury-selected artists and 40,000 visitors

to the Scottsdale Mall for entertainment, artist demonstrations, live music and exhibitions galore.

April

This city is a foodie mecca, so it's little wonder why the **Scottsdale Culinary Festival** (3939 N. Drinkwater Blvd., 480/945-7193, www.scottsdaleculinaryfestival.org) in April entices 40,000 people to eat, drink, and party. Taste the hard work of local restaurants and national celebrity chefs at the festival's Great Arizona Picnic on the Scottsdale Mall, or dine at one of the dozen events around town.

October

The small but surprisingly good **Scottsdale International Film Festival** (7001 E. Highland Ave., 602/410-1074, www.scottsdalefilmfestival.com) in October attracts audiences to Harkins Camehview Theater, with a global assortment of dramas, comedies, and documentaries.

Shopping

Scottsdale loves to shop. Luxury brands, cool boutiques, Native American crafts and jewelry, authentic cowboy boots and hats—this city has it all. Scottsdale is also home to the country's third-largest art market, with galleries featuring traditional Southwestern pieces as well as cutting-edge, contemporary installations that blend painting, sculpture, glass, and ceramics.

Spend some time browsing downtown shops and galleries to find those "only in Arizona" souvenirs. If you're in need, though, of an air-conditioned getaway in the summer, the colossal Scottsdale Fashion Square Mall has nearly 200 stores to keep your credit cards busy. The majority of the city's retail options are found at malls and open-air shopping centers along Scottsdale Road.

SHOPPING CENTERS AND DISTRICTS
Old Town and the Arts Districts

Park your car at the old hitching posts and make your way down the covered sidewalks. Next to the Scottsdale Civic Center Mall, **Bischoff's at the Park** (3925 N. Brown Ave., 480/946-6155, 10 A.M.–5:30 P.M. daily) is a terrific place to pick up Southwestern souvenirs, including books, rugs, Hopi kachina dolls, and Pima baskets and pottery. The store's brick walls and high ceilings originally housed a bank, which explains why Bischoff's doesn't feel as touristy as some of the other shopping options in Old Town. Pick up a few postcards inside, and head out to the charming shaded courtyard to jot down a few notes to friends.

The larger **Bischoff's Shades of the West** (7247 E. Main St., 480/945-3289, 9 A.M.–9 P.M. Mon.–Fri., 9 A.M.–8 P.M. Sat., 9 A.M.–7 P.M. Sun.) offers "everything needed to transform a bunkhouse into a Southwestern palace," from Mexican glasses and blankets to bronze hardware.

You can smell the leather when you walk through the door of **Saba's** (7254 E. Main St., 480/949-7404, 10 A.M.–7 P.M. Mon.–Fri., 10 A.M.–6 P.M. Sat., noon–5 P.M. Sun.). "Arizona's Original Western Store" has grown considerably since David Saba opened his first trading post in 1927, and you'll still find co-owner Roger Saba selling belt buckles and hats to real cowboys and old friends almost every day. Check out the wall of boots and children's fringe leather vests across the street at its sister store (3965 N. Brown Ave., 480/947-7664, same hours).

It seems like you can't turn a corner in Old Town without bumping into one of the **Gilbert Ortega Galleries,** mammoth emporiums filled with Navajo rugs, antler chandeliers, turquoise jewelry, equestrian art, and even headdresses, in a range of prices. The best of the bunch is the **Gilbert Ortega Gallery & Museum** (3925 N. Scottsdale Rd., 480/990-1808, 10 A.M.–6 P.M. Sun.–Tues., 10 A.M.–9 P.M. Wed.–Sat.). If you're looking for the perfect Southwest souvenir, you'll find something here.

Civil War buffs and Old West admirers should stop in at **Guidon Books** (7117 Main St., 480/945-8811, 10 A.M.–5 P.M. Mon.–Sat.). Proprietor Aaron L. Cohen packs his tiny bookstore with new and out-of-print specialty titles about Western America and the Civil War. Peruse the shelves, where you'll find categories that range from women of the West and Union generals to Indian crafts and Southwest furniture.

Between its Scottsdale store, catalog, and website, **The Poisoned Pen** (4014 N. Goldwater Blvd., 480/947-2974, 10 A.M.–7 P.M. Mon.–Fri., 10 A.M.–6 P.M. Sat., noon–5 P.M. Sun.) is the world's largest bookstore specializing in mysteries, crime, and espionage. Owner Barbara Peters says it comes down to one simple tenet: "You have to know your customers." In addition to the dozens of signed and first edition mysteries, the bookstore hosts some 200 events a year.

STRIP SEARCH

Travelers to Phoenix and Scottsdale at some point will visit the ubiquitous strip centers that line streetscapes across the Valley. Like many cities in the West, Phoenix came of age after the birth of the automobile and, as a result, the city's postwar building boom created a city tailor-made to serve the automobile.

Despite their bland facades, though, strip centers are frequently home to some of the city's most noteworthy mom-and-pop businesses, from ethnic restaurants to yoga studios and vintage shops. **Hilton Village** (6149 N. Scottsdale Rd.), near Paradise Valley, for example, features popular restaurants, trendy boutiques and salons, and even a gourmet cupcake shop.

Scottsdale Fashion Square

Shoppers, welcome to your temple. The nearly two-million-square-foot Scottsdale Fashion Square (Camelback Rd. and Scottsdale Rd., downtown, 480/941-2140, 10 A.M.–9 P.M. Mon.–Sat., 11 A.M.–6 P.M.) is one of the country's best shopping centers. High-end department stores like Nordstrom, Neiman Marcus, and a new Barneys New York anchor the vast air-conditioned megamall, and the impressive list of luxe boutiques should send any fashionista's heart racing: Burberry, Kate Spade, Gucci, Louis Vuitton, Tiffany and Co., Cartier, and Bottega Veneta, just to name drop a few. Shoppers will also find the usual mall standbys like Banana Republic and Anthropologie, along with local shops like Hub Clothing, a hipster favorite selling trendy jeans, cool jackets, and one-of-a-kind tees.

SouthBridge

This new complex of "mix-and-mingle-style" shops and restaurants along the Arizona Canal brought an ambitious concept to Scottsdale: a chain-free, walkable "urban village." SouthBridge's retail shops, collectively known as **The Mix** (5th Ave. and Stetson Dr.,

downtown, www.themixshops.com), blend into a dozen interconnected boutiques that neatly fall into four concepts: Nest (home furnishings), Live (fashion), Cherish and Treasure (beauty and treats), and Play (sporting goods and memorabilia). You'll find unique fashions and quintessential Scottsdale looks, like Ed Hardy hoodies, Affliction t-shirts, studded handbags, and Betsy Johnson creations.

The Mix's **Elan** (480/941-5575, 10 A.M.–8 P.M. Mon.–Sat., noon–5 P.M. Sun.) specializes in new designers from around the world, offering summer dresses, trendy jeans, and an in-house jewelry line. For the fashionable little one, **Garage: A Body Shop & Filling Station** (480/556-6900, 10 A.M.–6 P.M. Mon.–Wed., 10 A.M.–8 P.M. Thurs.–Sat., noon–5 P.M. Sun.) mixes rock-and-roll style with high-end designers like Little Marc by Marc Jacobs and Sonia Rykiel. Kids will want to pull up a seat to the Candy and Cupcake Bar.

Nestldown (480/941-5599, 10 A.M.–6 P.M. Mon.–Wed., 10 A.M.–8 P.M. Thurs.–Sat., noon–5 P.M. Sun.) stocks luxury European linens, which can be monogrammed, as well as bath accessories, baby items, and garden products.

See where the little dogs that ride in designer handbags go to get pampered at **Oh My Dog! Boutique + Spa** (480/874-1200, 10 A.M.–6 P.M. Mon.–Sat.). Pick up an organic treat or a couple of sweaters from lines such as Ruff Ruff Couture and Little Lilly (yes, that's Paris Hilton's "dog couture" line). OMD's spa has a glass window that allows pet owners to watch their furry babies get deep conditioning massages and custom hairstyles.

The Borgata

The Borgata (Scottsdale Rd. and Lincoln Rd., downtown, 602/953-6538, 10 A.M.–7 P.M. Mon.–Sat., noon–6 P.M. Sun.) is an intimate destination for shoppers who would prefer to avoid the crowds and big-name stores at Scottsdale Fashion Square. Inspired by the Italian hillside town of Borgata, the open-air mall's stone walls and turrets may look a little out of place in Scottsdale, but its 30 upscale shops, galleries, and restaurants are convenient options for visitors staying in Paradise Valley.

The eco-friendly Twig & Twill Boutique showcases organic maternity wear, children's apparel, and linens, many of which support environmental causes, while small resort wear boutiques like Fresh Produce, The Beach House Swimwear, and Lilly Pulitzer's Pink Paradise round out the retail offerings. There is live jazz on Friday evenings, and events are often scheduled for the weekends.

Kierland Commons

The perfectly manicured Kierland Commons (Greenway Pkwy. and Scottsdale Rd., North Scottsdale, 480/348-1577, 10 A.M.–9 P.M. Mon.–Sat., noon–6 P.M. Sun.) was the first mall in the Valley to kick off the "urban village" concept, updating the idea of small-town Main Street. Park streetside and stroll the complex's sidewalks, small gardens, and water fountains, where you'll see children playing on warm afternoons.

Restaurants, bars, and big-name chains like J. Crew, Juicy Couture, and French Connection set up shop on the ground floor, while residents live upstairs in steel-and-glass condos. Pop into Hemingway's Cigar Boutique for a quality stogie or Bacchus Wine Made Simple, which specializes in small boutique wines from around the world. Local boutiques like Jennifer Croll and glam-rock 42 Saint are fun stops at this oh-so-North Scottsdale outdoor pedestrian mall.

El Pedregal

The Moroccan-style El Pedregal (Scottsdale Rd. and Carefree Hwy., North Scottsdale, 480/488-1072, 10 A.M.–5:30 P.M. Mon.–Sat., noon–5 P.M. Sun.) fits nicely into the beautiful desert surroundings near Carefree. The open-air shopping center features 30 upscale restaurants and stores, including upscale boutique for men's and women's resort wear, leather goods, and jewelry. **D&G Contemporary Designs,** a local favorite for interior design and home furnishings, sells candles, home fragrances, and gifts. The **Paul's Pantry** specializes in

© MICA THOMAS MULLOY

Kierland Commons, an open-air shopping center in North Scottsdale culinary treats and unique hostess gifts. The plaza's outdoor amphitheater serves as a frequent venue for concerts, live theater, dances, and charity events.

Frontier Town

Whether you arrive by car or motorcycle, the shops at Cave Creek's Frontier Town (6245 E. Cave Creek Rd., North Scottsdale, 480/488-9129) will seem like another world compared to Scottsdale's high-end shopping centers. Join the "Creekers" and bikers who frequent the barber shop and saloon. Amble down the touristy wooden sidewalks, and pick up a few Arizona souvenirs at the Gloria Bee's or the Totem Pole (you can't miss its carved namesake out front). Leather Mill sells jackets, chaps, and other "motorcycle leather goods."

Just down the street, **The Town Dump** (6820 E. Cave Creek Rd., 480/488-9047, 10 A.M.–6 P.M. daily) is packed with furniture, old light fixtures, giant metal lizards, rusted gates, and brightly painted Mexican pottery. The indoor/outdoor shop almost lives up to its motto as "one of the world's most unusual stores."

◼ ART GALLERIES

Scottsdale's 100-plus art galleries are among the city's biggest attractions and an important center of commerce. Only New York and Santa Fe can tout larger art markets. Traditionally, Western and Native American art dominated the scene, but now a host of contemporary galleries showcase some of the art world's biggest names as well as emerging talent.

Most of the city's galleries are clustered in the Marshall Way, 5th Avenue, and Main Street arts districts, located just west of Scottsdale Road in Downtown. It's not too hard to find attractive pieces to take home, though prices aren't exactly "inexpensive" at the larger, more established galleries. Also, you can expect shorter hours at galleries in the summer, so be sure to call ahead for times.

The best way to become a part of the art scene—at least for an evening—is to join the weekly Thursday night **Scottsdale ArtWalk** (www.scottsdalegalleries.com). Socialize with

SCOTTSDALE ARTWALK

The best way to become a part of the art scene – at least for an evening – is to join the weekly Thursday night Scottsdale ArtWalk (www.scottsdalegalleries.com). Socialize with artists, collectors, curators, and Valley residents from 7 to 9 P.M., when almost all the downtown galleries open their doors for the popular event.

artists, collectors, curators, and Valley residents 7–9 P.M., when almost all downtown galleries open their doors for the popular event.

Contemporary

The beautifully curated paintings, sculptures, photographs, and drawings at **Bentley Gallery** (4161 N. Marshall Way, 480/946-6060, 9:30 A.M.–5:30 P.M. Tues.–Sat., www.bentleygallery.com) make it one of Scottsdale's best contemporary art galleries. Bentley's impressive roster of established artists includes Richard Serra, Dominique Blain, and Dale Chihuly.

The polished concrete floors, high ceilings, and natural light make **Calvin Charles Gallery** (4201 N. Marshall Way, 480/421-1818, 10 A.M.–6 P.M. Mon.–Sat., www.calvincharles.com) a terrific spot to view contemporary works by mid-career and emerging artists. Collectors will find modern works from China, Vietnam, and Japan, as well as Europe and the Americas. A smattering of Asian antiques rounds out the gallery, and the rooftop sculpture terrace offers a nice view of Camelback Mountain.

Gebert Contemporary (7160 E. Main St., 480/429-0711, www.gebertartaz.com, 10 A.M.–5 P.M. Mon.–Sat., noon–4:30 P.M. Sun.) specializes in abstract painting and sculpture by contemporary artists. Misha Gordin's stark black-and-white photography is particularly at home in the minimalist gallery.

Lisa Sette Gallery (4142 N. Marshall Way, 480/990-7342, 10 A.M.–5 P.M. Tues.–Fri., noon–5 P.M. Sat., www.lisasettegallery.com)

always puts on a good show—15 of them a year, in fact. The thoughtful artworks, often with a political or social comment, include painting, sculpture, photography, and mixed-media installation. Be sure to check out Matthew Moore's photographs of suburban sprawl, James Turrell's forays into capturing light, and William Wegman's quirky dog portraits.

If you don't have the deep pockets to invest in a piece of art, two terrifically low-key galleries highlight the works of emerging talent. **Art One** (4120 N. Marshall Way #1, 480/946-5076, www.artonegalleryinc.com, 10 A.M.–5:30 P.M. Tues.–Sat.) showcases reasonably priced paintings and sculpture by young and emerging artists, including local students. The regularly changing lineup can be a fun way to dip your toes into the art world.

Cowboy, Native American, and Southwestern
With more than 100 artists, **The Legacy Gallery** (7178 Main St., 480/945-1113, www.legacygallery.com, 10 A.M.–5:30 P.M. Mon.–Sat., 11 A.M.–5 P.M. Sun.) is one of Scottsdale's largest Southwestern art galleries. Survey the Native American portraits, Western landscapes, romantic pastels, and life-size bronze sculptures. You may even be tempted to take one home.

The gallery **Legacy Contemporary** (7178 Main St., 480/945-1113, www.legacy contemporary.com, 10 A.M.–5:30 P.M. Mon.–Sat., 11 A.M.–5 P.M. Sun.) filters Western imagery through a modern lens. You'll see pop-art colors, Dali-esque surrealism, abstracted images, and screened canvases inspired by Andy Warhol.

Trailside Galleries (7330 Scottsdale Mall, 480/945-7751, www.trailsidegalleries.com, 10 A.M.–5:30 P.M. Mon.–Sat.) offers classic Western art, with colorful paintings of wildlife, traditional scenes of the Old West, and expansive landscapes, as well as an extensive collection of bronze sculpture.

The small and understated **Duley-Jones Gallery** (7100 E. Main St., 480/945-8475, www.duleyjones.com, 10 A.M.–5 P.M. Mon.–Sat.) brings a fresh eye to its collection of Southwestern art. The gallery's paintings, ceramics, glassworks, and mixed-media sculpture range from the traditional to the whimsical and modern.

The oldest major fine art gallery in the West, **Biltmore Galleries** (7113 E. Main St., 480/947-5975, www.biltmoregalleries.com, 10 A.M.–5 P.M. Mon.–Sat.) specializes in 19th- and 20th-century American artists. The impressionistic cowboy paintings, blazing sunsets, and barren landscapes are evocative of another era.

Sports and Recreation

Resorts and nightlife aren't all Scottsdale has to offer. Its spectacular desert setting makes it an ideal place to get out and explore nature first-hand. The Sonoran Desert may only get an average of seven inches of rain per year, but its various plants and animals make it one of the most diverse ecosystems on Earth.

You've probably been lured to Scottsdale by the city's sweeping desert landscapes and color-saturated sunsets, but the best way to truly appreciate this unique locale is by experiencing it firsthand—whether on bike, on a raft, or on the links.

Oh, and be sure to drink lots of water, especially in the summer. Many visitors are easily caught off-guard by the heat and dehydrating arid climate.

ADVENTURE TOURS
When summertime temperatures soar, most animals in the Sonoran Desert go nocturnal. Catch a glimpse of this secret world by donning night-vision goggles with **Desert Storm Hummer Tours** (480/922-0020, www.dshummer.com, $125 adult, $100 child). Guides explain how plants and animals adapt to the

SCOTTSDALE

DO YOU LOVE THE NIGHTLIFE?

Sure, Scottsdale boasts lots of sunshine and clear, blue skies, but it's at night when the Sonoran Desert comes alive.

With the summer's scorching daytime heat, most of the desert's wildlife comes out to play at night. Catch coyotes, tarantulas, and owls prowling the rocky terrain by donning night-vision goggles with **Desert Storm Hummer Tours** (480/922-0020, www.dshummer.com, $125 adult, $100 child). Guides take you far from the city lights for an in-depth look at this fascinating ecosystem. Be sure to hunt down scorpions with the professional-grade UV lights that cause the arachnids to glow.

Thanks to the Southwest's minimal "light pollution," Arizona's skies twinkle with some of the best stargazing in the country. Venture with astronomers into the desert to survey the heavens with the aid of state-of-the-art telescopes and constellation charts. **Sky Jewels** (602/294-6775, www.gemland. com) features one- and two-hour astronomy tours, with some Scottsdale resorts offering the course free of charge for guests, includ-

ing The Four Seasons, which also equips its suites with telescopes.

Dance under the stars at **Greasewood Flat** (480/585-9430, www.greasewoodflat.net), a former stagecoach stop that now houses an open-air bar, stage, and dance floor. Head into the 120-year-old bunkhouse to order a beer and burger, then plop down at one of the picnic tables next to the regular bikers, cowboys, and businesspeople. And even if you're not the two-steppin' kind, the live country-western music will keep your foot tappin' late into the evening.

For design buffs, a twilight visit to **Taliesin West** (480/860-2700, www.franklloydwright. org, $38 adult, $34 Student) is a real thrill. The two-hour Night Lights on the Desert tour gives visitors the opportunity to see Frank Lloyd Wright's winter home lit from within, giving fresh perspective to the architect's masterful use of geometric forms and masonry materials. Perched in the foothills of the McDowell Mountains, the home's views of the city's glimmering lights can't be beat. Reservations are highly recommended, and be sure to call ahead for days, times, and prices.

extreme conditions of the desert and even lead kids in a safer-than-it-sounds scorpion hunt using UV lights that cause stinging insects to glow yellow.

Stellar Adventures (877/878-3552, stellaradventures.com) offers a variety of ways to get out in the desert and get dirty, from ATV rentals ($150 per rental) and Blazer tours ($95 adult, $75 child) of mining ghost towns and ancient Native American ruins to "advanced" Hummer tours ($165) that show off the rock-hopping, wall-climbing, hole-busting capabilities of the military vehicles.

For the next step in Jeep safaris, try driving your own Tomkat off-road vehicle with **Desert Wolf Tours** (877/613-9653, desertwolftours. com, $165). A cross between an ATV and a baby Hummer, the golf cart–sized vehicles were originally developed for the Israeli Defense Forces, but they'll take you over rocky roads

and through desert washes on a guided tour that brings new meaning to the word convoy.

BALLOONING

There are few better ways to get a new perspective on the desert than by gliding silently above it in a hot-air balloon. On calm days, the sky might be dotted with dozens of the colorful balloons, but inside the basket, the world feels like it's all yours.

A Balloon Experience by Hot Air Expeditions (480/502-6999, www.hotairexpeditions.com) flies its balloons about 400 feet above the desert floor, low enough to see critters like jackrabbits, roadrunners, and coyotes. But the best part might come after landing. A red-carpet welcome that includes either a champagne breakfast or full dinner catered by award-winning Arizona chef Vincent Gerithault's restaurant, Vincent's, awaits

($175). The company is FAA-certified and offers free hotel transfers.

Fliers on **A Great American Balloon Co.** (877/933-6359, www.wedoflyscottsdale.com) celebrate every flight with a champagne toast, with prices starting at $170 an hour. The company is FAA-certified and has 30 years of experience flying.

Anyone short on time or transportation might want to try a combined jeep tour/balloon flight with **Adventures Out West/ Unicorn Balloons** (480/991-3666, www.adventuresoutwest.com, $250 adult, $185 child). Jeeps pick you up at most hotels in Scottsdale, and guides fill the time driving out to the balloon-launch site by telling tales of Arizona's Old West past. Following the flight, guides lead extended desert tours focused on plants and wildlife—adventurous souls might even partake in eating a cactus. If you're not interested in the jeep tour you can opt for just the balloon flight ($135).

BIKING
Mountain Biking

Some of the finest mountain-biking trails in the U.S. snake their way up the rocky peaks and through the desert washes in and around Scottsdale. **The Pemberton Trail** is one of the best. Located just north of Scottsdale in the scenic **McDowell Mountain Regional Park** (www.maricopa.gov/parks/mcdowell), this 15.4-mile loop shoots riders up and down rolling hills along a trail that alternately narrows to single-track and widens to open speed-runs. It's easy enough for novice riders to navigate but varied enough to keep even the hard-core adventurer interested.

Another good destination for the intrepid mountain biker is the maze of trails beneath the power lines running north of **Pima and Dynamite Roads.** Pedal northeast of the parking area along a Jeep road. After a mile or so, single-track trails start to branch off to the right and left. Most go up and down the rocky hills nearby and eventually return to the access road under the power lines, so just pick your favorite and let it rip.

For a more organized experience—not to mention transportation and bike rentals—call **Desert Biking Adventures** (602/320-4602, www.desertbikingadventures.com). The company specializes in three- and four-hour biking tours that include bikes, helmets, and other attire, and a guide will pick you up at most Scottsdale resorts and hotels. Rides can be customized by skill level, and most are arranged so that pedaling uphill is optional. Tours start at $80.

Road Biking

Road bikers shouldn't feel left out, either. Speeding along **Pima Road to Bartlett Lake** (start anywhere north of Frank Lloyd Wright Boulevard) is popular with the skinny-tire crowd. The ride passes through stunning high desert and quite a few tony neighborhoods, but the full distance from Frank Lloyd Wright to the dam is about 60 miles. Park farther north along Pima for a quicker out-and-back.

Other good tips can be had at local bike shops, including **Rage Cycles** (2724 N.

mountain biking in McDowell Mountain Regional Park

SCOTTSDALE

Scottsdale Rd., 480/968-8116, www.ragecy-cles.com), or from the **Phoenix Metro Bicycle Club** (www.sportsfun.com/gaba), which schedules regular group rides.

GOLF

Golf may have been born in Scotland, but it has been transformed into a way of life in Scottsdale. The natural, rocky terrain and lack of rainfall may seem like an odd match for acre after acre of thirsty greens. Yet Scottsdale's residents and visitors will tell you that the region's year-round sunny skies and expansive landscape are far too tempting to let a little thing like water get in the way.

I'm only half joking, as water is a concern, believe it or not, for these courses. By law, only 90 acres of turf can be watered on new greens. This challenge, though, has only pushed the creativity of designers further, with new courses showcasing the stunning contrast between verdant green fairways and golden desert washes.

The city's nearly 50 courses span the gamut from municipal executive greens to PGA tournament stops. And though you'll find far more affordable options in Phoenix and its suburbs, none of them will match Scottsdale's premier courses.

Like hotel and resort rates, greens fees tumble as the heat rises, with even the best courses charging a fraction of their winter prices in the summer. Call ahead for current fees.

National magazines regularly rank the 36-hole **Boulders Golf Club** (34631 N. Tom Darlington Rd., 480/488-9009, www.the-boulders.com) as one of the best golf resorts in the country. It's a real desert course, so don't be surprised to see rabbits, coyotes, or javelina scurrying across the fairway as you tee off. The scenic South Course is a highlight of the property, with its greens nestled along the resort's signature rock formations. Also, the new Ladies First golf program, which is limited to four women per session, complements three days of instruction with social activities.

Camelback Golf Club (7847 N. Mockingbird Ln., 480/596-7050, www.camelbackinn.com) tees up 36 holes of championship golf. Try the

Boulders Golf Club

© SCOTTSDALE CONVENTION & VISITORS BUREAU

par-72 Padre Course, which is known for its challenging water holes, including the infamous 18th. The traditional links-style Indian Bend Course winds though a lush grassy wash, with fairways lined by palm and eucalyptus trees. After a hard game, pop into the terrific golf shop to cool off.

Who says you can't find a decent and affordable golf course in Scottsdale? The executive-style **Continental Golf Course** (7920 E. Osborn Rd., 480/941-1047, www.continentalgc.com) is a fun, par-60 course just a few blocks from Old Town. The long tees and narrow greens give the Continental a little character. Play a full 18 holes or hit the executive nine before your kids gets up. Be sure to call the pro shop to ask about any specials.

For a younger crowd, check out **Grayhawk Golf Club** (8620 E. Thompson Peak Pkwy., 480/502-1800, www.grayhawkgolf.com) in North Scottsdale. This rockin' 36-hole desert course blasts tunes from the Rolling Stones and offers live music and drink specials in the evenings as golfers wrap up their games. Don't be fooled, though; the two 18-hole courses, Talon and the Tom Fazio–designed Raptor, are among the best in the Valley.

Never one to be outdone, **Kierland Golf Club** (15636 N. Clubgate Dr., 480/922-9283, www.kierlandgolf.com) brings a lot of high-tech fun to the links, as it was the first course in Arizona to roll out the Segway GT (Golf Transporter), which carries a golfer and bag around the 27-hole course. Oh, and let's not forget the "air-conditioned carts" for those brutal summer temperatures. But Kierland doesn't let the toys get in the way of its challenging desert course, with literally hundreds of bunkers and desert washes. If you'd like some help with your game, the LaBauve Golf Academy and Foremax Training System pumps up anyone's golf game.

McCormick Ranch Golf Club (7505 E. McCormick Pkwy., 480/948-0260, www.mccormickranchgolf.com) is another reasonably affordable option, conveniently located near downtown Scottsdale and Paradise Valley. *Golf Illustrated* named its Palm Course's ninth hole as one of the top water holes in the country, and its practice facility has one of the Southwest's largest putting greens. Best of all, parents can bring their children to the Junior Golf Academy to learn golf rules and etiquette, as well as technique and strategy.

It's hard to believe this 27-hole, luxury golf sanctuary sits in the middle of the Phoenix/Scottsdale metropolitan area. **The Phoenician** (6000 E. Camelback Rd., 480/423-2449, www.thephoenician.com) has three USGA championship golf courses that sprawl below the red-hued Camelback Mountain, and the backdrop couldn't be better. The course is a fantastic splurge and a popular choice for golfers of all skill levels, thanks in part to its slightly shorter fairways.

The par-70 **Rancho Mañana Golf Club** (5680 E. Rancho Manana Blvd., 480/488-0885, www.ranchomanana.com) in Cave Creek will definitely wow you with its dramatic elevation changes and pristine desert surroundings. The rolling course's green lawns, sculptural cacti, and sweeping mountain views

make it the most scenic course in the Valley. You can't help but enjoy yourself on this challenging course, and its high Sonoran Desert setting outside of the city means slightly cooler temperatures on warmer days.

Who doesn't want to play like the pros—or at least play the golf course of the pros? The **TPC Scottsdale** (17020 N. Hayden Rd., 480/585-3600, www.tpc.com/scottsdale) lives up to its hype as one of the country's best courses. Tee off at the FBR Open's Stadium Course, designed by Tom Weiskopf and Jay Morrish, or head out to the New Championships course. Even if your game's a little off, you'll be rewarded with spectacular views of the McDowell Mountains. Plus, you can't beat the thrill of sinking a putt on the 16th hole "stadium" green. Private instruction and two-, three-, and five-day classes at the Tour Academy are available for any Phil Mickelsons in the making.

Tom Weiskopf and Jay Morrish teamed up again at **Troon North Golf Club** (10320 E. Dynamite Blvd., 480/585-7700, www.troonnorthgolf.com), and its two courses have emerged as the pinnacle of desert golf course

Troon North Golf Club

© SCOTTSDALE CONVENTION & VISITORS BUREAU

SCOTTSDALE

design. Rolling greens meander seamlessly through the natural ravines and unspoiled terrain. It will almost convince you that lush, perfectly manicured grounds grow naturally in this arid climate. The state-of-the-art Callaway Performance Center and chic clubhouse attract serious players and North Scottsdale's most affluent residents.

HIKING AND ROCK CLIMBING
Camelback Mountain
Even if you're not a "hiker," visitors to Scottsdale won't want to pass up the chance to explore the Sonoran Desert on foot. The challenging Camelback Mountain (www.phoenix.gov/parks/hikecmlb.html) is a must-climb destination for hikers, with two summit trails scaling the 1,200-foot slopes in a little over a mile. The popular **Echo Canyon Summit Trail** starts at the "camel's head" in the **Echo Canyon Recreation Area** (5700 N. Echo Canyon Pkwy., 602/256-3220, phoenix.gov/parks/hikecmlb.html). Expect rough terrain and loose rocks as you climb the trail, but the hidden caves and rock formations like the 80-foot-tall **Praying Monk** make the effort worthwhile. For an easier trek, try the quarter-mile **Ramada Loop Trail.**

The less popular **Cholla Trail** at the "camel's hump" offers a manageable ascent to Camelback's summit and views of the Eden-like Phoenician Resort. The trailhead starts on Cholla Lane; note that parking is limited.

McDowell Sonoran Preserve
Hikers, climbers, and horseback riders of all skill levels can trek through the McDowell Sonoran Preserve (480/998-7971, www.mcdowellsonoran.org) on the eastern edge of Scottsdale. The protected park serves as a wildlife corridor for the McDowell Mountains and Tonto National Forest, making it an important habitat for a host of desert plants and animals.

Hikers may explore the area on their own or join a guided tour for a more educational experience (call ahead for times or to create a customized tour). The 16,000-acre preserve has eight access areas, like the **Lost Dog Wash Trailhead** (on 124th St., just north of

Shea Blvd.). The new **Gateway Access Area** (on Thompson Peak Pkwy., west of Bell Rd.) has desert exhibitions, an amphitheater, lots of parking, and an ADA-approved trail—an accessible trail for those with limited mobility. Climbers wanting to scale one of the preserve's rock formations should contact the **Arizona Mountaineering Club** (www.amcaz.org) for information about choice locales or to book one of its beginner classes.

HORSEBACK RIDING
There's nothing like the desert to get visions of cowboys dancing in your head, and **Windwalker Expeditions, Inc.** (888/785-3382, www.windwalkerexpeditions.com, $165) can help you live out any Zane Grey (or even Billy Crystal, *City Slickers*–style) fantasies with trail rides atop guide-owned Arabian or quarter horses. Beginners can even get lessons on the trail. For experienced riders, the company also organizes multiday pack trips through the backcountry lasting anywhere from 2 to 10 days.

Cave Creek's **Spur Cross Stables** (480/488-

Explore the Sonoran Desert on the back of a horse.

© MICA THOMAS MULLOY

9117, www.horsebackarizona.com) can get even the newest cowpokes into the saddle. The ranch, located on the site of an 1870s gold mine, offers spectacular rides through the desert and mountain passes of Tonto National Forest, with rates beginning at $35 for an hour. Customize your horseback adventure, or select the Native American Ruin, Stagecoach Stop, or Sunset trail ride. Children can sign up for the all-day Trail Blazer Kids Camp or feed crackers to the pot-bellied pigs, mini donkey, and pygmy goats that roam the ranch.

Wanna push the herd? Maybe flank and brand a calf? Or perhaps do a little pickin' and singin' after a long day on the range? Well, have I got the place for you, cowhand. **Arizona Cowboy College** (30208 N. 152nd St., 480/471-3151, www.cowboycollege.com) offers honest-to-goodness, "no frills" lessons in cowboyin'. From half-day sessions on horseback riding and roping ($150) to the comprehensive six-day course ($2,250), you'll have the experience of a lifetime learning how Arizona's pioneers won the West.

RAFTING

See the Sonoran Desert from an unexpected perspective. Float down the Salt or Verde River with **Cimarron Adventures & River Company** (480/994-1199, www.cimarrontours.com, $45) on one of its two-hour expeditions 30 minutes east of Scottsdale. The Class I rapids (no white water) are pretty tame, but don't be surprised if a splash fight breaks out on a hot day.

Grab a paddle with **Desert Voyagers Guided Raft Tours** (480/998-7238, www.desertvoyagers.com, $68 adults, $58 kids) and meander along the banks of the lower Salt River, where you'll spot a surprising mix of wildlife, including otters, wild mustangs, and the most-active bald eagle nesting areas in Arizona. The two-person "funyak" excursions offer a more intimate journey and a bit more maneuverability ($78 adults, $73 kids).

◖ SPAS

Scottsdale is one of the spa capitals of the world, boasting some of the largest and most

lavish facilities that you'll find anywhere. Whether you're in the mood for a deep-tissue massage or Native American–inspired treatments, you'll find the perfect spa in Scottsdale to get scrubbed, rubbed, and buffed.

Although there are a host of day spas throughout the city, none offer the amenities of the big resorts (nor do you really save any money). Many locals book a facial or massage at a resort so that they can spend the entire day taking advantage of the spa's pool, fitness classes, on-site gym, and amenities like steam rooms and saunas. It's a great way to experience a five-star resort without having to pay to stay there. Basic hour-long massages begin at $125, and multi-treatment packages are available.

The Centre for Well-Being at The Phoenician Resort & Spa (6000 E. Camelback Rd., 480/941-8200, www.thephoenician.com, 7 A.M.–7 P.M. Sun.–Wed., 7 A.M.–8 P.M. Thurs.–Sat.) takes a holistic approach to spa-ing. In addition to the usual whirlpools, saunas, and Swiss showers, the Centre is one of the first spas in the country to offer homeopathic and wellness consultations by a naturopathic physician. The spa's massages and treatments utilize plants and minerals indigenous to the Southwest, like the Native American–inspired Well-Being Stone Ritual ($150) and the hydrating Desert Serenity Scrub, Wrap, and Massage ($240). For a New Age-y experience, a "circle of intuitive guides" offers personalized meditation, astrology, hypnotherapy, and sports-guided imagery sessions.

The 33,000-square-foot **Golden Door Spa** at The Boulders Resort (34631 N. Tom Darlington Dr., 480/595-3500, www.theboulders.com, 8 A.M.–8 P.M. daily) offers a fascinating mix of Japanese bathing customs and Native American traditions, set against Carefree's craggy desert landscape. Lounge in the *ofuro,* a traditional Japanese bath, before heading outside to the swimming pool and meditative labyrinth, which overlook the resort's namesake boulder formation. If you're intrigued by Native American healing traditions, book the Shamanic Meditation Journey in the Tipi ($260), during which the spa's on-site healer "will guide a meditative journey into

© SCOTTSDALE CONVENTION & VISITORS BUREAU

Sanctuary Camelback Mountain Resort & Spa

non-ordinary reality, a dimension of consciousness similar to a dream state." The spa also offers rock-climbing clinics ($135) if you like a little adventure with your pampering.

The Moroccan-inspired **Joya Spa** at the Intercontinental Montelucia Resort (4949 E. Lincoln Dr., 480/627-3020, www.joyaspa. com, 8 A.M.–7:30 P.M. daily) has set the bar in Scottsdale for an over-the-top spa experience. You'll want to spend the day (and evening) at this sprawling complex to take advantage of the hammam-style bathing facilities, which include a warming room, sauna, steam room, cold deluge shower, and whirlpool. In between treatments, enjoy the rooftop pool terrace with views of Camelback Mountain and the whisper lounges, a serene place to relax with friends on cushy daybeds, surrounded by candles and soft music. For a real splurge, try one of the suites, which feature private terraces and outdoor showers and copper tubs. Massages here start at $154.

A favorite of locals, the **Spa at Camelback Inn** (5402 E. Lincoln Dr., 480/596-7040, www. camelbackspa.com, 6:15 A.M.–7:30 P.M. daily) offers the most amenity bang for your spa buck. The saunas, steam rooms, whirlpools, and cold

plunge pools are beautifully bathed in natural light, and the outdoor sun decks provide a private retreat before and after treatments. The soothing massages and wraps ($125) feature techniques and nature-based ingredients indigenous to Native American cultures. Enjoy a healthy meal from Sprouts, Scottsdale's only spa restaurant, next to the outdoor Olympic-size pool, which offers uninterrupted views of the desert and mountains.

You would think that with a climate ready-made for reveling in the outdoors, more spas would take their amenities outside. **Spa Avania** at the Scottsdale Hyatt Regency Resort & Spa at Gainey Ranch (7500 E. Doubletree Ranch Rd., 480/483-5558, www.scottsdale.hyatt.com, 8:30 A.M.–8 P.M. daily) has created a seamless indoor/outdoor facility. Glass walls slide open onto terraces with outdoor showers, comfy lounge chairs, and hot and cold plunge pools. The facility incorporates elegant stonework, garden treatment rooms, and a co-ed French-Celtic mineral pool and lotus pond. Avania's "science of time" philosophy takes a holistic approach to relaxation, syncing treatments to the body's natural biorhythms and subtly incorporating herbal medicine and traditional Thai therapies into treatments. Massages here start at $165.

If you like chic design with your Swedish massage, **Sanctuary Spa** at Sanctuary Camelback Mountain Resort & Spa (5700 E. McDonald Dr., 480/948-2100, www.sanctuaryoncamelback.com, 6 A.M.–8:30 P.M. daily) won't disappoint. Design buffs will appreciate the stylish transformation of this 1960s "tennis ranch" into a Modernist Zen retreat, complete with men's and women's relaxation lounges that overlook a meditation garden and reflecting pond. The Asian-inspired treatments, which start at $170, are available in one of 12 indoor and outdoor treatment rooms. The heated Watsu massage pool, private outdoor suites, and location on the side of Camelback Mountain make this spa an extraordinary destination.

One of the finest spas in the world, **Willow Stream Spa** at the Fairmont Scottsdale (7575 E. Princess Dr., 480/585-2732, www.willowstream.com, 6 A.M.–10 P.M. daily) pays homage to the Arizona landscape, with indigenous stone and native architectural details. The domed men's and women's areas provide a welcome bit of privacy to enjoy the sauna, steam room, whirlpool, cold plunge pool, Swiss shower, and eucalyptus inhalation room. Make a trip through the red-stone Canyon Oasis, an outdoor waterfall treatment, and up to the rooftop Mesa Oasis Pool and cabanas. Try one of the seasonal or signature treatments, like the Havasupai Body Oasis Experience ($319), which includes a chamomile exfoliation, a eucalyptus herbal bath, an aromatherapy wrap with a face and scalp acupressure treatment, and a warm-oil massage.

The intimate **Spa at the Four Seasons Scottsdale** (10600 E. Crescent Moon Dr., 480/513-5145, www.fourseasons.com/Scottsdale, 6 A.M.–9 P.M. daily) doesn't offer the sprawling amenities of its competitors, but its desert-inspired treatments make it a worthwhile option. Try the Jojoba and Prickly Pear Body Polish or Soothing Sage Wrap.

Younger spa-goers looking for hipper crowds and some poolside excitement may want to check out the **VH Spa** at the Hotel Valley Ho (6850 E. Main St., 480/248-2000, www.hotelvalleyho.com, 8 A.M.–8:15 P.M. daily). Although a bit small, the mod decor, froufrou treatments, and poolside action will appeal to 20-somethings looking to splurge. Massages here start at $100.

SPECTATOR SPORTS

You'll find most of the Valley's sports action in Phoenix, but every March the Boys of Spring descend upon Scottsdale for the Cactus League spring training series. Baseball fans can catch the San Francisco Giants at **Scottsdale Stadium** (7408 E. Osborn Rd., 480/312-2586, www.scottsdaleaz.gov/stadium), battling one of 13 other MLB teams on the field, including the Chicago Cubs, Seattle Mariners, Los Angeles Dodgers, and hometown Arizona Diamondbacks. You can also grab a hot dog and a game at the downtown stadium during the Arizona Fall League in October.

Accommodations

There is no shortage of great places in Scottsdale to make your temporary home, and you'll find a rather broad spectrum of options and prices. The city doesn't offer much in the way of historic hotels or bed-and-breakfasts, though you'll find many retro-cool and newly renovated 1960s properties that were first built when Scottsdale came of age as a resort destination.

If you'd like to experience the city's best shopping and nightlife without the hassle of a car, stay downtown, where most hotels offer a free shuttle within a three-mile radius. However, if you're looking to escape to a desert playground, you have to try one of the city's mega-resorts, an Arizona specialty. Enjoy mornings on the tee, afternoons in the pool, and evenings under the stars.

SCOTTSDALE

Fortunately, even the most luxurious resorts become affordable in the summer, when the temperatures soar into the triple digits and visitors become a bit wary of making a trip to the Valley of the Sun. Locals, though, take advantage of these hometown oases, spending a "stay-cation" at the four- and five-star resorts, which often offer spa and food vouchers. Don't consider them out of your price range until you give them a call or check their websites.

DOWNTOWN
$50-100

Finding an inexpensive hotel in Scottsdale is challenging, though not impossible. The retro **Best Western Papago Inn & Resort** (7017 E. McDowell Road, 480/947-7335, www.bestwesternarizona.com, $60–90 d) offers a bit of personality and rooms that overlook a grassy, flower-filled courtyard and swimming pool. Its location near Tempe, Papago Park, and the airport makes it a handy option if you plan to explore the rest of the Valley of the Sun.

There's nothing like clean and functional when you are on a budget. **Motel 6 Scottsdale** (6848 E. Camelback Rd., 480/946-2280, www.motel6.com, $50–85 d) is downtown's cheapest hotel, and its location next to Scottsdale Fashion Square cannot be beat. Have breakfast at the on-site pancake house, which is frequented by locals on the weekend.

$100-250

The hip **Hotel Indigo** (4415 N. Civic Center Plaza, 480/941-9400, www.scottsdalehiphotel.com, $125–200 d) packs a lot of style into a converted motel. Younger guests will love its incredible location near Scottsdale's best bars and clubs, not to mention the boldly decorated rooms that were clearly inspired by more expensive boutique hotels. Guests can take advantage of the gym and outdoor swimming pool, or head out to the second-story terrace for cocktails by the fire pit on cool evenings. It's a bit of Scottsdale flash for not much cash.

Hyatt Place (7300 E. 3rd Ave., 480/423-9944, http://scottsdaleoldtown.place.hyatt.com, $100–175 d) also is conveniently located

within walking distance of Scottsdale Stadium and Old Town's shops, restaurants, and nightlife. The comfy, modern rooms feature a fridge, free Wi-Fi, and a 42-inch flat-screen TV. Downstairs, the convenient food counter prepares takeaway sandwiches and salads perfect for breakfast or a quick snack.

The budget-boutique **3 Palms** (7707 E. McDowell Rd., 480/941-1202, www.scottsdale-resort-hotels.com, $90–135 d) creates an intimate resort feel, thanks to its white-on-white lobby, mod guest rooms, inviting poolside bar, and neighboring park. The remodeled property, a 10-minute drive from Old Town, isn't perfect, but it's a terrific value. The in-room DVD player, refrigerator, and microwave make it practical for families, and its location near Tempe attracts parents and friends visiting students at Arizona State University.

Over $250

Classic mid-20th-century modern architecture and a chic decor make **❰ Hotel Valley Ho** (6850 E. Main St., 480/248-2000, www.hotelvalleyho.com, $225–300 d) a swanky place to hang your fedora. The 2005 overhaul restored the 1956 property to its golden age glory, when Hollywood celebrities like Tony Curtis and Janet Leigh lounged by the pool, and Robert Wagner and Natalie Wood held their surprise wedding reception at the hotel. The translucent walls, Philippe Starck tubs, and hip bar attract a younger crowd, but the large patios, mod rooms, and Trader Vic's restaurant are fun for everyone.

The too-cool-for-school **Mondrian** (7353 E. Indian School Rd., 480/308-1110, www.mondrianscottsdale.com, $275–300 d) epitomizes Scottsdale's love of trendy style over substance. Its nightclub vibe starts in the white-on-white lobby and continues throughout the property, with strategically placed alfresco lounges and oh-so-mod rooms that feel a little small. Count on spotting MTV-ready crowds at the always-packed pool or in the Euro-chic Red Bar. The hotel's handy location on the Scottsdale Mall means guests are within easy walking distance of downtown restaurants, bars, and shops.

CENTRAL SCOTTSDALE AND PARADISE VALLEY $100-250

Think of the family-owned **Smoke Tree Resort and Bungalows** (7101 E. Lincoln Dr., 480/948-7660, www.smoketreeresort. com, $150–175 d) as a Scottsdale-style bed-and-breakfast—in other words, a mini-resort. Smoke Tree is the longest-running independent hotel in Paradise Valley, and it's no wonder. The charming Arizona decor of the 26 recently remodeled private bungalows feels like you are staying in a friend's cozy guesthouse or at an exclusive retreat. There are one- and two-bedroom villas, some with small, full-service kitchens.

For more amenities, consider the Frank Lloyd Wright–inspired **Doubletree Paradise Valley Resort** (5401 N. Scottsdale Rd., 480/947-5400, www.doubletree.com, $125–175 d). The two large pools with whirlpools, racquetball and tennis courts, health club, and nine-hole putting green are fun for families and business travelers who would like a few distractions in between meetings. The spacious rooms are clean and bright, though a tad dated.

The charming **Hermosa Inn** (5532 N. Palo Cristi, 602/955-8614, www.hermosainn.com, $180–225 d) quietly exudes a taste of old Arizona. Cowboy artist Lon Megargee built the hacienda as his home and studio, and it was a converted into a small inn in the 1930s. Today, the intimate 35-room boutique hotel features authentic furnishings and artwork painted by Megargee, and guests should expect the quirks that come with a historic property, like small bathrooms and limited space for a pool and other amenities you'd find at the big resorts. The meticulously landscaped grounds, stunning views of Camelback Mountain, and prime location near Phoenix's Camelback Corridor can't be beat, though.

The **Scottsdale Cottonwood Resort and Suites** (6160 N. Scottsdale Rd., 480/991-1414, www.scottsdalecottonwoods.com, $160–180 d) offers quite a bit of size for its relatively small price: a huge pool, big suites, and sprawling, well-maintained grounds. The budget resort could use an update—inside and out—but its convenient location next to the Borgata and Hilton Village shopping centers makes it a worthwhile option.

Resorts

When **Camelback Inn** (5402 E. Lincoln Dr., 480/948-1700, www.camelbackinn.com, $375–425 d) first opened in 1936, wealthy travelers who arrived by train had to make a 12-mile journey across the desert to reach the hacienda-style resort. Fortunately, things are bit easier today, and thanks to a $50 million restoration, the five-star property has a new sheen of luxury. Celebrities from Jimmy Stewart and Bette Davis to Oprah Winfrey have decamped to the Paradise Valley institution. Guests can relax at the world-class spa, play golf at Camelback Golf Club's 36-hole course, or hike Mummy Mountain's desert terrain. Because of its age, the rooms have some quirks, but who doesn't want to "rough it" a bit in the Wild West?

The romantic **C FireSky Resort and Spa** (4925 N. Scottsdale Rd., 480/945-7666, www. fireskyresort.com, $250–300 d) is a terrific home base just north of Scottsdale Fashion Square. The recently renovated property is an excellent value, offering friendly service and amenities similar to those at the five-star resorts up the road. Couples appreciate the gorgeous stonework, cathedral ceilings, lush grounds, and complimentary evening wine hour, while kids love the sandy "beach pool" and nighttime s'mores kits. Families and groups of friends can book adjoining rooms.

The Spanish-themed **Intercontinental Montelucia Resort and Spa** (4949 E. Lincoln Dr., 480/627-3200, www.icmontelucia.com, $430–500) makes a convincing aesthetic tie between the Sonoran Desert and Andalucia's arid landscape and big skies. No expense was spared in creating this elegant mix of dark woods, Moroccan screens, and Moorish geometric patterns. The real attraction, though, is the resort's extraordinary views of the red-hued Camelback Mountain, particularly at sunset from the main pool, which makes reserving a room during high season worth the splurge.

Inside, rooms feature sunken tubs, walk-in showers, and high-tech hookups to link your laptop and iPod to the room's flat-screen TV and sound system. Also, kids will love the indoor/outdoor clubhouse with its bikes, air hockey, and video games. **The Phoenician Resort & Spa** (6000 E. Camelback Rd., 480/941-8200, www.thephoenician.com, $550–600 d) is the grande dame of Valley resorts, having hosted royalty, heads of state, A-list actors, and rock stars. The 250-acre property sprawls across the base of Camelback Mountain, with a 27-hole championship golf course, its renowned Centre for Well-Being spa, and a 12-court "tennis garden." The resort's nine swimming pools include a 165-foot water slide and a "signature" pool inlaid with handcrafted mother of pearl tiles. This is the good life—and secluded behind the landscaped grounds, you wouldn't know that you are only a five-minute drive to Scottsdale Fashion Square. For some of the best views of the Valley, enjoy a cocktail on the lobby terrace or dinner at chef Jean-Georges Vongerichten's new J&G Steakhouse.

When A-list actors and pop stars come to Scottsdale in search of style and discretion, they often hide away at ◖ **Sanctuary on Camelback Mountain Resort & Spa** (5700 E. McDonald Dr., 480/948-2100, www.sanctuaryaz.com, $445–550 d). Once a 1960s "tennis ranch," the chic resort maintains many of its architectural details, though a sleek update has given the property a mod overhaul. Subtle Asian touches carry throughout property, including the innovative restaurant and fashionable spa. The boutique resort's 105 luxury casitas—many with outdoor balconies, wood-burning fireplaces, and private outdoor soaking tubs—climb the side of Camelback, giving guests a cliffside view of Paradise Valley and Mummy Mountain. And in a tribute to the resort's history, Sanctuary offers daily clinics and personalized instruction at its five championship tennis courts.

Secluded in the elegant neighborhood of Gainey Ranch, the **Hyatt Regency Scottsdale** (7500 E. Doubletree Ranch Rd., 480/444-1234, www.scottsdale.hyatt.com, $300–400 d) is a blissful retreat that combines a manicured resort setting with an unbeatable location 10 minutes from Old Town and Scottsdale Fashion Square mall. Most days, the lobby's glass walls slide open, providing the lounge and bar with a soft breeze and views of the turquoise pools, golf courses, and McDowell Mountains. Spend your day getting pampered at the alfresco spa or lounging by one of the 10 interconnected pools, which feature sandy beaches, a three-story water slide, Jacuzzis, and a swim-through temple. In the evening, enjoy dinner at one of the four on-site restaurants before taking a romantic gondola ride around the lagoon or enjoying the nightly live music shows, which range from jazz to flamenco dancing.

NORTH SCOTTSDALE $100-250

For visitors who would like to stay near Scottsdale WestWorld or the FBR Open's TPC golf course, there are a few affordable options in North Scottsdale. **SpringHill Suites** (17020 N. Scottsdale Rd., 480/922-8700, www.marriott.com, $160–200 d) may lack quirky character, but its practical, large rooms are clean and have microwaves. The neighboring **Sleep Inn** (16630 N. Scottsdale Rd., 480/998-9211, www.sleepinn.com, $100–130 d) offers special packages during the Phoenix Film Festival. Both hotels are within walking distance of the TPC golf course and a host of restaurants and bars. They offer free daily breakfast, pleasant pools, and Wi-Fi access.

A former high-end apartment complex, the recently upgraded **Xona Resort Suites** (7677 E. Princess Blvd., 888/222-1059, www.xonaresort.com, $179–200 d) offers loads of space in North Scottsdale. Large groups of friends and business travelers with families in tow will appreciate the large living rooms, full kitchens, and one- to four-bedroom suites—not to mention the four pools and generous balconies.

Resorts

You're not in Kansas anymore—or anywhere

else on the planet, for that matter. **The Boulders Resort & Golden Door Spa** (34631 N. Tom Darlington Dr., 480/488-9009, www.theboulders.com, $360–400 d) sits at the foot of its namesake 12-million-year-old rock formation, a stunning testament to the geological scale of the Sonoran Desert. Pathways wind through the 1,300-acre property, where you're likely to come across quail, jackrabbits, lizards, and even javelina. The luxury resort still offers all the amenities of Scottsdale: shimmering pools, two championship golf courses, tennis courts, and one of the finest spas in the world. Still, the slightly dated rooms are charming (or in need of a remodel depending on your point of view). And if you get the courage, rock-climbing clinics are available for thrill-seekers wanting to conquer those impressive boulders.

The sprawling **Fairmont Scottsdale** (7575 E. Princess Dr., 480/585-4848, www.fairmont.com/scottsdale, $365–475 d) deftly marries luxury service with a casual atmosphere, making it an excellent choice for many. Kids love the National Geographic Explorers Camp, pet desert tortoise, and five swimming pools—complete with towering slides—while their parents appreciate chef Michael Mina's fashionable Bourbon Steak and the two 18-hole championship golf courses, home of the boisterous FBR Open. The resort is also a popular getaway for couples and friends who prefer to spend their days at the must-be-seen-to-be-believed Willow Stream Spa and their nights at Rande Gerber's posh Stone Rose Lounge.

The **(Four Seasons Resort Scottsdale at Troon North** (10600 E. Crescent Moon Dr., 480/515-5700, www.fourseasons.com/scottsdale, $425–500 d) overlooks the city from its stunning North Scottsdale perch at Pinnacle Peak, a 20-minute drive from Old Town. The adobe-inspired architecture and brilliant desert landscape feel like an elegant desert retreat, complete with two pools, a spa, and the popular Troon North Golf Club. The 25 casita buildings, each with a private balcony, were just redesigned to showcase the "colors of the Sonoran desert," and the multi-bedroom suites are perfect for families. Take advantage of the unique programs like desert stargazing and weekly tequila tastings. And for one of the single best Scottsdale experiences, order a prickly pear margarita on the terrace for a dazzling view of the Valley of the Sun.

If you're hoping for a vacation destination where your golf bag doesn't leave your side, **The Westin Kierland Resort & Spa** (902 E. Greenway Pkwy., 480/624-1000, www.kierlandresort.com, $430–470 d) delivers. Kierland Golf Club's 27 holes will satiate any diehard golfer, and its personalized instruction and Foremax Training System provide a comprehensive approach to improving your score. Of course, there's more than the putting green at Kierland. The informal resort's monstrous water slide and lazy river are popular with the kids, and the walls are lined with the mementos from Arizona history. The neighboring Kierland Commons mall is a shopping and dining option without having to get into a car.

Four Seasons Resort Scottsdale at Troon North

SCOTTSDALE

Food

Foodies know: Scottsdale is a mecca for great eating. First-time visitors will discover outposts of New York's best-known chefs, as well as homegrown talents who infuse their cooking with the indigenous flavors of the Southwest. Get ready for a culinary adventure. And though some of the best restaurants can be a little pricey, it's well worth loosening the purse strings for a culinary treat.

DOWNTOWN
American
If you make one culinary splurge in Scottsdale, make 🍷 **Cowboy Ciao** (7133 E. Stetson Dr., 480/946-3111, www.cowboyciao.com, 11:30 A.M.–2:30 P.M. daily, 5:30–10 P.M. Sun.–Thurs., 5:30–11 P.M. Fri.–Sat., $15–32) your stop. The Stetson Chop Salad is the stuff of culinary legend in the Valley, and the quote on the menu says it all: "I love that chopped salad so much that I put it on my screen saver." The exotic mushroom pan fry and Berkshire pork ribeye are almost as good. In fact, it seems like chef Bernie Kantak has done everything he can think of to offer guests bold flavors and unpredictable combinations of fresh ingredients. And few restaurants can compete with Cowboy Ciao's wine list. The restaurant is a 10-time *Wine Spectator* award winner.

Three of the Valley's top culinary forces teamed up in 2009 to open **FnB** (7133 E. Stetson Dr., 480/425-9463, www.digestifscottsdale.com, 5–10 P.M. Wed.–Thurs., 5–11 P.M. Fri.–Sat., $18–28). The unostentatious "gastropub"—helmed by heavy weights from Cowboy Ciao, Prado, and Rancho Pinot—features a seasonal, local menu with decidedly global influences, ranging from Mediterranean to Southwestern. Start with one of the fresh salads and sample from the hearty, roasted meats or fresh seafood, like the polenta-crusted shrimp with green goddess dressing. Wine lovers will not be disappointed by the extensive wine list, and you don't have to have a sweet tooth to appreciate the innovative desserts.

The smooth jazz music and New American cuisine should clue you in to the experience at **Estate House** (7134 E. Stetson Dr., 480/970-4099, 5–10 P.M. daily, $29–45). Order a bottle of red and dine with Scottsdale's well-heeled professionals indoors or on the rooftop patio, which is "well-misted" during the warmer months. The Shiraz molasses braised short ribs and sea bass with Catalan-style potatoes and sesame sugar snap peas are delicious. **Upstairs at Estate House** is a more casual option for cocktails and appetizers.

The slider craze has hit Arizona at **Stax Burger Bistro** (4400 N. Scottsdale Rd., 480/946-4222, 11 A.M.–midnight daily, $5–20), which serves up mini-hamburgers in a host of mix-and-match options. Select your meat(s)—beef, turkey, lamb, ostrich, buffalo, salmon, or veggie—and top it with your choice of bun, cheese, and condiments, including crispy bacon, fresh guacamole, and fancy aiolis. For the uninspired, there's an extensive menu of recommendations, including pesto-infused ostrich and lamb with feta. Oh, don't forget to order a few hearty sides, like the mac and jack, sweet potato fries, or tater tots.

Welcome to the new frontier of haute dining. **Posh** (7167 E. Rancho Vista Dr. Ste. 111, 480/663-7674, 5 A.M.–11 P.M. Tues.–Thurs., 5 A.M.–midnight Fri.–Sat., $45–75) pioneers into unchartered culinary territory with its seasonal, "improvised" cuisine. Translation: There is no menu. Instead, you fill out a sheet that lists tastes, preferences, allergies, number of courses, and requests for wine pairings. The restaurant's chefs take over from there, preparing an innovative lineup of genre-breaking dishes, including popcorn soup with clarified butter and smoked paprika, kangaroo in bacon broth, halibut with Meyer lemon aioli, and pear-cabernet sorbet. Everyone in your party gets something different, which means an epic meal that's as memorable as it is surprising. Try to grab a seat at the bar that overlooks the open kitchen, or simply have a plate or two, along with a swank cocktail, in the glass-walled lounge.

Salt Cellar (550 N. Hayden Rd., 480/947-1963, www.saltcellarrestaurant.com, 5–11 P.M. Sun.–Thurs., 5 P.M.–midnight Fri.–Sat., $25–60) is the place to go for fresh seafood in the desert. Enter through the white-and-blue shack and descend the antique wooden staircase leading underground to the dining area. Lobster is the house specialty, complemented by a wide variety of sea creatures that include mussels, mahimahi, scallops, and monkfish—all flown in fresh from across the country. Take the plunge and try the baked lobster stuffed with scallops and crabmeat, or go with the basic and appreciate the waiters' expert cracking abilities. This subterranean venue is the perfect place for a date, as it maintains a casual vibe with tasty cuisine.

Asian

Malee's Thai on Main (7131 E. Main St., 480/947-6042, www.maleesthaibistro.com, 11 A.M.–9 P.M. Mon.–Thurs., 11 A.M.–10 P.M. Fri.–Sat., noon–9 P.M. Sun., $10–18) attracts a devoted following of diners, who praise its comfy atmosphere, warm service, and reasonable prices. The Thai-inspired cuisine ranges from classic spring rolls, satays, and pad Thai to the "Tropical Pineapple," a spicy mix of shrimp, scallops, and minced chicken in coconut curry sauce. Speaking of which, curry-lovers will find a decent selection of dishes—served as hot as requested.

For a little bit of modern Tokyo on the grassy Scottsdale mall, try **Pure Sushi Bar + Dining** (7343 E. Scottsdale Mall, 602/903-1124, www.puresushibar.com, 11:30 A.M.–2 A.M. Mon.–Sat., 11 A.M.–7 P.M. Sun., $15–30). The minimalist, all-white decor provides the perfect setting for the best sushi in Scottsdale. This is good stuff. The extensive drink menu features sake from many regions in Japan, but the signature drinks, like the Lychee Lemon Drop, are light and refreshing. While the tuna and yellowtail nigiri shouldn't be missed, try a few of the house-specialty rolls, like the potato spicy tuna roll. This twist on an old favorite features

flash-fried julienne potatoes and a sweet-and-spicy chile sauce.

The lively **Stingray Sushi** (4302 N. Scottsdale Rd., 480/941-4460, www.stingraysushi.com, 11:30 A.M.–midnight daily) lures the trendy set into its sleek, orange dining room in Old Town. When you walk in the door, be sure to look down and check out the koi pond under the glass floor. Ask to eat in the bar area or head out to the large patio to kick back one of the restaurant's specialty cocktails. You'll find classic udon bowls and tempuras on the menu, along with an interesting lobster ceviche and seasoned calamari steak. Dive into the sushi list with wild abandon, as you're guaranteed a fresh, tasty selection.

Breakfast, Lunch, and Snacks

You don't have to be one of the Scottsdale "ladies who lunch" to appreciate **Arcadia Farms** (7014 E. 1st Ave., 480/941-5665, www.arcadiafarmscafe.com, 8 A.M.–3:30 P.M. Sun.–Tues., 8 A.M.–8 P.M. Wed.–Sat., $9–15). The charming, cottage setting provides a pleasant backdrop for breakfast, brunch, lunch, or dinner. Its fresh and organic omelets, sandwiches, and soups fail to disappoint, and the warm goat cheese salad with fresh raspberries is legendary—seriously. In fact, the salad's reputation earned Arcadia Farms permanent venues at the Phoenix Art Museum and Heard Museum.

The Breakfast Club and Barrista Bar (4400 N. Scottsdale Road, 480/222-2582, www.thebreakfastclub.us, 6 A.M.–3 P.M. Mon.–Fri., 8 A.M.–3 P.M. Sat.–Sun., $5–10) specializes in the most important meal of the day well into the afternoon. The polished concrete floors and contemporary decor forgo the dowdy country-kitsch of most breakfast places. Try the Southwest-inspired breakfast burrito with eggs, black refried beans, chorizo, and pepper jack cheese. And when it comes to omelets, "The Bird"—smoked turkey, avocado, mushrooms, and boursin cheese—is the word. Dishes are inexpensive and hearty, but the people-watching is the real treat, from older couples enjoying lattes to 20-somethings decked out in sunglasses and recovering from a late-night out.

You can't beat a good breakfast joint. **The Orange Table** (7373 E. Scottsdale Mall, 480/424-6819, 7 A.M.–10 P.M. Tues.–Sat., 7 A.M.–3 P.M. Sun.–Mon.) is tucked into a nondescript, white-stucco plaza on the Scottsdale Mall, but its bright orange tables make it easy to find. The large menu should appeal to most folks, including vegetarians. You or your dining companion needs to order the strawberry pancakes or corned beef hash—no exceptions. And if you stop in at lunch, select one of the quirky beers from the extensive list to enjoy with your sandwich, burger, or salad.

Stepping into the **Original Pancake House** (6840 E. Camelback Rd., 480/946-4902, 7 A.M.–2 P.M. daily, $7–12) is a bit of a time warp. The retro throwback hasn't been updated since the Nixon Administration, and the devoted regulars wouldn't have it any other way. This is the kind of place where you find sky-high pancakes, slabs of crispy bacon, and freshly squeezed orange juice, along with surprising treats like lingonberry crepes and the oven-baked Dutch Baby, served with whipped butter, lemon, and powdered sugar. Bring some cash, as credit cards are not accepted.

Farmers Market

On Saturday mornings, a small parking lot at the corner of Brown and 1st Street transforms into the **Old Town Farmers Market** (8:30 A.M. to 1 P.M., earlier in the summer). The relatively new market has become a popular shopping destination for locals year-round. Make a picnic from the seasonal specialties like local cheeses, fresh tamales, artisan breads, jams, and organic vegetables.

French

Metro Brasserie & Bar (7114 E. Stetson Dr., 480/994-3663, www.metrosouthbridge.com, 8 A.M.–midnight Mon.–Wed., 8 A.M.–2 A.M. Thurs.–Sun., $9–19) serves up French bistro classics at Scottsdale's new SouthBridge complex. Executive chef Matthew Taylor culls from his New Orleans cooking experience to create a rich and satisfying menu. The onion soup gratin and salmon rillettes are tasty starters, as is the house-made pâté. Stick with one of the salads or artfully crafted sandwiches at lunch. Once the sun sets, try the *moules frites* or beef burgundy. Thanks to the restaurant's extended hours, you can easily grab a snack or meal all day long.

Mexican and Southwest

You can't help but love the **Old Town Tortilla Factory** (6910 E. Main St., 480/945-4567, www.oldtowntortillafactory.com, 4–9:30 P.M. Sun.–Thurs., 4–10:30 P.M. Fri.–Sat., $12–32). Enjoy one of the fantastic house margaritas on the large flagstone patio shaded by citrus and pecan trees, or choose from one of 80 premium tequilas in the gazebo bar. Move inside the 75-year-old adobe home to sample the homemade tortillas, which come in two dozen flavors and are served with herb butter. Try the tangy achiote ribs, chile pork verde, or Pollo Margarita, stuffed with cheese and roasted peppers.

Grilled artichoke—it's so simple, but so good at **Bandera** (3821 N. Scottsdale Rd., 480/994-3524, www.hillstone.com, 4–10 P.M. Sun.–Thurs., 4–11 P.M. Fri.–Sat., $11–29). This contemporary Western restaurant delivers wood-fire-roasted chicken, ribs, and steaks, accompanied by enchiladas or Spanish rice. Try the steak and enchilada platter with Mexican cucumber salad (akin to Greek). And this is the kind of place where you save room for dessert, like the banana cream pie or the homemade Oreo ice cream sandwich with créme de cocoa and fresh whipped cream.

Frank and Lupe's Old Mexico (4121 N. Marshall Way, 480/990-9844, www.frank-andlupes.com, 11 A.M.–10 P.M. daily, $7–15) has been serving up delicious chicken enchiladas for more than 25 years. It's hard to beat the casual atmosphere and colorful patio, not to mention the reasonable prices in the middle of downtown. Order a Mexican beer or a prickly pear margarita, and dig into the green corn tamales, shredded beef tacos, or Lupe's enchilada plate. Oh, and be sure to ask for the hot salsa—if you can handle it.

Looking to try a different kind of Mexican cuisine? **Los Sombreros Cafe & Cantina** (2534 N. Scottsdale Rd., 480/994-1799, www.

delicious Mexican food at Los Sombreros Cafe & Cantina

SCOTTSDALE

lossombreros.com, 5–9 P.M. Tues.–Thurs., 5–10 P.M. Fri.–Sat., 5–9 P.M. Sun., $12–28) serves up dishes from southern, central, and northern Mexico. Owner Azucena Tovar's *queso fundido* with crab and crepes with goat and blue cheese in pomegranate sauce are inspired, especially when paired with a margarita made with fresh lime juice. Dine outside on the homey patio, and learn how Mexican food is more than just refried beans and tacos.

The combination may sound unusual, but **Medizona** (4240 N. Winfield Scott Plaza, 480/947-9500, www.medizonarestaurant.com, 5:30–10 P.M. daily, $16–26) manages to combine Mediterranean and Southwestern cuisines into an imaginative menu. Eggplant tacos with lamb, honey-glazed veal chops, and chiote-rubbed salmon and crayfish with corn risotto are just the beginning. It may take a bit of faith to get past the unattractive facade, but Medizona serves up a meal you're unlikely to find anywhere else. Go ahead—be bold and try something new.

A relative newcomer to the city's dining scene, **The Mission** (3815 N. Brown Ave., 480/636-5005, www.themissionaz.com,

11 A.M.–10 P.M. Sun.–Thurs., 11 A.M.–11 P.M. Fri.–Sat., $12–32) is a perfect Scottsdale combination of Latin flavors and chic style. You can't help but notice the restaurant's neighbor first: the domed Old Adobe Mission, which serves as the inspiration for the restaurant's modern-colonial decor. Start with one of the house cocktails and the amazing *almejas al vapor,* steamed clams with rock shrimp, chorizo, and yucca. The grilled street corn, pork shoulder tacos, and diver scallops are delicious.

The Corral family started **Los Olivos** (7328 E. 2nd St., 480/946-2256, www.losolivosrestaurant.com, 11 A.M.–10 P.M. Mon.–Thurs., 11 A.M.–1 A.M. Fri.–Sat.) more than 50 years ago and named it for the old olive trees along 2nd Street. This affordable Old Town Scottsdale favorite features the Sonoran-style Mexican food that Arizona natives grew up on. Enjoy your carne asada and steak picado (served with homemade flour tortillas hot off the griddle) in the Gaudi-esque Blue Room. Or go for a red chile burro enchilada-style along with the traditional margarita with a salted rim while being serenaded, on weekends, by mariachis.

CHILLY DRINKS AND COOL EATS

When it's summer in the city, cold drinks can look quite pretty in Scottsdale. Check out these hot spots for the best warm-weather food and libations.

At **AZ88** (7353 Scottsdale Mall, 480/994-5576, 11:30 A.M.-1:30 A.M. Mon.-Fri., 5 P.M.-1:30 A.M. Sat.-Sun.), select from the extensive list of cool cocktails, from classic martinis and sparkling cosmos to the cucumber-flavored Pimm's Cup, which is served in a chilled brass mug. Be sure to start with the tasty St. Petersburg Potatoes – house chips topped with cool Scottish smoked salmon, sour cream, radishes, and cucumber – or dive into the Picnic Chicken sandwich's cold sliced chicken breast, pears, pecans, and gorgonzola.

Thanks to its Latin roots, you're sure to find a cool meal from a sultry climate at **Deseo** (6902 E. Greenway Pkwy., 480/624-1030, www.kierlandresort.com, 6-10 P.M. Wed.-Sun., $12-35). Order the Ceviche Trio and a threesome of chef Douglas Rodriguez's 10 seafood appetizers, including the lobster escabeche with baby avocado or the ahi tuna with candied citrus, lime sorbet, and mustard oil. And don't forget to sidle up to the Muddle Bar to concoct a frosty blend of fresh fruits, herbs, and your favorite spirit.

The flavorful sashimi and *nigiri* at **Stingray Sushi** (4302 N. Scottsdale Rd., 480/941-4460, www.stingraysushi.com, 11:30 A.M.-midnight daily) are always refreshing, but it's the hip restaurant's "cold dish" menu that serves as the perfect remedy to triple-digit temperatures. Try the indulgent lobster ceviche or the seared *hamachi* drizzled with white truffle oil. Either dish can be exquisitely paired with an icy Japanese beer, chilled sake, or the Summer Sumo, a blend of lemongrass-infused Grey Goose vodka, vanilla syrup, ginger beer, and the citrus-flavored Licor 43. For dessert, top off the evening with green-tea or red-bean ice cream.

Praise to the tiki gods for this tropical oasis of cool. Polynesian-themed **Drift** (4341 N. 75th St., 480/949-8454, 11:30 A.M.-2 A.M.) serves up ice-cold treats with a kick, from pitchers of Hawaiian beer and minty *mojitos* to tropical mai tais, hurricanes, and piña coladas. And though there are plenty of psychedelic-colored punches to distract you, be sure to sample the chilled vegetarian spring rolls, crisp salads, and fresh tuna *poke* with mango, avocado, and cucumber.

◀ **Roaring Fork** (4800 N. Scottsdale Rd., 480/947-0795, www.eddiev.com, 4–10 P.M. Mon.–Sat., 4–9 P.M. Sun., $15–35) serves hearty cowboy grub fit for the most finicky foodies. In fact, former chef Robert McGrath won an "innovative menu" James Beard award for his work. Share the small iron kettle of green chile pork stew, and order the Roaring Fork "Big Ass" Burger, New Mexico fondue pot with little lamb chops, or grilled grouper fish tacos. You're sure to find a nice pairing for the Western cuisine on the restaurant's bold wine list.

Pizza

Try to get a seat on the patio of **Grazie Pizzeria & Wine Bar** (6952 E. Main St., 480/663-9797, www.grazie.us, 11 A.M.–10 P.M. daily). For some reason, the gourmet pizzas seem to taste better outside. The delicious selection of thin-crust pies, prepared with hand-tossed dough and housemade mozzarella, pop with simple ingredients like prosciutto, arugula, shaved parmigiano reggiano cheese, and kalamata olives. Select a bottle of sangiovese or chianti from the extensive wine list, and start thinking about how you're going to make room for the panna cotta.

Grimaldi's Coal Brick-Oven Pizzeria (4000 N. Scottsdale Road, 480/994-1100, www.patsygrimaldis.com, 11 A.M.–11 P.M. Mon.–Thurs., 11 A.M.–midnight Fri.–Sat., $10–16) brings a Brooklyn tradition to the Valley of the Sun with its coal-fired ovens and famous "secret" sauce. The simple menu offers salad starters, calzones, and pizzas, accompanied by list of fresh toppings. Kids will love the quarter-sized slices of pepperoni, and the ricotta cheese is incredible. Be prepared to build up an appetite—its reputation for unique flavor draws large crowds to this casual and family-friendly spot.

Steakhouses

Don and Charlie's Steakhouse (7501 E. Camelback Rd., 480/990-0900, www.donandcharlies.com, 5–9:30 P.M. Mon.–Sat., 5–9 P.M. Sun., $15–45) woos sports-history and red-meat aficionados alike. The upscale eatery is adorned with rich, dark woods and enough sports memorabilia and autographs to make Bob Costas's head spin. The Ned Colletti Chicken Schnitzel or the ribeye steak is a perfect accompaniment to a stiff cocktail from the full bar. Don't let the sports memorabilia fool you; Don and Charlie's is an old-Scottsdale gem, and the perfect place to fill your belly and lighten your wallet after a round of golf or a spring training baseball game.

Mastros City Hall Steakhouse (6991 E. Camelback Rd., 480/941-4700, www.cityhallsteakhouse.com, 5–10 P.M. Sun.–Thurs., 5–11 P.M. Fri.–Sat., $30–75) serves all the classics you'd expect at a high-end steakhouse: lobster cocktails, oysters Rockefeller, and a host of filets, poterhouses, ribeyes, and chops. The side dishes—sautéed asparagus, creamed spinach, au gratin potatoes—are ordered family style. The happening bar, which often has live music, attracts singles of all ages in the evenings.

CENTRAL SCOTTSDALE AND PARADISE VALLEY
Breakfast

Where to begin at **Butterfield's Pancake House & Restaurant** (7388 E. Shea Blvd., 480/951-6002, 6 A.M.–3 P.M. daily, $9–12)? The menu is an epic breakfast journey, with a dozen kinds of pancakes, omelets that range from Denver to Jambalaya, and enough egg dishes to shut down Denny's. That doesn't even count the French toast and crepes, Belgian waffles, Spanish frittatas, or the Dutch oven-baked pancakes. Order a cup of coffee—it's gonna be a while.

Italian

Veneto Trattoria Italiana (6137 N. Scottsdale Rd., 480/948-9928, www.venetotrattoria.

com, 5–10 P.M. Mon.–Sat., 4:30–9 P.M. Sun., $18–26) specializes in cuisine from Venice and northern Italy. Dine alfresco on the patio, and start with the spinach salad with warm goat cheese or *baccala* (cod whipped with cheese spread atop polenta). The house specials like *tagliolini* (clams, mussels, and shrimp with linguine) and sea bass with a lemon-dijon sauce are only surpassed by the osso buco over saffron risotto. For dessert, splurge and order the *affogato,* vanilla ice cream with white chocolate chips and a shot of Scotch-flavored espresso.

New American

They just don't make 'em anymore like **El Chorro Lodge** (5550 E. Lincoln Dr., 480/948-5170, www.elchorrolodge.com, 11 A.M.–10 P.M. Mon.–Thurs., 5:30–11 P.M. Fri.–Sat., 5:30–11 P.M. Sun., $25–35). This Paradise Valley institution has been serving fresh fish, roasted duck, beef stroganoff, and mesquite-broiled steaks since the 1930s. Come with that special someone, and order the "trailside specialty" Chateaubriand for two and cap the evening with El Chorro's famous sticky buns, a 65-year-old El Chorro tradition.

The panorama shot of Mummy Mountain at sunset is worth the reservation alone. From its perch atop Paradise Valley, **Elements** (5700 E. McDonald Rd., Paradise Valley, 480/607-2300, www.elementsrestaurant.com, 7–10:30 A.M., 11:30 A.M.–2 P.M., 5:30–9:30 P.M. daily, $17–32) is a treat in many respects. The mod decor is stylish, and the views are stunning. However, it's the simple and natural menu by *Iron Chef*-winner Beau McMillan, the friendliest chef you're likely to meet, that makes Elements special. His innovative dishes change with the season but always maintain a farm-fresh American flavor with Asian accents.

Lon's at the Hermosa Inn (5532 N. Palo Cristi Rd., 602/955-7878, www.lons.com, 11:30 A.M.–2 P.M. and 5:30–10 P.M. Mon.–Fri., 5:30–10 P.M. Sat., 10 A.M.–2 P.M. and 5:30–10 P.M. Sun., $15–35) prides itself on being the most authentic hacienda in Arizona. Once the home of cowboy artist Lon Megargee, the elegant yet cozy adobe and wood-finished interior captures the allure of Old Arizona. Grilled salmon with blackberry shellac, duck confit with chile-pomegranate glaze, and truffle-scented mac and cheese round out the menu, which features ingredients grown on the inn's grounds. Dine on the patio for beautiful views of the desert, and save room for dessert—the chocolate truffle torte with minted berries is incredible.

Slow food chef Chrysa Robertson's **Rancho Pinot** (6208 N. Scottsdale Rd., 480/367-8030, 5:30–10 P.M. Mon.–Sat., www.ranchopinot.com, $15–35) is a master class in using fresh, seasonal food without a lot of hoopla or Scottsdale flash. You can't help but love the vegetarian antipasto and diver scallops on cornbacon fritters. The Southwest decor and artful recipes may not be for everyone, but you can't help but admire the restaurant's use of local ingredients and experimental flavors.

Spanish

The dramatic painting of a flamenco dancer in the bar sets the tone for **Prado** (4949 E. Lincoln Dr., 480/627-3004, www.pradolife.com, 8 A.M.–10 P.M. Sun.–Thurs., 8 A.M.–11 P.M. Fri.–Sun.) at the Montelucia Resort. Chef Claudio Urciuoli boldly draws his inspiration from traditional Andalusian cooking, importing succulent hams and rich cheeses from Spain. The restaurant's wood-fired gilled meats, like the daily lamb trio and suckling pig, are tender and smoky, and the paella and prawns are perfect.

Steakhouse

Chef Laurent Tourondel's modern American steakhouse, **BLT Steak** (5402 E. Lincoln Dr., 480/905-7979, www.bltscottsdale.com, 6–10 P.M. Sun.–Thurs., 6–11 P.M. Fri.–Sat., $15–48) brings a bit of New York chic to Paradise Valley's Camelback Inn. The long, dark-wood bar and reclaimed mesquite wood floors seem to disappear, though, when the lineup of certified Black Angus, Kobe, and Wagyu steaks arrive, not to mention the signature gruyère popovers and twice-baked sweet potatoes. The three-course prix fixe Blackboard Menu ($60) allows diners to sample Tourondel's mastery in action.

NORTH SCOTTSDALE
Breakfast, Lunch, and Snacks

The bright and airy **Breakfast Joynt** (14891 N. Northsight Blvd., 480/443-5324, www.thebreakfastjoynt.com, 6:30 A.M.–2:30 P.M. daily, $7–10) serves up filling treats like Texas French toast, chocolate-chip pancakes, and home-style biscuits with sausage gravy. While you can get breakfast until close, their midday lunchtime menu features salads, burgers, classic monte cristos and tuna melts, and specialties like the Crazy-Big Trash-Can Lid pork sandwich.

The hipster diner and market **Chloe's Corner** (15215 N. Kierland Blvd., 480/998-0202, www.foxrc.com, 7 A.M.–6 P.M. Mon.–Fri., 8 A.M.–6 P.M. Sat., 9 A.M.–6 P.M. Sun.) is a fun place to get a quick and inexpensive meal at Kierland Commons. Grab an egg sandwich and coffee in the morning, or plop down at the butcher-block counter when lunch rolls around for the chopped salad with turkey, blue cheese, and candied pecans. For an midafternoon pick-me-up, the vanilla, chocolate, and strawberry hand-dipped milk shakes are delicious.

At **JP Pancake** (9619 N. Hayden Rd., 480/596-9369, www.jppancake.com, 7:30 A.M.–1:30 P.M. Tues.–Sun., $8–10) you'll find light and golden flapjacks topped with mounds of fruit, nuts, and chocolate, all made to order. Try the specialty oven-baked pancakes or dive into a short stack of orange poppy, coconut cranberry, lemon pecan, or strawberry hotcakes. There are waffles, French toast, eggs, and omelets as well.

Burgers and Sandwiches

Four Peaks Grill & Tap (15730 N. Pima Rd., 480/991-1795, www.fourpeaks.com, 11 A.M.–2 A.M. Mon.–Sat., 10 A.M.–2 A.M. Sun., $15–25) showcases its unique Tempe-brewed beers at this North Scottsdale location. The curious can find a full listing of beers, with their alcohol contents, on the chalkboard. The Kiltlifter and 8th Street ales are local specialties, but serious hopheads will enjoy the Hop Knot IPA. If you're hungry, the Tap Room Tenderloin with beer-battered fries is especially good when upgraded from the hoagie to "beer bread." And for those limiting their red meat intake, the veggie burger is one of the best in town.

French

Why travel to Scottsdale to have French food? Well, taste the onion soup at **Zinc Bistro** (15034 N. Scottsdale Rd., 480/603-0922, www.zincbistroaz.com, 11 A.M.–10 P.M. daily, $15–30) and we'll talk. The Kierland Commons restaurant feels like a Parisian neighborhood favorite, right down to the mosaic floor, red leather banquettes, mirrored walls, and 25-foot zinc bar. Grab a sidewalk table if you're up for a little people-watching, or head for the candle-lit garden patio if you'd like a more romantic setting to enjoy your bordeaux and braised lamb shank.

Italian

North (15024 N. Scottsdale Road, 480/948-2055, www.foxrc.com, 11 A.M.–9:30 P.M. Sun.–Thurs., 11 A.M.–10:30 P.M. Fri.–Sat., $8–17) at Kierland Commons offers a unique twist on northern Italian cuisine. The urban, loft-like design perfectly reflects the light, modern dishes. Guests can enjoy traditional antipasti and thin-crust pizzas or select from a variety of "plates of the day." Expect your rosemary chicken or braised duck risotto to be served alongside fresh, organic vegetables in satisfying portions. The wine-savvy servers can suggest a bottle of vino to round out your meal.

The entire staff at family-owned **Ristorante Giuseppe** (13610 N. Scottsdale Rd., 480/991-4792, 10 A.M.–8:30 P.M. Mon.–Sat., $10–30) makes you feel welcome. Start with the amazingly fresh bruschetta. Then move on to one of the delicious entrées that are named after family members, one of whom could very likely be your server (Franco claims you'll dream about him after eating his namesake dish). The menu may seem daunting due to its lack of descriptions, so when in doubt, ask. However, ordering one of their famous meatballs is a must. At the end of the night, you might end up enjoying a glass of wine with the server. The cash-only restaurant is BYOB, but there isn't a corkage fee.

Sassi (10455 Pinnacle Peak Pkwy, 480/502-9095, www.sassi.biz, 5:30–10 P.M. Tues.–Sun., $15–38) means "rocks" in Italian, a reference to its Pinnacle Peak location, but its food and service are anything but rocky. The southern Italian cuisine has been updated and re-imagined, earning praise from magazines and foodies alike. The gran reserva prosciutto from Parma and Sicilian-style eggplant baked with mozzarella antipasti are followed by pastas that range from hearty to subtle and delicate. Entrées include a wood-grilled filet and fresh halibut with olives, capers, and fingerling potatoes. Try to dine on the patio at sunset for the complete Sassi experience.

Latin American and Mexican

Deseo (6902 E. Greenway Pkwy., 480/624-1030, www.kierlandresort.com, 6–10 P.M. Wed.–Sun., $12–35) is really good—I can't say it more simply. James Beard Award–winning chef Douglas Rodriguez's survey of Nuevo Latino fare at The Westin Kierland spans Latin Mexican, Caribbean, and Native American cuisine. The impressive ceviche menu may convince first-timers to give the fresh seafood starter a try. Order a cocktail from the Muddle Bar, where fresh fruits and herbs are mashed together and given a little extra kick by an assortment of premium liquors. Then, dive into the goat cheese empanadas, Kobe meatballs, and brie potato mash.

Cave Creek may be famous for its cowboy steaks and burgers, but do not miss the casual **El Encanto** (6248 E. Cave Creek Rd., 480/488-1752, www.elencantorestaurant.com, 11 A.M.–10 P.M. Mon.–Sat., 9 A.M.–10 P.M. Sun., $9–17) for legitimate Mexican cuisine. Outdoor tables line a pleasant lagoon where palm trees grow and ducks wait patiently for a reward. It's been named one of the best places in the Valley to pop the question, but if you came for the food, not romance, you're in luck. The chef came from a coastal Mexican town and has perfected the art of seafood. He recommends the sea bass Vera Cruz—the "real flavor of Mexico"—and the chicken mole. True Mexican food buffs will salivate over the *carnitas poblana relleno,* a roasted chile stuffed with tender, slow-cooked pork and green chile sauce.

New American

Binkley's (6920 E. Cave Creek Rd., 480/437-1072, www.binkleysrestaurant.com, 5–10:30 P.M. Tues.–Sat., $25–32) may be the best restaurant in Arizona. Chef Kevin Binkley, who trained with superstar chef Thomas Keller, brings style and culinary panache to his eponymous Cave Creek eatery, changing his menu daily to showcase fresh, seasonal ingredients. What's all the fuss about? Order the four-, five- or six-course tasting menu, and you'll see. The carefully arranged arugula salad, sunchoke soup with pancetta, and brown-butter-crusted cod are punctuated by a series of *amuse-bouche* presentations, which range from fois gras to "frozen balls of carrots created through the magic of molecular gastronomy."

For a more causal option, consider **Café Bink** (36899 N. Tom Darlington Dr., 480/488-9796, 11 A.M.–9:30 A.M. Tues.–Sat., $8–20), which features superb mountain views, a cozy patio, and French bistro-inspired fare. You'll find a few of the usual Parisian suspects—cheese and spinach quiche, onion soup, heirloom tomato salad, flat iron steak—though chef Binkley shakes things up with some inventive additions. For instance, the lunchtime Cuban-style pork sandwich with Dijon mustard, gruyère cheese, and crunchy bread is incredible. In the evening, the dinner lineup expands to include roasted chicken legs with confit garlic, seared sea scallops, and a rich pork cassoulet.

Enjoy a glass of pinot noir in the unique North Scottsdale setting of DC Ranch Marketplace at **Armitage** (20751 N. Pima Rd., 480/502-1641, www.armitagewine.com, 11 A.M.–midnight Mon.–Thurs., 11 A.M.–1 A.M. Fri.–Sat., 10 A.M.–midnight Sun., $9–17). The wine bar and bistro has a little bit of everything, from tasty bruschetta and baked brie for the peckish to beer brat paninis, ahi tuna sliders, and whiskey butter ribeye steaks for the downright hungry. Sundays are ideal; the filling brunch menu lures neighbors from their million-dollar homes with the promise of bellinis and bloody marys, and the live music in the evening keeps the party going.

Next door, **Eddie V's** (20715 N. Pima Rd., 480/538-8468, www.eddiev.com, 4:30–11 P.M. Mon.–Sat., 5–10 P.M. Sun., $30–45) prepares the freshest catches of great seafood in town, with new deliveries of lobster, shrimp, and scallops arriving every morning. Go with Eddie V's oyster bar or the tower of iced shellfish before trying out the Chilean sea bass, steamed "Hong Kong style."

Slow down and sample the multi-course lineup at **Heirloom** (20775 N. Pima Rd., 480/515-2575, 6–9 P.M. Tues.–Sat., $30–50). Noted Valley chef Michael DeMaria's restaurant at DC Ranch Marketplace features an exquisite mix-and-match tasting menu shaped by seasonal ingredients, allowing diners to savor a variety of fresh flavors and textures. Begin with one of the locally grown starters, like the namesake heirloom tomato soup with tiny "pestoed" pasta or the organic beets with chianti-tossed arugula, lamb's lettuce, and *manchego* cheese. The bacon-seared Idaho trout, butter-poached lobster with garlicky spinach, and braised Kurobuta pork are also phenomenal. Thankfully, the portions are small, which means you'll have room for the custard-filled cake doughnuts on smooth lemon chiffon.

Mosaic (10600 E. Jomax Rd., 480/563-9600, www.mosaic-restaurant.com, 4:30–10 P.M. Tues.–Sat., $12–40) will delight even the most finicky and jaded taste buds. Chef/owner Deborah Knight's eclectic dishes are designed to be savored, and with the broad range of flavors and ingredients, you'll want to try it all. Consider the green chile and citrus-marinated lobster tail, followed by the truffle-seared veal tenderloin. The next course: Why not a cardamom-caramel fondue? Thankfully, diners who are having a hard time deciding what to order can select from three five-course tasting menus, in addition to à la carte options.

Steakhouses

It seems celebrity chefs can't resist the temptation to put their stamp on the Arizona steakhouse, and Michael Mina's chic-and-sleek **Bourbon Steak** (7575 E. Princess Dr., 480/513-6002, www.michaelmina.

net, 5:30–10 P.M. Tues.–Sat., $30–72) at the Fairmont Scottsdale Resort is as over-the-top as they come. Try the elegantly prepared Kobe steaks, spice-poached prawns, and crisp salads, which are almost overshadowed by the stunning Desert Modernist architecture. If you can pry yourself away from stone-and-glass design, survey the extensive list of side dishes, including brown-butter yam puree, truffled mac and cheese, and brussels sprouts with ham and apple. Order one of the classic, handcrafted cocktails for the perfect complement to the meaty experience. It's pricy, but the ambience and re-imagined comfort food are exquisite.

The Horny Toad (6738 E. Cave Creek Rd., 480/488-9542, www.thehornytoad.com, 11 A.M.–10 P.M. Sun.–Thurs., 11 A.M.–11 P.M. Fri.–Sat., $8–25) has been dishing out ribs and country fun long before tourists discovered Cave Creek. The Horny Toad is one of the few restaurants within riding distance of North Scottsdale where cowboy boots aren't for show. This is a meat lover's dream, especially on Monday, when the barbecue beef ribs are all-you-can-eat. Come hungry for the juicy 16-ounce porterhouse or the half-pound Tijuana Torpedo Burger, which might require a cooling-off period. In addition to the full lineup of barbecue, you'll find plenty of seafood. Polish your dancing boots Friday and Saturday night. Live country-western music goes from 6 P.M. until 10 P.M.

Since its inception in the 1880s as a stagecoach stop, **Reata Pass** (27500 N. Alma School Pkwy., 480/585-7277, www.reatapass.com, 11 A.M.–9 P.M. Tues.–Thurs., 11 A.M.–11 P.M. Fri.–Sat., noon–9 P.M. Sun., $8–18) has been serving meals to hungry travelers in one way or another for more than a century. The food isn't fancy, but the cowboy steakhouse radiates real Western atmosphere, even attracting Hollywood's attention as a frequent backdrop for movies. Grab a beer at the Branding Iron Saloon, and take your grub at one of the indoor or outdoor picnic tables. Afterward, head next door to Greasewood Flat for live country music and dancing under the stars.

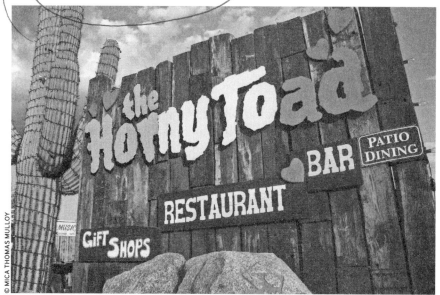

© MICA THOMAS MULLOY

The Horny Toad restaurant in Cave Creek

Information and Services

TOURIST INFORMATION

The **Scottsdale Convention and Visitors Bureau** (800/782-1117, www.scottsdalecvb.com) is one of the best in the country, distributing useful information to help you plan a customized trip to the city. Visit the extensive website or stop by its main office at the **Galleria Corporate Centre** (4343 N. Scottsdale Rd., Ste. 170, 8 A.M.–5:30 P.M. Mon.–Fri.). You also can pick up materials from the concierge desk at **Scottsdale Fashion Square** (7014 E. Camelback Rd., 10 A.M.–7 P.M. Mon.–Sat., 11 A.M.–4 P.M. Sun.) or the **Downtown Scottsdale office** (4248 N. Craftsman Ct., www.downtownscottsdale.com, 8:30 A.M.–5 P.M. Sat.).

LIBRARIES

The four branches of the **Scottsdale Public Library** (480/312-7323, http://library.scottsdaleaz.gov) can be handy resources for visitors. The **Civic Center Library** (3839 N. Drinkwater Blvd., 9 A.M.–9 P.M. Mon.–Thurs., 10 A.M.–6 P.M. Fri.–Sat., 1–5 P.M. Sun.) is a popular destination because of its free Wi-Fi, frequent events, and large children's section. The architecturally stunning **Arabian Library** (10215 E. McDowell Mountain Ranch Rd.,

9 A.M.–8 P.M. Mon.–Thurs., 10 A.M.–6 P.M. Fri.–Sat., 1–5 P.M. Sun.) brings Desert Modernism to North Scottsdale. Its rusted, metal facade seems to emerge like small mountain from its rocky site, and the glass walls allow natural light to bathe its reading rooms.

HOSPITALS AND EMERGENCY SERVICES

The renowned **Mayo Clinic** (5777 E. Mayo Blvd., 480/515-6296, www.mayoclinic.org/scottsdale) has a branch in North Scottsdale, serving as an important center for medicine in the Valley. In fact, the large medical complex attracts patients from around the world because of its respected doctors, high-tech equipment, and clinical trials.

Scottsdale Heathcare (www.shc.org) has three hospitals scattered around the city, each with emergency rooms and a spectrum of services. **Scottsdale Healthcare Osborn** (7400 E. Osborn Rd., 480/882-4000) is conveniently located in Old Town, while the **Scottsdale Healthcare Shea** (9003 E. Shea Blvd., 480/323-3000) and **Scottsdale Healthcare Thompson Peak** (7400 E. Thompson Peak Pkwy., 480/324-7000) are found further north.

Getting There and Around

AIR

Phoenix Sky Harbor International Airport (3400 E. Sky Harbor Blvd., 602/273-3300, www.phxskyharbor.com) is a short, 15-minute ride from downtown Scottsdale's restaurants, bar, and hotels. The airport serves as important regional hub for national and international flights, including direct flights to and from New York, London, and Mexico.

If you're able to fly by private jet, **Scottsdale Airport** (15000 N. Airport Drive, 480/312-2321, www.scottsdaleaz.gov/airport) is a handy,

headache-free option. The North Scottsdale airpark, a frequent choice of celebrities, is one of the busiest single-runway airports in the country.

CAR
Rental Cars

In all likelihood, you'll need a vehicle to get around Scottsdale, especially if you want to explore both Old Town and North Scottsdale's attractions. Take the free shuttle from any of the terminals to the **Rental Car Center** (1805

CAR CULTURE

Scottsdale displays its public art where the city's car-loving residents are sure to find it: streetside. Commuters driving Highway 101 (Loop 101) on the Pima Freeway can't help but notice the 60-foot-tall lizards and green-and-pink cacti that decorate the overpasses and retaining walls.

You can also drive by the rusted steel fish of the *Tributary Wall* on Goldwater Boulevard between Indian School and Camelback Roads, a tribute to the nearby Arizona Canal and water, the desert community's most important resource.

The Doors, a two-story collection of three wooden doors on the southwest corner of Scottsdale and Camelback Roads, doesn't seem like much. But get out of your car and go inside the piece, and you'll find a mirrored audio installation that muffles traffic and provides a "sound massage."

For a map of all the city's public art pieces, including works by Robert Indiana and Louise Nevelson, visit www.scottsdalepublicart.org.

with the reliable **SuperShuttle** (602/232-4610, www.supershuttle.com). Its bright blue vans are easy to spot at all of Sky Harbor's terminals.

AAA Sedans (602/454-7433) has a fleet of town cars that can ferry you to Scottsdale for about $50, plus tip. **Desert Knights Sedans & Limousines** (480/348-0600, www.desertknights.com) provides taxis, sedans, limos, and luxury minibuses, which can be a practical option for families or groups.

Also, you can grab a taxi at Sky Harbor with one of three contracted companies: **AAA Cab** (602/437-4000), **AllState** (602/275-8888), and **Discount** (602/266-1110). And if you want to hit the town at night, try **Courier Cab** (602/232-2222).

PUBLIC TRANSPORTATION
Trolley

If you're tired of driving or walking around downtown, the free **Scottsdale Trolley** (480/421-1004, www.scottsdaleaz.gov/trolley, 11 A.M.–9 P.M. daily) shuttles visitors throughout the area, with stops along 5th Avenue, Marshall Way, and Scottsdale Fashion Square.

Bus

Scottsdale is a part of the **Valley Metro** (602/262-7433, www.valleymetro.org) public transportation network, which connects the Phoenix metropolitan area. Its buses run throughout the city, but the new light-rail system, which links the communities of Mesa, Tempe, and Central Phoenix, doesn't stop in Scottsdale. Fares start at 1.25 for a single ride, and multiday passes are available. Visit the website for a comprehensive schedule and map.

E. Sky Harbor Circle, 602/683-3741). You'll find major companies, like **Budget** (602/267-4000, www.budget.com), **Hertz** (602/267-8822, www.hertz.com), and **Enterprise** (602/489-6898), which has convenient drop-off centers around Phoenix and Scottsdale and offers free pickup service. It can be hard to find a gas station near the rental car center, so be sure to fill up before returning your vehicle.

Limos, Shuttles, and Taxis

Join a shared-van ride to your resort or hotel

SCOTTSDALE

SEDONA

Hiking one of Sedona's dusty, red trails, you can't help but pause at the top of a rugged rock formation and appreciate the view. The landscape is simply stunning, especially when streaked a soft burnt orange by the setting sun. The sturdy, crimson mesas easily compete with Arizona's best-known geological wonders, both in terms of grandeur and beauty. As locals quip, "God created the Grand Canyon, but He lives in Sedona."

The red cliffs mark the southern rim of the Colorado Plateau, a massive expanse of land that rises 2,000 feet from the high-desert floor in Sedona and stretches into Utah, Colorado, and New Mexico. The variegated sandstone buttes, carved by wind and rain, feature a series of rounded formations and delicate spires that seem to defy gravity.

This evocative terrain attracts an eclectic following of visitors and residents, some of whom are almost as compelling as the area's famed red rocks. Hikers, climbers, and mountain bikers of all skill levels come to scale the colossal buttes, while cowboy painters and contemporary artists hope to be inspired by their beauty.

Religious pilgrims, from Native Americans to Christians to Buddhists, are drawn to the sacred spaces that have been carved into the landscape, amid dark-green Ponderosa pines and twisted cottonwoods. More recently, New Age followers, equipped with crystals and smudge sticks, have come in search of vortexes, which they believe are invisible centers of spiraling cosmic energy.

For others, the scenery merely serves as a backdrop for golf games, Southwestern cuisine, and rejuvenating spa treatments, while children

HIGHLIGHTS

◖ Chapel of the Holy Cross: Witness this iconic church, which appears to rise out the red rocks, creating a brilliant union of art, nature, and God. Its quiet interior is the perfect place to contemplate Sedona's majestic landscape (page 144).

◖ The Red Rocks: Explore the famous buttes from the road, on foot, or by bike. The massive red-rock buttes, which soar from the desert floor, captivate with intricate spires and rich colors (page 146).

◖ Tlaquepaque Arts and Crafts Village: Explore Sedona's charming shopping center, inspired by small artisan villages in Mexico. It features some of the city's best shops, galleries, and restaurants (page 152).

◖ Jeep Tours: Tour the red rocks from the back of an open-air Jeep. The guided journey is a must-do highlight, and a fun way to explore out-of-the-way formations and learn about Sedona's unique geology and wildlife (page 156).

◖ Oak Creek Canyon: Drive the scenic highway through this leafy refuge north of Sedona. The quiet, wooded setting is an ideal place to take a hike – though kids will want to slip down the natural chute at Slide Rock State Park (page 178).

◖ Jerome: Visit this hillside mining town in the Verde Valley, which locals like to tell you is haunted. The narrow streets that were once home to saloons and brothels now feature small restaurants, galleries, and shops (page 182).

◖ Montezuma Castle National Monument: Discover one of the best-preserved cliff dwellings in the country. The five-story, 20-room pueblo, which clings to side of a limestone wall 75 feet above the ground, is an impressive testament to the ingenuity of the Sinagua people (page 187).

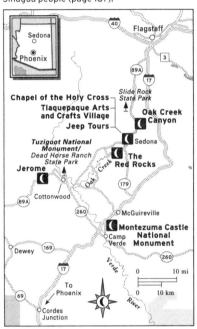

LOOK FOR ◖ TO FIND RECOMMENDED SIGHTS, ACTIVITIES, DINING, AND LODGING.

love the neighboring Oak Creek Canyon's swimming holes and Slide Rock State Park.

Situated about 90 minutes north of Phoenix, Sedona's larger-than-life fame as a travel destination belies its reasonably small size. The 19-square-mile city and its neighboring bedroom community can be broken into three distinct areas worth exploring.

Visitors driving from Phoenix on Highway 179 will arrive in the Village of Oak Creek, a small suburb that has mushroomed in the last decade with a host of new shopping centers, hotels, and restaurants along the main drag. The village is a handy option for exploring the red rocks and, pleasantly, feels a bit less congested than the rest of Sedona.

Continue north on Highway 179, and you'll see many of the area's most prominent rock formations along the seven-mile scenic drive. Once you cross over the leafy banks of Oak

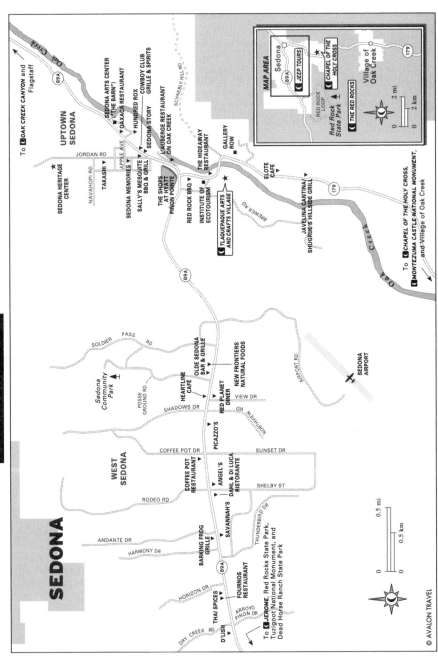

SEDONA

SEDONA

MAP AREA

Sedona
Village of
Oak Creek

JEEP TOURS
CHAPEL OF THE HOLY CROSS
THE RED ROCKS

Red Rock
State Park
RED ROCK
LOOP

2 mi
2 km

To OAK CREEK CANYON and
Flagstaff

Oak Creek

UPTOWN
SEDONA

SEDONA HERITAGE
CENTER

JORDAN RD

NAVAHOPI RD

TAKASHI

APPLE AVE

SEDONA ARTS CENTER
("THE BARN")

OAXACA RESTAURANT

HUNDRED ROX

COWBOY CLUB
GRILLE & SPIRITS

SEDONA STORY

SEDONA MEMORIES

SALLY'S MESQUITE
BBQ & GRILL

THE SHOPS
AT HYATT
PIÑON POINTE

RED ROCK BBQ

INSTITUTE OF
ECOTOURISM

TLAQUEPAQUE ARTS
AND CRAFTS VILLAGE

SCHNEBLY HILL RD

L'AUBERGE RESTAURANT
ON OAK CREEK

THE HIDEAWAY
RESTAURANT

GALLERY
ROW

BREWER RD

ELOTE
CAFE

JAVELINA CANTINA
SHUGRUE'S HILLSIDE GRILL

179

89A

To CHAPEL OF THE HOLY CROSS,
MONTEZUMA CASTLE NATIONAL MONUMENT,
and Village of Oak Creek

Oak Creek

179

To

SOLDIER   PASS   RD

Sedona
Community
Park

POSSE
GROUND RD

SHADOWS DR

HEARTLINE
CAFÉ

OLDE SEDONA
BAR & GRILLE

RED PLANET
DINER

NEW FRONTIERS
NATURAL FOODS

VIEW DR

NORTHVIEW RD

AIRPORT RD

SEDONA
AIRPORT

WEST
SEDONA

COFFEE POT DR

PICAZZO'S

SUNSET DR

COFFEE POT
RESTAURANT

RODEO RD

ANGEL'S

DAHL & DI LUCA
RISTORANTE

SHELBY ST

ANDANTE DR

HARMONY DR

BARKING FROG
GRILLE

SAVANNAH'S

THUNDERBIRD DR

89A

FOURNOS
RESTAURANT

HORIZON DR

THAI SPICES

D'LISH

DRY CREEK RD

ARROYO
PIÑON DR

To JEROME, Red Rocks State Park,
Tuzigoot National Monument, and
Dead Horse Ranch State Park

0.5 mi
0.5 km

© AVALON TRAVEL

© MICA THOMAS MULLOY

Uptown Sedona's shops, galleries, and restaurants

SEDONA

Creek, you'll hit the Y, a three-pronged round-about that splits West Sedona and Uptown Sedona on Route 89A. Touristy Uptown commands impressive views of the rock formations and caters to visitors with a diverse selection of accommodations, restaurants, galleries, and shops. You'll find locals, as well as less-expensive hotels and popular bars and bistros, in West Sedona.

It can be hard at times to get past the hordes of tourists, streaming convoys of brightly colored Jeep tours, and touchy-feely New Age mystics—complaining about the development boom and resulting traffic is a pastime shared by residents and visitors alike. But none of it can really distract or detract from the landscape. After all, no matter where you go or what you do in Sedona, the red rocks cast a powerful shadow that's hard to ignore.

PLANNING YOUR TIME

Sedona makes a terrific weekend getaway, offering natural beauty and some interesting sites within a relatively compact area. The city has grown with its legions of tourists in mind, and its pedestrian-friendly shopping areas, delicious restaurants, and impressively diverse galleries—all surrounded by the red rocks—make exploring the town hassle-free.

Couples yearning for a quick romantic trip with minimal stress can easily pop up from Phoenix for an overnight stay at one of Sedona's charming resorts that overlook Oak Creek. More adventurous travelers, though, may want to stay two or three nights in order to enjoy the natural attractions and historic sites throughout the Verde Valley. The nearby Slide Rock State Park, small mining town of Jerome, and Native American ruins that dot the area make Sedona a convenient home base for side trips.

Outdoor lovers could easily tack on a few extra days to explore Sedona's hiking and biking trails, horseback ride, play golf or tennis, or appreciate the red rocks from a hot-air balloon or biplane.

No matter what time of year you visit, Sedona's landscape fails to disappoint. Spring wildflowers and autumn leaves are irresistible incentives, not to mention balmy temperatures. Summer, on the other hand, is quite warm, with highs in the mid- to high-90s, but it cools off considerably at night. The occasional light snow in winter and annual holiday-light events make a winter trip to Sedona a compelling option.

HISTORY

To first-time visitors, Sedona may appear to be a newly inhabited boomtown. Sure, its red buttes are millions of years old, but the freshly stuccoed shopping centers and recently constructed housing developments don't inspire a sense of history. The truth is, though, settlers have been coming to Sedona and the Verde Valley for 6,000 years, lured by the dramatic landscape and mild climate.

The Sinagua were the first people to leave a lasting mark on the area in A.D. 900. While it doesn't appear that they lived in present-day Sedona, ruins of their pueblos can be found throughout the valley, the most striking being the cliffside Montezuma's Castle. The civilization mysteriously disappeared in 1350, but historians believe they blended into the Apache tribes that roamed northeast Arizona.

In 1876, the Apache were forced onto reservations by the U.S. government, and the first homesteader, John J. Thompson, arrived in Oak Creek Canyon. Additional ranching and farming families joined him, including T.C. Schnebly, an entrepreneurial settler who built his wooden house-cum-hotel where Tlaquepaque and the Los Abrigados Resort now stand. Schnebly established the area's first post office in 1902, which required him to submit a name for the burgeoning community. After the postmaster general in Washington rejected Schnebly Station and Oak Creek Crossing for being too long for a cancellation stamp, Schnebly followed his brother's advice and submitted his wife's name, Sedona.

After the turn of the century, Arizona pioneers built a dusty stagecoach trail through town, connecting the communities of Flagstaff and Prescott, and bringing the first regular tourists to Sedona. More settlers began to stream into the Verde Valley, where they found work as farmers or in Jerome's ore-rich mines.

However, it was another industry that made Sedona famous: the movies. Hollywood filmed many of its classic westerns against the backdrop of Sedona's massive rock formations, beginning with Zane Grey's *Call of the Canyon* in 1923. Since then, stars from John Wayne and Joan Crawford to Robert De Niro and Sharon Stone have shot nearly a hundred films in the area, and the rugged terrain is still attracting production companies.

The big-screen attention propelled Sedona into the national spotlight after World War II, and its tourism industry took off as Americans began to explore the country by car. By the 1980s and '90s, Sedona exploded as a retirement and vacation destination. Fortunately, more than half of the land in and around Sedona has been protected by state and national parks, which has driven up real estate values and pushed new residents into the neighboring Village of Oak Creek and Cottonwood. Still, some 11,000 people live in Sedona today—dwarfed by 3.5 million visitors every year—and the community manages to retain plenty of its frontier-town character.

Sights

Sedona's main attraction is its unique landscape. The red-rock buttes, evergreen pines, and blue skies dominate the horizon, while refreshing Oak Creek cuts through town, creating a peaceful, leafy axis. Make driving the scenic byways and hiking the numerous trails your top priorities, but be sure to carve out some time to visit one of its cultural attractions before heading to Uptown's shops and galleries.

UPTOWN
◖ Chapel of the Holy Cross

In a region renowned for natural beauty, it's hard for a manmade structure to compete for attention, which is why the Chapel of the Holy Cross (780 Chapel Rd., 928/282-4069, www.chapeloftheholycross.com, 9 A.M.–5 P.M. daily, free) seems to take an "if you can't beat 'em, join 'em" route to its design. The chapel's 90-foot-tall cross rises between two red rock formations, framed by a simple Modernist chapel. Perched high above Sedona and just south of Uptown proper, the elegant structure overlooks the valley's famed buttes and attracts visitors to its minimalist interior, embellished only by a floor-to-ceiling window behind the altar and flickering red votives lit by believers and visitors.

The inspiring edifice can be credited to the generosity and talents of Marguerite Brunswig Staude, a philanthropist and sculptor who envisioned a building that could glorify God through art. Her design was inspired by a trip in 1932 to New York City, where she saw a cross in the steel-and-glass facade of the recently constructed Empire State Building. Early sketches of her glass cathedral impressed Lloyd Wright, son of architect Frank Lloyd Wright, but the archbishop of Los Angeles ultimately rejected them for a proposed cathedral. When Staude and her husband bought a ranch in Sedona in 1941, she found the perfect home for her calling. Staude's plans were adapted, and the small chapel was completed in 1956.

KEEPING UP APPEARANCES

As Sedona has mushroomed from small town to tourist mecca, residents have become nearly fanatical in their determination to keep things "tasteful." When mounting road congestion called for traffic lights that could have marred the city's multimillion-dollar-earning views, planners solved the problem by constructing a series of roundabouts from the Village of Oak Creek to the Y intersection on Highway 179. Even global powerhouse McDonald's had to conform to the town's strict zoning ordinances, changing its iconic golden arches to teal at its West Sedona location. And when the sun sets, there are also ordinances for "light pollution" to protect the nighttime sky for stargazing.

SEDONA

© MICA THOMAS MULLOY

Chapel of the Holy Cross

Sedona Heritage Center

Get a glimpse of how Sedona's pioneers lived long before the tourists and art galleries arrived in **Jordan Historical Park.** Tour Jordan House, now the Sedona Heritage Center (735 Jordan Rd., 928/282-7038, www.sedonamuseum.org, 11 A.M.–3 P.M. daily, $3), to see the family's 1930 one-room cabin restored with some of its original furnishings. The home's additions now showcase exhibits about life in early Sedona, from the rough work of farmers and cowboys to an old-fashioned schoolroom. Visitors can also learn about the nearly 100 movies filmed in the area, many shot during Hollywood's Golden Age of westerns. Be sure to venture out to the Apple Packing Shed, which houses Walter Jordan's original apple grading machine, an ingenious bit of frontier ingenuity that sorted his orchard's fruit by quality and size.

Institute of Ecotourism

Located next to the Tlaquepaque Arts and Crafts Village, the Institute of Ecotourism (91 Portal Ln., 928/282-2720, www.ioet.org, 10 A.M.–6 P.M. Mon.–Fri., free) offers a useful overview of the region's natural history and indigenous cultures. The easy-to-digest information about the people, animals, and plants that inhabit area is enhanced by interactive exhibitions for adults and children about geology, astronomy, and Arizona's fragile ecosystem. The modest grounds feature native plants, and its weekly classes and lectures on topics range from Native American storytelling to vortexes. The nonprofit institute is more than a museum, though, as it serves as a think tank for environmentally sensitive travel and tourism.

Sedona Arts Center

Started in 1958 as a place for local artists to teach and share ideas, the Sedona Arts Center (15 Art Barn Rd., 928/282-3809, www.sedonaartscenter.com, 10 A.M.–5 P.M. daily) has evolved to into one of the region's leading cultural forces, helping transform Sedona into an art mecca. Visitors can survey galleries that feature local and regional artists, with rotating

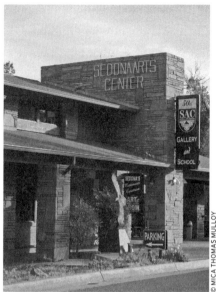
Sedona Arts Center

© MICA THOMAS MULLOY

exhibitions that include fine art, jewelry, sculpture, textiles, and photography. The center's Nassan Gobran School of the Arts offers more than a hundred art classes every year, for a host of media and skill levels. Its three- to five-day intensive art workshops and field expeditions are handy for artistically minded travelers in town for a short period of time.

◖ THE RED ROCKS

It's called Red Rock Country for a reason. The mammoth buttes surround Sedona, towering over the desert and attracting visitors from around the world. You won't need to search for the rocky, prehistoric formations—you'll see them everywhere: from the highway, through your hotel-room window, on the patio at a small restaurant, and even while you're getting a Watsu massage in an outdoor pool.

Their monolithic size, craggy spires, and deep-rust color create an otherworldly landscape, especially when contrasted against the brilliant blue sky and forest-green pine trees and scrub that burrow into the terrain. Most

© BOB CLEMENZ / SEDONA CVB

Bell Rock and Courthouse Butte

SEDONA

of the formations are named after shapes their silhouettes resemble—though you should expect a little creative license.

It doesn't take much effort to get an up-close view of these formations. Simply pull off one of the highways and you'll find a parking spot and a trail ready to hike, bike, horseback ride, or four-wheel drive.

Village of Oak Creek

If you're driving north from Phoenix on Highway 179, the first major butte you'll recognize is **Bell Rock,** the easiest formation to match to its namesake silhouette. Behind the Liberty Bell–shaped butte, you can spot the stout **Courthouse Butte.**

On the opposite side of the highway to the west, you'll discover the enormous **Castle Rock,** as well as the more modest **Cathedral Rock,** a multi-spired, photogenic formation. Pull off Highway 179 and drive up Chapel Road to the Chapel of the Holy Cross, where you can get a clear view of three small formations: the beaked **Eagle Head Rock,** the

double spires of **Twin Nuns,** and the charming **Mother and Child Rock.** To see the low-lying **Submarine Rock,** head east on Morgan Drive. You'll need to hike in on your own to climb the formation or take a Jeep tour.

Uptown Sedona

Once you drive into town, you can see **Thumb Butte and the Bench.** Kids will get a kick out of **Snoopy Rock** from the perspective of Uptown Sedona, where they'll recognize the famous beagle asleep on his back. If you continue north on Highway 89A, you'll locate **Steamboat Rock** towering west of the road.

West Sedona

Travel back down Highway 89A to West Sedona and turn south on Airport Road, where you'll be treated to one of Sedona's best panoramic views on **Airport Mesa.** You can make out most of the major formations as well as find easy hiking trails and one of Sedona's best-known vortexes.

Continuing west on Highway 89A, look north

and you'll see the telltale spout of **Coffeepot Rock** before spotting the spire of **Chimney Rock** and the domed **Capitol Butte.**

Parks and Recreation Areas

Crescent Moon Recreation Area (928/282-4119, www.fs.fed.us/r3/Coconino, $7 per vehicle) is a popular picnic spot, thanks to the cool waters of Oak Creek and postcard views of Cathedral and Castle Rocks. Hiking trails meander from the creek and through the trees to Cathedral Rock.

Oak Creek flows to the 286-acre **Red Rock State Park** (928/282-6907, http://azstateparks.com/parks/rero, $6 per vehicle) on the western edge of town. The former Smoke Trail Ranch was opened to the public as a state park in 1991 and now serves as a protected riparian habitat for native wildlife and plants. Both parks can be accessed via Red Rock Loop Road.

WHY SO RED?

The red rocks' famous color is just part of the story that created this dramatic landscape. Much of the credit goes to the area's unique geology – and a few hundred million years of work. Over the eons, this part of Arizona has sat under the ocean, endured volcanic eruptions, and fluctuated between muggy swamp and Sahara-like desert. With each climatic and geological upheaval, a new layer of sediment was added, producing layer upon layer of limestone and sandstone.

Oak Creek began the work of exposing these layers, splitting the buttes from the massive Colorado Plateau, which extends well into the Four Corners region. Erosion, caused by wind and rain, did most of the shaping and sculpting of those buttes, creating the intricate formations and tall, slender spires seen today.

As for that trademark color; not surprisingly, the rusty red rocks get their tint from dissolved iron that has drained through the porous sandstone layers. That classic mixture of iron and water produced iron oxide, staining the brilliantly colored buttes red. In most formations, you'll see rings that reveal each of Sedona's previous lives. The hard, white limestone formed at the bottom of the sea, while the porous, red sandstone was created from the dry sands that once blew across the landscape. To make things a bit more complicated, shifting tectonic plates caused some of the land to buckle, shifting these layers. Fortunately for visitors, all of that work has resulted in one of the most beautiful landscapes on Earth.

Sedona's red rocks, from the Village of Oak Creek

Cathedral Rock and Oak Creek

Coffeepot Rock

Entertainment and Events

Despite the millions of tourists who visit annually, Sedona is still a small town, and its slow pace and relaxed atmosphere mean you won't discover a ton of events or a buzzing nightlife. But that's not a bad thing. In fact, a quiet evening under the stars with a locally brewed beer in hand can provide a nice complement to a day full of hiking and exploring the red rocks.

NIGHTLIFE

Couples will find plenty of romantic restaurants in which to enjoy a glass of wine, though the big resorts expertly set the mood with cozy fireplaces and leafy patios. Make the 15-minute drive to **Enchantment Resort** (525 Boynton Canyon Rd., 928/282-2900), which is nestled in the horseshoe-shaped Boynton Canyon. The red-rock walls glow at sunset

and provide a memorable backdrop for the resort's signature prickly pear margaritas. The creekside wine bar at **L'Auberge de Sedona Resort** (301 L'Auberge Ln., 928/282-1661) in Uptown Sedona creates an intimate, alfresco spot to share a bottle of wine.

Join the locals at **Full Moon Saloon** (7000 Hwy. 179, 928/284-1872, 11 A.M.–2 A.M. daily) at Tequa Marketplace in the Village of Oak Creek. What Full Moon lacks in rustic character, the relatively new watering hole makes up for with a friendly crowd and casual vibe that extends from the bar to the billiards tables. Don't be surprised to see the small dance floor fill up when the occasional live band is playing.

You don't have to look far to find a decent beer in Red Rock Country. **Oak Creek Brewery and Grill** (2050 Yavapai Rd., 928/203-9441,

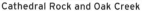

© MICA THOMAS MULLOY

4–11 P.M. Mon.–Thurs., noon–1 A.M. Fri.–Sun.) in West Sedona serves up a slew of award-winning handcrafted beers, like its popular amber ale, pilsner-style gold lager, and refreshing hefeweizen. Check out the cabinet where members stow their personal mugs before heading out to the patio to listen to live music, which ranges from rockabilly and bluegrass to "off-kilter jazz fusion."

The **Olde Sedona Bar & Grille** (1405 W. Hwy. 89A, 928/282-5670, 11 A.M.–2 A.M. daily) is a West Sedona mainstay. The self-described family restaurant may not have the best food in town, but its live music and funky Western atmosphere can't be beat. Grab a local brew at sunset and head to the second-story patio for a view of the red rocks. You could easily spend the rest of the night drinking, shooting pool, dancing, and listening to a blues band with new friends.

PJ's Village Pub & Sports Lounge (40 W. Cortez Dr., 928/284-2250, 10 A.M.–2 A.M. daily) is a laid-back watering hole in the Village of Oak Creek that packs in locals with live music on Saturday nights. As at any good neighborhood bar, you'll find regulars playing darts and video games, as well as three pool tables that are free on Sunday evenings.

You never know what you'll find at the spirited **Relics Restaurant & Nightclub at Rainbow's End** (3235 W. Hwy. 89A, 928/282-1593, 4 P.M.–2 A.M. daily), a former homestead, general store, and stagecoach stop. Thankfully, the dancehall—which retains much of its rustic ambience and northern Arizona's largest wooden dance floor—is still attracting Sedonans with weekly events, including Johnny Cash tributes, Latino nights, and DJ dance parties that range from Motown to country. If the barroom looks a little familiar, you may have seen it in the 1965 Western *The Rounders,* starring Henry Fonda and Glenn Ford.

The **Rooftop Cantina** (321 N. Hwy. 89A, 928/282-4179, 11 A.M.–9 P.M. daily) at Oaxaca Restaurant serves tasty margaritas and a fine menu of 50 tequilas. Best of all, the views of Snoopy Rock are as much fun as the atmosphere at this Uptown Mexican restaurant.

If you want to catch a big game on TV, **Stakes and Sticks Sports Bar and Celebrity Grill** (160 Portal Ln., 928/204-7849, 8 A.M.–3 P.M. 5–9 P.M. Mon.–Thurs., 11 A.M.–midnight Fri.–Sat., 8 A.M.–9 P.M. Sun.) at the elegant Los Abrigados Resort and Spa has two dozen screens broadcasting the wide world of sports. True to its promise of "pilsner, pool, and ponies," here you can wager on horse races at the automated betting stations inside the billiards room or enjoy a beer on the more subdued patio.

PERFORMING ARTS

Chamber Music Sedona (928/204-2415, www.chambermusicsedona.org) presents an eclectic series of artists year-round at venues throughout Sedona, from pianists and string quartets to Latin guitar and small jazz bands. Check its website for performance dates and locations. **Canyon Moon Theatre Company** (6601 Hwy. 179, 928/282-6212, www.

canyonmoontheatre.org) stages an eclectic mix of dramas, comedies, and musicals at its theater in the Village of Oak Creek.

FESTIVALS AND EVENTS
February
Sedona boasts a rich selection of outdoor festivals throughout the year. Serious runners converge the first week of February for the **Sedona Marathon** (800/775-7671, www.sedonamarathon.com). Unlike big-city races, the challenging run wends part of its course onto dirt roads in West Sedona, offering spectacular views and a few wildlife sightings. The full- and half-marathon runs, as well as the more manageable 5K option, are open to runners of all levels.

Around the last week of February, the **Sedona International Film Festival** (2081 W. Hwy. 89A, 928/282-1177, www.sedonafilmfestival.com) presents more than 100 movies from around the world, including big-budget features, documentaries, shorts, and student films. Some have even gone on to earn Academy Award nominations. The screenings are open to the public, with directors, producers, and stars frequently in attendance.

August-September
The **Red Rock Music Festival** (877/733-7257, www.redrocksmusicfestival.com) in late August and early September attracts classical musical lovers for a vibrant showcase of chamber and orchestral music, as well as shows by flamenco and Native American performers. Concerts and events are held at venues throughout Sedona.

For fans of bebop, swing, and soul, **Sedona Jazz on the Rocks** (928/282-0590, www.sedonajazz.com) in late September showcases live outdoor performances of jazz classics under the red rocks. Call or visit the website for locations and events.

October
In early October, look for the sea of white tents in West Sedona. The **Sedona Arts Festival** (995 Upper Red Rock Loop Rd., 928/204-9456, www.sedonaartsfestival.org) assembles more than 100 artists for a showcase of contemporary paintings and sculpture, colorful jewelry, and works by Native American artists and craftspeople. Children can create their own masterpieces from paint, glitter, beads, and feathers in the Kid Zone.

Sedona's residents know how to live the good life, and the **Luxury Home & Classic Car Tour** (928/284-3034, www.azopera.com) in mid-October offers a peek into some of the area's most lavish homes. Tour the beautifully designed residences and survey the mint-condition vintage autos during the weekend-long event. Proceeds benefit the Arizona Opera League of Northern Arizona.

The **Sedona Plein Air Festival** (928/282-3809, www.sedonapleinairfestival.com) in late October attracts about 30 painters from around the country to create art "in the open air," a technique made famous by the French Impressionists. The weeklong event—at trailheads, creeks, and parks throughout town—includes demonstrations and workshops for painters hoping to develop their technical abilities, as well art lovers who would like a behind-the-scenes peek.

November-December
When the weather turns chilly in late November, more than a million lights go up at Los Abrigados Resort and Spa for the **Red Rock Fantasy** (1090 W. Hwy. 89A, 928/282-1777, www.redrockfantasy.com). Participants compete by creating traditional and quirky nighttime displays that twinkle through the holiday season. And to see a unique Southwestern holiday tradition, visit Tlaquepaque Arts and Crafts Village for the **Festival of Lights** (336 Hwy. 179, 928/282-4838, www.tlaq.com) in mid-December. Some 6,000 glowing luminarias—small paper bags filled with sand and a single lit candle—flicker in the charming shopping complex.

SEDONA

Shopping

After tracking down impossibly perfect views of the red rocks, shopping is probably Sedona's most popular activity, with the vast majority of stores targeting the out-of-state visitors who flock here for a taste of Arizona—or to experience the New Age energy. Small specialty stores selling cactus jellies, cowboy boots and hats, colorful pottery, and mystical gemstones line Highways 179 and 89A. And you won't have to search long to find Native American arts and crafts, like handmade Navajo rugs and kachina dolls.

Also, Sedona's thriving gallery scene attracts serious collectors as well as first-time buyers. The 50-some galleries range from mammoth, light-filled spaces selling large-format bronzes and contemporary pieces to intimate studios specializing in Western-themed canvases. Even if art isn't your "thing," the gallery scene is a quintessential part of Sedona and shouldn't be missed.

You'll find the greatest concentration of souvenir shops, metaphysical boutiques, and galleries in Uptown. If you're looking for gifts for friends and family back home, the gourmet salsas, outdoor wind sculptures, silver jewelry, and "healing" crystals can be fun and a little kitschy. You may even want to consider splurging on a handcrafted piece of furniture or canvas to remember your trip.

UPTOWN
◖ Tlaquepaque Arts and Crafts Village

Rarely does a shopping center become an attraction in its own right, but the charming Tlaquepaque Arts and Crafts Village (336 Hwy. 179, 928/282-4838, www.tlaq.com, shops open 10 A.M.–5 P.M. daily) is considered a Sedona landmark. Tlaquepaque (pronounced tuh-LAH-kuh-PAH-kee) was the mission of Abe Miller, who bought the 4.5-acre homestead on the banks of Oak Creek in the early 1970s, promising its original owners that he would do his best to preserve the property's mature sycamore grove.

Tlaquepaque Arts and Crafts Village

© MICA THOMAS MULLOY

Miller envisioned an artists' enclave where visitors could see craftspeople at work. He traveled around Mexico with an architect and designer, visiting towns and villages to observe how shoppers and artisans interacted in the small plazas and markets. He replicated the colonial-style buildings and courtyards, decorating them with colorful tiles and flowers, and incorporating truckloads of iron work, carved doors, and clay pots and lanterns that he had shipped north from Mexico. He was particularly proud of the chapel, a romanticized confection of stained-glass windows, hand-carved leather pews, and adobe walls, which now hosts weddings year-round.

True to his word, Miller built the complex around the property's old sycamore and cypress trees, giving the shopping village a timeless feel. And though Miller's vision of a live-work artists' village didn't come to full fruition, Tlaquepaque—which means "best of everything"—now houses many of Sedona's finest boutiques, galleries, cafés, and restaurants.

ART GALLERIES
Tlaquepaque's **Andrea Smith Gallery** (928/203-9002, www.andreasmithgallery. com) features "uplifting" pieces from cultures around the world, including colorful Native American–inspired canvases, imported religious sculpture from Asia and India, and jewelry made with turquoise, topaz, and crystals.

Eclectic Image Gallery (928/203-4333, www.eclecticimage.com) specializes in framed travel photography. The black-and-white landscapes and brilliantly colored images of Arizona's canyons, rivers, and forests make terrific souvenirs.

You'll find South American folk art at **El Picaflor** (928/282-1173, www.elpicaflor.com), a quirky gallery that stocks handcrafted ceramics, intricate patchwork tapestries, and beautifully woven garments made from Peruvian alpaca wool.

The indoor-outdoor **El Prado by the Creek** (928/282-7309, www.elpradogalleries.com) overlooks Sedona's peaceful Oak Creek, though it's hard to be distracted from El Prado's large metal sculptures that twist and revolve in the wind. The elegant gallery also showcases contemporary and Western paintings, pottery, and mixed-media pieces.

For a colorful collection of hand-blown glass art, visit **Kuivato Glass Gallery** (928/282-1212, www.kuivato.com). The delicate glass sculptures, fountains, and chandeliers sparkle in light, tempting many buyers to ship one of the fragile pieces home.

Renee Taylor Gallery (928/282-7130, www.reneetaylorgallery.com) regularly draws celebrities and serious art collectors with an eclectic mix of contemporary paintings, jewelry, and sculpture. The abstract works and modern interpretations of Western landscapes are particularly strong.

BOUTIQUES AND SPECIALTY SHOPS
There are a few clothing boutiques at Tlaquepaque. **Isadora** (928/282-6232) stocks woven coats with bold prints in copper, silver, and black, as well as Native American–inspired shawls and scarves. **Biada's Fine Clothing** (928/282-5665) is a bit hipper, with a modern interior space that could best be described as "Sedona loft."

One of Abe Miller's original tenants, **Cocopah** (928/282-4928) bills itself the "oldest bead store in Arizona," though the store also carries an impressive array of Art Nouveau and Art Deco estate jewelry, antique Tibetan beads, and Native American jewelry and accessories. **Hyde Out Fine Leathers** (928/282-1292) sells handbags, jackets, luggage, and belts in buttery tans and browns, deep reds, and rich blacks.

For housewares and furnishings with a "south of the border" look, stop into **Cosas Bonitas de Mexico** (928/204-9599). Shoppers can order rustic-looking furniture or browse the extensive collection of Talavera pottery—richly painted in deep blues, golds and reds, similar to the tiles that decorate Tlaquepaque.

The Shops at Hyatt Piñon Pointe
On a small bluff overlooking the Y intersection of Highways 179 and 89A, The Shops at Hyatt

SEDONA

SEDONA'S ARTISTIC TRADITION

One look around Sedona, and it shouldn't come as a surprise why so many artists have flocked to the area. The sculptural rock forms and bold color palette of deep scarlet rocks, cerulean blue skies, and forest-green ponderosa pines can be powerful inspiration. Sedona didn't emerge as an artistic haven, though, until Hollywood's epic westerns first publicized the vivid landscape in big-screen, Technicolor glory. Surrealist Max Ernst was among the first to arrive, briefly making his home here in the 1940s. Before long, a growing artistic community would help shape the town and define its identity. In fact, it was a sculptor, Marguerite Brunswig Staude, who would give Sedona its most iconic landmark, the Chapel of the Holy Cross.

The burgeoning art scene really began to take hold in 1958, when Egyptian émigré Nassan Groban and a few like-minded artists established the "Canyon Kiva" at the old Jordan Apple and Peach Packing Barn in Uptown Sedona. This studio/exhibition space, where artists could gather and teach, evolved into the Sedona Arts Center. Just a few years later,

cowboy artist Joe Beeler arrived in Sedona brandishing his Western canvases and sculpture. He met with Charlie Dye, George Phippen, Robert MacLeod, and John Hampton in 1965 at the Oak Creek Tavern (now the Cowboy Club Grille & Spirits), where they formed the Cowboy Artists of America, a Western school of art still highly sought by serious collectors.

Soon galleries began popping up across town with the growing hordes of tourists eager to take home a Sedona souvenir. Even today, the expanded Sedona Arts Center continues its mission to serve as a resource for local artists, providing gallery and classroom space, as well as hosting festivals and events year-round. To temporarily immerse yourself in the art scene, join the First Friday of the Month evening art walk. Many of Sedona's galleries – which feature the contemporary and Southwestern art found in Scottsdale and Santa Fe – host receptions and technique demonstrations from 5 to 8 P.M. The Sedona Trolley offers free transportation between galleries. For more information, contact the **Sedona Gallery Association** (928/282-7390).

Piñon Pointe (101 N. Hwy. 89A, 928/254-1006, www.theshopsathyattpinonpointe.com) include some interesting independent boutiques along with a few chains, which are quickly creeping into Sedona. **Marchesa's Fine Shoe Salon** (928/282-3212, 10 A.M.–6 P.M. daily) stocks heels, boots, and sandals by high-end designers like Marc Jacobs, Betsey Johnson, Christian LaCroix, and Stuart Weitzman, as well as more affordable options. **George Kelly Fine Jewelers** (928/282-8884, 10 A.M.–6 P.M. daily) carries imaginative and contemporary necklaces and rings. And for a tasty souvenir or gift, pick up a bottle of Arizona vino at **The Art of Fine Wine** (877/903-9463, 10 A.M.–6 P.M. Mon.–Wed., 10 A.M.–8 P.M. Thurs.–Sun.).

Continue north on Highway 89A into the heart of Uptown to find **Cowboy Corral** (219 N. Hwy. 89A, 928/282-2040, 10 A.M.–6 P.M. daily). Inside the stone-facade building,

wannabe desperados and cowgirls can buy re-production badges, leather holsters, spurs, riding skirts, and even long-johns. Try on one of the handmade hats, such as the Big Sky or Lonesome Charley, a beaver-fur creation straight out of the Old West and decorated with original buffalo nickels and turkey hackle feathers.

Gallery Row

Just south of Oak Creek, you'll find Gallery Row, a strip of small art galleries and Southwestern-looking shopping centers lining Highway 179. For an elegant selection of Native American arts and crafts, visit **Garland's Navajo Rugs** (411 Hwy. 179, 928/282-4070, 10 A.M.–5 P.M. Mon.–Sat., 11 A.M.–5 P.M. Sun.) on Gallery Row. The large stone building houses the world's largest selection of Navajo rugs, including antique pieces and hard-to-find large floor rugs. Garland's offers an extensive assortment of tastefully displayed Navajo sand paintings, hand-carved Hopi kachina dolls, Pueblo pottery, and hand-woven baskets.

Shoppers looking for a sweeping survey of art in Sedona should pop into **Exposures International** (561 Hwy. 179, 800/526-7668, 10 A.M.–5 P.M. daily), Arizona's largest fine art gallery. The sprawling indoor/outdoor exhibition space showcases the works of more than 100 artists, including large-format original oils, photographic wall murals, fountains, jewelry, and art pieces in metal, wood, and glass.

The Santa Fe-style **Hozho Distinctive Shops & Galleries** (431 Hwy. 179) features a diverse lineup of three galleries. Art collectors and shoppers will find Native American canvases, sculpture, and jewelry at **Turquoise Tortoise Gallery** (928/282-2262, www.turqtortsedona.com, 10 A.M.–5:30 P.M. Mon.–Sat., 11 A.M.–5 P.M. Sun.). Next door, **James Ratliff Gallery** (928/282-1404, www.jamesratliffgallery.com, 10 A.M.–5 P.M. Mon.–Sat., 11 A.M.–5 P.M. Sun.) sells high-end bronzes, colorful canvases, and modern Southwestern works, while **Lanning Gallery** (928/282-6865, www.lanninggallery.com, 10 A.M.–5:30 P.M. Mon.–Sat., 11 A.M.–5 P.M. Sun.) features more contemporary oils, acrylics, and encaustics, as well as ceramics and handmade furniture.

The neighboring **Hillside Sedona** (671 Hwy. 179, 928/282-4500, www.hillsidesedona.net, 10 A.M.–6 P.M.), an upscale shopping center overlooking Oak Creek, features unique restaurants, galleries, and shops. Be sure to check out **Gordon's** (928/204-2069), a "unique gallery of clocks, arts and crafts, home accents, and gifts."

Native American Arts and Crafts

There's no shortage of shops in Sedona selling Native American goods, but only **Joe Wilcox Indian Den** (320 N. Hwy. 89A Ste. J, 928/282-2661, www.joewilcoxsedona.com, 9:30 A.M.–8 P.M. Mon.–Sat., 9:30 A.M.–6 P.M. Sun.) offers such a vast array of gifts and souvenirs. The Sinagua Plaza boutique features jewelry crafted by Hopi artists, as well as Zuni fetishes

and Navajo sand paintings and alabaster carvings. Shoppers also will find Southwestern wall art, delicate pottery, vibrantly colored throws and pillows, and a variety of kitchen goods. And if your desire for Southwest tchotchkes hasn't been sated, duck into **Zonie's Galleria** (215 N. Highway 89A, 928/282-5995, www.zoniesgalleria.com, 9:30 A.M.–7 P.M. daily). The tiny shop's Southwestern housewares, sculpture, wooden fetishes, and wind chimes may be just what you are looking for.

Drive five minutes south of Gallery Row on Highway 179 and you'll find one of Sedona's best stores, **Son Silver West Gallery** (1476 Highway 179, 928/282-3580, www.sonsilverwest.com, 9 A.M.–5:30 P.M. daily). The kitschy shop manages to avoid a touristy feel, selling brightly colored glassware and ceramics, petrified wood, bells and wind chimes, imported Mexican crafts, and dried chile peppers. Meander through a pleasant outdoor pottery garden, where contemporary and Southwestern pots are stacked alongside vintage signs and an assortment of religious carvings and sculpture.

Jewelry

Looking for a piece of turquoise jewelry? There's no better place to find this classic Southwestern blue-green stone than at the **Turquoise Buffalo** (252 N. Hwy. 89A, 928/282-2994, www.turquoisebuffalo.com, 9 A.M.–6 P.M. Tues.–Wed., 9 A.M.–7:30 P.M. Thurs.–Mon.), which stocks more than 1,700 unique pieces. The helpful staff guides buyers—and curious browsers—through dozens of varieties of turquoise specimens available, from the green-veined Lone Mountain and the copper-flecked Morenci to the creamy white variations. It's a fascinating stop even if you haven't considered buying a piece.

For jewelry "traditionally inspired but with a contemporary flair," peruse the selection at the **Blue-Eyed Bear** (450 Jordan Rd., 928/282-9081, www.blueeyedbear.com, 9 A.M.–5:30 P.M. daily). The small Uptown shop specializes in handmade pieces made of sterling silver, gold, and semiprecious stones, all designed by Native

American and Southwestern artists. The neck-laces, bracelets, and earrings evoke Arizona's indigenous roots while the clean lines and bold color give the work a modern feel.

WEST SEDONA
Antiques
Tucked behind a white picket fence and shaded by large sycamore trees, **Hummingbird House** (100 Brewer Rd., 928/282-0705, 10 A.M.–5 P.M. Mon.–Sat., 11:30 A.M.–3:30 P.M. Sun.) offers shoppers a nostalgic slice of old Sedona. The 1926 general store was recently refurbished, and it now sells country knickknacks, as well as antiques and custom furniture. Children will appreciate the vintage signs and old waterwheel that still churns just outside the store.

New Age
Explore Sedona's New Age side at **Crystal Magic** (2978 W. Hwy. 89A, 928/282-1622, www.crystalmagicsedona.com, 9 A.M.–9 P.M. Mon.–Sat., 9 A.M.–8 P.M. Sun.), "a resource center for discovery and personal growth." Take home some healing crystals or stock up on aromatherapy oils and candles, feng shui supplies, incense, books, or music.

Mystical Bazaar (1449 W. Hwy. 89A, 928/204-5615, www.mysticalbazaar.com, 9 A.M.–8 P.M. Sun.–Wed., 9 A.M.–9 P.M. Thurs.–Sat.) sells jewelry made in Sedona, as well as a host of metaphysical items, including New Age books, music, tarot cards, and a diverse selection of gemstones and crystals. The shop also offers a new version of aura photography, which comes with two aura photos, a 23-page report, and chakra information. If you'd like a more complete experience, though, you can book one of the "facilitated spiritual tours" that range from treks to Sedona's vortexes and sacred spots to personalized shamanic journeys and starlight fire ceremonies.

Native American Arts and Crafts
Kachina House (2920 Hopi Dr., 928/204-9750, www.kachinahouse.com, 8:30 A.M.–4:30 Mon.–Fri., 8:30 A.M.–2:30 P.M. Sat., 10 A.M.–2 P.M. Sun.) is Arizona's largest distributor of Native American arts and crafts—many for rather reasonable prices. The Native American emporium sells hundreds of kachina dolls, ceremonial masks, horsehair pottery, Hopi baskets, and sand paintings, all made by Native American artisans.

Sports and Recreation

If you're not content viewing Sedona's majestic red rocks from the roadside—or from the comfort of a hotel balcony or a restaurant patio—there are plenty of ways to get outside and get a little dirty. Hikers and bikers could spend weeks, if not months, exploring the miles and miles of trails that wind through Sedona's protected state and national parks. The region's deep canyons, meandering creeks, and ponderosa pine forests can be irresistible, and the diverse topography and wildlife frequently surprise visitors.

A Jeep tour is one of Sedona's must-dos. The bumpy and occasionally dusty trips are a lot of fun, giving visitors a taste of how the pioneers who arrived by stagecoach more than a century ago must have felt. Of course, there are more

refined ways to sneak in your time outdoors: a round of golf, an alfresco massage at a four-star spa, or a hot-air balloon trip.

Not matter what you do, be sure to wear sturdy shoes, a hat, and sunscreen when you venture outside. Despite the shady trees, this is still the high desert, and the sun can be brutal, especially for visitors who underestimate its power. Also, bring water—and lots of it—as it's not uncommon to dehydrate quickly in this arid climate.

TOURS
Jeep Tours
Taking a ride with iconic **Pink Jeep Tours** (204 N. Hwy. 89A, 928/282-5000, www.

pinkjeep.com) is the most popular way to romp over Sedona's red rocks. Charismatic guides describe the geology and ecosystem surrounding Sedona as they drive beefed-up Jeep Wranglers over steep boulders and occasionally treacherous passes. The tours provide excellent photo opportunities and, surprisingly, a deeper appreciation for the animals, fauna, and red-rock vistas surrounding the city center. The popular Broken Arrow Tour ($75 adults, $56.25 children) explores the submerged-below-the-treetops Submarine Rock and scouts out postcard-perfect views. For a little history with your nature, the three-hour Ancient Ruins Tour ($72 adults, $54 children) stops at an ancient Sinaguan cliff dwelling and tracks down prehistoric rock art. Plush motorcoach tours to the Grand Canyon are also available ($125 adults, $115 children). Advanced reservations are recommended, though walk-ins can frequently get same-day tours.

Red Rock Western Jeep Tours (270 N. Hwy. 89A Ste. 2, 928/282-6826, www.redrockjeep.com) offers four-wheeling excursions

Go off-road with a Jeep tour through Sedona's backcountry.

and much more. The cowboy guides may look like cheesy anachronisms, but these local experts enrich a traveler's appreciation for Sedona's complex geology and wildlife. Red Rock's various outings range from romping with wine tasting and romantic private tours *à deux* to Western-themed treks that trace Apache and cowboy trails. The company also provides horseback riding, ranch cookouts, and sunset trips to the Grand Canyon. Basic Jeep tours are about $50 per person. Parties of 10 or more may qualify for group rates.

Adventure Tours

If you're not content letting the scenery pass you by from the seat of a Jeep, **Sedona Adventure Outfitters & Guides** (2020 Contractors Rd., 928/204-6440, www.sedonaadventuretours.com) leads tours that highlight the area's diverse outdoor activities, including hiking, kayaking, and water tubing. The Water to Wine Tour ($133 adults) combines a four-mile guided kayaking trip down the Verde River with a side trip to Alcantara Vineyard for a pleasant afternoon of Arizona wine-tasting. The family-friendly Cathedral Rock Mellow Hiking & Vortex Tour ($60 adults, $45.50 children 12 and under) starts at Airport Mesa, which offers panoramic views of Sedona and a chance to "feel" the energy of a vortex before making it down to Oak Creek and Cathedral Rock.

Eco-Rides and Rentals at Hillside Sedona (671 Hwy. 179, 928/204-0628) maintains a stable of Earth-friendly vehicles for exploring Sedona's great outdoors. Pick up a mountain or road bike for an afternoon ride, or if you'd like a little kick to your adventure, try out an electric bike or scooter. Younger travelers will love the e-bikeboard, a combination skateboard-scooter-tricycle that offers off-road capabilities and a quiet electric engine. For longer journeys, the rechargeable Zenn Electric Car and Vectrix Maxi-Scooter provide eco-sensitive transportation for day trips throughout red-rock country.

Helicopter and Biplane Tours

Get a different perspective on the Verde Valley

region's natural beauty. **Arizona Helicopter Adventures** (235 Air Terminal Dr., 928/282-0904, www.azheli.com) skims the massive buttes and green forests that proliferate the area, descending into canyons and climbing over rugged mountains. The Red Rock Roundup ($65 per person) surveys the area's best-known formations, like Bell and Snoopy Rocks, as well as the Chapel of the Holy Cross

DID YOU FEEL THAT? IT COULD BE A VORTEX.

They're as ubiquitous as the red rocks and pink Jeeps, but not nearly as easy to spot. Sedona's vortexes embody much of the city's New Age culture: an ever-present phenomenon that earns curiosity from locals and visitors alike. For believers, vortexes are spiraling centers of cosmic energy that lead to heightened self-awareness and spiritual improvement. You may be familiar, though, with more common vortexes, like tornadoes, whirlwinds, or water going down a drain.

In Sedona, these funnels of the Earth's inner-energy are prime spots for meditation. According to with whom you speak, numerous sites are scattered around town, but there are four well-known and easy-to-reach vortexes near Airport Mesa, Boynton Canyon, Bell Rock, and Red Rock Crossing/Cathedral Rock. Some feature more masculine energy, improving strength and self-confidence, while others are more feminine, boosting patience and kindness.

If you'd like a guided journey, contact **Sedona Vortex Tours** (150 Hwy. 179, 928/282-2733, www.sedonaretreats.com), which can customize a trip to multiple vortexes, visit a medicine wheel, or organize a Native American ceremony. Most Jeep and adventure tour operators offer vortex tours, and the New Age bookstores and crystal shops can also make recommendations.

and Bear Wallow Canyon. For a look at prehistoric Native American ruins in Boynton Canyon, take the Ancient Ruins Tour ($115 per person), which also visits Secret Canyon and provides some context to the enormous size of the Mogollon Rim and Colorado Plateau.

Take to the skies in a helicopter or Red Waco biplane with **Sedona Air Tours** (1225 Airport Rd., 928/204-5939, www.sedonaairtours.com). The popular biplane flights can accommodate two passengers at a time, with a pilot providing commentary about the changing landscape. Tours range in price and length from the 20-minute Classic Tour ($99 per person)—which soars past Bell Rock, the Chapel of the Holy Cross, Mund's Canyon, and Devil's Kitchen—to an hour-long flight through Sedona and Oak Creek ($489 per person). The signature Ancients Way helicopter journey (25 minutes, $116 per person) surveys Secret Canyon, Fay's Arch, and the Sinaguan cliff dwellings of Boynton Canyon. Combination trips that incorporate jeep tours, fishing, whitewater rafting, and flights to the Grand Canyon and Monument Valley are available.

Astronomy Tour

Sedona's dark skies provide the perfect backdrop for shimmering planets, galaxies, and star clusters. **Evening Sky Tours** (928/203-0006, www.eveningskytours.com, $60 adults, $20 children, free under 8) surveys the nighttime canopy with custom-built telescopes that offer so-close-you-can-touch-it views of the moon, meteor showers, and even Saturn's rings. Professional astronomers use high-powered laser pointers to guide you around the night sky without getting too technical.

BALLOONING

Sedona's landscape, punctuated by soaring buttes and green forests, seems made-to-order for a gentle hot-air balloon flight. That said, only a handful of ballooning companies are permitted by the Coconino National Forest to fly in the red-rock area, so be sure to check when booking a tour operator not listed here. **Northern Light Balloon Expeditions**

(928/282-2274, www.northernlightballoon. com, $195 per person) is the oldest and largest ballooning company in Sedona, offering red-rock air tours since 1974. The daily sunrise flights provide visitors with one of those "only in Sedona" experiences. And unlike some other tour operators that maintain fleets of larger balloons that accommodate more than a dozen people, Northern Light's balloons hold up to seven passengers, making for a less touristy feel. The free hotel pickup is a handy option, especially after the champagne picnic after landing. Day-before reservations are usually available.

Promising the closest views of the Sedona's famed buttes from the air, **Red Rock Balloon Adventures** (800/258-3754, www.redrockballoons.com, $195 person) offers stunning sunrise-only tours. The 60- to 90-minute adventures—depending on weather—drift through Sedona skies and conclude with a mimosa picnic. Brides and grooms may want to consider the Wedding Package ($2,500), which can accommodate up to six people on a private flight and includes a "commemorative picnic" with wedding cake.

© OSAMU HOSHINO / SEDONA CVB

Spectacular views are a hiker's reward for a climb up one of Sedona's buttes.

HIKING

Hikers, welcome to nirvana. It's easy to use a succession of clichés to describe the views from Sedona's trails (breathtaking, heart-stopping, etc.), but it's hard to convey just how rich and dynamic Sedona's landscape is, especially when explored on foot. Thanks to spectacular buttes, massive geological formations, and acres upon acres of protected land, there seems to be a world-class trail wherever you pull over your car in Sedona. And, even if you're not a hiker, you can't help but enjoy a little on-foot time kicking up some red dust on the paths that wind for miles throughout the Sedona area.

Serious hikers looking for just the right trails that suit their particular skill level or topographical interests should call the Coconino National Forest's Red Rock Ranger District at 928/203-7500 for a complete map or visit www.redrockcountry.org.

Beginners may want to consider the four-

mile **Bell Rock Pathway,** the single best introductory trail in Sedona. Conveniently located just north of the Village of Oak Creek on Highway 179, the frequently crowded trail is popular for good reason: it's beautiful. The leisurely trek circles the delicate Bell Rock and the nearby Courthouse Butte, making for a can't-miss trek for families and first-time hikers.

About a mile north on Highway 179, turn into the Back O'Beyond housing development, where the **Cathedral Rock Trail** offers a bit more solitude and a bigger challenge. The short but steep hike to the "saddle" of Cathedral Rock can be tough, but the rewarding views of the multi-spired formation are incredible. Follow the basket cairns (stacked-rock markers), and be prepared to use the toeholds carved into the rock at one spot. At the top of three-quarters of a mile, some believe a vortex swirls with cosmic energy.

For panoramic views of Sedona and its red-rock buttes, the 3.5-mile **Airport Mesa Trail** provides a host of camera-ready vistas. It's best

SEDONA

Unbeatable views await hikers without a fear of heights.

Kachina Woman Rock at Boynton Canyon

to hit this trail early in the morning before the parking lot—just off of Highway 89A in West Sedona—fills up.

In West Sedona, take Dry Creek Road north to Forest Road 152, where you'll need a four-wheel-drive vehicle to access to the trailhead for **Devil's Bridge,** Sedona's largest natural stone arch. Halfway through the moderate, mile-long hike, the trail splits, with the right trail going to the top of the soaring Devil's Bridge and the left winding below the arch. A warning for those with a fear of heights: Be prepared to climb the well-used stone stairs, which do not have handrails.

Farther north on Dry Creek Road, you'll find two stunning canyon trails on Boynton Pass Road. Park just outside Enchantment Resort to trek the **Boynton Canyon Trail,** an easy to moderate hike that traverses several different terrains, from cactus-dotted desert to pine-shaded forest. The hike is about five miles round-trip, and you'll pass Native American ruins in cliffside caves as you make

your way up the canyon. Unlike some of the other panoramic trails that offer sweeping views of Sedona, the cocooning box canyon feels more intimate. Plus, its reputation as a vortex site and the belief by the Apache that the canyon was the birthplace of their ancestors gives the area a spiritual vibe. Look for the tall, elegant spire called Kachina Woman Rock, which watches over the canyon.

Just west on Boynton Canyon Road, you'll come across the trailhead for **Fay Canyon Trail.** Oak and pine trees shade parts of this flat, easy hike, which runs about three miles roundtrip to the canyon's red sandstone walls. Less than a mile into the trek, look for an easy-to-miss side trail, which leads to a natural stone arch that looks like it has been tunneled into the bottom of a large canyon wall. The diverse geology and rich ecosystem are quite scenic.

BIKING

Strap on your helmet and get ready for some of the best off-roading in the country. Mountain bikers will find a terrain every bit as diverse and challenging as meccas in Moab, Utah, and Durango, Colorado—though far less crowded. The singletrack trails lure diehards and beginners alike, thanks to challenging combinations of dirt, sand, and slickrock.

Many of Sedona's hiking trails allow biking, the most notable exceptions being designated wilderness trails where it is strictly forbidden. Consult signage at trailheads before starting. Also, the terrain can be a bit unpredictable, so exercise caution on rock formations and near cliff sides.

For a moderately challenging half-day trek, try **Submarine Rock Loop** at the end of Morgan Road, located just off of Highway 179 between Sedona and the Village of Oak Creek. The 10-mile loop starts with a singletrack trail that varies between dirt and hard clay, leading to slickrock at Submarine Rock and Chicken Point.

The **Jim Thompson Trail** can be accessed from the end of Jordan Road in Uptown

RED ROCK PASS

Before you set out to explore Sedona's famous buttes and hiking trails, be sure to purchase a Red Rock Pass, which is required to park your vehicle in national forest areas. Most of the pull-offs on Highways 89A and 179 will require the pass, as well as parking lots at trailheads. The pass must be displayed in the windshield of your vehicle, though it is not required if you are simply pulling over for a quick stop or photo-op. You can purchase the $5 daily and $15 weekly passes at visitors centers, many hotels, and automated kiosks at parking areas and trailheads, including Bell Rock and Boynton Canyon. Money generated from the passes is used to maintain and protect this "high-impact recreation area." For more information call 928/203-2900 or visit www.redrockcountry.org.

SEDONA

© JANISE WITT / SEDONA CVB

mountain bikers exploring Red Rock Country

Sedona or a couple of miles north at the Wilson Canyon Trailhead at the Midgley Bridge on Highway 89A. Thompson built the trail in the 1880s as a wagon road to his home, which is why it tends to be a bit wider than most trails in these parts. Loose rocks cover much of the terrain, and the ride is pleasant.

In West Sedona, the **Upper and Lower Red Rock Loop Trails** off of Highway 89A explore Red Rock State Park and Oak Creek. Also off of 89A, take Coffee Pot Road north to Thunder Mountain Road, where you'll find trailheads for **Little Elf Trail** and **Sugar Loaf Park,** which access numerous trails that range from short loops to demanding climbs.

If you need to rent some wheels, **Sedona Bike & Bean** (6020 Hwy. 179, 928/284-0210, www.bike-bean.com, 8 A.M.–5 P.M. daily) in the Village of Oak Creek offers convenient access to trails near Bell, Courthouse, and Cathedral Rocks. The laid-back shop rents mountain and road bikes starting at $25 for two hours, and same-day reservations are welcome on any bike for any length of time. The coffee's pretty darn good, too, and makes a great way to fuel up on caffeine before or after a ride. Inquire about the Bean's tours, which include family-friendly mountain biking and road tours to wineries and galleries. A new location near Uptown (671 Hwy. 179, 928/204-5666, 8 A.M.–5 P.M. daily) specializes in road bikes.

Mountain Bike Heaven (1695 W. Hwy. 89A, 928/282-1312, www.mountainbikeheaven.com, 8 A.M.–6 P.M. Mon.–Fri., 8 A.M.–5:30 P.M. Sat., 8 A.M.–4:30 P.M. Sun.) is popular with the fat-tire crowd, offering adventure rides and dual suspension rentals. Prices start at $40 per day and $25 for each additional day. If you'd like a guided tour, the shop's **Sedona Bikapelli Mountain Bike Adventure Tours** offers outings that range from one-on-one instruction to group tours that scout out some of Sedona's lesser-known trails.

BIRDING

More than 300 bird species flock to the Verde Valley's lush riparian areas and protected forests, making Sedona a prime spot for bird-watching.

Throughout the year, it's not uncommon to see a host of colorful birds perched on the ponderosa pine and cottonwood trees, including bald and golden eagles, herons, orioles, hawks, and even Canadian geese in the winter. For a guided outing, **Sedona Adventure Outfitters & Guides** (2020 Contractors Rd., 928/204-6440, www.sedonaadventuretours.com) explores the Verde Valley's best spots. Hop on one of the shuttles in the early morning or early evening when birds are most active. You'll be equipped with a pair of binoculars so that you're sure to catch the seasonal flocks and permanent residents that make their home in the area.

GOLF

For those who appreciate the pleasure of a golf course's natural landscape as much as the thrill of a challenging game, Sedona won't disappoint. The lush fairways provide a brilliant contrast to the crimson buttes that surround the area's courses. Unprotected land that can be developed is at a premium in Sedona, so expect slightly shorter drives and imaginatively designed tees and greens.

One of the best golf courses in the state, **Seven Canyons** (755 Golf Club Way, 866/367-8844, www.sevencanyons.com) has earned much critical acclaim, including being named one of America's 50 Greatest Golf Retreats by *Golf Digest Index* and one of the Top 100 Modern Courses by *Golfweek* magazine. Tom Weiskopf designed the par-70 course to emphasize the natural topography of the landscape, with tees that take advantage of changes in elevation, naturally rolling fairways, and small, quick greens. The rock walls, water features, bridges, mature trees, and high-desert landscaping are eclipsed only by the red-rock formations that surround the course. The instructional Performance Center and two-tiered Practice Park—which features a 20,000-square-foot teeing space, four target greens, and a chipping area with a practice bunker—round out the world-class facility.

If the scenery looks familiar at the **Sedona Golf Resort** (35 Ridge Trail Dr., 928/284-2093, www.sedonagolfresort.com), you may recognize it from one of the classic Westerns that were filmed here in the 1930s and 1940s, long before the carefully manicured greens and sandy bunkers arrived. The championship course in the Village of Oak Creek features long, rolling fairways and scenic vistas—the view of the red rocks at the par-3 10th hole can be particularly distracting while teeing off. *Golf Digest* regularly bestows the 6,646-yard, par-71 course with a well-deserved four-star rating. And for duffers in need of a quick refresher or extensive instruction, the clubhouse offers clinics, private and group lessons, and even a club-fitting analysis. Before you leave, be sure to check out the remains of the red-rock wall from an early homestead between the first and 18th holes.

Another top course can be found in the Village of Oak Creek. The par-72, 18-hole **Oak Creek Country Club** (690 Bell Rock Blvd., 928/284-1820, www.oakcreekcountryclub.com) will appeal to purists who prefer a traditional layout: tree-lined fairways that dogleg, slightly elevated greens, and lakes that pose the occasional hazard. Robert Trent Jones Sr. and Robert Trent Jones Jr. designed the championship golf course to be a tough play, and the signature fourth hole, which is complemented by terrific views of the red rocks, will push most golfers to earn a par 3. Recent renovations added new concrete cart paths and greenside bunkers, though it hasn't sacrificed the natural setting.

The par-3 executive course at the **Radisson Poco Diablo Resort** (1752 S. Hwy. 179, 928/282-7333, www.radissonsedona.com) provides an excellent opportunity to work on your short game while taking in some impressive views along Oak Creek. The duck ponds, willow and pine trees, and low-key atmosphere offer a refreshing break from Uptown's crowds. The water hazards and fast greens can be challenging, but the real draw to this 9-hole course is its manageable size, offering a quick and affordable way to fit in a game of golf on a short trip to Sedona.

SPAS

One of the finest spas in the world, **Mii Amo** (525 Boynton Canyon Rd., 888/749-2137, www. miiamo.com, 6 A.M.–10 P.M. daily) regularly tops magazine "best of" lists for its comprehensive

COURTESY OF ENCHANTMENT RESORT

Mii Amo spa

SEDONA

treatments, chic decor, and incredible setting in Boynton Canyon. The one downside: The luxury spa is only open to guests staying at Mii Amo or its sister resort, Enchantment. If you're a diehard spa-goer, consider splurging on a stay here—you won't be disappointed. Mii Amo's design and treatments are inspired by Native American, Asian, and New Age practices. You'll want to spend days relaxing by indoor and outdoor pools, enjoying a fitness class on the yoga lawn, or taking a moment for quiet contemplation in the Crystal Grotto, which perfectly aligns with the sun's light during the summer solstice. Day packages for Enchantment guests start at $390, and prices for an all-inclusive three-day journey begin at $1,905.

Hilton Sedona Spa (10 Ridge View Dr., 928/284-6900, www.hiltonsedonaspa.com, 5:30 A.M.–9 P.M. Mon.–Fri., 7 A.M.–8 P.M. Sat.–Sun.) is a rather unpretentious facility that boasts a devoted local membership. The 25,000-square-foot facility includes three tennis courts, an outdoor heated lap pool, a fully equipped gym, and fitness classes that range from basic cardio to tai chi, Kundalini yoga, and qui gong. Be sure to try one of the aromatherapy massages ($125) before taking advantage of the separate men's and women's steam rooms, saunas, and rooftop sun decks.

Younger spa-goers may appreciate **The Spa at the Sedona Rouge** (2250 W. Hwy. 89A, 928/203-4111, www.sedonarouge.com/spa, 11 A.M.–6 P.M. Mon.–Thurs., 10 A.M.–7 P.M. Fri.–Sun.). The modern, boutique option offers a bit of style and substance, as therapists are trained in a host of techniques, including Ayurvedic services, Thai massage, cranial sacral reflexology, and cupping massage. Even wellness guru Deepak Chopra hosts his

five-day SynchroDestiny Retreat at the spa. In addition to gender-specific steam rooms and alfresco whirlpools, guests can enjoy the co-ed tranquility room and garden. Massages here start at $120.

Amara Spa (100 Amara Ln., 800/891-0105, www.amararesort.com, 10 A.M.–7 P.M. daily) is another mod boutique-resort option, with a decidedly luxe atmosphere. Guests can create a custom-tailored massage or select from a menu of full-body treatments, like the Blissful Sage Body Wrap ($190) or Deep Blue Lavender Embrace ($130). Daily yoga classes or fitness private sessions are available.

Sedona Spa (160 Portal Ln., 928/282-5108, www.sedonaspa.com, 6 A.M.–9 P.M. Mon.–Sat., 8 A.M.–6 P.M. Sun.) at Los Abrigados Resort offers an impressive selection of therapeutic massages that begin at $95, as well as acupuncture and full-body polishes, herbal wraps, and soothing mud masks. Get to the spa early to relax in the eucalyptus steam room, sauna, and whirlpool, or to fit in a game of tennis or pilates class.

Therapy on the Rocks (676 N. Hwy. 89 A, 928/282-3002, www.myofascialrelease.com, 9 A.M.–5 P.M. daily) takes a holistic approach to massage therapy. The cabin-like center, just north of Uptown on Oak Creek, specializes in the myofascial release, a massage technique practitioners say relieves pain and increases range of motion. There are half-hour, hour, and half-day sessions, as well as comprehensive two-week programs for people with chronic pain conditions. If it's warm enough, you can enjoy a creekside treatment or the outdoor whirlpool on the sun deck. Customized treatments vary from person to person. Call ahead for individual treatment prices.

Accommodations

T.C. and Sedona Schnebly built the town's first hotel in 1900, a cozy homestead that is now the home of the Tlaquepaque shopping plaza. More than a century later, visitors are still flocking here, and though there are a host of motels, hotels, resorts, and inns to suit every taste, Sedona's specialty is the romantic getaway. Accommodations tend to be steep year-round, with rates peaking in the winter and spring. Still, there are bargains to found in Sedona, but they tend to be occasionally moderate prices at the more expensive hotels and resorts. No matter where you stay, though, you can almost be guaranteed a room with a view.

UPTOWN
$50-100

Star Motel (295 Jordan Rd., 928/282-3641, $79–89 d) is an ideal spot for budget travelers looking for affordability with a little character, and its prime locale in pedestrian-friendly Uptown can't be beat. The converted 1955 homestead maintains many of the original home's retro features, and its 11 units are bright and clean. The hospitable owners, Marcelle and Anne, couldn't be sweeter. Families will love the second-floor suite's two queen beds, full kitchen, and private patio with views of the red rocks. The ground floor unit in the original home features two bedrooms, a kitchen, and a living room with foldout couch.

Centrally located one block south of the Y, **The Sedona Motel** (218 Hwy. 179, 928/282-7187, www.thesedonamotel.com, $90–110 d) is a good value. The dated rooms could use a makeover, but you probably won't be spending much time in them anyway, especially with the commanding views of the red rocks from the motel's terraced patio.

$100-250

Just down the hill from Uptown's shops and galleries, ◖ **Amara Hotel, Restaurant & Spa** (100 Amara Ln., 928/282-4828, www.amara-resort.com, $185–215 d) brings a bit of big-city chic to Red Rock Country. The posh boutique hotel stands out in Southwest-crazed Sedona, though its minimalist design doesn't try to overshadow its spectacular natural setting on the banks of Oak Creek. In fact, the mod furniture, elegant black-and-white photography, and Zen design touches provide a quiet backdrop to the property's giant sycamore trees and spectacular views. You'll find all the usual luxury-amenity suspects at Amara—300-thread-count linens, oversized soaking tubs, private balconies, elegantly manicured grounds—but the hotel ups the game with a heated saltwater pool and the AAA Four Diamond Hundred Fox restaurant.

Los Abrigados Resort & Spa (160 Portal Ln., 928/282-1777, www.ilxresorts.com, $185–215 d) used to be Sedona's gold standard for top accommodations. And though it has been eclipsed by more luxurious options in the last decade, the resort still sits quite literally in the heart of Sedona, next to the Tlaquepaque shopping center and Oak Creek. Walking the 22-acre, beautifully landscaped resort, you'll find plenty of diversions: two swimming pools, a whirlpool spa, tennis and basketball courts, a fitness center, and a creekside miniature golf course. Plus, the on-site Sedona Spa features some fine treatments for guests looking for a little R&R. The rooms were undergoing a much-need remodeling in 2009, which should bring a refreshing dose of style back to the resort.

You can't beat the Uptown location of ◖ **The Orchards Inn** (254 N. Hwy. 89A, 928/282-2405, www.orchardsinn.com, $110–170 d). Perched hillside, every room overlooks the valley, with patios and decks that offer spectacular views of Snoopy Rock and the surrounding buttes. If a "room with a view" is a priority and budget is a concern, this motel tucked behind a row of shops on Sedona's main street may be an ideal place to hang your hat. Plus, most of Uptown's shops, restaurants, and bars are just outside your front door. The

SEDONA

spacious, newly renovated rooms have been refreshed with a modern Southwest feel: dark oak furniture, leather-upholstered headboards, and warm earth tones.

Best Western Arroyo Roble Hotel & Creekside Villas (400 N. Hwy. 89A, 928/282-4001 or 800/773-3662, www.bestwesternsedona.com, $179–189 d) may be a mouthful to say, but the five-story hotel next to Sedona Arts Center has a lot to offer, providing a host of amenities you typically would find at a large resort: tennis and racquetball courts, a fully equipped exercise room, and an indoor/outdoor heated swimming pool. The recently updated rooms are spacious and nicely decorated—some even have fireplaces and whirlpool tubs. The 1,300-square-foot, two-bedroom creekside villas could use an overhaul, though. The price may seem a little steep for a chain hotel, though the complimentary full breakfast and the hotel's incredible setting—complete with red-rock views and private paths on the banks of Oak Creek—are well worth the money.

For a woodsy experience, try the **Briar Patch Inn** (3190 N. Hwy. 89A, 928/282-2342, www.briarpatchinn.com, $205–259 d). Its 19 cabin-like rooms are furnished with rustic wood tables, big beds, old rocking chairs, and brightly colored Native American blankets and rugs, all lovingly cared for by the incredibly friendly and hardworking staff. The accommodations range from quaint one-room hideaways to the sprawling four-bedroom Ponderosa cabin, which is large enough to accommodate 20 people. Wood-burning fireplaces and hearty morning breakfasts round out the decidedly rustic environment—there are only three TVs on the property. Splurge for a cottage that overlooks Oak Creek, where you can fish for trout and jump into the private swimming hole during the summer. Also, be sure to make time to meet Briar Patch's permanent guests, Wooly and Bully, two sheep that tend the property's meadow.

Victorian doily. I can't think of a better way to describe **Creekside Inn at Sedona** (99 Copper Cliffs Dr., 928/282-4992, www.creeksideinn.net, $199–269 d). The rather feminine bed-and-breakfast is decorated with period antiques, and its cheerful rooms are bright and clean. The mammoth, ceiling-high walnut bed in the Creekview Suite is a showstopper, and the room's French doors, private deck, and large bathroom overlooking Oak Creek provide an ideal setting for a romantic weekend. Guests can pass the time by fishing in the creek, relaxing on the porch with a glass of wine, or taking a short walk to Gallery Row.

The Matterhorn Inn (230 Apple Ave., 928/282-7176, www.matterhorninn.com, $129–159 d) sits right in the heart of Uptown, which means you can explore many of Sedona's shops, galleries, and restaurants without having to get into your car. The recently updated rooms are nice, and thanks to the hotel's hillside location, all rooms have a private balcony or terrace with panoramic views of the red rocks.

Over $250

The charming **(€ El Portal Sedona** (95 Portal Ln., 928/203-9405, www.elportalsedona.com, $250–350 d) is one of Arizona's finest hotels, marrying Arts and Crafts–period design with Southwestern hacienda architecture. Owners Connie and Steve Segner have created an intimate, luxury inn, and even the smallest details reflect their vision, like rough-hewn beam ceilings, cozy fireplaces, 18-inch thick adobe walls, and a grassy central courtyard. Each of the 12 unique rooms echoes El Portal's eclectic historical style—the vaulted log-beam Grand Canyon and handsome Santa Fe suites are particularly exquisite. Situated next to the Tlaquepaque shopping center, the inn is conveniently located near some of Sedona's best restaurants and galleries, but you may not want to leave this elegant hideaway. The Segners welcome four-legged friends, and they're happy to recommend pet-friendly trails and parks.

Thanks to a $25 million renovation and expansion, **(€ L'Auberge de Sedona** (301 L'Auberge Ln., 800/905-5745, www.lauberge.com, $325–395 d) continues to seduce guests, many of whom return annually for romantic pilgrimages along the banks of Oak Creek. The intimate resort feels hidden away under giant sycamores, and the morning duck feedings and relaxing spa feel a world away from the congestion and crowds just up the hill in Uptown. Cozy rooms are available in the main lodge, though the creekside cabins are worth the splurge. The new hillside cottages are refreshingly modern, boasting outdoor showers and large observation decks. You can't help but appreciate the warm and social atmosphere, which is helped along by the nightly wine receptions and stargazing on Friday evenings.

WEST SEDONA
$50-100

Sky Ranch Lodge (1105 Airport Rd., 928/282-6400, www.skyranchlodge.com, $80–125 d) feels like a hazy version of a 1970s ranch or vacation home. Small ponds, bridges, and grassy lawns dot the six-acre property, with quaint stone paths leading to quiet gardens and a secluded swimming pool. Best of all, the inn is perched on Airport Mesa, 500 feet above Sedona, providing elevated views of the town and its red-rock formations and green valleys. And when you're ready for a little excitement, a five-minute drive will drop you back in the heart of Uptown. The large rooms are quite outdated, but clean. Be sure to ask for a private deck when you make a reservation.

Cheap, clean, and convenient, **Sugar Loaf Lodge** (1870 W. Hwy. 89A, 928/282-9451, www.sedonasugarloaf.com, $60–90 d) provides the basics just off of Highway 89A and even throws in a few frills like a pool, free Wi-Fi, and in-room refrigerators. The motel isn't fancy, but its low price is hard to beat, as is the convenient access to neighboring hiking and mountain biking trails. And if you're planning on bringing your pooch to Sedona, Sugar Loaf has a few pet-friendly rooms.

$100-250

The Santa Fe-style **Southwest Inn at Sedona** (3250 W. Hwy. 89A, 928/282-3344, www. swinn.com, $94–154 d) is a terrific value if you're looking for a quiet, comfortable place to sleep between hiking, shopping, and visiting galleries. The converted motor lodge has been

nicely updated with excellent bedding and gas fireplaces, but don't expect a resort-like setting. Be sure to ask for a room with a view of the red buttes.

Visitors who appreciate a more modern style may want to check in at the **Sedona Rouge Hotel & Spa** (2250 W. Hwy. 89A, 928/203-4111, www.sedonarouge.com, $167–197 d). The hotel combines clean lines and Sedona's distinctive color palette of warm earth tones and deep red accents. The comfortable rooms are well appointed, though those on the second and third level have bathrooms that feature generous walk-in showers with dual heads. Sedona Rouge has a more urban vibe than some of its competitors, but you'll still get amazing views of the red rocks, particularly from the Observation Terrace that's open at night for stargazing. Plus, you'll find other amenities, like a large outdoor seating area with fireplace, a heated swimming pool and Jacuzzi, and a topnotch spa with programs by New Age guru Deepak Chopra.

With a name like **Boots and Saddles** (2900 Hopi Dr., 928/282-1944, www.oldwestbb.com, $225–305 d), you can expect a heavy dose of cowboy style at this popular bed-and-breakfast. Innkeepers Irith and Sam Raz have created a rabid following, thanks to their warm hospitality and gourmet breakfasts. Each of the inn's seven rooms is unique, decorated in Western themes like Ghost Rider and El Dorado, and with amenities that vary from fireplaces and outdoor air-jet tubs to telescopes for stargazing. The 600-square-foot City Slickers room includes a sunrise nook with a large window, a cheery place to read the paper and enjoy a morning cup of coffee.

The Lodge at Sedona (125 Kallof Pl., 928/204-1942, www.lodgeatsedona.com, $189–229 d) is an unexpected treat in West Sedona. The quaint stone-and-timber lodge features Arts and Crafts–style decor, Mission furnishings, and cozy, fireside seating areas. Make time to explore the gardens, which include water features and red-rock views, before heading out to the meditative labyrinth that is based on Native American traditions.

SEDONA

The handsome Star Gazer suite features a large deck with garden views and an outdoor shower, while the Red Rock Crossing king suite offers a jetted in-room tub that's perfect for a romantic weekend.

The red-stucco **Alma De Sedona Inn** (50 Hozoni Dr., 928/282-2737, www.almadesedona.com, $189–260 d) is a lovely bed-and-breakfast for those who appreciate a little privacy with their red-rock views. The 12 large rooms have king-size beds, gas fireplaces, and two-person tubs. The grounds are well maintained and feature a host of desert cacti and agave, along with shady old sycamore trees. You may take a dip in the heated pool—or at least enjoy your breakfast poolside if it's a little too chilly.

The independent **Sedona Real Inn & Suites** (95 Arroyo Dr., 928/282-1414, www.sedonareal.com, $105–119 d) lacks character, but the clean, spacious rooms and suites are a nice option for families and big groups, especially for the price. You also get some perks not found at budget competitors: free high-speed Internet, an outdoor pool and spa, free continental breakfast, and private balconies.

The **Best Western Inn of Sedona** (1200 W. Hwy. 89A, 928/282-3072, www.innofsedona.com, $130–150 d) offers views that would cost you a pretty penny anywhere else in the world. Although the recently renovated rooms are clean and comfortable—and have surprising touches like glass-bowl sinks in the bathroom—you'll want to spend most of your time on the communal balconies, which feature panoramic views of the red rocks. There's also plenty of convenient parking and a pool, as well as a free shuttle to/from Uptown.

Cathedral Rock Lodge & Retreat Center (61 W. Los Amigos Lane, 928/282-5560, www.cathedralrocklodge.com, $150–300 per cabin) isn't fancy, but its views are among the finest in the world. Situated near Red Rock State Park about 15 minutes from Uptown, the three secluded "retreat homes" are surrounded by green lawns and wooded grounds—though their lookouts onto Cathedral Rock are the real draw. The Homestead House—which is the largest, sleeping up to six people—has a large kitchen, two bedrooms, two bathrooms, and a collection of westerns filmed in Sedona to enjoy.

Over $250

You won't find a hotel in Sedona with a more stunning backdrop than **Enchantment Resort** (525 Boynton Canyon Rd., 928/282-2900, www.enchantmentresort.com, $250–350 d). Situated 10 minutes outside of town, the resort is nestled into the horseshoe-shaped Boynton Canyon. Its soaring cliff walls envelop the resort, creating a sense of seclusion and protection—or it could be the Kachina Woman rock formation that Native Americans believe watches over the canyon. The hacienda-inspired design features 220 rooms scattered across the property, which began as a homestead before being transformed into a tennis ranch and later a luxury resort. Guests have exclusive access to swimming pools, tennis courts, private hiking trails, and the adjacent Mii Amo spa, one of the finest facilities in the world. Kids will enjoy Camp Coyote, which explores Native American culture and the Southwest environment.

(Mii Amo (525 Boynton Canyon Rd., 928/282-2900, www.miiamo.com) sets the bar for destination spa-going, blending holistic wellness treatments, Native American traditions, and luxury pampering. The resort creates three-, four- and seven-night "personal journeys" that are tailored to a guest's goals: de-stress, optimum aging, spiritual exploration, etc. The total price includes accommodations in one of 16 spa casitas and suites, three meals a day, and two spa treatments every day, as well as the use of fitness classes, spa facilities, swimming pools, and activities like tennis, hiking, and mountain biking. The small, communal setting is perfect for solo travelers who want to balance personal time and socializing with new friends. Mii Amo's seamless indoor/outdoor design blends chic, modern style with the Boynton Canyon's soaring red walls and the desert landscape. Rates begin at $1,905 for a three-night package.

COURTESY OF ENCHANTMENT RESORT

Enchantment Resort

Subtlety isn't a word that is used at **Adobe Grand Villas** (35 Hozoni Dr., 928/203-7616, www.adobegrandvillas.com, $349–450 d). The over-the-top, bigger-is-better suites start at 850 square feet, and each has at least one king-size bed, two fireplaces, and enough Western kitsch to re-create the sets of *Tombstone* and *Bonanza*. Still, you've got to love any hotel that can decorate with wagon-wheel beds and lantern chandeliers. Some rooms feature tubs for two and steam showers, while others offer red-rock views, private patios, and wood-beam ceilings.

VILLAGE OF OAK CREEK
$50-100

Adobe-inspired **Wildflower Inn** (6086 Hwy. 179, 928/284-3937, www.sedonawildflower-inn.com, $99–139 d) is bit a nicer than your standard motel fare, and its prime location across the street from Bell Rock…well, rocks. Expect a few pleasant perks like flat-screen TVs and continental breakfast, and be sure to call the motel directly for any late-breaking deals.

$100-250

Loaded with character, **(Adobe Village Graham Inn** (150 Canyon Circle Dr., 928/284-1425, www.adobevillagegrahaminn.com, $200–250 d) promises a bit of "rustic luxury" and doesn't disappoint. The boutique inn's unique rooms and villas earn kudos for their Western decor and romantic ambience. Try to reserve the Sundance Room, which offers a fireplace, wood-plank flooring, king-size canopy bed, and large bathroom with a rainforest shower and jet tub. For a real splurge, go with the Wilderness Villa, a picturesque gem with log walls, a charming periwinkle-blue sleigh bed, and a river-rock fireplace that connects the bedroom with a two-person tub. The small gardens and incomparable views of Bell, Cathedral, and Courthouse Rocks make this bed-and-breakfast a real find.

Adobe Hacienda Bed & Breakfast (10 Rojo Dr., 800/454-7191, www.adobe-hacienda .com, $199–239 d) bills itself as "Sedona's most authentic Southwest-style bed and breakfast inn," and it may just be. The small bed-and-breakfast's five guest rooms are each decorated with traditional Southwestern touches, like lodge pole beams, Saltillo tile floors, Native American rugs, hand-painted Mexican sinks, and cozy Pendleton blankets. Owners Pauline and Brad Staub are the consummate hosts, happy to point you in the direction of an easy hiking trail or to serve up a hearty breakfast on the flagstone patio that overlooks the adjacent golf course and the red rocks. Call for last-minute discounts or to request a specific room.

Families will appreciate the recently renovated **Hilton Sedona Resort & Spa** (90 Ridge Trail Dr., 928/284-4040, www.hiltonsedona.com, $209–239 d), which provides an impressively diverse assortment of amenities for its price, including a championship golf course, a fitness center, a full-service spa, and multiple pools. Guest rooms and one-bedroom suites—which can accommodate up to five people—are tastefully decorated with Southwestern accents and boast gas fireplaces and small balconies. The helpful and friendly staff is happy to provide recommendations on local restaurants, tours, and hiking trails. Perched on a hill overlooking the Village of Oak Creek and Bell Rock, the hotel's location far from the crowds of Uptown can provide a nice change of pace.

Las Posadas of Sedona (26 Avenida De Piedras, 928/284-5288, www.lasposadasofsedona.com, $179–219 d) calls itself a bed-and-breakfast, though the sprawling property and all-suite hotel feels more like a large condo complex. It's a not a bad choice if you are planning to spend more than a few days in Sedona and need a home away from home. The French-trained chef goes above and beyond every morning to create a tasty three-course breakfast, and some of Oak Creek's best restaurants are within walking distance.

Families will appreciate the spacious rooms at Hilton Sedona Resort & Spa.

© MICA THOMAS MULLOY

About halfway between Uptown and the Village of Oak Creek, **Radisson Poco Diablo Resort** (1752 S. Highway 179, 928/282-7333, info@RadissonSedona.com, $149–195 d) offers travelers a hint of luxury without breaking the bank. Aside from red-rock views and lots of nearby hiking, the "Little Devil" lures its visitors with a fitness center, a swimming pool, a nine-hole golf course, and pristine tennis courts. Worried about catching your ZZZ's after all that action? Don't be. The standard room offers a Sleep Number bed, and for a few bucks more you can relax in your own private whirlpool bath.

Food

As in many tourist towns, Sedona's dining options range from the sublime to the ridiculously expensive. Hole-in-the-wall cafés, mom-and-pop diners, crowded brewpubs, and four-star restaurants duke it out for your taste buds—and your money. You'll want to sample Sedona's Mexican and Southwestern cuisine for a taste of authentic Arizona, and fortunately, there are delicious options for every price range. Also, be sure to splurge at least once while you're in Red Rock Country at one of the romantic dining spots that make a stay in Sedona such a treat.

UPTOWN
American
Trendy Cal-Ital cuisine has hit Sedona at the mod **C Hundred Rox** (100 Amara Ln., 928/340-8820, 5–9 P.M. daily, $23–34), Amara Resort's AAA Four Diamond restaurant. Chef David Schmidt uses fresh organic produce to create an innovative and delicious menu. Start with the toasted bruschetta or the *fritto misto,* a medley of fried artichokes, broccoli, squash, and mozzarella, served with a lemon-caper aioli. Then, move on to the brown-butter-braised yellow fin hamachi with a citrus-herb salad or the caramelized potato gnocchi with crispy pork and brussels sprouts. For dessert, forgo the classic tiramisu and try the black raspberry panna cotta, popped with a few drops of aged balsamic vinegar.

Saturday evenings, the luxury inn **El Portal Sedona** (95 Portal Ln., 928/203-4942, 5:30–8 P.M. Sat., $25–45) opens its doors to the public for a culinary tour de force. Rich cheeses, fresh fish, roasted meats, and local organic vegetables and spices highlight an ever-changing menu. When the weather cooperates—and it frequently does in Sedona—meals are served in the hotel's grass-and-stone courtyard. Diehard foodies will want to book one of the limited reservations.

Enjoy Sedona's very own award-winning microbrew at **Oak Creek Brewery & Grill** (336 Hwy. 179, 928/282-3300, 11 A.M.–9 P.M. daily, $11–26). The casual second-floor pub at Tlaquepaque has a darn good menu of sandwiches, salads, pastas, burgers, and "fire-kissed" pizzas, like the feta-and-artichoke Oak Creek Greek Pizza. The smoked pork tenderloin with prickly pear-chipotle glaze and rotisserie chicken are always good choices. Check out the delicious ales and pilsners brewing in copper tanks behind the bar before heading out to the large patio, which has a nice view of Snoopy Rock.

You'll find plenty of great dishes at the popular **Shugrue's Hillside Grill** (671 Hwy. 179, 928/282-5300, 11:30 A.M.–3 P.M. and 5 P.M.–8:30 daily, $21–32), but it's the sunset views from the deck that pack the place. Order a glass of wine and enjoy the sight before you dig into the whiskey-barbecued duck, lemon-seared scallops, or the signature flame-broiled shrimp scampi. The menu includes a wide selection of pastas, salads, fish, and steaks.

Asian
Under the glow of paper lanterns, **Takashi** (465 Jordan Rd., 928/282-2334, 4–9 P.M. Tues.–Sun., $19–25) serves traditional Japanese cuisine, including teppanyaki, sushi, teriyaki, and tempura. You'll find all the classics in the understated dining room, which resembles a small, Japanese cabin, or you can enjoy your edamame and yellowtail nigiri on the patio.

Breakfast and Lunch
The laidback **Secret Garden Café at Tlaquepaque** (336 Hwy. 179, 928/203-9564, 9 A.M.–5 P.M. daily, $8–15) is a pleasant place to enjoy breakfast, especially outside by the charming fountain. Order a cup of the Kona coffee and try the fluffy French toast dipped in Grand Marnier or the filling breakfast burrito. In the afternoon, the café serves salads, sandwiches, hearty quiches, and burgers. And if you were thinking about indulging in a red-rock picnic, you can get your order to go at the counter.

Finding an inexpensive lunch in Uptown can be a challenge. Fortunately, the sandwiches and salads at **Sedona Memories** (321 Jordan Rd., 928/282-0032, 10 A.M.–2 P.M. Mon.–Fri., $4–7) are cheap and delicious. Expect generous portions and fresh ingredients at this cash-only, mom-and-pop shop. There are a few tables outside, though you may want to call ahead to order a picnic to go.

Café

For a little metaphysical fine-tuning and a snack, pop into **Sedona Story** (207 N. Hwy. 89A, 928/282-3875, 8:30 A.M.–7:30 P.M. Mon.–Sat., 8:30 A.M.–6:30 Sun., $3–5). The small café offers "chakra-healing" smoothies, shakes, coffees, and teas, along with reflexology and massages. Try the peach-and-strawberry smoothie.

Desserts

How Sweet It Is (336 Hwy. 179, 928/282-5455, 10 A.M.–6 P.M. daily) sells delicious chocolates, fudges, marshmallows, lollipops, and unique candies. Kids will have a field day perusing the rows of jellybeans and gummy confections in this small sweet shop, and you may want to treat yourself to a fresh fruit smoothie or shake.

French

In a city of "spectacular views," ◖ **L'Auberge Restaurant on Oak Creek** (301 L'Auberge Ln., 928/282-1661, 7 A.M.–9 P.M. Mon.–Sat., 9 A.M.–9:30 P.M. Sun., $6–12 breakfast, $15–40 lunch and dinner) stands out. The flagstone patio of the elegant restaurant and wine bar creeps right up the banks of Oak Creek, creating a leafy, romantic setting. The menu's seasonal ingredients reflect the changing scenery, from wild game and hearty soups in winter to fresh salads with wild greens and creamy cheeses in the summer. Even *Wine Spectator* magazine is a fan, bestowing L'Auberge with its "Best of Award of Excellence" for 14 consecutive years for its large selection of vintage wines.

The formal dining room at **René at Tlaquepaque** (336 Hwy. 179, 928/282-9225,

11:30 A.M.–2:30 P.M. and 5–8:30 P.M. daily, $15–42) attracts locals and visitors celebrating weddings, anniversaries, and birthdays, although it's the Southwestern-inspired French cuisine that keeps them coming back. Feast on traditional Gallic treats like escargots, onion soup, and steak au poivre, or try surprising dishes like the seared Ostrich René, topped with béarnaise sauce, king crab, and asparagus.

Italian

The Hideaway Restaurant (251 Hwy. 179, 928/282-4204, 11 A.M.–9 P.M. daily, $7–15) is just that, tucked into a small shopping center near Tlaquepaque. This is where the locals go for cheap and delicious subs, pastas, and pizzas, piled high with toppings like homemade sausage. Be sure to go at lunch or before dark so that you can enjoy the views of Oak Creek and the red rocks. There are plenty of kid-friendly choices—and even some crayons to keep the little ones happy—while the adults may want to sneak upstairs to the lively bar.

Mexican and Southwest

If you ventured all the way to Sedona to find some good Mexican food, look no further than ◖ **Elote Cafe** (771 Hwy. 179, 928/203-0105, 5–9 P.M. Tues.–Sat., $13–20). Chef Jeff Smedstad has traveled through Mexico for more than 15 years, creating a flavor distillation of the country's diverse cuisine, which runs deeper than tacos and refried beans. Be gluttonous and order an appetizer, entrée, and dessert. The *elote* is a must: fire-roasted corn with spicy mayo, lime, and *cotija* cheese. Try the jicama and orange salad, and follow it up with the sweet-and-spicy lamb adobo or the braised pork in a tomatillo and pumpkinseed mole, a savory chocolate sauce native to Puebla, Mexico. The restaurant's flavors will make a lasting impression on you.

If you're in the mood for classic tacos or quesadillas, try **El Rincon** (336 Hwy. 179, 928/282-4648, 11 A.M.–9 P.M. Tues.–Sat., 11 A.M.–8 P.M. Sun., 11 A.M.–4 P.M. Mon., $5–15). The Mexican village atmosphere of Tlaquepaque provides a pleasant backdrop for the classic Sonoran-style cuisine that most Americans will recognize, like shredded-beef burritos, green chile and cheese enchiladas, and sweet corn tamales, served enchilada style with red or green chile sauce. The combination platters are a convenient way to taste a few highlights from the menu—complemented by a prickly pear margarita or Mexican beer, of course.

Javelina Cantina (671 Hwy. 179, 928/203-9514, 11:30 A.M.–8:30 P.M. daily, $10–17) serves the best fajitas in town. A pan of beef, chicken, fish, or shrimp is brought to your table sizzling and popping alongside sautéed onions and peppers. The dish is served with plenty of warm tortillas, guacamole, and crème fraîche. *¡Dios mio!* The restaurant is large but gets busy with families and large parties around dinnertime. And it's no wonder that business is booming—the restaurant's patio provides views of the majestic red rocks.

Oaxaca Restaurant (321 N. Hwy. 89A, 928/282-4179, $8–14) boasts a healthy approach to south-of-the-border fare. The menu was designed by a dietician and provides many

COURTESY OF OAXACA RESTAURANT SEDONA CVB

a sizzling plate of fajitas at Oaxaca Restaurant

guilt-free entrées, like grilled Arizona cactus with a zesty sauce of roasted tomatoes, red peppers, chiles, and almonds. The restaurant's patio offers stunning views of Sedona's red rocks, and there is great people-watching along the city's main drag. If you just want to sip a margarita while you feast on nature's eye candy, this is the place, as the views are better than the food.

Steakhouses and Barbecue

Where else can you get cactus fries and rattlesnake? Slip into one of the big booths at **Cowboy Club Grille & Spirits** (241 N. Hwy. 89A, 928/282-4200, 11 A.M.–10 P.M. daily, $10–28) and admire the "second-largest set of Longhorn horns in the United States." It may not be true, but they're fun to appreciate while digging into the buffalo chili, fresh seafood, and delicious barbecue. This is definitely the place to go for cowboy-worthy steaks and ribs. Next door, the more upscale sibling, **Silver Saddle Room** (5–9 P.M. daily, $16–44), features a slightly more elegant menu in a less-touristy atmosphere.

Every town needs a hole-in-the-wall barbecue joint. Drop into **Sally's Mesquite BBQ & Grill** (250 Jordan Rd., 928/282-6533, 11 A.M.–7 P.M. daily, $8–15) for a pulled pork sandwich, smoked beef brisket, or St. Louis-style ribs that are as good as you'll get anywhere in Arizona. The relaxed lunch and dinner spot has been serving up tasty sides like fresh-cut fries and homemade baked beans and cole slaw for more than 20 years.

Get your hands dirty at **Red Rock BBQ** (150 Hwy. 179, 928/204-5975, 11 A.M.–9 P.M. Sun.–Thurs., 11 A.M.–10 P.M. Fri.–Sat., $9–18). Dive into the hickory-smoked pork sandwiches, spicy wings, and juicy hamburgers. Even the thick shakes and sweet berry cobbler will have you reaching for more napkins. The casual restaurant is a nice place to kick back on the patio with a beer and take in the red-rock views.

WEST SEDONA
American

Housed in a former cabin that once served as Sedona's first sheriff's station, **Savannah's**

SEDONA

(2545 W. Hwy. 89A, 928/282-7959, 5–9 P.M. daily, $23–41) oozes local charm. The cozy restaurant, tucked into an old grove forest, is well known by locals for having the best steaks in town, grilling tender filets and marbled ribeyes. Non-beefeaters will find chicken dishes and an impressive selection of seafood, expertly prepared. And for a little fun, all entrées come with a choice of toppings, including sautéed mushrooms, gorgonzola-walnut butter, and pepper-brandy sauce.

The garlic-sautéed lobster blinis at **Heartline Café** (1610 W. Hwy. 89A, 928/282-0785, 4:30–10 P.M. daily, $15–32) are a Sedona classic. The hard-to-categorize restaurant features Southwestern flavors, Asian touches, and a little continental flair, like the roasted pear and butternut squash soup or the tea-smoked chicken dumplings with spicy peanut sauce. There are seafood, pasta, and vegetarian dishes on the menu, and plenty for meat eaters.

Breakfast and Lunch

When you're on vacation, this is just the kind of place you want to go for breakfast. Locals have been making **Coffee Pot Restaurant** (2050 W. Hwy. 89A, 928/282-6626, 6 A.M.–2 P.M. daily, $4–9) a morning ritual for years, and the small breakfast joint doesn't disappoint. You'll find all the morning staples, like fluffy pancakes and crispy bacon, as well as 101 omelets. The fun atmosphere may be a credit to the friendly service, or it could be the mimosas and bloody marys. Try to get a table on the patio for a view of the diner's namesake, Coffee Pot Rock. The cozy café regularly earns the distinction of "best breakfast" in local magazines.

The aliens are among us at **Red Planet Diner** (1655 W. Hwy. 89A, 928/282-6070, 10 A.M.–11 P.M. daily, $7–14), a kitschy little greasy spoon in West Sedona. Kids will love the 1950s-diner-meets-outer space motif, as well as the burgers, fries, and milkshakes. Adults will appreciate the full bar and filling sandwiches. Look for the UFO out front.

New Frontiers Natural Foods (1420 W. Hwy. 89A, 928/282-6311, 8 A.M.–9 P.M. Mon.–Sat., 8 A.M.–8 P.M. Sun.) is an excellent grocery store if you'd like to pick up some supplies for a picnic or if you're planning an extended stay in Red Rock Country. They sell an impressive selection of organic produce, naturally raised meats, and fresh breads, as well as vegan products and fresh salads at the well-stocked deli.

Greek

Usually, a restaurant this good would come with an impossibly chic decor and long waiting list. Fortunately, that hasn't happened yet at **Fournos Restaurant** (3000 W. Hwy. 89A, 928/282-3331, 6–8 P.M. Tues. and Thurs.–Sat., closed Sun. and Tues.–Wed., $16–21). The delightfully relaxed Mediterranean-influenced restaurant features some of the best food in Sedona, with a menu that is bold and focused. There will, no doubt, be some hard-to-resist special, but be sure to start your meal with the rich lobster bisque with black trumpet mushrooms. After that, the rest of the meal—whether you go with the lamb or fresh fish—will play out beautifully.

Italian

Dahl & Di Luca Ristorante (2321 W. Hwy. 89A, 928/282-5219, 5–10 P.M. daily, $19–30) is always packed with locals and visitors, who swear by the crispy calamari and fresh pasta. Be sure to start with the incredible antipasti menu, which includes roasted heads of garlic, grilled asparagus wrapped with prosciutto, and fried Greek olives, stuffed with cheese. There's often live music and a lively atmosphere in the bar, though you may want to skip the Tuscan-inspired dining room.

I've never seen so many options for a pizza. Order an Oak Creek Nut Brown beer and dive into **Picazzo's** (1855 W. Hwy. 89A, 928/282-4140, 11 A.M.–9 P.M. Sun.–Mon., 11 A.M.–10 P.M. Fri.–Sat., $11–22) epic menu. Ingredients range from the meaty (sausage, pepperoni, Canadian bacon) to the cheesy (ricotta, parmesan, mozzarella) to the spicy (yellow peppers, red chile flakes, fresh jalapeños). Or you can go the gourmet route with shrimp, applewood-smoked bacon, and gorgonzola. The modern-but-casual restaurant is also known for its big salads and insanely decadent desserts.

Mexican and Southwestern

The colorful and relaxed **Casa Bonita** (164 Coffee Pot Dr., 928/282-2728, 11 A.M.–9:30 P.M. Mon.–Thurs., 11 A.M.–10 P.M. Fri.–Sun., $8–15) is a favorite with locals, and though it may not look like much, it's hard to beat the tasty margaritas, fresh salsa, and refreshing escape from the tourists of Uptown. The homey, reasonably priced restaurant is hidden in a grocery store plaza, and its diverse menu includes chicken poblano and bacon-wrapped shrimp smothered in a flavorful cream sauce.

Named for the croaking amphibian that lives in southeastern Arizona, **Barking Frog Grille** (2620 W. Hwy. 89A, 928/204-2000, 5–10 P.M. daily, $14–20) serves Southwestern favorites that don't seem tired or dated. Kick off happy hour with a prickly pear mojito and stay for dinner to enjoy the chicken tortilla soup, fish tacos, or enchiladas. If you're looking for something more filling, try the campfire ribs or maple-juniper pork chop. Conclude the night with the tequila-laced crème brûlée.

For cheap, straightforward Mexican food, give **Angel's** (2245 W. Hwy. 89A, 866/826-9515, 7 A.M.–9 P.M. daily, $6–12) a try. Don't let the Denny's-esque ambience fool you—this is classic Sonoran food: hot tamales, crispy beef tacos, burritos, and a host of enchiladas. The friendly staff is happy to walk you through the menu, though you really can't make a bad pick. Think basic, not fancy.

Vegetarian

Vegetarians rave about **D'lish** (3190 W. Hwy. 89A, 928/203-9393, 11 A.M.–8 P.M. daily, 9–noon Sat.–Sun. for breakfast, $7–10) and its innovative vegan cuisine, which includes many raw and gluten-free options. Order one of the soups, sandwiches, salads, or daily specials at the counter, and pull up a chair on the large patio overlooking the red rocks. The decor is quite modern, and it can be a fun place on the weekend to grab breakfast, complete with organic coffee and homemade chai. There are

also lots of healthy snacks—or gooey desserts for post-hike treats.

Thai Spices (2986 W. Hwy. 89A, 928/282-0599, 11:30 A.M.–9 P.M. Mon.–Sat., $8–13) is a well-loved choice of Sedona vegetarians. The healthy Thai cuisine features hot noodle dishes, fresh spring rolls, and flavorful soups. The inexpensive lunch specials are quite popular, and meat eaters will find several chicken and shrimp dishes.

VILLAGE OF OAK CREEK
American

A relative newcomer to Sedona's gourmet dining scene, **Fork in the Road–American Bistro** (7000 Hwy. 179, 928/284-9322, 4–9 P.M. Tues.–Sun., $14–28) has quickly established itself as a culinary force to be reckoned with. The modern, understated decor of white banquettes and dark woods sets the tone for the elegant, brilliantly crafted menu. Start with the Guinness Irish onion soup with herb croutons and Irish cheddar cheese or the apple and arugula salad with mint, toasted walnuts, radicchio, and crème fraîche-lemon dressing. The entrées are innovative takes on bistro classics, like duck cassoulet, roasted chicken, and lamb with an orange, honey-soy marinade. Try to get to the restaurant early to enjoy a cocktail and the creative tapas at the bar.

For delicious, no-fuss steak sandwiches and reubens, join the locals at **PJ's Village Pub** (40 W. Cortez Dr., 928/284-2250, 10 A.M.–2 A.M. daily, $8–14). You'll find bikers, hikers, and golfers huddled around the closely packed tables or at the popular bar. The tavern is known for its nightly specials—Pot Roast Tuesdays, Baby Back Rib Wednesdays, etc.—though the Friday night fish frys have become a weekly ritual in the Village of Oak Creek.

Breakfast and Lunch

The cheerful **Village Griddle** (7000 Hwy. 179, 928/284-4123, 7–8 P.M. daily, $6–15) in the Tequa shopping center is a must for hungry breakfast eaters. Grab a table or one of the "tractor" seats at the counter, and gobble down the generous fresh-off-the-griddle platters: eggs with

SEDONA

hash browns, huevos rancheros, and omelets with melted cheese and homemade chorizo.

Hidden away in a small strip center, the down-home **Blue Moon Café** (6101 Hwy. 179, 928/284-1831, 7 A.M.–9 P.M. daily, $6–10) is a great way to start your day before a hike or round on the links at the Sedona Golf Resort. You can also stop by afterward to refuel with the hearty Philly sandwiches, subs, burgers, and hand-tossed pizzas. You'll find a few Southwestern specialties and a decent beer and wine list.

Also in the Tequa plaza, **Café Jose** (7000 Hwy. 179 Ste. A108, 928/284-4123, 7 A.M.–8 P.M. daily, $6–10) is a modern cross between a classic dinner and a Mexican restaurant. You'll find eggs and bacon, short stacks and waffles, and healthy omelets in the morning, and a diverse lineup in the afternoon: fish and chips, burgers, and vegetarian dishes, along with burritos, enchiladas, nachos, and carne asada. The café is also an inexpensive option for dinner.

Every town should have **Dahl & Di Luca A'Roma** (7000 Hwy. 179, 928/284-1556, 10:30 A.M.–6:30 P.M. Mon.–Sat., 11 A.M.–5 P.M. Sun., $6–15). The gourmet deli and wine boutique is stylish and stocked with some of the best "deli" food that you'll find in Sedona. Create a romantic red-rock picnic or in-room hotel feast with sandwiches, panini, homemade soups, and sides like potato salad with lemon and dill, fresh caprese salad, and grilled vegetables. Pick up a bottle of wine and artfully prepared pastry for the perfect meal.

Italian

 Cucina Rustica Dahl & Di Luca (7000 Hwy. 179 Ste. 126 A, 928/284-3010, $13–28) is a crowd-pleaser. The salads, soups, and meat dishes are delicious, but it's the fresh, homemade pasta that has made the restaurant a hit with Sedona diners. Try the linguine Bolognese, tortellini with portobello mushrooms and white truffle cream sauce, or the gnocchi with slipper lobster meat and a creamy tomato vodka sauce. Eat at the bar or have a seat in the romantic dining room, which features a twinkling, starry sky.

Cucina Rustica Dahl & Di Luca in the Village of Oak Creek

© MICA THOMAS MULLOY

Information and Services

TOURIST INFORMATION

The **Sedona Chamber of Commerce** (331 Forest Rd., 928/282-7722 or 800/288-7336, www.visitsedona.com, 8 A.M.–5 P.M. Mon.–Sat., 8 A.M.–3 P.M. Sun.) has a convenient office in Uptown that supplies visitors with maps, directions, and suggestions for getting the most out of your time in Sedona. You can also purchase a Red Rock Pass here. The expanded **Red Rock Ranger Station** (8375 Hwy. 89A, 928/203-2900, 8 A.M.–5 P.M. daily), just south of the Village of Oak Creek, may be a more convenient option if you are driving in from Phoenix.

LIBRARIES

"A community without a library is a community without culture and without the backup needed by local education," said Sen. Barry Goldwater in 1968 at groundbreaking ceremonies of the **Sedona Public Library** (3250 White Bear Rd., 928/282-7714, www.sedonalibrary.org, 10 A.M.–6 P.M. Mon.–Thurs., 10 A.M.–5 P.M. Fri.–Sat.). Goldwater spoke again at the dedication of the new stone-clad building in 1994, a natural light-filled space in West Sedona, where he praised the community for all that it had accomplished in its short history. Since then, a second branch, the **SPL In the Village** (56 W. Cortez Dr., 928/284-1603, www.sedonalibrary.org, 1–5 P.M. Mon.–Fri., 9 A.M.–1 P.M. Sat.) has opened up in the Village of Oak Creek.

HOSPITALS AND EMERGENCY SERVICES

The **Verde Valley Medical Center–Sedona Campus** (3700 W. Highway 89A, 928/204-4100, www.verdevalleymedicalcenter.com) offers 24-hour emergency services in West Sedona, as well as primary and specialty health care. It's a part of the nonprofit Northern Arizona Healthcare, a collection of larger institutions, like the Verde Valley Medical Center in Cottonwood, Flagstaff Medical Center, and Northern Arizona Homecare and Hospice.

Getting There and Around

Sedona is a small town, and almost all of the area's natural attractions, cultural sights, and restaurants can be reached within a 10-minute drive of Uptown. And with so much neck-craning scenery, you won't mind your time behind the wheel, though the weekend traffic, especially during holidays, can test your patience. The scenic drive between the Y intersection in Uptown and the Village of Oak Creek on Highway 179 is particularly inspiring, and you'll be tempted to pull over more than few times to check out the mammoth formations and to investigate if even the dirt is that red (it is).

AIR

You'll need to fly into **Phoenix Sky Harbor International Airport** (3400 E. Sky Harbor Blvd., 602/273-3300, www.phxskyharbor.com) and in all likelihood drive the 90 minutes north to Sedona on I-17 to Highway 179. If you don't want to rent a car, take the **Sedona Phoenix Shuttle** (800/448-7988, www.sedona-phoenix-shuttle.com), which offers service via van from Sky Harbor to the Village of Oak Creek and West Sedona for $50 one-way and $90 round-trip. Also, chartered jet services are available to **Sedona Airport** (235 Air Terminal Dr., 928/282-4487, sedonaairport.org).

CAR
Rental Cars

To really explore Sedona, Red Rock Country, and the Verde Valley, you'll need a car. At Phoenix's Sky Harbor Airport, take the free

SEDONA

shuttle from any of the terminals to the **Rental Car Center** (1805 E. Sky Harbor Circle, 602/683-3741). You'll find major companies, like **Budget** (602/267-4000, www.budget.com), **Hertz** (602/267-8822, www.hertz.com), and **Enterprise** (602/489-6898), which has convenient drop-off centers around Phoenix. **Hertz** has a rental center in West Sedona (3009 W. Hwy. 89, 928/774-4452, www.hertz.com) and will make pickups within a 15-minute drive.

To make the most of your visit to Red Rock Country, you may want to consider renting a vehicle with four-wheel drive, especially as many of Sedona's off-highway destinations go off-road.

TROLLEY

If you're tired of driving, catch the **Sedona Trolley** (276 Hwy. 89A, 928/282-4211, www.sedonatrolley.com, $12 adults, children under 12 free) at its Uptown depot for one of two hour-long, narrated tours. The Sedona Highlights Tour visits Gallery Row and Tlaquepaque Arts and Crafts Village before making a 15-minute stop at the Chapel of the Holy Cross. The Seven Canyons Scenic Tour heads out to West Sedona, making a stop at Enchantment Resort in Boynton Canyon. Call or visit the website for times.

Vicinity of Sedona

The red rocks steal a lot of attention, but there's plenty to see outside of Sedona, which makes an excellent home base to explore some of the region's other notable natural attractions and historic sites. Within 10 minutes of Uptown Sedona, you can drive Arizona's first officially designated scenic highway through the leafy forests of Oak Creek Canyon. Head 25 minutes south, and you'll find one of the country's most impressive Native American ruins, the cliffside Montezuma Castle. And if you travel 30 minutes east, you'll land in the historic—and haunted—mining town of Jerome. Even if you're in Sedona for just a few days, be sure to make some time to visit one of these areas.

◖ OAK CREEK CANYON

Drive north from Uptown Sedona on Highway 89A and you'll discover one of Arizona's most picturesque drives. Oak Creek Canyon may not offer the scale of the Grand Canyon or the sculptural beauty of Sedona's red-rock formations, but its intimate scale is far more approachable and equally fun to explore. The scenic highway, which meanders from Sedona to Flagstaff through a series of lingering turns, traces much of the 12-mile-long river gorge. Running water along a geological fault line

© MICA THOMAS MULLOY

Oak Creek Canyon's leafy forests are very different from the rest of Sedona.

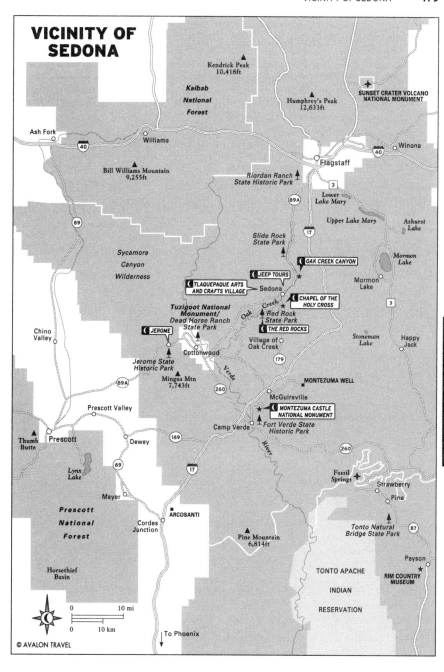

VICINITY OF SEDONA

Kendrick Peak
10,418ft

Kaibab
National
Forest

Humphrey's Peak
12,633ft

SUNSET CRATER VOLCANO
NATIONAL MONUMENT

Ash Fork

Williams

40

Winona

40

Flagstaff

Bill Williams Mountain
9,255ft

Riordan Ranch
State Historic Park

3

89A

Lower
Lake Mary

89

Sycamore
Canyon
Wilderness

Slide Rock
State Park

Upper Lake Mary

Ashurst
Lake

17

OAK CREEK CANYON

Mormon
Lake

JEEP TOURS

TLAQUEPAQUE ARTS
AND CRAFTS VILLAGE

Sedona

Mormon
Lake

3

CHAPEL OF THE
HOLY CROSS

Tuzigoot National
Monument/
Dead Horse Ranch
State Park

JEROME

Red Rock
State Park

THE RED ROCKS

Stoneman
Lake

Happy
Jack

Chino
Valley

Jerome State
Historic Park

Cottonwood

Village of
Oak Creek

179

Mingus Mtn
7,743ft

260

MONTEZUMA WELL

McGuireville

89A

MONTEZUMA CASTLE
NATIONAL MONUMENT

Prescott Valley

Camp Verde

Fort Verde State
Historic Park

260

Thumb
Butte

Prescott

Dewey

169

Lynx
Lake

69

17

Fossil
Springs

Strawberry

Pine

Mayer

Prescott

Cordes
Junction

ARCOSANTI

87

National

Forest

Pine Mountain
6,814ft

Tonto Natural
Bridge State Park

Payson

Horsethief
Basin

TONTO APACHE

RIM COUNTRY
MUSEUM

INDIAN

RESERVATION

0   10 mi

0   10 km

↓ To Phoenix

© AVALON TRAVEL

SEDONA

formed the canyon, creating sheer walls that range from 800 to 2,000 feet tall.

The wooded canyon was first made popular—like Sedona—in the 1920s and '30s when Hollywood arrived. Films like Jimmy Stewart's *Broken Arrow* captured its red-rock walls, leafy forests, and cascading waters. Today, Oak Creek Canyon attracts visitors in search of some rest and relaxation—though you won't escape the crowds, especially in summer. Fall is particularly lovely, when many of the sycamore trees turn golden yellow, shimmering against the evergreen pines and red rocks. No matter the time of year, it's still possible to find a quiet area for a picnic or hike without running into other people. Much of the area is part of the Coconino National Forest or state park land, ensuring its protection from development.

Slide Rock State Park

When the temperatures start to climb in late spring, the cool waters of Oak Creek can be irresistible. Take the plunge at Arizona's best swimming hole in Slide Rock State Park (6871 N. Hwy 89A, 928/282-3034, www.azstateparks. com, 8 A.M.–6 P.M. May–Sept., 8 A.M.–5 P.M. Oct.–April, $8–10 per vehicle), situated seven miles north of Sedona. Glide down the 80-foot-long natural rockslide, which was carved into the granite and red sandstone canyon floor by Oak Creek. The chilly water that started as snowmelt on neighboring mountains can be a little brisk—and the ride can be a little hard, so be sure to bring an old pair of sneakers to navigate the slickrock. There are small wading pools for a more relaxed swim, or you can sunbathe like a lizard on one of the warm red rocks. The **Slide Rock Market** sells snacks and water, though you may want to bring a picnic and cooler if you plan to stay the day.

Like any well-loved attraction, Slide Rock has become too popular for its own good in recent years. Families from Phoenix and across Arizona descend upon the park on weekends and during holidays in the summer, causing temporary closings when the parking lots fill up or when daily water tests reveals high levels

Slide Rock State Park

© BOB CLEMENZ / SEDONA CVB

of E. coli bacteria. In the fall and winter, the park can be blissfully quiet, providing a nice opportunity to explore the former homestead's historic buildings and apple orchard.

A little bit closer to Sedona and just over **Midgely Bridge,** you'll find **Grasshopper Point,** another popular swimming hole and picnic area. In the summer, be sure to get there early before it gets too crowded, as the deep pool attracts cliff-jumpers on the weekends. Head down the access road off of Highway 89A and follow the signs. There is an $8 parking fee unless you have a Red Rock Pass.

West Fork of Oak Creek

There are plenty of great **hiking** spots in Oak Creek Canyon, but West Fork is by far the best. The trail, which starts in a small meadow, follows the creek through lush riparian areas and shady groves before it slices into a narrow slot canyon. The large trees and 200-foot-tall canyon walls provide lots of shade, which is a blissful relief during the hot summer. The initial three-mile trek will suit most visitors, and even first-time hikers will enjoy the easy, flat trail. Serious explorers, though, can penetrate even farther into the deep, forested canyon, where they'll need to wade into the creek—and even swim in some spots. The vegetation gets thicker and the trail less defined, and it takes a full day to make the additional 11 miles.

To find the trail, take Highway 89A past mile marker 385 to the Call of the Canyon Recreation Area, named after the classic Western novel Zane Grey wrote after a visit to the area. There is a fee of $8 per vehicle, and you must notify the rangers if you are planning to backpack overnight.

Shopping

Two classic Native American trading posts can be found in Oak Creek Canyon. Step inside **Garland's Indian Jewelry** (3953 N. Highway 89A, 928/282-6632, www.garland-sjewelry.com, 10 A.M.–5 P.M. daily), and you'll see walls of intricately crafted silver-and-leather belts, woven baskets, kachina dolls, and jewelry. The designs lean toward the traditional,

though you'll find some impressive pieces like chunky bracelets inlaid with stones and necklaces with simple pieces of turquoise. The store sells antique pieces as well as new designs by emerging artisans from Hopi, Navajo, and Zuni tribes.

For more than 60 years, **Hoel's Indian Shop** (9589 N. Arizona 89A, 928/282-3925, www.hoelsindianshop.com, 9:30 A.M.–5 P.M. daily) has bought directly from Native American artisans, and their first-rate inventory is a testament to this tradition. The shop specializes in Native American arts and crafts, including jewelry, hand-carved kachina dolls, hand-woven baskets, and Navajo rugs and blankets. The innovative pottery designs are especially rich.

Accommodations

Garland's Oak Creek Lodge (8067 N. Hwy. 89A, 928/282-3343, www.garlandslodge.com, $290 per cabin) provides guests with the romance of a cabin in the woods and all the style of a small resort. The 1908 homestead is a well-kept Arizona secret, though you may have a hard time getting a reservation for one of the 16 cabins. And like any good summer hideaway, the lodge's on-site restaurant—simply called The Dining Room—will keep you coming back night after night. Breakfast and dinner are included with your stay. The resort is open early April through mid-November and closed on Sundays. If possible, try to book one of the large cabins with a fireplace.

Escape into the woods at the quirky **Forest Houses Resort** (9275 N. Hwy. 89A, 928/282-2999, www.foresthousesresort.com, $90–145 per house). The 15 cabins, A-frame homes, and stone cottages are scattered on 20 wooded acres. Some of the houses could use some updating, but they're all a lot of fun. Try to reserve one of the creekside cottages, the charming Rock House, or the arty Studio, a former sculpting workshop that overlooks a grassy meadow. The homes range in size, accommodating 2 to 10 people. Be sure to ask about the resort's charming history—there's a monkey involved.

Small and pleasantly rustic, **Canyon Wren Cabins** (6425 N. Hwy. 89A, 928/282-6900,

SEDONA

ww.canyonwrencabins.com, $155–175 d) attracts guests six miles north of Uptown. Its three chalet-styled cedar cabins are designed to accommodate two people comfortably, with a small living room, kitchen, bath, and wood-burning fireplace downstairs, and an open loft bedroom with queen bed upstairs. The Honeysuckle Log Cabin is a bit smaller, but it can be a fun way to live out your Zane Grey fantasies for a week. Proprietors Milena and Mike provide coffee and muffins in the morning, and they are happy to recommend tips for sightseeing and shopping.

Food

If you're planning a creekside picnic, pop into **Garland's Indian Garden** (3951 N. Hwy. 89A, 928/282-7702). The small deli and market prepares fresh sandwiches, salads, and baked goods. You can also stock up on lunchtime essentials like water, soda, and chips, as well as locally grown apples and fresh juice.

The elegant **Dining Room** at Garland's Oak Creek Lodge (8067 N. Hwy. 89A, 928/282-3343, $40 per person) serves up a communal culinary experience. A single prix-fixe menu is presented each night, with a changing gourmet lineup that may include coconut crabmeat chowder, rack of lamb, or grilled salmon with sweet corn and bacon relish. Guests—most of whom are staying at the lodge—share tables, creating a warm atmosphere. Cocktails are served at 6 P.M. by the fire or out on the lawn, depending on weather, and the dinner bell rings at 7 P.M. Reservations are required, and the restaurant is open early April through mid-November and closed on Sundays.

Getting There

Oak Creek Canyon may be one of the easiest day trips you've ever taken. Simply head north of Uptown Sedona on Highway 89A; in minutes, you'll be wending your way through one of Arizona's most beautiful forests, with roadside views of red-rock formations and cool, running waters. The drive to Slide Rock should take less than 20 minutes from Sedona, and with another 20 minutes or so in the car, you can reach the mountain retreat of Flagstaff, the unofficial capital of northern Arizona.

THE VERDE VALLEY

When Spanish explorers first rode into this part of central Arizona in the 16th century, they were immediately struck by the tall, green *(verde)* grasses and mighty cottonwoods that flanked the banks of its small river. The conquistadors named the area Verde Valley, a testament to its contrast against the brown Sonoran desert.

The Sinagua had known of this temperate oasis for hundreds of years, making their homes in cliffside dwellings and hilltop pueblos until they disappeared in the 1400s. By the late 19th century, Anglo settlers arrived and clashed with the Apache Indians who roamed the land, prompting the construction of Fort Verde. In their zeal to appease the settlers, though, Fort Verde's civilian and military commanders changed the landscape forever. Local pioneers took full advantage of the Native Americans' relocation to reservations and moved wave after wave of cattle and farms onto the land. So many head of cattle were brought in that the waist-high grasses that prompted Army-contracted hay cutters and gave the Verde Valley its name were soon gone. The topsoil washed away, leaving much of the land so denuded that the hard cacti and low grasses seen today were all that survived.

Fortunately, though, you can still see the vestiges of Verde Valley's green landscape and reminders of its dramatic history. Visit the national monuments at Montezuma Castle and Tuzigoot to see the protected pueblo villages of the Sinagua. Learn what life was really like in the Old West by exploring the haunted mining town of Jerome or the frontier military installation at Fort Verde. And be sure to see how the valley earned its green moniker at Dead Horse Ranch State Park, a lush riparian reserve between Sedona and Jerome.

◖ Jerome

Jerome is a rough-and-tumble town with a colorful history and penchant for surviving disaster. Once dubbed the "Wickedest Town in the West," the hillside community has endured the ravages of fire, landslides, and an influenza epidemic—not to mention Prohibition and the boom-and-bust business of mining.

There is a whole lot of history packed into Jerome, despite its small, walkable size. The town was founded in 1876 after prospectors Angus McKinnon and M.A. Ruffner filed the first mining claims. Six years later, the United Verde Copper Company mine was established by entrepreneur William Andrews Clark. It became the richest individually owned mine in the world, and Clark made a fortune. Workers arrived in droves, and the city became a melting pot of cultures, with Irish, Greek, and Chinese immigrants appearing in search of jobs and opportunity.

In its heyday, the city's population topped at 15,000. Saloons, opium dens, and brothels lined the streets and transformed the mining camp into a lively boomtown. Jerome flourished like this for decades, but after more than

By the time Jerome's mine closed in the 1950s, more than one billion dollars worth of ore had been hauled out.

© JEFF FICKER

WHO IS JEROME?

The city was named for New Yorker Eugene Murray Jerome, a United Verde Copper Company investor and cousin to Winston Churchill's mother. Jerome never visited his namesake, believing the camp and the rabble who worked in it would be too crude for his refined tastes.

$1 billion had been milked from the mines, the bust came to town. The UVCC mine closed for good in 1953, having producing enough copper to put 13 pounds of it into the hand of every person living at the time. Jerome became a ghost town overnight. It wasn't until the 1970s that settlers started to return, but this time they were hippies and artists who found the quaint atmosphere and cheap rent appealing.

Small shops, bars, and hotels still cling to the side of Cleopatra Hill, though today they mainly cater to tourists. The winding streets are filled with visitors on the weekends—and they're not alone. Jerome is rumored to be haunted by a slew of ghosts, including the spirit of Jennie Banters, a former madam, once considered the wealthiest woman in northern Arizona. She was murdered by her opium-addicted boyfriend in 1905. Banters was a beloved figure in Jerome—at least in part because she was often the first to rebuild after the repeated fires that often consumed local businesses.

Plan to spend a couple of hours in Jerome, a National Historic Landmark. Explore the narrow streets and alleys that climb the steep slopes and pop into its small galleries and stores. The must-see **Mine Museum** (200 Main St., 928/634-5477, www.jeromehistoricalsociety.com, 9 A.M.–5 P.M. daily, adults $2, children free) is small but jam-packed with information, giving a great overview of Jerome's sordid past. Exhibitions trace the complex hierarchy of prostitutes, immigrants, and shopkeepers who made their home in Jerome, and

SEDONA

© JEFF FICKER

The small Mine Museum is the perfect primer before exploring Jerome.

the displays of rusty old tools quickly school onlookers in the rigors of life in the mines.

Out front, bikers frequently park their hogs on **Main Street** while, inside the saloons, they compete with tourists for space at the bar and a view of the band. Jennie Banter's old brothel has been replaced by **Nellie Bly** (136 Main St., 928/634-0255, 10 A.M.–5:30 P.M. daily), a small store selling jewelry and arty gifts. Down the street, **Laughing Mountain** (116 Main St., 928/634-8764, 10 A.M.–5:30 P.M. daily) offers expansive views of Verde Valley, along with Native American leather goods, wind chimes, and Southwestern sculptures and wooden crosses.

ACCOMMODATIONS

A National Historic Landmark, the haunted **Jerome Grand Hotel** (200 Hill St., 928/634-8200, www.jeromegrandhotel.com, $120–205 d) sits high above town on Cleopatra Hill. The 12-room **Hotel Connor** (164 Main St., 928/634-5006, www.connorhotel.com, $90–165 d), built in 1898 by David Connor, offers

respite from the high-spirited happenings in the Spirit Room saloon below.

The Miner's Cottage (553 Main St., 928/254-1089, www.theminerscottage.com, $950 per week) is a sophisticated throwback to Jerome's Victorian past, with two master suites available for rental by the week. Shorter stays are available upon request.

FOOD

The Asylum Restaurant and Lounge (200 Hill St., 928/639–3197, 11 A.M.–3 P.M. and 5–9 P.M. daily, $16–28) at the Jerome Grand Hotel has earned rave reviews for its Southwestern-inspired dishes, like prickly pear barbecue pork tenderloin and the vegetarian sesame tofu and roasted butternut squash. The New American cuisine is complemented by a terrific view of Verde Valley and an extensive wine list, which has earned kudos from *Wine Spectator* magazine.

Though the hours may be a bit scattered, the casual **Mile High Grill & Spirits** (309 Main St., 928/634-5094, 8 A.M.–4 P.M. Sun.–Mon.,

© JEFF FICKER

Hotel Connor and the must-visit Spirit Room saloon

11 A.M.–4 P.M. Wed.–Thurs., 8 A.M.–9 P.M. Fri.–Sat., closed Tues., $6–12) is one of Jerome's best bets for a good meal. Breakfasts range from cinnamon oatmeal to Mile High Eggs, an English muffin topped with crab cakes, eggs, cheese, bacon, and a red pepper aioli. At lunch and dinner, you'll find delicious sandwiches, salads, wraps, and burgers.

Belgian Jennie's Bordello Bistro & Pizzeria (412 Main St., 928/639-3141, www.belgianjennies.com, 11:30 A.M.–8 P.M. Thurs.–Mon.) fixes hearty pastas like fettuccine alfredo, lobster ravioli, and tortellini carbonara. The wickedly good thin-crust pizzas live up to the restaurant's namesake, the infamous madam Jennie Banters. Next door, the **Flat Iron Café** (416 Main St., 928/634-2733, 8:30 A.M.–3 P.M. Wed.–Mon., $4–9) serves breakfast and lunch, as well as a decent cup of joe for a quick pick-me-up.

You can't leave Jerome without having a drink at **The Spirit Room** (166 Main St., 928/634-8809, 11 A.M.–1 A.M. daily). Beers and bands abound at this Jerome mainstay, which feels every bit as bad as the old saloons that used to serve up whiskey to miners after a long day underground.

GETTING THERE
To make the easy road trip to Jerome from Sedona, take Highway 89A west to the Cottonwood. The highway drifts south before looping north through town. You can stay on Highway 89A straight through to Jerome, where it winds up the side of Cleopatra Hill, or you can opt for the more scenic drive through Old Town Cottonwood on Highway 260, which is also called Main Street. Highway 260 passes by exits for Dead Horse Ranch State Park and Tuzigoot, as well as through the town of Clarksdale, where it rejoins Highway 89A to make the ascent up to Jerome.

Tuzigoot National Monument
Sitting on the summit of a desert hilltop, Tuzigoot National Monument (off of Broadway between Clarksdale and Old Town Cottonwood, 928/634-5564,

www.nps.gov/tuzi, 8 A.M.–5 P.M. daily Sep.–May, 8 A.M.–6 P.M. daily Jun.–Aug., $5 adults, children free) was once the home of the Sinagua people, who lived in the 110-room village between 1125 and 1400. The three-story pueblo ruins, constructed from limestone and sandstone rocks, formed an intricate complex of living, cooking, and large storage spaces that were used by Sinaguan farmers, who traded with communities hundreds of miles away. Unlike at the cliffside Montezuma Castle, visitors can explore the ruins' rooms up close and trace its well-preserved walls, which rise a few feet high. The largest room at the top of the complex has been reconstructed, giving views of the surrounding landscape and a sense of what it must have been like living in this close-knit community. Be sure to check out the nearby tailings pond, which Jerome's former United Verde Copper Mine used to deposit leftover minerals and sediment. The impact on the landscape is quite extraordinary.

GETTING THERE

A trip to the monument can be easily paired with a visit to Jerome by following Highway 89A to Highway 260, which turns into Broadway between Clarksdale and Old Town Cottonwood. Look for the turnoff just south of Clarksdale.

Dead Horse Ranch State Park

To catch a glimpse of what the Verde Valley looked like before the settlers and cattle herds arrived, head to Dead Horse Ranch State Park (675 Dead Horse Ranch Rd., 928/634-5283, www.azstateparks.com, 8 A.M.–5 P.M. daily), a nearly pristine stretch of Verde River that offers camping, hiking, mountain biking, fishing, and equestrian areas. Don't let the name fool you. This is some of the most verdant land in the area. Officially classified as a cottonwood and willow riparian gallery forest—one of only 20 such ecosystems left in the world—the 423-acre park protects one of the last stretches of free-running river in the Sonoran Desert and more than 100 species of migrating birds, including the black hawks and golden eagles that

come every year to feast on the trout released into the river.

GETTING THERE

From Sedona, take Highway 89A southwest to Cottonwood. Once you enter the town, the highway loops north and turns into Main Street. At the Y intersection, stay on Main Street, which is also called Highway 260. Turn right on 10th Street and head north to Tuzigoot Road. Make a right at Dead Horse Ranch Road, where you'll see the entrance to the park.

Cottonwood

Enjoy a bit of roadside charm on a quick ride through **Old Town Cottonwood,** a terrific throwback to the 1950s small towns you would expect to find off Route 66. The district's quaint Main Street—which is also called Old Highway 89A or Highway 260 depending on the sign—is a pleasant drive, especially for travelers on their way from Sedona to Jerome, Tuzigoot, or Dead Horse Ranch State Park. Many of its storefronts are being restored as Cottonwood tries to recapture a bit of its former glory. And though the town of 11,000 residents has strong agricultural roots that are still alive, modern Cottonwood also serves as a bedroom community for Sedona's workers, who can't afford to live in pricy Red Rock Country.

ACCOMMODATIONS

You'll find a few chain motels in Cottonwood, but frankly, you're better off staying in Sedona or Jerome. If you need to say in town, though, **Pines Motel** (920 Camino Real, 928/634-9975, www.azpinesmotel.com, $50–90) is better than your average roadside hotel. Its clean, bright rooms are cheery, and the new mini suites, equipped with full-sized refrigerators, are great for larger groups or big families.

FOOD

Hankerin' for an Old West cookout? Well, even if themed dining isn't your thing, **Blazin' M Ranch** (599 N. 10th St., 928/634-

0334, www.blazinm.com, 5–8:30 P.M. daily, closed Jan. and Aug., adults $34.95, children $24.95) serves up darn good "cowboy vittles, stories, tomfoolery," and it's a destination in its own right for many Sedona tourists. Arrive at 5 P.M. when the gates open so that you can enjoy the full Wild West experience, including a shooting gallery, train ride, petting zoo, and roping. The dusty streets and wooden sidewalks may not be authentic, but it's hard to resist browsing the old-fashioned shops—or dressing up as rough-and-tumble cowboys and saloon madams for an "Olde Tyme" photo. The dinner bell rings at 6:30, when you'll find chuckwagon grub like barbecued meats, cowboy beans, chunky applesauce, and homemade biscuits. After supper, the Blazin' M Cowboys carry on the Old West tradition of twangy music and storytelling. Call for reservations.

Willy's Burgers & Shakes (794 N. Main St., 928/634-6648, 11 A.M.–7 P.M. Mon.–Sat., 11 A.M.–3 P.M. Sun., $5–8) in Old Town Cottonwood re-creates the classic diner ambience of the 1950s, right down to the black-and-white checkered floor and swell jukebox. Look for the converted gas station's old pumps at out front, which welcome nostalgic boomers or those who want to refuel on classic burgers, gooey grilled cheese sandwiches, and malts that range from chocolate-banana to strawberry. If you're in a rush, grab a seat at the counter; otherwise slide into the vinyl booths for a tasty lunch.

The bustling **Nic's Italian Steak & Crab House** (925 N. Main St., 928/634-9626, 5–9 P.M. Mon.–Thurs., 5–10 P.M. Fri.–Sat., 5–9 P.M. Sun., $9–17) packs in Cottonwood residents with solid seafood dishes and topnotch steaks. Grab a drink at the saloon-like bar if there's a wait, and consider whether to start with the little neck clams simmered in white wine and garlic butter or the baked Crabby Mac-n-Cheese, pasta tossed in a cheddar-alfredo sauce with sweet lump crab. And as at any good Italian restaurant, you can't go wrong with the eggplant parmesan, classic lasagna, or lemon-and-caper chicken piccata.

GETTING THERE

A quick day trip to Cottonwood is quite easy, and it's a great place for a meal in between stops at Tuzigoot National Monument or Dead Horse Ranch State Park. From Sedona, take Highway 89A west. You'll notice the landscape changes quite starkly from red-rock buttes, high-desert cacti, and ponderosa pines to tawny grasslands and flat plains. Once you get into Cottonwood, the highway loops north and turns into Main Street or Highway 260. You can opt to take Highway 260 south to Camp Verde and Montezuma Castle.

◖ Montezuma Castle National Monument

Walking up the shady, creekside path to Montezuma Castle (I-17 Exit 289, 928/567-3322, www.nps.gov/moca, 8 A.M.–5 P.M. daily, 8 A.M.–6 P.M. daily Jun.–Aug., $5 adults, children under 16 free), you can't help but imagine what it must have been like to live in the five-story pueblo, one of the best-preserved cliffside dwellings in North America.

From about 1250 to the 1400s, the 20-room village served as the home of the Sinagua people, who cultivated the land along Beaver Creek by day and scaled tiered ladders 75 feet above the ground every night. The Sinagua used the mud, stone, and wood-timbered rooms and balconies for sleeping, preparing food, weaving, and storing goods that they would trade to surrounding communities. The vertical limestone cliff wall also functioned as a natural defense against rival tribes.

As many as 35 people lived in the structure, with an additional 100 people living in the 45-room **A Castle** at the bottom of the cliff. Montezuma Castle—built into a deep, carved-out recess in the cliff and sheltered from the elements—is in much better shape than A Castle, as well as the hundreds of other Sinaguan sites throughout the Verde Valley. A 1997 stabilization project by Native American workers added a fresh, chestnut-brown layer of mud to the facade. Incidentally, there is no connection to Montezuma. American explorers who discovered the site in the 1800s speculated

SEDONA

© JEFF FICKER

From about 1250 to 1400, the cliffside Montezuma Castle served as the home of the Sinagua people.

that the Aztecs and their legendary emperor built the impressive structure. The small museum at the visitors center provides a nice overview of the site and the Sinagua people.

MONTEZUMA WELL

The Sinagua were experts at making the most of the Verde Valley's natural landscape. Just 11 miles north of Montezuma Castle, you can witness their ingenuity at another of Arizona's natural wonders, Montezuma Well (I-17 Exit 293, 928/567-4521, 8 A.M.–5 P.M. daily, 8 A.M.–6 P.M. daily Jun.–Aug., $5 adults, free). Small cliffside ruins and canals are clustered around the site, which once provided a vital source of water to the agrarian community. Underground springs still feed 1.5 million gallons of water every day into the well, which actually is a large sinkhole, 365 feet across and 55 feet deep. The constant supply of 74-degree water has created an ecosystem with several plants and animals not found anywhere else in the world. Unique species of crustaceans, water scorpions, and turtles thrive in the warm,

carbon dioxide-rich water that is inhospitable to most fish and aquatic life. Walk through the forested grounds to the water's edge, where the temperature can be as much as 20 degrees cooler than in the surrounding grasslands. There are also ruins of small pit houses built by the Hohokam, who first constructed the still-running canals in the 8th century.

ACCOMMODATIONS AND GAMING

Feeling lucky? Scratch that gambling itch at **Cliff Castle Casino** (555 W. Middle Verde Rd., 928/567-7900, www.cliffcastlecasino.net), at Exit 289 off of I-17. The gaming facility, owned by the Yavapai-Apache Nation, offers slots, poker, blackjack, and keno, as well as live entertainment at the outdoor **Stargazer Pavilion** and inside at its nightclub, **Dragonfly Lounge.** Next door, you can find a clean, quiet room at **The Lodge at Cliff Castle** ($80–90 d).

GETTING THERE

If you're coming from Sedona, head south on Highway 179 to the I-17. Take Exit 289, and

© OSAMU HOSHINO / SEDONA CVB

Montezuma Well is a geological anomaly and an ancient Sinaguan site.

SEDONA

drive east through two roundabouts for less than a mile, where you turn left on Montezuma Castle Road. Plenty of signs will make navigating the narrow two-lane road quite easy. From Phoenix, follow the I-17 north about an hour and turn right at Exit 289, where signs will direct you through two traffic circles to the monument's entrance. To reach Montezuma Well, drive the I-17 to Exit 293, which is four miles north of the turnoff for Montezuma Castle. Follow the signs through the towns of McGuireville and Rimrock to the park's entrance.

Fort Verde State Historic Park

Wyatt Earp never shot it out with lawless gunslingers on its dusty streets, but Fort Verde (125 E. Hollamon, 928/567-3275, azstateparks.com, 9 A.M.–5 P.M. Thurs.–Mon., $3 adults, $1 children) is the place to go for a glimpse of the real Old West—especially of life among the soldiers sent out West after the Civil War. Originally built in 1871, the fort housed as many as 300 soldiers who were stationed here to protect

Anglo settlers from Apache and Yavapai raiders. What remains of the old fort today is considered the best-preserved example of Indian War-era military architecture in the state.

The territorial-style houses that line the dusty parade ground look more like the remains of a Midwestern main street than the stockade-fenced forts seen in old westerns. The three surviving historic houses are decorated with 1880s-period furnishings, and the former Military Headquarters building now houses a museum with artifacts and photographs from the soldiers, civilians, and Native Americans who once lived in the region. Exhibitions describe how many of the area's Native Americans were eventually confined to a reservation in the Verde Valley, then evicted wholesale to the San Carlos Apache reservation in 1875.

Today, more than 10,000 people live in the modern town of Camp Verde. The main drag is lined with a few forgettable antique shops and restaurants, though the fort is a nice stop if you need a break between Phoenix and Sedona.

GETTING THERE

From Sedona, drive south on Highway 179 through the Village of Oak Creek to the I-17, where you'll merge right and head southwest. Take Exit 287, and turn left onto Highway 260, also called the Camp Verde Payson Highway. Turn left a few minutes later on Finnie Flats Road, which will take you directly into the town of Camp Verde. You'll see signs directing you to the fort. If you are driving from Phoenix, simply take the I-17 north to Exit 287, where you'll follow Highway 260 south to Finnie Flats Road and Camp Verde.

Arcosanti

The utopian village of Arcosanti (928/632-7135, www.arcosanti.org, 10 A.M.–4 P.M. daily) was designed and built by Italian architect Paolo Soleri as the embodiment of his principles of "arcology"—a mixture of architecture and ecology. Soleri's goal is to create a "lean alternative" to the wastefulness of modern cities by making them more compact and self-sustaining. His real-world experiment began in 1970, more than two decades after Soleri first came to the Southwest to study with Frank Lloyd Wright at Taliesin West. Today, Arcosanti is perched in rural splendor on a bluff in Arizona's high desert and is home to just a few hundred people at any one time. From a distance, it looks like an unlikely combination of Italian hill town and sci-fi movie. But up close, the small, hand-crafted details of its buildings and the community's perfectly human scale make it a delight to visit, not to mention a pioneering example of urban sustainability. Guided tours are $10.

GETTING THERE

From Phoenix, drive north some 60 miles on I-17. Take Exit 262 for AZ-69 toward Prescott and turn right on Cordes Lakes Road. From there, signs for Arcosanti should direct you left on Stagecoach Trail, which is unpaved after a brief asphalt stretch, then onto Cross I Trail.

From Sedona, head south on AZ-279 to I-17. Take it 36 miles south to Exit 262, then follow the directions above.

WIKIMEDIA COMMONS / CODYR.

Arcosanti is an architectural and ecological experiment in the Arizona desert.

BACKGROUND

The Land

"Mountains complement desert as desert complements city, as wilderness complements and completes civilization," Edward Abbey wrote in his autobiographical work, *Desert Solitaire*. If the word "desert" conjures up images of sand dunes, camels, and parched, monochromatic landscapes, then get ready for a surprise. Phoenix and Scottsdale sit in the northeastern corner of the Sonoran Desert, the most ecologically diverse desert region on the planet. It stretches more than 100,000 square miles from central Arizona south into Mexico and west into California and is home to more than 1,000 native species of plants, 60 species of mammals, 350 kinds of birds, 20 amphibians, and 100 or so reptiles. It's also the only place in the world where the towering saguaro cactus—made famous in so many westerns—grows naturally. Sure, it's a desert that's usually hot from May to September and sunny most of the year, but Lawrence of Arabia would be lost here.

GEOGRAPHY AND GEOLOGY

The Phoenix metro area is ringed with mountains, deep canyons, and broad, alluvial valleys watered by rivers than can go from shallow trickles to raging torrents in a matter of minutes. This landscape is part of the vast basin

© MICA THOMAS MULLOY

The Sonoran Desert features rugged mountains and dramatic rock formations.

and range zone born 15 million years ago when the Earth's crust beneath what is now the western United States was pulled apart by shifting tectonic plates. It stretched as much as 50 percent, pushing up and pulling down the land to form a regular pattern of small but steep mountains and broad, flat valleys. Today, a ring of such mountain ranges around metro Phoenix gives the area its nickname: the Valley of the Sun. The major ranges surrounding the Valley are the White Tank Mountains to the west, the Sierra Estrella to the southwest, South Mountain to the south, the Superstitions to the southeast, the Usery Mountains to the east, the McDowell Mountains to the northeast and the Hieroglyphic Mountains to the northwest. Smaller ranges also ring the center of the city, including the Phoenix Mountains, South Mountain, and the Papago Buttes. Most of the rock that forms these craggy hills is volcanic, but they were created less by geysers of lava than by the inexorable seismic shifting that tilted up huge blocks of the Earth's crust.

To the north lies the high, flat Colorado

Plateau. Sedona sits in the southwestern part of this high-desert region, which covers the four corners area where northeastern Arizona, southeastern Utah, southwestern Colorado, and northwestern New Mexico meet. But to get there from Phoenix, you have to climb the Mogollon Rim, a long, snaking cliff that bisects the state from east to west. This dramatic drop-off separates the low desert surrounding Phoenix from the grasslands and Ponderosa pine forests of this vast plateau, and the trails along its edge offer fabulous views of the Sonoran Desert below. The area around Sedona is known as Red Rock Country thanks to the red-tinged sandstone cliffs towering above Oak Creek Canyon. The color comes from iron deposits that rust as the rock weathers and exposes them to air and water. But the majestic formations, called "fins," came to be thanks to a much simpler process: the combination of weak ground and flowing water. Oak Creek tumbles down from the north through a fault line. Over the millennia, thousands of small earthquakes fractured the ground above the fault, and water seeped in and carried away layer after layer of rock to form Oak Creek Canyon. The strongest rock formations stood up to this liquid attacker and now soar far above the canyon floor.

RIVERS AND LAKES

Phoenix owes its very existence to the Salt River (or Rio Salado as it is called in Spanish). The snaking stream runs 200 miles from the White Mountains in eastern Arizona to join the Gila River about 15 miles west of downtown Phoenix, and farmers from ancient times to the present have come to the Valley of the Sun for its life-giving water. A series of dams have left the lower half of the riverbed mostly dry since the first, the Roosevelt Dam, was built in 1911, but the Salt's natural flow is more than 2,500 cubic feet per second, about three times the amount of water in the Rio Grande. Except for overflow released after storms, most of this water now goes into hundreds of miles of irrigation canals scattered around the region, and the dams themselves provide flood control and produce electricity. The one exception to this is the 2-mile-long Tempe Town Lake, created in 1999 by building two inflatable dams in the bed of the Salt River and filling the area between them with a combination of upstream storm runoff and treated wastewater. Perhaps not surprisingly, no swimming is allowed, but kayaking, rowing, sailing, and paddle-boating are all popular pastimes, and the lake is stocked with fish regularly.

Central Arizona's other major river, the Gila, is even longer and more powerful than the Salt. It flows almost 650 miles from the White Mountains near the border with New Mexico all the way to the Colorado River, which forms the border between Arizona and California. Dams and irrigation diversions reduce the river to a trickle in several areas, but in its natural state, the Gila carries more than 6,000 cubic feet of water per second and once was navigable from the Colorado nearly to the New Mexico border. For five years, from the end of the Mexican War to the Gadsden Purchase in 1853, the Gila River actually formed the border

Tempe Town Lake

© MICA THOMAS MULLOY

between the U.S. and Mexico. Today, significant portions of the river run through Native American communities.

All the dams on the Salt and Gila Rivers have created a surprising number of lakes. An oft-repeated but completely unverified statistic that Arizonans love to repeat is that Maricopa County has one of the highest per capita rates of boat ownership in the nation. Whether or not this is true, the somewhat incongruous sight of a large pickup truck towing a water-ski or fishing boat through the desert is surprisingly common, and it's possible to learn how to sail, kayak, and even scuba dive at Lake Pleasant and a few of the other large lakes in the area.

CLIMATE

It's probably the Valley of the Sun's greatest claim to fame: the near-perfect weather—well, at least for a good portion of the year. In February, blue, sunny skies and balmy temps in 70s and 80s delight residents and visitors alike. The good times last well into April, as

MONSOON MADNESS

Triple-digit heat is to be expected during the summer months in Phoenix, but there's a weather phenomenon in the desert Southwest that makes the sweltering afternoons slightly unpredictable. The Arizona monsoon season begins June 15 and ends September 30, bringing volatile afternoon storms that can range from blowing dust to torrential downpour. The term monsoon is taken from the Arabic word for season, *mausim*, referring to a seasonal shift in wind flow. In Arizona, the typically westerly winds shift to a southerly flow, which pulls in moisture from the Gulf of California. Combine that moisture with the intense afternoon heat, and you get thunderstorms.

In May, the average afternoon high temperature is about 93 degrees, with relative humidity averaging 15 percent or below. By July, the mercury will rise each afternoon to about 105 degrees, and relative humidity doubles to an average of about 30 percent. That makes it tougher for the human body to cool down during the sweltering heat. But heat is only one of the dangers of the monsoon.

About a third of Phoenix's yearly rainfall occurs in the summer, and sometimes it comes dangerously quickly. The sandy desert floor can-not absorb rainfall that sometimes amounts to an inch or more in just a few hours. Flash-flooding becomes a problem as normally dry washes fill with water and careless drivers attempt to cross them. Traffic is often halted on highways too, as massive dust storms sweep across town. This happens when we see dry thunderstorms. Their strong winds pick up the dry desert soil and push it into town, sometimes bringing visibility to near zero. Finally, thunderstorms often send hikers and golfers hurrying for cover, as lightning lights up the desert horizon.

Monsoon thunderstorms are most likely during the afternoon and evening hours but can erupt any time of the day. They are more common the further south and east you go in Arizona. Although they can be very dangerous, they're essential to the desert ecosystem. Many desert creatures, including tarantulas, toads, and quail, have adapted their breeding cycles to benefit from the monsoon rain. And in May and June you will notice saguaro cacti blooming with beautiful white flowers, letting their fruit seeds ripen just in time to soak up the summer rains.

(Contributed by April Warnecke, meteorologist, KTVK 3TV)

A late-summer rainstorm builds over the mountains in the Santa Cruz Valley of southern Arizona.

hiking trails, golf courses, and restaurant patios fill up with people hoping to spend every last second soaking in the spring nirvana. And because this is the desert, the arid climate's low humidity means nighttime temps fall 20 to 30 degrees, providing a cool counterpoint to the warm days.

The Sonoran Desert heats up quickly in May, and its reputation for sizzling summer temps isn't an exaggeration, with an average high in the 90s and lows in the 70s. Still, the low moisture means that it actually feels quite a bit cooler than comparable days in New York, Miami, or Houston. By July, though, watch out. It's hot—as in a 115-degree kind of hot. Phoenix has the warmest climate of any major metropolitan area in the country, and its record high of 122 degrees on June 26, 1990, caused even the toughest of desert-tested Phoenicians to break out in one heck of a sweat. Most people cope by switching to an early morning or nocturnal schedule in the summer, as overnight lows drop into the 80s. Also, there are frequent breaks from the scorching heat and constant sunshine in the late summer, when the monsoon storms roll into the city from the desert. These afternoon showers, caused by a seasonal change in weather patterns, can be sudden and torrential, stranding motorists and even mountainside hikers. The dramatic bolts of lightning force golfers off the course and swimmers out of the pool.

By October, a "second spring" emerges with lush, green plants and colorful wildflowers. The triple-digit temps become a memory with fall temperatures dropping back into the 80s, which means you'll be able to fit in plenty of outdoor time. In the high deserts of Sedona, which is typically 15 to 20 degrees cooler than Phoenix throughout the year, the sycamore trees along Oak Creek begin to turn, revealing golden yellow and fiery red leaves against the green ponderosa pines.

Believe it or not, there is a winter in the Sonoran Desert. Don't laugh—there is. The 60-something highs and 40-something lows chill Phoenicians to the bone. OK, the weather is darn-near perfect, and residents love nothing

more than calling up snowed-in relatives in other parts of the country to gloat. Still, nighttime lows do fall below freezing a few times a year, and a rare light snow does happen, especially in Sedona.

ENVIRONMENTAL ISSUES

Mayor Phil Gordon announced an ambitious plan in 2009 to make Phoenix "the greenest city in America." Though admirable, the plan will have to solve at least two of the metro area's most daunting environmental problems if it's to be more than rhetoric—namely air pollution and suburban sprawl. In winter, a "brown cloud" of dust, car exhaust, and other particulates often hangs over the city for days at a time thanks to the surrounding mountains, which block the wind and trap warmer air near the ground. In summer, strong sunlight and extreme heat interact with chemicals in car exhaust to form ozone, a colorless pollutant that affects breathing and often leads to warnings from health officials that people with respiratory illnesses should stay inside. It's a problem that defies easy solution in a metro area that sprawls over more than 1,000 square miles and forces residents to drive almost everywhere. But that's not the only problem with the way one of America's fastest-growing cities is planned and built. The new subdivisions, office parks, and shopping malls sprouting up on the edge of town are paving over the desert at the rate of more than an acre per hour. This destroys wildlife habitat and native plants (though damaging or even moving a saguaro cactus without a permit can result in hefty fines and even jail time), not to mention the views of pristine desert that draw so many people to Arizona in the first place.

Water and where to get it has always been a top concern in the desert, but metro Phoenix has fewer problems in this area than might be expected. Rivers and streams that flow out of the mountains to the north and east fill roughly half the metropolis's water needs, while a 350-mile canal from the Colorado River delivers the other half. Local officials say the billions of dollars spent on this water

© SCOTTSDALE CONVENTION & VISITORS BUREAU

the saguaro cactus blossom, Arizona's state flower

infrastructure can supply more than the area currently needs, but a long drought could create serious problems. The complicated legal agreement that apportions water from the Colorado River to states along its banks is actually based on historically high levels of water, and with California at the front of the line, Arizona cities could get very thirsty if the mountain snows that feed all the rivers around the state get much lighter. Draining rivers so completely also creates a slew of environmental problems. Even under current conditions, very little of the water from the Salt and the Gila Rivers makes it to the Colorado, and the mighty river itself now dries up long before it reaches its mouth at the Sea of Cortez.

Another major problem comes from wildfires sparked by lightning, campers, and other human activities. Huge blazes in recent years have charred hundreds of square miles at a time. Though none of the fires have reached Phoenix, Scottsdale, or any of the surrounding suburbs, homes and businesses in small, remote communities are burned nearly every year, and it seems like only a matter of time before some of the northeastern suburbs of metro Phoenix that back up to the Tonto National Forest get hit.

State and local officials are trying to address these problems by changing the way people live and travel in the region. A new light-rail line running through Phoenix, Tempe, and Mesa opened in 2008. It surpassed ridership expectations in its first six months, and it promises to ease congestion and attract more businesses and residents in the neighborhoods it passes through. There's also an effort afoot to establish the metro area as a major player in the solar-power industry. Abundant sunshine makes the region a shoo-in for production—one of the largest solar-power plants in the country is planned for a landfill outside the city—but many business leaders are hoping for clean solar-manufacturing plants, too. These will hopefully attract high-paying engineering jobs to a metro area that's always been big in computer-chip manufacturing and engineering. But they may also help bring the next wave of technology to a place that's been uniquely affected by it. From the precise levels used by the Hohokam to build ancient irrigation canals from the Salt River to the air-conditioning-inspired real estate boom of the 1950s and '60s, metro Phoenix has been uniquely affected by new ideas and products—and there's no reason to think that the future won't repeat the cycle.

Flora and Fauna

FLORA
Cacti

They may seem prickly at first, but the Sonoran Desert's cacti are quite lovable once you get know them. These ingenious plants are prime examples of form meeting function in Arizona's harsh environment, having developed resourceful means to mitigate the hot, arid climate. In fact, many of their well-known features are simply an effort to conserve water. Their leaves have evolved into hard, slender spines, which provide shade and defend against animals foraging for food and water. Their trunks have become spongy repositories to store water, and their green skins have taken on the duties of photosynthesis.

The saguaro (pronounced "sah-WAH-roh") cactus is the king of the Sonoran Desert, an iconic figure that can only be found in this part of the world. The spiny giant can grow up to 60 feet tall and live to be more than 150 years old, with some of the oldest specimens living two centuries. Its clever root system tunnels only a few feet deep, but radiates out a distance equal to the saguaro's height, allowing the camel-like plant to capture the maximum amount of water possible after a rainstorm. These slow-growers can take up to 50 to 75 years to develop branches, or arms, with some growing as many as 25 and others never producing any. The saguaro is an important resource to the desert's ecosystem. In late spring, the cactus blooms with white flowers at night, taking advantage of nocturnal pollinators like moths and bats. They produce sweet, red fruits, which have been eaten by animals and indigenous people for thousands of years. Also, the saguaro's thick trunk often provides a home for a borrowing gila woodpecker—or the occasional desert owl that takes over an abandoned "apartment." Native people once used the plant's wooden ribs in the construction of their shelters, and desert animals still take up residence in their dry skeletons.

Of course, there are other barbed species in the desert. The paddle cactus, more commonly known as the prickly pear, has flat, rounded pads that are quite edible once cooked. The cactus produces a sweet, pink fruit, or fig, that is often used to make candy, jelly, and even a syrup that flavors the popular prickly-pear margarita. The stout barrel cactus can be

Cacti often serve as a home for small birds and rodents.

spiny cholla cactus

© MICA THOMAS MULLOY

found along desert washes, growing 1–3 feet wide and 2–4 feet high. The barrel-shaped body is easy to recognize, though you won't want to get too close to its fishhook spines. Interestingly, the cactus is also called the "compass barrel," as older plants frequently lean toward the southwest. The cholla cactus is also a common inhabitant of the Sonoran Desert, a shrubby-looking plant that comes in 20 varieties, like buckhorn cholla, the deceptively cuddly teddy bear cholla, and the jumping cholla, which doesn't so much jump as easily cling to anything that touches it.

Trees and Bushes

First-time visitors to Arizona are familiar with the Sonoran Desert's cacti, but they are often surprised by the numerous trees and bushes that are native to the area. The green-barked palo verde tree is a gorgeous example. The drought-deciduous tree, which is often found in floodplains and washes, sheds its tiny leaves during dry spells, leaving its "green wood" to take over photosynthesis. In the spring, the canopy blooms in an explosion of tiny yellow flowers. The hardy mesquite tree easily adapts to limited water conditions, thanks in part to a deep taproot that can easily tunnel 25–50 feet underground. Generations of pioneers or artisans have used the hard, dense wood in furniture and as a smoky flavoring in barbecues. Also, there are several varieties of acacia, including the whitethorn acacia, which produces fuzzy, yellow flowers. Farther north, in Sedona and Oak Creek Canyon, you'll see dark-green ponderosa pines, as well as white and Douglas firs, leafy oaks, old sycamores, and distinctive species like the scaly alligator juniper.

There are smaller shrubs to enjoy, too. The waxy creosote bush, a prevalent sight throughout the desert, produces a unique, herbal scent after much-appreciated rainstorms. In the spring, the silver-leafed brittlebush blooms with delicate yellow flowers, while the woody jojoba produces a nut that cosmetic companies covet for its natural oil. The long, slender ocotillo, which is also called vine cactus, is easy to spot. Its cane-like stems grow from the desert floor, and bright-red, tube-shaped flowers appear on the tips. Also, the ornamental agave is used as a decorative plant in many gardens. The thick leaves grow from a central core, often in a symmetrical pattern, and ending in a sharp point. The slow-growing agave produces a single flower only once, on a tall mast that grows from the center of the plant, and, like a romantic Western tragedy, dies after it blooms.

Wildflowers

Nothing dispels the misperception of a lifeless, beige landscape in the Sonoran Desert like wildflower season, when a torrent of psychedelic colors washes across the desert floor. Thanks to *Arizona Highways* magazine, the Grand Canyon state is famous for its vibrant wildflowers, which typically appear after a rainstorm in late February or March and can last well into April or early May. Get your camera ready for the apricot-colored globemallow, desert lavender, golden desert sunflower, violet purplemat, red-flowered chuparosa, and lemon-yellow desert senna. It's not hard to find these seas of color, as any of the mountain preserves that surround the city will teem with polychromatic life, although the best spots are east of Phoenix in the Superstition Mountains at the far end of Highway 60 or in North Scottsdale in the McDowell Mountains and Cave Creek. You can also catch a secondary round of blooms in the fall when summer's hot weather gives way to spring-like temperatures.

FAUNA
Reptiles and Amphibians

Only the tough survive in the Sonoran Desert, and the millennia-old reptile family has adapted to the harsh landscape like no other animal. The rattlesnake may be the area's most famous resident, with some 20 species slithering around Arizona's rocky canyons and dusty desert floors, including the western diamondback, tiger, and sidewinder. They're best known for their ominous rattles, a series of hollow segments made of keratin—like fingernails—that rub against one another at the end of their tails.

© ALYSSA A. MOORE
small agave

© MICA THOMAS MULLOY
leafy oaks in Oak Creek Canyon

© THE PHOENIX ZOO

tiger rattlesnake in the Phoenix Zoo

When threatened, the snakes strike a defensive posture and shake their tails to warn predators of their potent venom, which has an enzyme that paralyzes nerves and destroys tissue and blood cells. What is rarely appreciated about the rattlesnake, though, is its heat-sensing pits. These sensory organs near the eyes and nostrils produce a "heat image" that allows the rattlesnakes to spot prey in the pitch black of a desert night. You may also come across other desert snakes, like the banded sand snake, king snake, or gopher snake.

Lizards scurry around the desert as well, consuming insects, leaves, and springtime blossoms. Visitors are likely to see some of these harmless creatures sunning themselves on mountainsides and rocks, or even searching for shade on patios. The dozens of varieties include the Sonoran collared lizard and desert iguana, as well as whiptails, geckos, chuckwallas, and spiny lizards. North America's only venomous lizard, the gila monster, also makes its home in Arizona. This large reptile, which can grow up to two feet long, spends most of its life underground. The black lizards are covered in spots or bands, in shades of pink, orange, yellow, or red. A host of toads, frogs, and desert tortoises also inhabit Arizona.

Mammals

Despite the extreme heat, many warm-blooded mammals thrive in the desert, like mountain lions, bighorn sheep, and desert cottontail rabbits, a common sight in desert landscapes in and around the city. Bobcats look very similar to domestic cats, though they're about two to three times larger and extremely fierce, as they are able to hunt down rabbits, squirrels, rodents, and even pronghorn antelope and mule deer. Also, don't be surprised if you see coyotes roaming the deserts at night—or at least hear these small canines howling in the distance. Their tan and beige coats, along with their keen hearing and sense of smell, help them hide from predators in the day and search for prey at night. Additionally, brown, furry javelinas roam the desert in groups, searching for leaves, cacti, and grasses.

Bats, nature's only flying mammal, serve an important role in the desert's ecosystem.

© MICA THOMAS MULLOY

More than 100 species of birds roost in Arizona.

Migrating species, such as the lesser long-nosed bat from Mexico, travel to Arizona in the spring to pollinate plants and cacti, like the saguaro cactus. They also eat many of the small insects that could plague the desert without their hungry colonies. The 18 species live in caves throughout the deserts of the Southwest.

Birds

Arizona is a bird-watcher's paradise, with more than 100 avian species soaring across the state's blue skies, including cardinals, finches, eagles, hawks, hummingbirds, and sparrows. And as Phoenix resident Stevie Nicks once sang, "just like the white-winged dove sings a song," you can actually hear these birds, which flock to the desert every spring to pollinate blooming saguaro cacti. And they're not alone. Arizona's state bird, the brown-and-white cactus wren, is a frequent guest in backyard trees and on patios throughout the Valley of the Sun. There are also a half dozen species of owl in the desert, like the ghost-faced barn owl and the great-horned owl—though a more apt name would be the "great-eyebrowed owl."

Beep beep! If we've learned anything from cartoons, it's that where there are wily coyotes, there are speedy roadrunners. The long-legged cuckoos dash across the desert, happily chasing down lizards and insects. Their unique feet—four toes on each foot, two facing forward and two facing backward—make their tracks easy to recognize. And though you won't find that other great cartoon bird, Woody the Woodpecker, the gila woodpecker burrows into trees and cacti in the Sonoran Desert. Its black-and-white-striped wings help distinguish the bird from other species, as does the male's small red "cap" on the top of its head. The ground-dwelling Gambel's quail, crowned by a curled "topknot," is often seen in the late spring with its small chicks following in an orderly line.

Insects, Arachnids, and Centipedes

These creepy, crawly creatures may be the earliest residents of the Sonoran Desert. And once you get over the initial heebie-jeebies, you may be able to appreciate Arizona's insects. The easiest to love, of course, are the graceful butterflies that populate the desert in the spring or those that migrate from Mexico in late summer and early fall. The great purple hairstreak, orange sulphur, and scandalous painted lady are colorful specimens to keep an eye out for. It may be a bit harder, though, to channel the warm fuzzies for the giant desert centipede and the cactus longhorn beetle, which feasts on the cholla and prickly pear cacti.

There are also a few spiders lurking in the desert, like the Arizona blond tarantula and the more common desert tarantula. Typically, they're hiding underground in their silk-lined holes, but like Scottsdale club-goers, they do come out in search of mates. The same is true of the unnerving scorpion, which causes even the toughest of travelers (and cowboys) to halt. Luckily, of the 30 species in Arizona, only the bark scorpion produces venom that can be lethal. Stingers aside, tracking down these pinchers is a bit of a sport in Arizona, and hunters can search for the scorpions with an ultraviolet "black" light that causes their bodies to glow, or fluoresce.

History

ANCIENT CIVILIZATIONS

Despite its inhospitable appearance, the Sonoran Desert has proven to be an irresistible temptation for waves of settlers, beginning with early Native American hunters and followed by a succession Spanish explorers, Catholic missionaries, 19th-century miners and ranchers, and modern-day pioneers, all searching for opportunity. These generations of immigrants define much of Arizona's history, beginning 12,000 years ago when the first humans roamed the area. These Paleo-Indian people followed big game around the region, hunting them in small groups. However, it wasn't until 300 B.C. that permanent civilizations began to form, thanks in large part to the development of agriculture, which requires a long-term, communal effort.

Two major groups emerged during this time, leaving a lasting legacy. The Hohokam laid the foundations for modern Phoenix. They migrated from Mesoamerica (present-day Mexico) just before the birth of Christ, bringing with them crops like corn and beans. Small groups settled along the banks of the Salt River, and over time, they dug miles and miles of canals to create a dependable source of water for their fields. Villages developed, and residents lived in pit houses, igloo-like structures that were built over holes 1–2 feet deep and covered by a dome of sticks and brush, then plastered with mud. As the population grew, a complex culture developed, with elaborate pottery, organized competitions on ceremonial ball courts, and a sophisticated understanding of mathematics and astronomy, which allowed them to expanded their canals and track crop cycles.

Just north, the Sinagua people were developing their own civilization, having expanded from northern Arizona into the Verde Valley and Sedona region in about A.D. 900. This complex society sustained itself by hunting, farming, and gathering indigenous plants. They constructed large hilltop villages made of rock and mud, as well as cliffside dwellings to shelter their communities. Unlike the earthen mounds of the Hohokam, these pueblo ruins still dot the high Sonoran Desert, as well as rocky outcroppings near Flagstaff. The Sinagua thrived from about 1100 to 1350, as they sat at the crossroads of several trade routes that stretched from California to the Four Corners region to the Hohokam villages in the south.

This golden age came to an abrupt end, though. Around 1400, the Hohokam and Sinagua civilizations began to collapse. The causes are a bit murky, though it may have been triggered by a combination of drought, floods, and perhaps internal strife. Some anthropologists have suggested that the civilizations had grown too large, too complex, and too interdependent to sustain themselves. With as many

© USERY MOUNTAIN REGIONAL PARK / GREATER PHOENIX CVB

Hikers can find petroglyphs left by Arizona's ancient inhabitants at many protected parks throughout Phoenix.

as 50,000 people living in Phoenix alone, the desert's resources may have been stretched beyond their limits. By the end of the 1400s, the Hohokam and Sinagua had abandoned their pueblos and canals, with some establishing compact farming villages scattered across the region and others blending into smaller tribes. The modern Pima (Akimel O'odham) trace their roots to the Hohokam, as do the Papago (Tohono O'odham), while the Hopi, Yavapai, and six other tribes consider the Sinagua to be their ancestors.

THE EUROPEANS ARRIVE

Spanish explorers, who first swept through the Sonoran Desert in the 16th century, seemed initially to be unimpressed with region. That is, until tales of the Seven Cities of Gold began to circulate. In 1539, the viceroy of New Spain (now Mexico) organized a small expedition that included friar Marcos de Niza, who returned with stories of a golden city that had homes decorated with jewels and semiprecious stones. A second expedition, headed by Francisco Vázquez de Coronado, was quickly dispatched,

and the two-year odyssey stretched to the Grand Canyon and as far away as present-day Kansas. In the end, it revealed the legendary golden cities to be nothing more than myths.

Coronado's failed expedition also fizzled most interest in Arizona for 150 years, with the exception of a few explorers and missionaries, the most famous being Father Eusebio Francisco Kino, an Italian Jesuit who began his lifelong calling in 1687 to spread Catholicism through the Sonoran Desert. He introduced Native Americans to European plants, animals, and farming methods as he built a string of colonial missions, two of which became the first permanent European settlements in present-day southern Arizona. It was Padre Kino who mapped and named Phoenix's Salt River (Rio Salado), a moniker earned because of the salty taste of the water's high mineral content.

Mexico gained its independence from Spain in 1821, and a couple decades later, the Mexican-American War broke out. It ended in 1848, with Mexico ceding what is now the American Southwest, including most of Arizona, as a part of the Treaty of Guadalupe

Hidalgo. The new Mexican-American population shaped much of the state's art, culture, and cuisine.

THE TERRITORIAL BOOM

In 1849, the California Gold Rush broke out. Prospectors, eager to strike it rich, flooded across Arizona, which was officially part of the New Mexico Territory. Boomtowns sprung up overnight, and calls to make Arizona a separate territory went unheeded as the country plunged into the Civil War. Residents made the bold move in 1862 to form the Confederate Arizona Territory, which stretched across the southern half of the New Mexico Territory, giving Confederate troops in Texas access to California. However, Union troops easily seized control of the desert renegades, prompting the U.S. Arizona Territory with its current boundaries to be established the following year.

In 1867, former Confederate soldier Jack Swilling passed through the Salt River valley and decided that it looked like a good place for farming. The broad, fertile landscape was filled with desert grasses and mesquite, willow, and cottonwood trees, all fed by a wide, winding river, prompting the one-time scout, gold miner, cattle rancher, and saloon owner to return home to Wickenburg, a mining town about 50 miles northwest of present-day Phoenix, to seek financial backing. He got it from a group of local residents and organized a company to dig irrigation canals and establish farms. It wasn't long before he and the dozens of settlers who followed discovered that digging up the Hohokam canal system was an easier way to bring water to their fields than starting from scratch. It was his friend, British-born Lord Darrell Duppa, who suggested they name their new town Phoenix after the mythical bird that rises from its own ashes after being consumed by flame, a poetic tribute to the city's Hohokam roots.

It was still very much the Wild West in the Arizona Territory, though. Fort Verde was built in 1871 to house as many 300 soldiers, who were stationed at the military outpost to protect Anglo settlers from Apache and Yavapai raiders who were being forced onto reservations. Just

© MICA THOMAS MULLOY

remains of Phoenix's pioneering past

north, Jerome was founded in 1876 after pros- pectors filed the first mining claims. Workers arrived in droves, and soon saloons and broth- els lined the streets, transforming the mining camp into a lively boomtown. By comparison, Swilling's Phoenix seemed a "proper" Victorian town, so much so that Arizona's territorial capi- tal moved from Prescott in 1889, and in just a decade, the young city's population grew to 5,554. Shortly after the turn of the century, Arizona pioneers built a dusty stagecoach trail through the new town of Sedona, connecting the communities of Flagstaff and Prescott, and bringing the first regular tourists to the area.

STATEHOOD

Arizonans were clamoring for statehood by the early 20th century. After rejecting a 1906 congressional decision that Arizona and New Mexico enter the Union as a single state, Arizonans took political matters into their own hands. In 1910, they elected 52 delegates (41 Democrats and 11 Republicans) to a state constitutional convention. Many of the repre- sentatives—who included Arizona's first gover- nor, George W.P. Hunt, and Barry Goldwater's grandfather—had progressive, populist lean- ings. They drew up one of the nation's most liberal state constitutions, with provisions meant to give greater political voice to average Arizonans, including voter initiatives, referen- dums, and recalls. President William Howard Taft, who thought recalling judges would com- promise judicial independence, threatened to veto Arizona's admission unless the provision was removed. It was, and Arizona was granted statehood. Voters, however, had the last laugh when they passed a constitutional amendment in the state's first general election in November 1912 that restored the controversial measure. It was Wild West democracy in action.

The Western landscape also created prob- lems. Snowmelt and rain regularly sent the Salt River over its banks. Luckily, President Theodore Roosevelt was ready to ride to the rescue with a bold plan and several million dollars. Roosevelt tasked the newly formed federal Bureau of Reclamation with building a hydroelectric dam on the Salt River in 1911 to control flooding and generate electricity. It was the first project the new agency tackled, and the Roosevelt Dam tamed the free-flow- ing river by diverting the whole flow from its banks into an expanded canal system, leading to one of the city's first big boom periods. With an economy fueled by the "Five C's"—citrus, cotton, cattle, copper, and climate—Phoenix's population mushroomed to nearly 30,000 peo- ple by 1920, then added almost 20,000 more by 1930, matching the Hohokam's previous re- cord of 50,000 inhabitants in just 50 years.

The state came of age during World War II with the bombing of the USS *Arizona* at Pearl Harbor. The Sonoran Desert's terrain was an ideal spot for training soldiers to fight in the deserts of North Africa, and thanks to the state's blue skies and open stretches of land, new airfields were constructed, 60 in all by the end of the war. Moreover, the large, land-locked state also provided space for 23 prisoner-of-war camps, which were scattered around Arizona, including one at Phoenix's Papago Park, the site of the largest mass escape of POWs in the United States during the war. When they weren't escaping, the German POWs helped with projects like canal maintenance and har- vesting cotton crops. Also, due to the state's proximity to large Japanese-American popu- lations in California, several Japanese reloca- tion and work camps were built, including one just south of Phoenix on the Pima–Maricopa Indian reservation.

During this time, one of the most impor- tant pieces of legislation in American history was drafted by an Arizona senator, Ernest W. McFarland. The World War I veteran, having witnessed the poverty many servicemen were forced to endure after returning home, fought to pass a bill that granted tens of thousand of veterans financial assistance for education and housing. As the primary sponsor of the GI Bill, McFarland was a major force behind its unanimous passage in the Senate and House, although it's unlikely he anticipated the sweep- ing effects it would have on the nation when President Franklin D. Roosevelt signed the bill

BARRY GOLDWATER:
THE GOOD, THE BAD, AND THE UGLY

Arizona has had its share of rough-and-tumble politicians. At the top of the list stands the Grand Old Man of the Republican Party, Barry Goldwater, who brought Arizona into the national spotlight in the 1960s. The politically inclined might notice the famed U.S. senator's name etched onto the Phoenix airport's busiest terminal, but Goldwater's legacy extends far beyond the state's front door.

WIKIMEDIA COMMONS

Barry Goldwater in 1986

THE GOOD

Goldwater, with his trademark horn-rimmed glasses, ascended to the U.S. Senate in 1953. During his five terms and 30 years in Washington, the senator espoused a new form of conservatism. His politics carried a libertarian flare. Like most good Republicans he valued a strong military and held a profound mistrust of the Soviet Union in the Cold War Era. But he did not defer to the Republican politics of personal choice and religion that so often define the GOP. He famously said of one well-known evangelist, "I think every good Christian should kick [Jerry] Falwell right in the ass."

THE BAD

In 1964, Goldwater proved his star status when he snagged the Republican nomination for president. Opposition was fierce. Lyndon B. Johnson branded Goldwater as an extremist. Critics said he would bring the country to the brink of a nuclear war. Black voters turned

into law in 1944. McFarland eventually served in the state's three highest offices: U.S. senator, governor, and chief justice of the Arizona Supreme Court.

THE NEW LAND RUSH

In its early days, downtown Phoenix served as the city's commercial and residential district, surrounded by thousands of square miles of farmland and undeveloped desert. Its churches, theaters, and department stores attracted distant farmers and ranchers who would "go into town" for supplies and entertainment, all of which lent itself to a lively downtown familiar to most American cities. The postwar building boom changed all of that. Servicemen, who were captivated by Arizona's climate and

landscape while stationed at one of the state's many military training facilities, returned to Phoenix after the war with their Midwestern families and 1950s expectations of a three-bedroom home and a green lawn. The Valley of the Sun's burgeoning housing industry was happy to oblige, and developers conjured cookie-cutter track housing and large master-planned communities with amenities like parks and golf courses that appealed to young families as well as retirees.

As air-conditioning became widely available and early technology-manufacturing companies also moved to the city in search of cheap land, the population grew past 100,000 by 1950 and neared an almost-unimaginable 440,000 by 1960. Former agricultural land on Goldwater after he voted against the Civil Rights Act of 1964. The damage was done. Goldwater won his home state of Arizona, but only five others in the South, and the election ended in a landslide in Johnson's favor. After the drubbing, pundits said the Republican Party was doomed, fractured, and conservatism all but dead. Goldwater left office for four years after the election and remained largely out of the spotlight after his return to Washington.

THE UGLY

Barry Goldwater reemerged, however, during the Watergate crisis. As the call for Richard Nixon's resignation grew louder, Goldwater applied the pressure that presumably helped tip the scale. The senator visited Nixon at the White House and told the president that Congress could do nothing to stop his impeachment. Goldwater broke the news that few Senate Republicans still backed the president. He later said of the disgraced president, "Nixon was the most dishonest individual I have ever met in my life. He lied to his wife, his family, his friends, his colleagues in the Congress, lifetime members of his own political party, the American people, and the world."

THE LEGACY

Goldwater left the Senate for the final time in 1986. Twelve years later, at the age of 89, he died at his Paradise Valley home, in the early stages of Alzheimer's disease. Goldwater will be remembered for his individualism — as the one of the few politicians who was unafraid to speak his mind, even if it meant criticizing the power structure of his own party. Historians say that Goldwater's credo paved the way for Ronald Reagan's ascent to the White House in 1980. It's believed that a speech Reagan delivered on behalf of Goldwater during the 1964 campaign helped spark the future president's political career and ultimately allowed the next generation of conservatism to thrive. Today, numerous think tanks bear the senator's name, including the Goldwater Institute in Phoenix. These groups recall Goldwater's staunch belief in the Constitution and his principles of limited government as they shape public policy more than 50 years after Goldwater's rise.

(Contributed by Peter O'Dowd, reporter/host, KJZZ)

was quickly consumed by thousands of ranch houses, forcing new home-buyers further and further out into the suburbs. All of this sprawl and, some would argue, poorly managed growth has created a few unexpected consequences. A brown smog cloud often chokes the Valley's famed blue skies in the winter, and the dry desert air that once attracted health-seekers suffering from asthma and tuberculosis is now burdened in the spring with pollen from nonindigenous plants brought in from other parts of the country. Formerly independent towns and suburbs now blend from one into another, with regional malls and business districts that have sapped away much of downtown Phoenix's urban appeal.

Things are changing, though. Some 1.5 million people live in Phoenix, making it the country's fifth-largest city, and the U.S. Census Bureau estimates an additional 3 million residents in the surrounding communities. Many of these folks are driven by the same optimism and pioneering spirit that attracted the waves of settlers who preceded them, pushing these new Arizonans to dream up solutions to 21st century problems. Phoenix, Scottsdale, and Sedona now seemed determined to harness their growth responsibly, forcing developers to be mindful of the desert landscape and developing green-minded enterprises like solar-powered energy. Downtown Phoenix is once again a center of activity, thanks to $3 billion worth of new projects, including condo and hotel towers, restaurants, stadiums, museums, and a 20-mile light-rail system that many hope will curb the city's love affair with the automobile. And it's anyone's guess what seemingly impossible feats the residents of this dynamic city will tackle next—a looming water crisis likely tops the list. Nevertheless, Arizona's landscape has sparked hope, art, and opportunity for generations. Now its citizens are working to ensure it inspires generations more.

Government and Economy

GOVERNMENT

In its relatively short history, Arizona has experienced no shortage of political milestones, defining moments, or shameful antics. For instance, more than 80 years before Bush vs. Gore, the state faced its own contentious court battle for chief executive. A gubernatorial battle broke out in 1916 when Arizona's first governor, George W.P. Hunt, demanded a recount when his challenger, Thomas Campbell, was declared the winner by 30 votes. Hunt refused to vacate the governor's chair, and both men took the oath of office. The Arizona Supreme Court eventually settled the case, declaring Hunt the winner. However, both men would go on to serve multiple—and individual—terms as governor.

By the 1960s, Arizona's political titans were working hard to transform the Grand Canyon State into a national player. Morris "Mo" Udall took office in 1961 after winning the U.S. House seat vacated by his brother, Stewart, who had been appointed Secretary of the Interior by President John F. Kennedy. The Udall brothers, Representative John Rhodes, Senators Barry Goldwater and Carl Hayden, and Governor Paul Fannin formed a bipartisan group of political giants who reached across party lines and used their collective power to turn the state from a never-has-been into a united political power.

That's not to say there hasn't been scandal. When former car dealer Evan Mecham was

Arizona State Capitol in Phoenix

© MICA THOMAS MULLOY

ARIZONA'S POLITICAL TITANS

ARIZONANS WHO MADE (UNSUCCESSFUL) BIDS FOR PRESIDENT

- Barry Goldwater, Republican: 1964
- Morris "Mo" Udall, Democrat: 1976
- Bruce Babbitt, Democrat: 1988
- John McCain, Republican: 2000 and 2008

CABINET MEMBERS

- Morris "Mo" Udall, Democrat: Secretary of the Interior, Kennedy Administration
- Bruce Babbitt, Democrat: Secretary of the Interior, Clinton Administration
- Janet Napolitano, Democrat: Secretary of Homeland Security, Obama Administration

SUPREME COURT JUSTICES

- William Rehnquist
- Sandra Day O'Connor

women have enjoyed a great deal of independence and opportunity in Arizona. They were granted the right to vote in the year of Arizona's statehood in 1912, eight years before the Nineteenth Amendment. In 1981, President Ronald Reagan made history—and fulfilled a campaign promise—when he appointed the first female Supreme Court justice, Arizonan Sandra Day O'Connor. Following her groundbreaking confirmation, O'Connor emerged as one of the most influential voices on the Court, serving as a swing vote in many of its most controversial and closely watched cases, from abortion to affirmative action. Nearly two decades later, in 1998, Arizona made national headlines again when voters elected the country's first all-female line of succession: governor, secretary of state, attorney general, treasurer, and superintendent of public instruction. The media dubbed the unprecedented lineup the "Fabulous Five," which included then-Attorney General Janet Napolitano, who would later serve as governor and U.S. Secretary of Homeland Security.

Another important constituency is beginning to emerge. The release of the 2000 U.S. census heralded a demographic shift and potentially strong new political voice in Arizona. Latinos accounted for 25 percent of Arizona's population that year, and that number is increasing 88 percent a year. Latino voters will likely flex ever-more-considerable political influence in the coming decades, which is why they are being courted by both Republicans and Democrats. This swing group could prove to be a deciding voice as the once staunchly red, conservative Arizona begins to turn purple.

ECONOMY

The "Five C's"—copper, cotton, cattle, citrus, and climate—fueled Arizona's early economy, signifying the state's early reliance on agriculture and mining as its main economic engine. The Valley of the Sun became an important farming center, thanks to the canals originally built by the Hohokam and resurrected by Jack Swilling—so much so that, at one time, the state was the country's largest producer of

removed from office in 1988, it extinguished a political firestorm that ignited almost as soon as he was sworn in a year earlier. During his brief-but-infamous tenure, Mecham rescinded the Martin Luther King Jr. holiday, defended the use of the word "pickaninny," blamed working women for increasing divorce rates, and managed to insult minority groups from Asians to gays. With Mecham's impeachment came one bright spot, though: Arizona swore in its first female governor—and only the 10th in U.S. history—Rose Mofford. Strangely, it wasn't her first time in the chair. During the early days of Governor Bruce Babbitt's 1988 presidential bid, Mofford served as acting governor while he campaigned out of state.

In fact, true to the state's Wild West roots,

© MICA THOMAS MULLOY

Phoenix City Hall

during World War I to earn the title "Hay Capital of the World." Today, Arizona can still call itself the "Copper State," with its mammoth open-pit and underground mines producing about two-thirds of nation's total yield of the peachy-gold metal.

Thanks to more than 325 days of sunshine a year, it's possible to grow oranges and grapefruit, but the endless sunny days also mean dining alfresco, lying by the pool, and playing golf year-round—in short, tourism, which accounts for $18.5 billion annually. The sun may even be the basis of a new sustainable solar economy as the country searches for energy independence—a particularly critical need for this region, which is dependent on air-conditioning during the triple-digit summer months. High-tech innovation in the desert isn't new, though. After World War II, early technology manufacturing companies set up shop in Phoenix, including Motorola, which opened a research and development laboratory in 1948. Other computer-chip manufacturers and engineering firms followed, and within the past decade, Arizona political and business leaders have enticed medical research and biotechnology firms, like T-Gen, to take the state's economy—and its health care—to new heights.

cotton. Even the small farming community of Gilbert—now a Phoenix suburb of 100,000 people—produced enough alfalfa in its fields

People and Culture

Phoenix is a city of immigrants, and that, perhaps more than any other factor, save the unrelenting sun, has shaped the city's character. Sydney has its convicts, and Boston its Puritans. Phoenix, though, was founded by a different breed: the pioneer. These trailblazing optimists left their homelands for the Wild West, an open frontier where opportunity and the promise of a better life outweighed the difficulties of a harsh terrain. And these expatriates continue to arrive, thousands every year. Frozen transplants from the East Coast and Midwest mix with Mexican nationals who cross an unforgiving desert on foot for a chance at the American Dream. They're all driven by a thirst for more and an independent spirit that's

best embodied by the state's original icon, the cowboy, a figure that has come to represent not only Arizona, but also the Western attitude of "live and let live."

So many people have pulled up stakes and moved to the Valley of the Sun that residents like to joke that a native Phoenician is hard to find. Some newbies are initially tempted by the warm climate, moving to Phoenix to attend school at Arizona State University or to spend their years on the golf course. Even visitors popping in to see their college kids or retired parents can be easily seduced to make a move, not to mention the millions of tourists who travel to the state every year.

More than half of Arizona's 6.5 million

ARIZONA STATE FACTS

- **State Nickname:** The Grand Canyon State
- **Statehood:** February 14, 1912
- **Capital:** Phoenix
- **Area:** 113,998 miles
- **State Flower:** Saguaro cactus flower
- **State Bird:** Cactus wren
- **State Tree:** Palo verde
- **State Fossil:** Petrified wood
- **State Gemstone:** Turquoise
- **State Amphibian:** Arizona tree frog
- **State Reptile:** Arizona ridge-nosed rattlesnake
- **State Neckwear:** Bolo tie
- **Famous Arizonans:** Labor leader César Chávez, Apache chief Geronimo, novelist Zane Grey, singer Stevie Nicks, and architect Frank Lloyd Wright

example of a bolo tie, the official state neckwear of Arizona

© NORA JANG

residents live in the Greater Phoenix Metropolitan Area, and according a Brookings Institution study, only about half are white, reflecting the city's changing demographics. Latinos make up most of the other half of the population. And though the city still attracts retirees, only 11 percent of the population is over age 65. Younger people are moving to valley, and some 35 percent of adults are single, which may help explain Scottsdale's vibrant nightlife scene.

Several Native American communities govern tribal land around Phoenix and Sedona. These sovereign tribes act in many ways like independent nations, with the right to form their own governments, try legal cases within their borders, and levy taxes. Although these communities still cling to their agricultural roots, many now own and operate successful casinos, which have expanded in recent years to include resorts, restaurants, golf courses, amusement parks, and museums. Among them,

the Gila River Indian Community spans 584 square miles south of Phoenix, from the Sierra Estrella in the West Valley to the communities of Florence and Coolidge in the east. The 11,000 members are from the Pima (Akimel O'odham) and the Maricopa (Pee-Posh) tribes. Its most famous son, Ira Hayes, was one of the five Marines depicted in the iconic 1945 photograph "Raising the Flag on Iwo Jima."

The Pima and the Maricopa also make their home on the Salt River Pima–Maricopa Indian Community just east of Scottsdale. Some 8,700 individuals are enrolled as tribal members, living on 52,000 acres surrounded by Scottsdale, Tempe, Mesa, and Fountain Hills. The adjacent Fort McDowell Yavapai Nation is bordered by McDowell Mountain Park and the Tonto National Forest. Its 950 members are one of three Yavapai tribes in Arizona. Just north, in the Verde Valley near Sedona, the Yavapai have also aligned with the Tonto Apache at the Yavapai-Apache Nation, where

© SCOTTSDALE CONVENTION & VISITORS BUREAU

Perry Thompson dances at Scottsdale's *Native Trails*, a celebration of Native American dances and music.

many of its 750 members live on four noncontiguous parcels of land.

RELIGION

Arizona has a rich religious tradition, beginning with the spiritual practices of Native Americans who first worshipped in the region thousands of years ago. European missionaries introduced Catholicism to the Southwest in the 16th century, with Franciscan and Jesuit priests traveling throughout the Sonoran Desert to convert many of its indigenous people. Today, about 25 percent of Arizonans identify themselves as Catholic, according to the Pew Center, due in large part to the sizable Latino population. There are still cultural reminders in Arizona of the Southwest's unique style of Catholicism, which incorporates indigenous customs, such as Día de los Muertos, or Day of the Dead. Some Latino families celebrate the holiday October 31 through November 2 by visiting the graves of their ancestors or building small altars decorated with sugar skulls, artwork, flowers, and favorite foods. At Christmastime,

luminarias, small votive candles in paper bags, are lit to celebrate the holiday season.

As for the rest of Arizona, more than a third of the state is Protestant. About 4 percent of the population is Mormon, or members of the Church of Jesus Christ of Latter-day Saints. Mormon pioneers settled the East Valley town of Mesa in 1878, and the Valley of the Sun has the nation's largest concentration of Mormons outside of Utah. Also, there are small Jewish, Muslim, Buddhist, and Hindu populations throughout the state. New Age followers have flocked to Sedona in recent years, as well, citing the area's "spiritual energy" and Native American traditions.

LANGUAGE

Language can be a hot topic in the Arizona desert, fueled largely by the controversial immigration debate that flares up on a regular basis in this border state. Nearly 75 percent of Arizonans speak only English at home, and the Modern Language Association estimates more than 20 percent speak Spanish. In

Saint Mary's Basilica, founded in 1881, is the oldest Catholic parish in the Valley of the Sun.

addition to the occasional voter initiative to make English the state's official language, politicians have made efforts to revamp the public school system's English as a Second Language (ESL) program, which often faces opposition and produces mixed results. A recent Supreme Court case even debated if the state was spending enough to aid children who are learning to speak English, though it was kicked back down to a lower court. Travelers will hear Spanish spoken throughout the state, particularly in Phoenix, where Spanish-language media, even billboards, are fairly commonplace. Native American languages may be heard on Indian lands, though almost all Native Americans in urban areas speak English.

THE ARTS

Arizona has been called lot of things—the Wild West, retirement haven, desert oasis, sweltering inferno—but "cultural hotbed" is not one of them. Oh, how wrong reputations can be. Even among the air-conditioned locals who frequent malls and big-box stores chains,

the state's rich artistic tradition seems hidden, if not forgotten. The truth is, Arizona's rich cultural tradition reaches back thousands of years, beginning with the state's original inhabitants, Native Americans. Some of the 20th century's greatest artists produced work here, from Ansel Adams and Max Ernst to Frank Lloyd Wright, having been inspired by the dramatic Sonoran Desert landscape.

Arts and Crafts

Arizona's arts and crafts trace their origins back to the earliest Native American residents, who decorated rocks and everyday objects with graceful patterns and anthropomorphic images. Today, artisans continue the tradition, creating work that is firmly rooted in their tribal customs. That wasn't always the case, though. Following the postwar tourism boom, some Native American artisans began producing work that sightseers wanted Indian art to look like, such as spearheads, teepees, and mass-produced baskets. Fortunately, many artists have abandoned this practice and are once again creating artwork in styles unique to their individual tribes. Some contemporary artists are even moving beyond traditional imagery, which they dismiss as kitsch, and are pushing the definitions of Native American art by imagining innovative, contemporary pieces.

Buyers shopping for authentic Native American arts and crafts should keep a few things in mind. First, when possible, buy directly from the designer. There are markets and festivals throughout the year that feature Native American artists, such as the Heard Museum's annual Indian Fair and Market. Also, ask about the materials and how pieces were made, and be sure to get a certificate of authenticity. Quintessential arts and crafts include hand-woven baskets, turquoise jewelry, pottery, Navajo rugs and sand paintings, and Hopi kachina dolls, which have become more elaborate in recent years due to their popularity.

Architecture and Design

Arizona, and Phoenix in particular, suffered for years from a dearth of quality, geographically relevant architecture. Beginning with the Victorian buildings constructed in the original 1870s Phoenix townsite, architects have tried to impose misappropriated styles onto the Sonoran Desert. It took one of the greats, Frank Lloyd Wright, to break them of the habit—or at least introduce them to relevant ways of designing for the desert. Wright took his cues from the architecture of ancient Native Americans, building with materials from the desert and designing buildings around the sun's orientation.

Phoenix grew big, quickly, and developers responded to demand by building large, faceless ranch houses in many of parts of the Valley. By the 1990s, though, architects—inspired by Wright and a group of midcentury Modernist designers like Al Beadle and Bennie Gonzales—pioneered a new style, Desert Modernism, which respected Phoenix's harsh summer climate. These minimalist buildings blend indoor/outdoor spaces, use innovative materials, and embrace the desert's hallmark light and space. The best-known example, the Will Bruder-designed Burton Barr Central Library, features a rectangular, rusted-steel facade that resembles a red-hued mesa. On the equinox, the sun shines directly through overhead skylights in the fifth-floor reading room, "lighting" its graceful, white columns.

Interior designers are also employing many of Wright's design techniques, banishing the howling coyotes, flute-playing Kokopelli icons, and pastel colors that had come to define "Southwestern" design in the 1980s. Instead, many of Valley's best designers are now employing a more subtle style that incorporates light as a central element. Large glass windows, natural stone and wood elements, and polished concrete floors that remain cool in the summer are turning posh restaurants and resorts into showplaces for chic desert style.

Literature

The myth of the West has proven to be a fertile source of literary inspiration. For generations, stories were often related orally, heightening their romance and intimacy. Native Americans would pass their histories and folklore from one generation to the next, while cowboys shared stories over campfires or whiskies. Novelist Zane Grey may not have been the first to put these tales to paper, but he was certainly one of the most prolific, having produced 60 books, from which 110 films were made. Many of them were set in Arizona, and later filmed in Sedona, like *Call of the Canyon*. Grey's popular stories portrayed an idealized version of the Old West, with big heroes and bigger landscapes.

Author and environmental essayist Edward Abbey, the "Thoreau of the American West," extolled the virtues of the Southwest and the occasionally radical means one might take to protect it in his works, *The Monkey Wrench Gang* and *Desert Solitaire*. These days, a new breed of Arizona writer is building on Grey's frontier legacy, with equally adventurous stories, albeit not in very different settings; examples include adventure writer Clive Cussler and Stephenie Meyer, author of the *Twilight* vampire series.

ESSENTIALS

Getting There and Around

BY AIR

Most visitors to the Valley of the Sun arriving by air land at **Phoenix Sky Harbor International Airport** (3400 E. Sky Harbor Blvd., 602/273-3300, www.phxskyharbor.com). It's the country's ninth busiest airport in terms of traffic, with some 100,000 passengers arriving and departing every day. Tempe-based **US Airways** (800/428-4322, www.usairways.com) and **Southwest Airlines** (800/435-9792, www.southwest.com) account for more than half of Sky Harbor's traffic, though 18 other carriers provide service, including international airlines like **British Airways** (800/247-9297, www.britishairways.com), **Aeromexico** (800/237-6639, www.aeromexico.com), and **Air Canada** (888/247-2262, www.aircanada.com). Free shuttles connect Terminals 2, 3, and 4 (Terminal 1 was demolished in 1990), and visitors can also catch buses to the rental-car center and the light rail stop at 44th Street. Sky Harbor sits smack-dab in the middle of the Valley, just three miles east of downtown Phoenix and 20 minutes from Old Town Scottsdale. Two entrances link the airport to the city: one on the west side that connects to I-10 and 24th Street, and another on the east side that joins Highways 143 and 153 (44th Street) and Highway 202 (Loop 202).

Travelers arriving by private jet can use

© MICA THOMAS MULLOY

Scottsdale Airport (15000 N. Airport Dr., 480/312-2321, www.scottsdaleaz.gov/airport), a handy, headache-free option. This north Scottsdale airpark, a frequent choice of celebrities, is one of the busiest single-runway airports in the country. **Phoenix-Mesa Gateway Airport** (6033 S. Sossaman Rd., 480/988-7600, www.phxmesagateway.org) in east Mesa serves as a small hub for regional carrier **Allegiant Air** (702/505-8888, www.allegiantair.com), with service to northern parts of the country. As the Valley continues to grow, the airport will likely relieve growing congestion at Sky Harbor.

BY CAR AND BUS

The car, in some ways, continues the grand tradition of exploring the West on horseback or by stagecoach, as it gives travelers the solitary experience of seeing the wide open spaces that stretch between Arizona's towns and cities. That's the romantic take, at least. In truth, most visitors to Phoenix and Scottsdale will need a car, especially those planning to make the trip to Sedona. The Valley of the Sun is expansive, and unlike densely populated centers in New York and San Francisco, there is too much space and too little public transportation to see it all in an efficient manner. Embrace the spirit of the Great American Road Trip, and be prepared to spend some time behind the wheel when plotting trips to Jerome, Oak Creek Canyon, and Montezuma Castle.

Phoenix and Scottsdale were built with the car in mind. The streets follow an efficient and easy-to-navigate grid pattern, which is interconnected

by a large web of highways. The I-10 snakes from the southern part of the city, through downtown Phoenix, before heading to the West Valley. Highway 60, also called the Superstition Freeway, provides an important artery to the East Valley, which is encircled by the new Highway 202 (Loop 202). Its counterpart, Highway 101 (Loop 101), wends from Chandler to Tempe and Scottsdale, where it turns west and travels to the West Valley communities of Peoria and Sun City, before veering south through Glendale and connecting to the I-10. Finally, "the 51" freeway connects Central Phoenix to the northern part of the city and Highway 101 (Loop 101).

This book covers only a small portion of the Grand Canyon State, and there is plenty to see within few hours' drive of Phoenix. Further afield, the I-10 connects Phoenix to Tucson in the south and Palm Springs and Los Angeles in the west. The scenic I-17 crosses Phoenix into the high deserts and grasslands of Camp Verde and Flagstaff, where you can catch other highways to the Grand Canyon and Las Vegas or to the other Four Corners states of New Mexico, Colorado, and Utah.

Greyhound (2115 E. Buckeye Rd., 602/389-4200, www.greyhound.com) provides bus service to major cities throughout the state and Southwest, though you will not find terminals in Scottsdale or Sedona. To reach Red Rock Country without a car, you can catch a van service from Phoenix's Sky Harbor airport. **Sedona Phoenix Shuttle** (800/448-7988, www.sedona-phoenix-shuttle.com) offers a direct link to the Village of Oak Creek and West Sedona.

Tips for Travelers

ECOTOURISM

It's only natural that tourists be mindful of the environment when visiting Arizona, as the state's main attraction is its rugged, yet surprisingly delicate, landscape. Increasingly, ecotourists—travelers who are drawn to a natural locale and try to minimize their environmental impact—are choosing to explore the Sonoran

Desert. To capitalize on this movement and ensure that future generations are able to appreciate the desert, Arizona's tourism community has started to make green-minded changes to how they operate. In Sedona, the **Institute of Ecotourism** (91 Portal Lane, 928/282-2720, www.ioet.org) serves as a think tank for environmentally sensitive travel and tourism. Its

ETHICAL TRAVEL

Travel is perhaps the most valuable means by which we learn about the world and our place in it. But as we explore red-rock buttes and marvel at ancient ruins, our consideration of the impact we make on the cultures and landscapes we encounter becomes increasingly important. Observe a responsible and sustainable approach to travel by following these guidelines:

- **Plan ahead and prepare:** Arriving with a sense of the social, political, and environmental issues in your destination makes your travels more meaningful. Educate yourself about the region's geography, customs, and cultures, and remember to respect local traditions.

- **Minimize your environmental impact:** Always follow designated trails. Do not disturb animals, plants, or their natural habitats. Learn about and support local conservation programs and organizations working to preserve the environment.

- **Leave what you find:** Take only photographs. Leave only footprints. The impact of one person may seem minimal, but the global effect of removing items from their native place can be decimating.

museum showcases the indigenous plants and animals that inhabit the Sonoran Desert, and its interactive exhibitions highlight just how fragile Arizona's ecosystem can be.

The Scottsdale Convention and Visitors Bureau has introduced an online resource, as well. **Scottsdale Green By Design** (www.scottsdalegreenbydesign.com) outlines environmentally conscious travel ideas and resources, including cultural attractions and outdoor activities. The site also provides a list of individual hotels, resorts, and restaurants that are incorporating sustainable tourism practices, from water conservation and recycling programs to organic menus and spa treatments. Even Scottsdale's impossibly thirsty golf courses are turning… well, green, by using nonpotable water for

irrigation. Some are also replacing traditional turf with more drought-tolerant grasses.

FOREIGN TRAVELERS

International travelers should expect a warm welcome to Arizona, though you will encounter some long lines and a little paperwork at immigration when entering the country. Citizens from most North American, European, and Latin American countries do not need a visa for stays up to 90 days. However, all international visitors, including Canadians, are required to show a valid passport. For more information about visas and requirements to enter the United States through the Visa Waiver Program, visit the U.S. State Department's website at www.travel.state.gov.

Travelers exchanging foreign currency can do so at small kiosks inside the airport or at most banks. ATMs (automated teller machines) offer the best exchange rates, charging a $2 fee for the convenience. Be sure to inquire with your home bank to see if they charge an exchange fee, which usually ranges 1–2 percent. You'll find ATMs at a host of locations, including banks, shopping centers, and gas stations. Also, almost all hotels, restaurants, and stores accept travelers checks from well-known institutions like American Express and Visa.

TRAVELERS WITH DISABILITIES

In the Valley of the Sun and Sedona, hotels, restaurants, attractions, and public transportation are easy to access thanks in large part to the Americans with Disabilities Act. However, the Sonoran Desert's rugged terrain can be difficult to navigate. That said, some state and city parks are building ADA-accessible trails, like the new **Gateway Access Area at the McDowell Sonoran Preserve** (480/998-7971, www.mcdowellsonoran.org) in Scottsdale. Up north, Sedona's Jeep tours offer an excellent opportunity to explore Red Rock Country's monolithic buttes up close. The off-the-highway trails can get quite bumpy, so those with disabilities may want to request a front seat, which offers a bit of neck and back support. Also, the National

WHAT TO TAKE

A resort mentality and a Wild West attitude pervade much of Arizona, and overall, visitors will find Phoenix and Sedona to be pretty casual. Jeans are acceptable in most places, and in the summer shorts and flip-flops become de rigueur. That said, Scottsdale's nicer restaurants, bars, and clubs require that you "dress to impress," which almost never means a suit or tie. Also, visitors planning to take advantage of Arizona's myriad outdoor activities should come prepared: sneakers and hiking boots, swimsuits, and golf shoes and clubs.

The desert's arid climate can create a bit of confusion, as temperatures can swing as much as 20 to 30 degrees from an early-morning low to a late-afternoon high. Fall through early spring, be sure to bring along a sweater or jacket if you plan on staying out when the sun goes down. And it can be downright cold in the winter, with overnight temperatures sometimes falling below freezing.

Oh, don't forget the sunscreen. Or at least stock up when you get to Phoenix. The Sonoran Desert's powerful sun shouldn't be underestimated, particularly in the summer, when in late afternoons, the sun's rays are most intense and can cause fair skin to burn in less than 10 minutes. Be sure to wear a sunblock with a high SPF by the pool or on the golf course.

Parks Service offers free admission to visitors with permanent disabilities. The lifetime **America the Beautiful–National Parks and Federal Recreational Lands Pass–Access Pass** (www.nps.gov) includes Arizona sights like Montezuma Castle. The passes are available at all national parks, and documentation is required. For more information, visit www.disabledtravelers.com, an Arizona-based website that offers advice, tips, and recommendations for guided tours—and not just in Arizona.

TRAVELING WITH CHILDREN

With summer comes the all-important family vacation, and travelers with children shouldn't let the heat detour them from planning a trip to Arizona. In fact, most kids will revel in the season's prime attraction: the swimming pool. Families can easily spend days by the pool or at the Valley's three major water parks, which offer mammoth wave pools, multistoried slides, and lazy rivers for tubing. Also, most of the big resorts have built their own water parks, and the hotels offer adults a bit of respite thanks to well-organized kids' camps, which pack days full with morning hikes, arts and crafts, trips to the pool, and games in air-conditioned clubhouses. The whole family can enjoy one of the rafting trips on the Salt River northeast of Phoenix. These outdoor adventures are nothing more than a leisurely float, as the "rapids" never exceed a Class I (almost no white water). There are also kid-approved museums like the interactive Arizona Science Center and the Children's Museum of Phoenix.

In the cooler months, the state's parks and easy hiking trails can be fun to explore, especially on horseback. The Phoenix Zoo delights kids with 1,300 birds, slithering reptiles, and furry mammals, as well as a small petting area and the walk-through Monkey Village. For a taste of the Wild West, Rawhide Western Town delivers 1880s-themed family fun, with stunt shows, stagecoach rides, and old-fashioned chuck-wagon cookouts under the stars. And if you plan to head north, Sedona may not wow the little ones, but older kids and teenagers will appreciate the bouncy Jeep tours and dozens of mountain-biking trails.

SENIOR TRAVELERS

Arizona's blissfully warm weather makes the state a popular destination for seniors, particularly active travelers who hit tennis courts, swimming pools, and the more than 200 golf courses. In the summer, many avoid the extreme heat at the half dozen casinos scattered around the Valley on Native American lands. Most Phoenix, Scottsdale, and Sedona attractions offer discounts for seniors, including the Desert Botanical Garden, which is an excellent opportunity to survey the Sonoran Desert's diverse plant life without having to leave paved sidewalks. Also, travelers 62 and older can obtain the **America the Beautiful–National Parks and Federal Recreational Lands Pass–Senior Pass,** a lifetime pass to all national parks. It can be purchased for $10 at any national park (www.nps.gov).

GAY AND LESBIAN TRAVELERS

Like most major metropolitan areas, the Valley has an active gay community that is centered around Central Phoenix, where travelers will find many of the city's gay-friendly restaurants and bars, including those on Central and 7th Avenues, between Indian School and Camelback Roads. The **Greater Phoenix Gay & Lesbian Chamber of Commerce** (602/266-5055, www. gpglcc.org) is a convenient resource for travelers, producing an online business directory that lists hotels and restaurants, as well as a thorough relocation guide for new transplants. *Echo Magazine* (www.echomag.com) and *'N Touch News Magazine* (www.ntouchaz.com) provide news and information on upcoming events.

Health and Safety

SUN AND HEAT

Phoenix is the Valley of the Sun, and for good reason. With more than 300 days of sunshine a year, the warm rays of light can be hard to avoid—not that winter visitors trying to escape frozen climates find that a problem. Still, the Sonoran Desert's powerful sun shouldn't be underestimated, particularly in the summer, when in late afternoon the sun's UV rays are most intense, causing fair skin to burn in less than 10 minutes. Excessive exposure can cause real, and potentially fatal, health problems. Fortunately, it's all quite avoidable.

Shield yourself from the sun by covering up. Try to wear protective clothing, like long-sleeved shirts and pants. The sun easily damages sensitive skin on your face and neck, so be sure to bring a broad-rimmed hat and sunglasses when you are planning to spend extensive time outside, like on the golf course or while hiking. Poolside, long sleeves and pants may seem unreasonable, which makes a sunscreen with a high SPF a crucial ingredient. Be sure to slather on a thick coat 15 minutes before going out and reapply throughout the day. Also, seek shade when possible and get out of the sun occasionally. It's best to avoid the sun during the hottest part of the day, from 11 A.M. to 3 P.M., when the UV rays are at their peak.

Although everyone is at risk of getting a sunburn, no matter the skin tone, fair-skinned people and children are particularly susceptible. In fact, those with light skin, blue or green eyes, blond or red hair, freckles, or moles are at a greater risk of skin cancer. Should a burn occur, though, cool the skin by applying ice or taking a cold shower or bath. Apply an alcohol-free aloe vera gel and stay out of the sun.

The desert's hot, arid climate can take its toll on the body in other ways. You may not even feel particularly "sweaty" in Arizona, especially compared to more humid climates, but perspiration evaporates quickly in the dry air, depleting the body of moisture and leading to **dehydration.** Drink lots of water, about a gallon a day in the summer or when outside for long periods of time. Many Phoenicians carry a bottle of water with them and instinctively drink throughout the day. On the golf course, you'll see lots of drinking fountains and giant water coolers—take advantage of them. Again, try to limit exertion during the hottest parts of the day.

Should you find yourself dizzy, weak, or nauseated, it may be **heat exhaustion,** which is caused when the body is unable to replace fluids. Other symptoms include sweating profusely, paleness, muscle cramps, headaches, and fainting. Find a cool place immediately, sit down, and drink a beverage with electrolytes, like Gatorade. If the body is unable to cool down, it may suffer from **heatstroke,** a potentially fatal form of hyperthermia. Heat stroke is often marked by the body reaching 104 degrees and an inability to sweat or release heat. The skin may be red or hot to the touch. Also, look for an increased heart rate, dizziness, fatigue, unconsciousness, or convulsions. Get immediate medical help, and try to cool the body down with water, ice, or cold compresses. Staying hydrated and avoiding the extreme heat will stave off these serious ailments.

FLOODS, LIGHTNING, AND DUST STORMS

The Sonoran Desert's weather, like its landscape, can be severe. Blue, sunny skies can quickly turn ominous when a storm rolls across the horizon, with sheets of rain and forked bolts of lightning. During monsoon season, a wall of dust may even move in from the desert and sweep across the city with impressive speed and not a drop of rain despite a perceptible increase in moisture. These powerful storms are impressive displays of the desert's strength, and they can leave motorists, golfers, and swimmers scurrying for cover. Should one of these climatic events occur, don't take any chances. Immediately get out of a swimming pool or any body of water if you see lightning or even hear thunder. You should also abandon any mountain biking or hiking expeditions (heights!) or rounds of golf (metal clubs!).

Even residents fail to use their best judgment and learn from the experiences of others. These quick deluges can dump inches of rain on the dry desert floor, which is unable to absorb that much water so quickly. As a result, usually dry washes become swiftly moving rivers, trapping cars that attempt to cross them. Freeways can become makeshift canals, filling with water and stranding commuters. When pouring rain or dust storms limit visibility, pull over to the side of the road and wait for conditions to improve, as most storms sweep through quickly.

REPTILES AND SCORPIONS

Most travelers don't mind a little sun or rain, but nothing makes a tourist second-guess a trip to Arizona more than the creepy-crawlies that bite (or sting) in the Sonoran Desert. If you stay on trails and use good judgment when hiking, a painful encounter with a snake or insect is unlikely. Keep an eye out for rattlesnakes, though you may be more likely to hear their rattling tails first. They usually don't attack unless provoked, so simply keep a safe distance from the slithering desert dwellers and move along.

Scorpions tend to hide under rocks or in holes, and they typically sting people when they are inadvertently touched. If you're particularly concerned about scorpions, shake out your shoes before putting them on and pay attention to what you grab when exploring the desert. Gila monsters are also venomous, but bites from these slow-moving creatures are rare.

If you're stung or bitten by any poisonous desert dweller, don't panic. Remove constricting jewelry and limit movement of the affected area in order to minimize venom from flowing into the rest of the bloodstream. Seek medical attention immediately.

Information and Services

MAPS AND TOURIST INFORMATION

The **Arizona Office of Tourism** (1110 E. Washington St. Ste. 155, Phoenix, 602/364/3700, www.arizonaguide.com) is happy to help visitors plan a trip to the Grand Canyon State, and its comprehensive guide and website, which includes videos and slide shows, are excellent resources for tailoring a trip to your individual interests. The **Greater Phoenix Convention & Visitors Bureau** (602/254-6500, www.visitphoenix.com) offers loads of information for visitors and new residents about the Valley of the Sun. Its **Downtown Phoenix Visitor Information Center** (125 N. 2nd St. Ste. 120, 8 A.M.–5 P.M. Mon.–Fri.)

LOCAL MEDIA

NEWSPAPER

• *The Arizona Republic*

NATIONAL PUBLIC RADIO

• KJZZ 91.5 FM

TELEVISION

• 3 KTVK (Independent)

• 5 KPHO (CBS)

• 8 KAET (PBS)

• 10 KSAZ (FOX)

• 12 KPNX (NBC)

• 15 KNXV (ABC)

• 45 KUTP (Independent)

• 61 KASW (CW)

is conveniently located across from the main entrance of the Hyatt Regency Phoenix.

Arizona's top attraction is its incredible landscape, and there seems to be a stunning formation or unique geological feature off every highway exit. To chart out the state's national parks and monuments, visit the website for the **National Park Service** (www.nps.gov/state/az). Not to be outdone, the **Arizona State Parks** system (1300 W. Washington St., Phoenix, 602/542-4174, www.azstateparks.com) is among the best in the country. Learn more about the parks' diverse habitats and natural attractions by visiting the website or the office in downtown Phoenix.

AREA CODES AND TIME ZONES

The Grand Canyon State has five area codes, three of which are dedicated to the Phoenix metropolitan area: 602 for Phoenix proper, 623 for the West Valley, and 480 for the East Valley, including Scottsdale. Sedona and the rest of northern Arizona are assigned 928, while Tucson and southern Arizona were given 520.

Free-spirited Arizona is never one to be told what to do by the rest of the country, and that sentiment extends to something as basic as time. Officially, the state is a part of the mountain standard time (MST) zone, along with Utah, Colorado, New Mexico, Wyoming, Idaho, and Montana. Unlike the rest of its western brethren, though, Arizona does not observe daylight saving time, and instead of its clock springing forward in March, it instead syncs up with Pacific daylight time. Why the difference? Well, in the hot desert, the last thing Arizonans need is more daylight. The "extra" hour of darkness at night means residents can take advantage of cooler temperatures earlier in the evening.

There is one exception to the exception: The Navajo reservation, which takes up a sizable portion of the northeastern part of Arizona, does observe daylight saving time, so that all of its land, which stretches into the neighboring Four Corners states, is on the same schedule.

RESOURCES

Glossary

ancho chile (AHN-cho CHILL-ee) a dried poblano chile that has turned a deep black-red color; its smoky-sweet flavor is found in many dishes

asada **(ah-sah-dah)** broiled over hot coals or roasted, such as carne asada

burrito (buhr-REE-toh) a flour tortilla wrapped around any number of ingredients, from beans and cheese to meat, vegetables, and salsa; also called burro

camarón **(cah-mah-ROHN)** shrimp

carne **(CAR-nay)** meat, usually beef

cerveza (ser-VAY-sah) beer, the most popular Mexican brands in Arizona being Corona, Dos Equis, Modelo, Pacifico, and Tecate

ceviche (seh-VEE-chay) citrus-marinated seafood, raw or cooked, and tossed with spices and vegetables, like onions, chilies, and tomatoes

chile relleno (CHILL-ee ray-YAY-no) a mild green chile stuffed with cheese, lightly fried, and topped with a spicy red sauce

chimichanga (chih-mee-CHAHN-gah) a deep-fried burrito filled with meat and typically garnished with lettuce, salsa, sour cream, and guacamole

chipotle (chih-POHT-lay) a hot, smoke-dried jalapeño chile pepper

chorizo (CHOH-ree-zoh) a spicy pork (or sometimes beef) sausage, flavored with chilies and spices

churro (CHOOR-roh) a fried-dough pastry, coated with Mexican cinnamon and sugar

cilantro (SIH-lahn-troh) a fresh, slightly spicy herb used in salsas and as garnish

cotija **(coh-TEE-ha)** an aged, crumbly white Mexican cheese

elote **(eh-LOH-tay)** roasted corn on the cob, often topped with butter, *cotija* cheese, lime juice, and chile pepper

empanada (em-pah-NAH-da) a baked pastry filled with meat, cheese, or fruit

enchiladas (en-chih-LAH-das) corn or flour tortillas, dipped in red sauce and wrapped around shredded beef, chicken, or cheese; they are topped with more red sauce and cheese, and then baked

fajitas (fah-HEE-tas) grilled beef or chicken, served on a sizzling platter with onions and green peppers; warm flour tortillas and fresh tomatoes and lettuce accompany the dish

flauta (FLOU-tah) a flour or corn tortilla stuffed with chicken or beef, then deep-fried

frijoles (free-HO-lays) beans, typically pinto or black; most dishes come with a side of frijoles, the most common being refried beans, which are fried, mashed, and "refried" with lard

guacamole (gwah-kah-MOH-lay) a dip or condiment made of mashed avocado, lime juice, and diced chilies, onions, tomatoes, and cilantro; served with tortilla chips

habanero (hah-bah-NEH-roh) Mexico's hottest pepper, used sparingly; adds a feisty kick to salsas and dishes

helado **(eh-LAH-do)** ice cream

horchata **(or-CHAH-tah)** a sweet, vanilla-and-cinnamon-flavored drink made with ground rice and water or milk

huevo **(WAY-voh)** egg

huevos rancheros (WAY-vose rahn-CHAIR-ohs) eggs, ranch-style – fried or scrambled eggs, topped with a red chile sauce or chunky salsa; served with tortillas and beans

jalapeño (hah-lah-PEH-nyo) a popular, medium-hot chile pepper best known for topping nachos

machaca **(mah-CHA-ca)** shredded beef

margarita (mar-gah-REE-tah) a classic Mexican drink made with fresh lime juice and tequila, and sometimes an orange liqueur like cointreau; served blended or on the rocks, in a salt-rimmed glass

mariscos **(mah-REE-skos)** seafood, usually shellfish

masa (MAH-sah) a traditionally stone-ground corn dough, used in tamales

menudo (meh-NOO-doh) a spicy, chunky soup flavored with chiles, tripe, onion, and spices; routinely served with warm tortillas and fresh avocado and lime

mole (MOH-lay) a rich, dark sauce made with chilies, Mexican chocolate, nuts, fruit, spices, and vegetables

nachos (nah-CHOSE) a popular snack and appetizer featuring corn tortilla chips topped with a selection of ingredients, including melted cheese, meat, onion, olives, lettuce, tomatoes, beans, sour cream, guacamole, and salsa

nopales (noh-PAHL-lays) prickly pear cactus pads that are stripped of their spines and then grilled or boiled; they're added to soups, served like fries, or stuffed into tacos

pico de gallo **(PEE-coh dah GUY-yoh)** a fresh chunky salsa, made from chopped tomato, onion, chiles, and cilantro

poblano (POH-blah-no) a dark-green, fresh chile pepper that is very mild

pollo **(POY-yoh)** chicken

posole (pah-SOHL-lay) a hearty, moderately spicy soup with pork or chicken, hominy, onions, and spices; a delicious red stew sometimes garnished with cabbage, radish, onion, avocado, and lime juice

puerco **(PWEAR-coh)** pork

quesadilla (kay-sah-DEE-yah) a flour tortilla, stuffed with cheese, folded in half, pressed, and warmed; chicken or beef, onions, bell peppers, and chilies are sometimes added to the filling

queso **(KAY-soh)** cheese

salsa (SAHL-sah) literally, "sauce," though salsa usually describes the tomato-based condiment that includes chopped onions, chilies, and cilantro; many restaurants serve green tomatillo and mild red versions with tortilla chips

serrano chile (seh-RAH-no chili-ee) a small green chile from northern Mexico that can be quite hot; used in moderation in a host of dishes and salsas

taco (TAH-koh) a corn or flour tortilla folded and loaded with meat, cheese, lettuce, tomato, and salsa; either soft or hard (fried)

tamale (TAH-mah-lay) masa dough, stuffed with meat or vegetables, wrapped in a corn-husk and steamed

tequila (teh-KEE-lah) distilled liquor made from the agave; the golden or clear alcohol is sipped neat or blended into cocktails like the margarita

tomatillo (toh-mah-TEE-yo) a fruit similar in appearance to a small, green tomato; its bright, acidic flavor adds a pleasant punch to many dishes and salsas

torta **(TORR-tah)** a crusty Mexican sandwich, served hot or cold, and filled with any number of ingredients

tortilla (tor-TEE-yah) a thin, circular flatbread made of either corn or flour, and lightly cooked

tostada (tos-TAH-dah) a flat, fried corn tortilla topped with layer of beans, meat, lettuce, tomato, cheese, and salsa

Suggested Reading

HISTORY

Buscher, Linda, and Dick Buscher. *Historic Photos of Arizona.* Nashville: Turner Publishing Company, 2009. See how early pioneers, soldiers, and frontier families lived in the Wild West. The collection of 200 rare and historical images begins with Arizona's territorial days in 1850s and moves through statehood and the postwar population boom.

Dutton, Allen A. *Arizona: Then & Now.* Englewood, CO: Westcliffe Publishers, 2002. Get a sense of the Arizona's dramatic evolution from the 19th century to the 20th. Historical photographs, stories, and essays document the Grand Canyon State's cities and towns, mining industry, railroads, and ranching and farming traditions.

Johnson, James W. *Arizona Politicians: The Noble and the Notorious.* Tucson: University of Arizona Press, 2002. A former University of Arizona journalism professor sketches colorful portraits of the politicians who shaped the state and the country, including Barry Goldwater, Mo and Stewart Udall, Bruce Babbitt, John McCain, William Rehnquist, Sandra Day O'Connor, and disgraced former governors Evan Mecham and Fife Symington.

Lauer, Charles D. *Arrows, Bullets, and Saddle Sores: A Collection of True Tales of Arizona's Old West.* Phoenix: Golden West Publishers, 2005. The Wild West was built on a rich tradition of storytelling, from Native American myths to cowboy yarns. Learn about the events from the real West, including street-clearing gunfights, outlaw gangs, fatal poker games, stolen gold, and dirt-floored prisons.

Martin, Douglas D. *An Arizona Chronology: The Territorial Years, 1846–1912.* Tucson: University of Arizona Press, 1962. They didn't call it the Wild West for nothing. Learn how Arizona evolved from Mexican territory to America's 48th state.

Trimble, Marshall. *Roadside History of Arizona.* Missoula, MT: Mountain Press Publishing Company, 2004. Arizona's state historian takes a road-trip approach to exploring the Grand Canyon State's past. Because it's organized geographically and along highways, travelers can easily cruise to cultural sites, like old missions and Civil War battlefields.

NATIVE AMERICANS

Betancourt, Marian, Michael O'Dowd, and Jack Strong. *The New Native American Cuisine: Five-Star Recipes from the Chefs of Arizona's Kai Restaurant.* Dallas: Three Forks Press, 2009. Only a handful of restaurants in the U.S. have earned AAA's Five Diamond rating and Mobil's Five Star designation, but it's little surprise given the innovative and elegant cuisine at Kai Restaurant at the Sheraton Wild Horse Pass Resort. Try out some of the Native American-inspired recipes at home, including those for cocktails, soups, salads, deserts, and entrées, like grilled elk chop with truffles and sweet corn panna cotta with venison carpaccio.

Circle of Light Navajo Education Project. *Our Fathers, Our Grandfathers, Our Heroes... The Navajo Code Talkers of World War II: A Photographic Exhibit.* Gallup, NM: Circle of Light Navajo Education Project, 2004. This rich collection of photographs chronicles the incredible story of the Navajo Code Talkers, who transmitted U.S. Marine Corps messages in their native language during World War II. See the letters documenting the program's inception, newspaper clippings, a guide to the Navajo language, and historic photos of recruitment visits to the reservation and scenes from the Pacific Theater battlefields.

Hodge, Carle. *Ruins Along the River: Montezuma Castle, Tuzigoot, and Montezuma*

National Monuments. Tucson: Western National Parks Association, 1986. Explore the rich history and heritage of the Sinagua people and how they were able to build a series of impressive monuments that still stand as a testament to their sophisticated civilization.

LITERATURE AND MEMOIRS

Guerrero, Pedro E. *Pedro E. Guerrero: A Photographer's Journey with Frank Lloyd Wright, Alexander Calder, and Louise Nevelson.* New York: Princeton Architectural Press, 2007. Guerrero, a Mexican-American and Arizona native, documents the lives and work of some of the giants of the 20th century art world. Here, 190 black-and-white photographs—some of them iconic images—tell the stories not only of these artists, but of the midcentury Modernist movement that flourished during the photographer's heyday and Guerrero's incredible, seemingly impossible life.

McCain, John, and Mark Salter. *Worth the Fighting For.* New York: Random House, 2002. Following his release from imprisonment in Vietnam, John McCain returned home to the U.S., where he launched his formidable political career, which has included two-plus decades in Congress and two bids for the presidency. In this autobiography, the Grand Canyon State's senior senator shares profiles of the mavericks who inspired him: Theodore Roosevelt, Ernest Hemingway, Ted Williams, and Marlon Brando.

Notaro, Laurie. *The Idiot Girls' Action-Adventure Club: True Tales from a Magnificent and Clumsy Life.* New York: Viliard, 2002. The hilarious writer chronicles a world of hourly wage jobs, Phoenix's subcultures, high school reunions, and hangovers that leave her surprised she woke up in the first place.

O'Connor, Sandra Day, and H. Alan Day. *Lazy B: Growing up on a Cattle Ranch in the American Southwest.* New York: Random House, 2005. The former Supreme Court justice and her brother recount their lives growing up on an Arizona ranch near the New Mexican border, highlighting how their parents, fellow cowhands, and the environment taught them hard lessons and fundamental values. The warm, engaging memoir demonstrates how the Arizona landscaped forged one of the country's greatest minds.

NATURE

Bearce, Neil R. *Minerals, Fossils, and Fluorescents of Arizona: A Field Guide for Collectors.* Tempe, AZ: Arizona Desert Ice Press, 2006. Arizona's vast mineral wealth is a dream for rockhounds, and this guide to the state's geological treasures provides advice and maps on where to find agates and geodes, amethysts and malachites. For those new to rock hunting, there are photos and a thorough outline of mineral basics, like shape, size, and color, as well as a how-to primer on scavenging.

Johnson, Tom, and Hoyt C. Johnson. *Sedona: The Most Uniquely Beautiful Site on Earth.* Sedona, AZ: Sedona Publishing Company, 1998. A picture's worth a thousand words, and it's the only way to truly comprehend Sedona's incredible beauty on the printed page. Discover the region's red rocks, stunning formations, and craggy canyons, as well as its fall leaves and springtime flowers.

Maxa, Christine. *Arizona's Best Wildflower Hikes: The Desert.* Englewood, CO: Westcliffe Publishers, 2002. The noted travel writer and outdoor enthusiast shares her tips on where to find colorful wildflowers, from mountainside hideaways to the vast, open spaces carpeted with orange, yellow, pink, and violet blossoms.

Tessmer, Martin. *50 Hikes in Arizona.* Woodstock, VT: The Countryman Press, 2004. There's no shortage of great hikes in Arizona, and this illustrated guide highlights the state's diverse landscapes and best trails, including treks through the Grand Canyon and around the Valley of the Sun.

PHOENIX

Ellin, Nan. *Phoenix: 21st Century City*. London: Booth-Clibborn Editions, 2006. The richly photographed book chronicles Phoenix's evolution into a cosmopolitan metropolis, replete with cutting-edge architecture, a burgeoning fashion scene, modern design, and vibrant public art. Local writers, photographers, and designers create a rich tapestry that documents the city's cultural evolution.

Gober, Patricia. *Metropolitan Phoenix: Place Making and Community Building in the Desert*. Philadelphia: University of Pennsylvania Press, 2006. Phoenix, like its sister desert megalopolises in Las Vegas and Dubai, has transformed an arid landscape into a diverse, urban community. Learn how the Valley of the Sun and its citizens have tried to avoid becoming "another L.A." and what building a major metropolitan area in the desert means.

Scharbarch, Paul, and John H. Akers. *Phoenix: Then and Now*. San Diego, CA: Thunderbay Press, 2005. A fascinating before-and-after look at the Valley's growth, the richly illustrated book contrasts historical images against contemporary shots of Phoenix, Tempe, Mesa, and Glendale. The consistent theme: growth.

TRAVEL

Cheek, Lawrence W. *Arizona*. Oakland, CA: Compass American Guides, 1997. The dense guide takes a more literary approach to exploring Arizona, with a thoughtful collection of essays about the state's history and geographical regions, as well as its natural attractions, Native American culture, and art and architecture. The archival photos from Arizona's early territorial days are particularly fascinating.

Kutz, Jack. *Mysteries & Miracles of Arizona: Guide Book to the Genuinely Bizarre in the Grand Canyon State*. Corrales, NM: Rhombus Publishing Company, 1992. The Arizona desert hides a mystical side, or at least that's what generations of Native American shamans, fireside cowboys, and Sedona's New Agers say. Discover the curse of the Superstition Mountains east of Phoenix and the old ghost towns on the frontier.

Lindahl, Larry. *Secret Sedona: Sacred Moments in the Landscape*. Phoenix: Arizona Highways, 2005. Sedona's red-hued landscape takes center stage in this lavishly illustrated book, with stunning photography and poetic descriptions that showcase the region's massive formations, ancient Native American history, and rich geology and wildlife.

Lowe, Sam. *Arizona Curiosities: Quirky Characters, Roadside Oddities, & Other Offbeat Stuff*. Guilford, CT: The Globe Pequot Press, 2003. Lowe, a former Arizona newspaperman, provides a humorous survey of the Grand Canyon State's kooky history, people, and roadside attractions. Most Arizonans don't know even half of the oddball stories, like concrete religious shrines, alien abductions, and "wild" burros that roam the streets of one town.

Treat, Wesley. *Weird Arizona: Your Travel Guide to Arizona's Local Legends and Best Kept Secrets*. New York: Sterling, 2007. Uncover the Wild West's weird and wacky side, from outlaws and outhouses to rattlesnake-inspired bridges.

Internet Resources

TOURISM SITES
Arizona Office of Tourism
www.arizonaguide.com
Featuring video tours, itinerary options, travel deals, and a calendar of events, the AOT website is a valuable resource and great place to start planning your visit.

Arizona State Parks
www.pr.state.az.us
A guide to the Grand Canyon State's myriad parks, plus volunteer programs, junior ranger activities, and a Green Guide to Arizona. Also, weather forecast information and directions on how to obtain an annual parks pass.

Greater Phoenix Convention & Visitors Bureau
www.visitphoenix.com
With its "Shine On" logo, the Greater Phoenix CVB provides news and information on everything from golf to accommodations to assistance in relocating to Arizona. The site also hosts a blog called The Hot Sheet, which is "written for Phoenix locals and visitors alike."

Scottsdale Convention and Visitors Bureau
www.scottsdalecvb.com
A comprehensive website for all things Scottsdale: attractions, shopping, resorts, and hotels, as well as special packages available year-round. Visitors can book their entire trip at this one-stop shop.

Sedona Chamber of Commerce
www.visitsedona.com
The definitive site for visiting Red Rock Country, it also provides information and assistance for planning your Sedona wedding. Something you'll be hard-pressed to find elsewhere is its spiritual/personal enrichment webpage.

Sedona Verde Valley Travel Council
www.sedona-verdevalley.com
This visitor guide and information center covers the area surrounding Sedona, including Jerome and Camp Verde, and provides suggestions for arts and cultural activities, along with news on events and festivals, hotels, dining, shopping, and tours.

NEWS AND CULTURE
The Arizona Guardian
www.arizonaguardian.com
Started by a group of former newspaper reporters, this in-depth news site explores Arizona politics and government, with regular coverage of both sides of the aisle. The site can be a little esoteric for visitors, but it's a terrific resource if you want to dive head first into the state's political scene.

Arizona's Family
www.azfamily.com
Local television station 3TV's website features news, entertainment, and weather and traffic information, as well as stories on real estate, airport news, and flight maps. Slideshows and readers' photos make this hometown site a real Arizona "family" affair.

azcentral
www.azcentral.com
The website for *The Arizona Republic* newspaper, azcentral bills itself as "Arizona's Home Page." It covers news in the nation and the world, along with the latest in sports, food, and the weather, plus a "Things to Do" link that serves as an essential resource for tourists.

KJZZ
www.kjzz.org
Phoenix's National Public Radio station offers this multimedia website, a great resource to learn more about the city's news, politics, people, and culture.

Index

List of Maps

Acknowledgments

Like raising a child, producing this book took a village, and I couldn't have completed it without my family and friends who donated their time and efforts. In fact, the recommendations in this guide represent the cumulative research of countless meals, road trips, and nights out with the people listed below.

First, I would like to thank my parents, Stephen and Susan Ficker, who brought me to Phoenix more than two decades ago and have been a constant source of support, as well as my brother, Daniel, our native Phoenician. Thanks to my favorite travel companion and steadfast friend for nearly 20 years, Alyssa Moore. Thank you to David Proffitt, my Sedona buddy, who is the best writer and friend I know. I must thank my "pro-soul," Leigh Flayton, for being my "fresh eyes" and indispensable adviser. Also, a special thanks to April Warnecke, Mark McClune, and Peter O'Dowd for their contributions and friendship. Thank you, as well, to Mica Mulloy and Kris Califano.

I should also thank Mike and Theresa Rassas, Bryan Vorkapich, Erica Heartquist, the Flynns, the Lockerys, and the Ericksons; Joe and Jennifer Vazquez; Josh Krist and Helene Goupil; Marci Knebel and Denna Musser; and the teams at McMurry and Avalon Travel. Also, a big thanks to Ally Califano, Ayrel Clark, Nate Crocker, Drew Herndon, Steph Lindstrom, Leslie Mulloy, Katelyn Parady, and the NCP gang. And thank you to the Knudsons, the Kahus-Saccios, and my extended family.